MOUNTAIN BIKE!
Virginia

MOUNTAIN BIKE!
Virginia

A GUIDE TO THE CLASSIC TRAILS

SECOND EDITION

RANDY PORTER

Menasha
Ridge
Press

Library of Congress Cataloging-in-Publication Data:
Porter, Randy
Mountain bike! Virginia: a guide to the classic trails/
Randy Porter. 2nd Ed.
p. cm.
Includes index.
ISBN 0-89732-376-9 (alk. paper)
1. All terrain cycling—Virginia—Guidebooks
2. Trails—Virginia—Guidebooks
3. Virginia—Guidebooks
I. Title
GV1045.5.V8 P67 2001
917.5504'44—dc21   2001018311
CIP

Photos by the author unless otherwise credited
Maps by Brian Taylor at RapiDesign
Cover and text design by Suzanne Holt
Cover photo by Dennis Coello

Menasha Ridge Press
P.O. Box 43673
Birmingham, Alabama 35243
www.menasharidge.com

All the trails described in this book are legal for mountain bikes. But rules can change—especially for off-road bicycles, the new kid on the outdoor recreation block. Land access issues and conflicts between bicyclists, hikers, equestrians, and other users can cause the rewriting of recreation regulations on public lands, sometimes resulting in a ban of mountain bike use on specific trails. That's why it's the responsibility of each rider to check and make sure that he or she rides only on trails where mountain biking is permitted.

CAUTION
Outdoor recreational activities are by their very nature potentially hazardous. All participants in such activities must assume the responsibility for their own actions and safety. The information contained in this guidebook cannot replace sound judgment and good decision-making skills, which help reduce risk exposure, nor does the scope of this book allow for disclosure of all the potential hazards and risks involved in such activities.

Learn as much as possible about the outdoor recreational activities in which you participate, prepare for the unexpected, and be cautious. The reward will be a safer and more enjoyable experience.

CONTENTS

Map Legend   ix
Ride Location Map   x
List of Maps   xii
Acknowledgments   xv
Foreword   xvii
Preface   xix
Ride Recommendations for Special Interests   xxvii

INTRODUCTION   1

Trail Description Outline   1
Abbreviations   3
Topographic Maps   4
Trail Etiquette   6
Hitting the Trail   7

COASTAL VIRGINIA   11

1   False Cape State Park   13
2   First Landing State Park   19
3   Great Dismal Swamp   22
4   Carrollton Nike Park   26
5   Newport News Park   29
6   Harwoods Mill Trail   32
7   Beaverdam Reservoir Park   36
8   York River State Park   40
9   Marl Ravine Trail   43
10   Waller Mill Park   45

VIRGINIA'S PIEDMONT   49

11   Belle Isle   51
12   Chimbarazo Park   53
13   Dogwood Dell   56
14   Powhite Park   59
15   Pocahontas State Park   62
16   Poor Farm Park   66
17   Petersburg National Battlefield   69
18   Occoneechee State Park and Wildlife Management Area   71
19   Carter Taylor Trail   74
20   Cumberland State Forest   79
21   James River State Park   81
22   Walnut Creek Park   85
23   Observatory Hill   88

NORTHERN VIRGINIA   91

24   Wakefield and Lake Accotink Parks   93
25   Fountainhead Regional Park   96
26   W&OD Railroad Regional Park   99
27   C&O Canal National Historic Park   102
28   Mount Vernon Trail   106
29   Great Falls Park   109
30   Prince William Forest Park   112

THE MOUNTAINS OF WESTERN VIRGINIA   117

31   Elizabeth Furnace   121
32   Massanutten Campout   126
33   Duncan Hollow   137
34   Brandywine Lake Overnighter   141
35   Lake to Lake   146
36   Slate Lick Lake   149
37   Long Run   153
38   Blueberry Trail   157
39   Sandspring Mountain Trail   160
40   The Long Way to Reddish Knob   164
41   North River Gorge Trail   168
42   Little Bald Knob Climb   174
43   Great Lakes Loop   176
44   West Augusta Trail   180
45   Deerfield Horse Trail   183
46   Elliott Knob   186

47 Walker Mountain   190
48 Williamsville Loop   194
49 Wallace Tract   198
50 Hidden Valley   202
51 Laurel Fork   206
52 Lake Robertson   212
53 Longdale Recreation Area   215
54 North Mountain Ridge   217
55 Dry Run   223
56 Fore Mountain Trail   226
57 Blue Suck Falls   228
58 Middle Mountain Ridge   231
59 Big Levels Reservoir Loop   233
60 Big Levels to the Blue Ridge   237
61 Pedlar River Loop   242
62 Shady Mountain   246
63 Cave Mountain Lake   248
64 Thomas Mountain   251
65 Pine Mountain Trail   255
66 Otter Creek Outing   257
67 Spec Mines   261
68 Carvins Cove Reservoir   265
69 Dragon's Back   268
70 Barbours Creek Wilderness   271
71 Fenwick Mines   276

VIRGINIA'S BLUE RIDGE HIGHLANDS   281

72 Breeze across Brush Mountain   283
73 Poverty Creek Trail   286
74 Mountain Lake Trail System   289
75 Mountain Lake to Butt Mountain   292
76 Flat Top Mountain   296
77 Tract Fork and Polecat Trails   299
78 Grayson Highlands State Park   302
79 New River Trail State Park   305
80 Mountain Bike Heaven   310
81 Skulls to Hurricane Gap   313
82 Rowlands Creek Falls Circuit   316
83 Barton Gap   318
84 Whitetop Mountain   321
85 Beartree Recreation Area   324
86 Feathercamp Ridge   326

87 Virginia Creeper Trail 329
88 Guest River Trail 333
89 Breaks Interstate Park 337
90 Sugar Hill Loop Trail 340
91 Heart of Appalachia Bike Route 343

Glossary 347
Index 353
About the Author 364

AMERICA BY MOUNTAIN BIKE   MAP LEGEND

Ride trailhead

Primary bike trail

Direction of travel

Optional bike trail and trailhead

Other trail

Hiking only trail

Interstate highways (with exit no.)

US routes

State routes

Other paved roads — Taylor Rd.

Unpaved, gravel or dirt roads — 4WD (may be 4WD only)

US Forest Service roads

Columbus
Cities

Mt. Vernon ●
Towns or settlements

Dam
Lake

Intermittent stream

Perennial stream

0   1/2   1
MILES
Approximate scale in miles

N
True north

WILDERNESS AREA
Public lands*

State or county border

✈ Airport

♥ Archeological or historical site

🚤 Boat ramp

▲ Campground (CG)

≡ Cattle guard

✝ Cemetery or gravesite

♠ Church

Cliff, escarpment, or outcropping

🐾 Drinking water

🗼 Fire tower or lookout

🗻 Falls or rapids

🅾 Food

✉ Gate

🏠 House or cabin

🛏 Lodging

Mountain or butte

Mountain pass

△ Mountain summit
3312 (elevation in feet)

✗ Mine or quarry

🔭 Observatory

🚩 Park office or ranger station

🅷 Picnic area

Power line or pipeline

🚻 Rest rooms

◖ Spring

🐎 Stable, corral, or ranch

🏊 Swimming Area

Transmission towers

Tunnel or bridge

Remember, private property exists in and around our national forests.

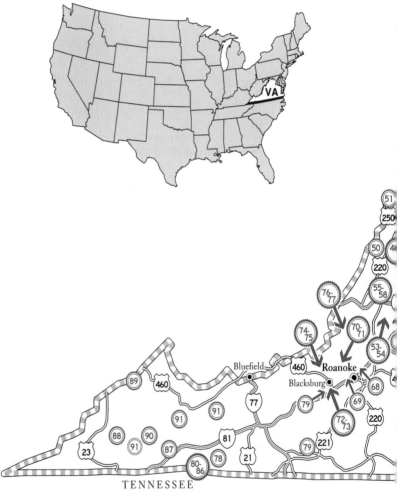

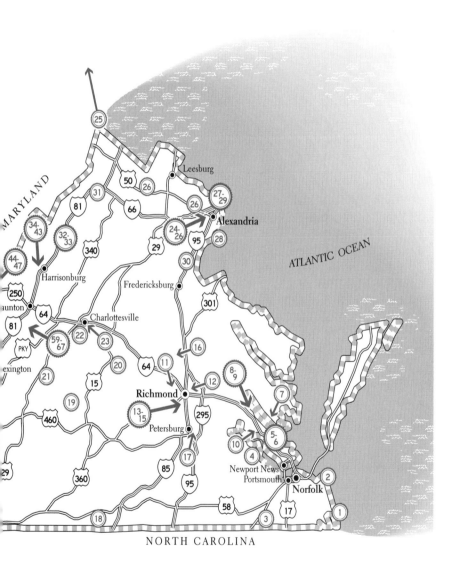

LIST OF MAPS

1 False Cape State Park   14–15
2 First Landing State Park   20
3 Great Dismal Swamp   23
4 Carrollton Nike Park   28
5 Newport News Park   30
6 Harwoods Mill Trail   34
7 Beaverdam Reservoir Park   38
8 York River State Park   42
9 Marl Ravine Trail   42
10 Waller Mill Park   46
11 Belle Isle   52
12 Chimbarazo Park   55
13 Dogwood Dell   57
14 Powhite Park   60–61
15 Pocahontas State Park   64
16 Poor Farm Park   67
17 Petersburg National Battlefield   70
18 Occoneechee State Park and Wildlife Management Area   73
19 Carter Taylor Trail   75
20 Cumberland State Forest   80
21 James River State Park   82
22 Walnut Creek Park   86
23 Observatory Hill   89
24 Wakefield and Lake Accotink Parks   94
25 Fountainhead Regional Park   97
26 W&OD Railroad Regional Park   100

27 C&O Canal National Historic Park   103
28 Mount Vernon Trail   107
29 Great Falls Park   110
30 Prince William Forest Park   114–15
31 Elizabeth Furnace   122–23
32 Massanutten Campout   128, 132, 135
33 Duncan Hollow   138
34 Brandywine Lake Overnighter   142–43
35 Lake to Lake   147
36 Slate Lick Lake   150
37 Long Run   154
38 Blueberry Trail   158
39 Sandspring Mountain Trail   162
40 The Long Way to Reddish Knob   165
41 North River Gorge Trail   172–73
42 Little Bald Knob Climb   172–73
43 Great Lakes Loop   172–73
44 West Augusta Trail   181
45 Deerfield Horse Trail   184
46 Elliott Knob   187
47 Walker Mountain   191
48 Williamsville Loop   195
49 Wallace Tract   199
50 Hidden Valley   203
51 Laurel Fork   207
52 Lake Robertson   213
53 Longdale Recreation Area   220–21
54 North Mountain Ridge   220–21
55 Dry Run   225
56 Fore Mountain Trail   225
57 Blue Suck Falls   230
58 Middle Mountain Ridge   230
59 Big Levels Reservoir Loop   234
60 Big Levels to the Blue Ridge   238
61 Pedlar River Loop   244
62 Shady Mountain   244
63 Cave Mountain Lake   252–53
64 Thomas Mountain   252–53
65 Pine Mountain Trail   252–53
66 Otter Creek Outing   258
67 Spec Mines   262
68 Carvins Cove Reservoir   266

69 Dragon's Back 269
70 Barbours Creek Wilderness 272
71 Fenwick Mines 277
72 Breeze across Brush Mountain 284
73 Poverty Creek Trail 287
74 Mountain Lake Trail System 290
75 Mountain Lake to Butt Mountain 293
76 Flat Top Mountain 297
77 Tract Fork and Polecat Trails 300
78 Grayson Highlands State Park 303
79 New River Trail State Park 306–7
80 Mountain Bike Heaven 311
81 Skulls to Hurricane Gap 315
82 Rowlands Creek Falls Circuit 315
83 Barton Gap 319
84 Whitetop Mountain 322
85 Beartree Recreation Area 327
86 Feathercamp Ridge 327
87 Virginia Creeper Trail 330
88 Guest River Trail 334
89 Breaks Interstate Park 338
90 Sugar Hill Loop Trail 341
91 Heart of Appalachia Bike Route—no map

ACKNOWLEDGMENTS

I never could have completed a project of this magnitude without the support and assistance of a number of folks who helped in many different ways. The first and last thanks goes to the staff at Menasha Ridge Press, especially Dennis Coello, Molly Burns, and Holly Brown, who coached and cajoled me through the process of compiling two and a half years of notes, maps, and scribbles into a first-rate guidebook. Thanks especially to Holly, who showed uncommon patience during a time in my life when it seemed all else was coming apart. I'd also like to thank Nancy Sorrells, my coauthor on A Cyclist's Guide to the Shenandoah Valley.

There are so many people in the field who, in large and small ways, helped give this book thorough coverage of the mountain biking wave that's sweeping over Virginia in a very positive direction. I apologize ahead of time for those I may have omitted , but whose input was no less appreciated or valuable: David Rhodes, Bob McKinney, Kathy Hall, Jerry Jacobson, Mike Gallegly, Bill Compton, Robert Boardwine, and Bonnie Crush (George Washington and Jefferson National Forest); Mark Schuppin and Dan Soper (Virginia State Parks); Wayne Bowman (Virginia Department of Forestry); Ralph White (Richmond Parks Department); Stan Thorne (Hanover Parks Department); Debra Weir (Isle of Wight Parks Department); Angela Leigh (Gloucester Parks Department); Gary Morgan, Noel Loesen, Daniel Barnaby, Mark Kohlmorgan, Dick Howard, and Doug Wilkins (Mountain Bike Virginia); Patrick Powell (Eastern Virginia Mountain Bike Association); Mark Nissley (Mark's Bike Shop); Gerald Knicely (Mole Hill Bikes); Tim Carruthers (Mid-Atlantic Off-Road Enthusiasts); Kyle Fedler (Mountain Bike Club at the University of Virginia); Dan Comber (Atlantic Event Productions); Mark Gordon (The Bike Factory); Tim Gathwright (Performance Bike Shop); Tom Brody

(Endless Mountain Retreat Center); Rick Lambert (Highland Adventures); Tom Horsch (Iron Mountain Trail Club); Chris Pohowsky (East Coasters Bicycle and Fitness); Andy Hunter (Lexington Bike Shop); Wil Kohlbrenner (Potomac Appalachian Trail Club); Matt McCall (Rockfish Gap Outfitters); Lanny Sparks (New River Bicycles); and Lori Finley, Joe Surkiewicz, Dave Shipp, Scott Steele, Paul David, Dave Glendening, Susan Sura, Tim Wion, Jean and Frank Kilgore, Larry E. Grossman, and Jerry Bryant.

I'd like to dedicate *Mountain Bike! Virginia* to my family—Chris, Stuart, and Susi Porter—who saw me through some rough times during the final stages of this book's production. Contrary to what Forrest Gump would have us believe, life is more like a long mountain bike ride. With the often unpredictable nature of weather, terrain, energy level, and equipment, we don't always have as much control as we'd like over each day's ride. But still, we try to remain on top of the bike instead of face down in the mud. Thanks to the Porters for helping to keep me in the saddle.

FOREWORD

Welcome to *America by Mountain Bike*, a series designed to provide all-terrain bikers with the information they need to find and ride the very best trails around. Whether you're new to the sport and don't know where to pedal, or an experienced mountain biker who wants to learn the classic trails in another region, this series is for you. Drop a few bucks for the book, spend an hour with the detailed maps and route descriptions, and you're prepared for the finest in off-road cycling.

My role as editor of this series was simple: First, find a mountain biker who knows the area and loves to ride. Second, ask that person to spend a year researching the most popular and very best rides around. And third, have that rider describe each trail in terms of difficulty, scenery, condition, elevation change, and all other categories of information that are important to trail riders. "Pretend you've just completed a ride and met up with fellow mountain bikers at the trailhead," I told each author. "Imagine their questions, be clear in your answers."

As I said, the *editorial* process—that of sending out riders and reading the submitted chapters—is a snap. But the work involved in finding, riding, and writing about each trail is enormous. In some instances our authors' tasks are made easier by the information contributed by local bike shops or cycling clubs, or even by the writers of local "where-to" guides. Credit for these contributions is provided, when appropriate, in each chapter, and our sincere thanks goes to all who have helped.

But the overwhelming majority of trails are discovered and pedaled by our authors themselves, then compared with dozens of other routes to determine if they qualify as "classic"—that area's best in scenery and cycling fun. If you've ever had the experience of pioneering a route from outdated topographic maps, or entering a bike shop to request information from local riders who would much prefer to keep their favorite trails secret, or know how it is to double- and triple-check data to be positive your trail info is correct, then you have an idea of how each of our authors has labored to bring about these books. You and I, and all the mountain bikers of America, are the richer for their efforts.

You'll get more out of this book if you take a moment to read the Introduction explaining how to read the trail listings. The "Topographic Maps" section will help you understand how useful topos will be on a ride, and will also tell you where to get them. And though this is a "where-to," not a "how-to" guide, those of you who have not traveled the backcountry might find "Hitting the Trail" of particular value.

In addition to the material above, newcomers to mountain biking might want to spend a minute with the Glossary, page 368, so that terms like *hard-pack*, *single-track*, and *waterbars* won't throw you when you come across them in the text.

Finally, the tips in the Afterword on mountain biking etiquette and the land-use controversy might help us all enjoy the trails a little more.

All the best.

Dennis Coello
St. Louis

PREFACE

Just as America's first settlers at Jamestown found an adventurous and challenging new world in 1607, mountain bikers will find in Virginia a place that welcomes travel, exploration, and discovery on two wheels. The geography of the Old Dominion offers a diverse land from the Atlantic Ocean to the Blue Ridge and Allegheny Mountains and beyond where mountain bikers will find an ever-expanding variety of terrain on which to ride.

Mountain Bike! Virginia covers the state's 40,815 square miles with a wide range of biking options from technical single-track to state and federal forest roads. The conversion of abandoned railroad lines into recreational trails has also benefited Virginia's mountain bikers, and in this guide you'll learn about converted rail trails which range in length from 5 to 55 miles. Former Virginia first lady Susan Allen listed biking on one of Virginia's rail trail conversions as the first of 28 *Great Ways to Enjoy Virginia* on the state's "VISIT Virginia" Web site on the World Wide Web. (To see the rest of the list, sign on to www.virginia.org/cgi-bin/vis.)

Virginia's topography is such that you can use this guide to pedal on secluded beaches along the Atlantic Ocean at False Cape State Park on one day, and the next day you can bike on rocky single-track at an elevation above 5,000 feet across the state's highest mountains in the Blue Ridge Highlands, in the southwest corner of the state. And, of course, there's everything in between these two extremes.

I've sectioned the rides in this guide into five commonly accepted regions: Coastal Virginia, Virginia's Piedmont, Northern Virginia, the Mountains of Western Virginia, and Virginia's Blue Ridge Highlands. More specific descriptions will precede each particular section, but I'll offer some brief information here to help distinguish one from another.

The coastal region lies between the Chesapeake Bay and Interstate 95 running north and south. It's relatively flat, and the hills you'll encounter vary markedly from the three-mile-plus climbs and downhills you'll find in the mountains of Western Virginia and the Blue Ridge Highlands. Each trail presents a challenge of its own, and it's hard to rate one against the other in terms of degree of difficulty. It's all a matter of what you're accustomed to and how much work you're willing to do.

Virginia's Piedmont begins where the coastal area leaves off at a north-south line drawn by Interstate 95. Extending west to the foothills of the famed Blue Ridge Mountains, its terrain is largely rolling. In the Piedmont you'll have access to Virginia's largest state forests and state parks. Although there are state forests and parks elsewhere in Virginia, in the Piedmont they combine to form the greatest proportion of public land in the state.

Northern Virginia is defined more by sociocultural aspects than geographic ones. It's located in the northernmost part of Virginia's Piedmont. The Potomac River to the northeast and east and the Blue Ridge Mountains to the west form natural cutoffs. The southern edge is a bit harder to distinguish, and for the purpose of this guide I've used a continuous line from Fredericksburg to Culpeper along VA 3 which, if continued west from Culpeper, would reach the Blue Ridge Mountains and Shenandoah National Park around Old Rag Mountain. At first glance, this northernmost tip of the state seems to be a high-rent bedroom community for the District of Columbia's federal workers. Because of the premium placed on land, there are relatively few public parks or forests offering large natural areas in which to ride. As a result, much of Northern Virginia mountain biking takes place on man-made paths, both dirt and hard surface. This doesn't necessarily translate into a lack of challenging single-track, though, and the region's newest trail at Fountainhead Regional Park is convincing testimony.

The mountains of western Virginia are my home turf and include the Blue Ridge and Allegheny Mountains that frame the Shenandoah Valley. The Blue Ridge Mountains separate this region from central Virginia to the east and the Roanoke River separates it from the Blue Ridge Highlands to the south. This region includes over one million acres of George Washington National Forest and part of the 700,000-acre Jefferson National Forest, although the majority of the Jefferson lies in the Blue Ridge Highlands.

The Blue Ridge Highlands, Virginia's final frontier, are tucked away in the southwest corner of the state. The region is bounded by the states of Kentucky, Tennessee, North Carolina, and West Virginia on the north, west, and south. The Blue Ridge Mountains and Blue Ridge Parkway form the eastern edge, with the Roanoke River forming the northeastern boundary. This region takes in demanding, rocky single-track in the Mount Rogers National Recreation Area, as well as more rider-friendly former rail beds that now form the Virginia Creeper, New River, and Guest River Trails.

A map comes in
handy in mountainous
western Virginia, where
trail signs and blazes
are infrequent.

The Commonwealth of Virginia includes several types of public lands
open to mountain biking. Part of my selection process for including rides in
this guide was the exclusion of private property on which mountain bike riding might be a common but not strictly legal practice. I also did not include
public land whose managers' stance on mountain biking was ambiguous.
Some of you who are more familiar with a specific area may know of a great
spot that is not included in this guide. If you wish to share your favorites for
future inclusion, please send them along to me, care of Menasha Ridge Press.
After all, that's why there are revised editions.

I've found that many people are confused about the difference between
national parks and national forests. This becomes even more problematic
when you add state parks and state forests such as those throughout Virginia.
This is especially true in the western Virginia mountains, where Shenandoah
National Park, George Washington National Forest, Skyline Drive, and the
Blue Ridge Parkway seem to merge. A few words of clarification will go a long
way toward untangling this bureaucratic ball of string. Shenandoh National

Virginia's George Washington and Jefferson National Forests' 1.7 million acres offer unlimited mountain biking opportunities (photo by Larry E. Grossman).

Park and all other national parks are administered by the United States Department of the Interior. Mountain biking off Shenandoah National Park's hard-surface roads is presently not allowed in this much-visited park, which surrounds the 105-mile Skyline Drive along the crest of the Blue Ridge Mountains.

In 1911, the Weeks Act laid the foundation for national forests to grow. They were set up for timber production and watershed protection, but recent initiatives have placed higher priorities on wildlife management, recreation, and wilderness preservation. In the mid-1990s, the Jefferson and George Washington were consolidated into one national forest, at least in terms of overall administration; but as of the fall of 1997, both forests have retained their own names and identities as well as those of their individual ranger districts. (In some sort of unofficial tribute to the African-American character played by actor Sherman Helmsley on the 1970s situation comedy *The Jeffersons*, the only name for the newly consolidated forest that I've heard tossed around, albeit tongue in cheek, is the George Jefferson National Forest.)

With more than 2,000 miles of roads and 200 miles of trails in George Washington alone, there are innumerable possibilities for mountain biking, and I generally encountered very few people in the Jefferson and George Washington forests while developing routes for this guide. This included rides on trails as well as along gravel Forest Service roads open to vehicular traffic.

With the exception of federally designated wilderness areas, you can ride a bicycle anywhere in the national forests unless it is otherwise prohibited by a regulation specific to that particular area. Mountain bikers are allowed to ride on gated roads, even those closed to vehicular traffic. I've heard that bikes are not allowed on some trails within major recreation areas serving large numbers of people, but I've never seen that in print. In Virginia, all national forest land is in the western part of the state.

State forests, on the other hand, are administered by the Virginia Department of Forestry as a self-sustaining branch of the state government. The four largest state forests are in the central part of the state and allow mountain biking unless there is a regulation that prohibits riding on a specific trail or road. State forests range in size from the 77-acre Matthews State Forest to the 19,535-acre Appomattox-Buckingham State Forest.

State parks are administered by the Virginia Department of Conservation and Recreation and deal with trail use by mountain bikers on a park-by-park basis. If you're unsure about the status of riding in a particular Virginia state park, it's best to call the individual park you plan to visit or ask when you get there. Recently Virginia's state parks have really begun to embrace, or at least address, the question of bikes on trails. When I began my research three years ago this was not the case, and I often got varying answers to the question of mountain bike access depending on which staff member I spoke with. But on the whole, Virginia's state parks have begun to take a harder look, and a very positive one, at the question of how mountain bikers can utilize their individual sites.

A single day or overnight visit to York River, False Cape, Seashore, Holliday Lake, Bear Creek Lake, Pocahontas, or Grayson Highlands State Park can add up to a nice family camping/biking vacation. In addition, New River Trail State Park is a 55-mile converted rail bed that offers easy pedaling for riders of all ability levels. You can opt to ride as little or as much as you like by utilizing shuttle services and easy access to the trail where it intersects various state roads.

Throughout the Commonwealth there are also wildlife management areas (WMAs), which are managed by the Virginia Department of Game and Inland Fisheries. These are open to mountain biking. Users should ride with caution and with the knowledge that hunting is the highest priority of usage in the WMAs. Their trail systems are designed for hunters and generally consist of short spurs branching off from the main trail. As a result, you'll generally end up doing a lot of short out-and-back riding in WMAs, which range in size from 400 to more than 33,000 acres.

There are also numerous county and regional parks whose managers are addressing the manner in which growing numbers of users—mountain bikers, hikers, and equestrians—can utilize limited recreational space in a safe, equitable, and environmentally sound manner.

In regard to the vagaries of weather forecasting and charts that give seasonal averages, I'll say only that Virginia's seasons may display certain trends, but warm and cold fronts can move in quickly to tip the scales in one direction or the other. I've ridden in shorts and a T-shirt during atypical 80-degree weather in December, and I've also gotten snowed on at high elevations in April when the spring jonquils were opening their yellow and white petals. Neither is typical, but the extremes do occur. Mountain bikers should anticipate the unexpected, whether planning to ride a short section of single-track along the coast or to take a four-day camping trip across the Massanutten mountain range.

A certain amount of this guide was the result of following leads and suggestions from those who were more familiar with a given trail, trail system, or particularly enticing area. These rides are the tried-and-true "classic rides" whose enjoyment factor is more or less a matter of public record. In the last several years, the trend in Virginia has been to develop mountain biking trails through partnerships between responsible mountain bike organizations and the municipalities that hold dominion over specific recreational locales. You'll find a number of classic rides in the making.

Many rides were the trial-and-error result of studying maps from western Virginia's two national forests, George Washington and Jefferson, and then venturing forth into the "great beyond." That made my two-and-a-half-year odyssey to ferret out Virginia's finest mountain biking destinations an interesting but very time-consuming undertaking. In most cases I didn't merely follow in the tire treads of thousands of riders who had gone before me on trails and gravel roads. I forged ahead into unknown territory. Quite frankly, some routes appeared far better on paper than they were in reality, while others surprised me with the high quality of off-road or rough-road experience.

I'll resist the temptation to compare my twentieth-century exploration to that of John Smith, Meriwether Lewis and William Clark, Daniel Boone, and others who pushed into a far less friendly wilderness several centuries ago. But I often enjoyed that feeling of discovery. At other times I grew weary of this trial-and-error approach, especially when roads and trails disappeared into the forest after they'd appeared to be such promising routes on Forest Service and topographic maps.

One particularly exciting discovery was a 25-mile rail bed that had been abandoned years ago; its right-of-way had been taken over by the Virginia Department of Transportation (VDOT). This former rail line was not identified as such on any map nor had any source told me about it. It happened to appear just where a particular western Virginia route-in-the-making needed a connection back to the start. Although not everyone's cup of tea, a relatively flat, wide, smooth surface through the woods is, for many of us, a great way to get from point A to point B without mixing it up with vehicular traffic or threading a way across single-track that may not be maintained for mountain biking, or even walking, for that matter.

To really know and understand Virginia and Virginians, you must also have some knowledge of the considerable role that the Commonwealth of Virginia has played in the birth, early years, and adolescence of the United States. The first Jamestown settlers indelibly etched Virginia's place in America's future. The final battle of the Revolutionary War was fought at Yorktown, and 85 years later the final engagement of the Civil War occurred near Appomattox. Virginia has offered more U.S. presidents (eight) than any other state; the first Thanksgiving was held at Berkeley Plantation more than one year before the Pilgrims landed in New England; more Civil War battles were fought in Virginia than in any other state; and Douglas Wilder, a descendent of slaves, was the first African-American governor in the country's history. Other Virginians went on to achieve prominence elsewhere, including such noteworthy figures as Cyrus McCormick, Sam Houston, Steven Austin, and explorers Meriwether Lewis and William Clark. Virginians like myself can take pride in the role that the Old Dominion has played in our country's growth.

As you drive and ride through these areas to one or more of the destinations described in this book, you may better appreciate the state if you dig a little deeper into the historical surroundings of some great mountain biking geography. Although it's possible to enjoy these routes by simply riding them, it's more exciting when you have a deeper understanding of the rich history of their surroundings.

Stop to read historical roadside signs, spend some extra time exploring historical attractions, and then go into the woods with a better appreciation of the way the sandy soil or red clay under your two wheels figured into earlier times. Virginia's history is inseparable from her present. So I'll present the state's history along with trail descriptions, and hopefully you too will appreciate Virginia in its totality—not just for great mountain biking, nor merely for its rich history and natural treasures, but for all three.

Unlike the tendency toward trail closings that has affected many recreational lands throughout the country, Virginia's trend has been to move cautiously, with partnerships forming between responsible mountain bike groups like Mid-Atlantic Off-Road Enthusiasts (MORE), the Eastern Virginia Mountain Bike Association (EVMA), and Mountain Bike Virginia. They've developed positive working relationships with municipalities to build, maintain, and even police trails to make sure they are used responsibly and remain good places to ride. Similar actions by the Mountain Bike Club at the University of Virginia brought Observatory Hill back from the brink of exclusion to cyclists and improved the condition of both the trail system and the relationship among diverse users.

To help perpetuate this trend you should always follow the Rules of the Trail of the International Mountain Bike Association found in the series Introduction.

Ours is a relatively inexpensive sport that in most places is devoid of specific user fees. Put your money to good use by joining IMBA, MORE, EVMA, Mountain Bike Virginia, your local mountain bike club, or all of the above. Minimally you should become a dues-paying member, but even better, become an active participant in the trail-building and maintenance process. And encourage others to do the same.

A few words of warning are appropriate lest you ride off in the great beyond with no concern except to satisfy your own pleasures. Multi-use trails are generally the rule on most of the rides in *Mountain Bike! Virginia*. In the case of rides in the national forests, state forests, and WMAs, at certain times of the year hunters constitute a large proportion of the other users. The exact opening and closing dates of Virginia's hunting seasons vary depending on whether you're east or west of the Blue Ridge Mountains, the type of weapon used (rifle, bow, or black powder), and the type of game animal hunted. Rather than providing a list of dates that are subject to change, I suggest you call the Virginia Department of Game and Inland Fisheries (804-367-1000) for the most up to date and accurate information. If you decide to ride in the woods during one of the hunting seasons, you should wear brightly colored attire with a healthy sampling of blaze orange, just as hunters are required to do.

We all have our favorite kinds of rides, and yours and mine may not be the same. But Virginia's riding opportunities are as diverse as its geography. I have tried to present helpful information in an objective manner, while still letting my own biases come through unfettered. Perhaps that's a tall order, but our mountain biking experiences are but a function of our own subjective opinions. Objective data may or may not speak for itself, but my riding impressions are distinctly my own.

This guide is not an end in itself; it's merely a passport to get you out riding in initially unfamiliar terrain. Keep an open mind and try to judge each ride for what it is, not for what it isn't. Above all else, ride to have fun without getting too wrapped up in organizational squabbles, equipment controversies, schools of debate over various trail configuration preferences, and any number of other fractious areas of debate that *Homo sapiens* inevitably manage to devise just to show how different we can be.

Wildlife Viewing
1 False Cape State Park
3 Great Dismal Swamp
18 Occoneechee State Park and
   Wildlife Management Area

Climbers' Delights
35 Lake to Lake
39 Sandspring Mountain Trail
40 The Long Way to Reddish Knob
42 Little Bald Knob Climb
60 Big Levels to the Blue Ridge

61 Pedlar River Loop
76 Flat Top Mountain
84 Whitetop Mountain
86 Feathercamp Ridge

Fishing and Biking
42 North River Gorge Trail
44 Great Lakes Loop
49 Williamsville Loop
51 Hidden Valley

52 Laurel Fork
53 Lake Robertson
69 Carvins Cove Reservoir

Short and Sweet
4 Carrollton Nike Park
38 Blueberry Trail

Rail Trails
26 W&OD Railroad Regional Park
27 C&O Canal
   National Historic Park
71 Fenwick Mines
   (section that parallels VA 615)

79 New River Trail State Park
86 Virginia Creeper Trail
88 Guest River Trail

Entry Level Single-track
4 Carrollton Nike Park
6 Harwoods Mill Trail
7 Beaverdam Reservoir Park

74 Poverty Creek Trail
90 Breaks Interstate Park

Family
2 First Landing State Park
5 Newport News Park
8 York River State Park
11 Belle Isle (perimeter loop)
15 Pocahontas State Park
   (Old Mill Trail)
21 James River State Park

26 W&OD Railroad Regional Park
27 C&O Canal National Historic
   Park
68 Carvins Cove Reservoir
79 New River Trail State Park
87 Virginia Creeper Trail

(continued)

RIDE RECOMMENDATIONS FOR SPECIAL INTERESTS *(continued)*

Technical Single-track

9 Marl Ravine Trail
10 Waller Mill Park
13 Dogwood Dell
14 Powhite Park

16 Poor Farm Park
22 Walnut Creek Park
23 Observatory Hill
25 Fountainhead Regional Park

On Top of the World

40 The Long Way to Reddish Knob
42 Little Bald Knob Climb
46 Elliott Knob

54 North Mountain Ridge
69 Dragon's Back

Downhillers' Delight

40 The Long Way to Reddish Knob
61 Pedlar River Loop
87 Virginia Creeper Trail (Whitetop Station to Damascus section)

MOUNTAIN BIKE!
Virginia

INTRODUCTION

Each trail in this book begins with key information that includes length, configuration, aerobic and technical difficulty, trail conditions, scenery, and special
comments. Additional description is contained in 11 individual categories. The
following will help you to understand all of the information provided.

Trail name: In some instances, trails are named by the author. In others, trail
names are as designated on United States Geological Survey (USGS) or Forest Service or other maps, and/or by local custom.

At a Glance Information

Length/configuration: The overall length of a trail is described in miles,
unless stated otherwise. The configuration is a description of the shape of
each trail—whether the trail is a loop, out-and-back (that is, along the same
route), figure eight, trapezoid, isosceles triangle, decahedron . . . (just kidding), or if it connects with another trail described in the book. See the Glossary for definitions of *point-to-point* and *combination*.

Aerobic difficulty: This provides a description of the degree of physical exertion required to complete the ride.

Technical difficulty: This provides a description of the technical skill
required to pedal a ride. Trails are often described here in terms of being
paved, unpaved, sandy, hard-packed, washboarded, two- or four-wheel-drive,
single-track or double-track. All terms that might be unfamiliar to the first-
time mountain biker are defined in the Glossary.

　　Note: For both the aerobic and technical difficulty categories, authors
were asked to keep in mind the fact that all riders are not equal, and thus to
gauge the trail in terms of how the middle-of-the-road rider—someone
between the newcomer and Ned Overend—could handle the route. Com-

ments about the trail's length, condition, and elevation change will also assist you in determining the difficulty of any trail relative to your own abilities.

Scenery: Here you will find a general description of the natural surroundings during the seasons most riders pedal the trail and a suggestion of what is to be found at special times (like great fall foliage or cactus in bloom).

Special comments: Unique elements of the ride are mentioned.

Category Information

General location: This category describes where the trail is located in reference to a nearby town or other landmark.

Elevation change: Unless stated otherwise, the figure provided is the total change in elevation as measured from high point to low point. Total gain, that is, the cumulative total feet in which the trail ascends, is difficult to measure accurately, but suffice it to say that it generally exceeds the simple difference between high and low points. In an effort to give you a sense of how much climbing is involved in a particular ride, brief but general descriptive phrases are used in conjunction with elevation change.

Season: This is the best time of year to pedal the route, taking into account trail conditions (for example, when it will not be muddy), riding comfort (when the weather is too hot, cold, or wet), and local hunting seasons.

Note: Because the opening and closing dates of deer, elk, moose, and antelope seasons often change from year to year, riders should check with the local Fish and Wildlife Department or call a sporting goods store (or any place that sells hunting licenses) in a nearby town before heading out. Wear bright clothes in the fall, and don't wear suede jackets while in the saddle. Hunter's-orange tape on the helmet is also a good idea.

Services: This category is of primary importance in guides for paved-road tourers and is far less crucial to most mountain bike trail descriptions because there are usually no services whatsoever to be found. Authors have noted when water is available on desert or long mountain routes and have listed the availability of food, lodging, campgrounds, and bike shops. If all these services are present, you will find only the words, "All services available in . . ."

Hazards: Special hazards like hunting season, rattlesnakes, mountain lions, bears, ticks, poison oak, earthquake, lightning, other trail users, and vehicular traffic are noted here. Other hazards which are considered a regular part of a ride, such as steep cliffs, boulder stair-steps, or scree on steep downhill sections are discussed in the "Notes on the trail" section.

Rescue index: Determining how far one is from help on a particular trail can be difficult due to the backcountry nature of most mountain bike rides. Authors therefore state the proximity of homes or Forest Service outposts, nearby roads where one might hitch a ride, or the likelihood of other bikers being encountered on the trail. Phone numbers of local sheriff departments or hospitals have not been provided because phones are almost never available. If you are able to reach a phone, the local operator will connect you with emergency services.

Land status: This category provides information regarding whether the trail crosses land operated by the Forest Service, the Bureau of Land Management, or a city, state, or national park; whether it crosses private land whose owner (at the time the author did the research) has allowed mountain bikers right of passage; and so on. A note regarding fees for land usage: There is no standard by which use-fees are charged. Some land agencies charge a fee to park within designated areas, others charge a fee regardless of where you park your car. Some areas are free year-round, others only during the off-season or during the week. Some parks charge a day-use fee, regardless of whether you park a car or not. Most national forests do not charge a day-use fee, nor do most BLM districts. State parks almost always charge a day-use fee at the very least.

Note: Authors have been extremely careful to offer only those routes that are open to bikers and are legal to ride. However, because land ownership changes over time, and because the land-use controversy created by mountain bikes still has not completely subsided, it is the duty of each cyclist to look for and heed signs warning against trail use. Don't expect this book to get you off the hook when you're facing some small-town judge for pedaling past a "Biking Prohibited" sign erected the day before you arrived. Look for these signs, read them, and heed the advice. And remember, there's always another trail.

Maps: The maps in this book have been produced with great care and, in conjunction with the trail-following suggestions, will help you stay on course. But as every experienced mountain biker knows, things can get tricky in the backcountry. It is therefore strongly suggested that you avail yourself of the detailed information found in the USGS (United States Geological Survey) 7.5 minute series topographic maps. In some cases, authors have found that specific Forest Service or other maps may be more useful than the USGS quads, and they tell how to obtain them.

Finding the trail: Detailed information on how to reach the trailhead and where to park your car is provided here.

Sources of additional information: Here you will find the address and/or phone number of a bike shop, governmental agency, or other source from which trail information can be obtained.

Notes on the trail: This is where you are guided carefully through any portions of the trail that are particularly difficult to follow. The author also may add information about the route that does not fit easily in the other categories. This category will not be present for those rides where the route is easy to follow.

ABBREVIATIONS

The following road-designation abbreviations are used in this series:

CR	County Road	I-	Interstate
FR	Farm Route	IR	Indian Route
FS	Forest Service road	US	United States highway

State highways are designated with the two-letter state abbreviation, followed by the road number. Example: VA 20 = Virginia State Highway 20.

RIDE CONFIGURATIONS

Combination: This type of route may combine two or more configurations. For example, a point-to-point route may integrate a scenic loop or an out-and-back spur midway through the ride. Likewise, an out-and-back may have a loop at its farthest point (this configuration looks like a cherry with a stem attached; the stem is the out-and-back, the fruit is the terminus loop). Or a loop route may have multiple out-and-back spurs and/or loops to the side. Mileage for a combination route is for the total distance to complete the ride.

Loop: This route configuration is characterized by riding from the designated trailhead to a distant point, then returning to the trailhead via a different route (or simply continuing on the same in a circle route) without doubling back. You always move forward across new terrain but return to the starting point when finished. Mileage is for the entire loop from the trailhead back to trailhead.

Out-and-back: A ride where you will return on the same trail you pedaled out. While this might sound far more boring than a loop route, many trails look very different when pedaled in the opposite direction.

Point-to-point: A vehicle shuttle (or similar assistance) is required for this type of route, which is ridden from the designated trailhead to a distant location, or endpoint, where the route ends. Total mileage is for the one-way trip from the trailhead to endpoint.

Spur: A road or trail that intersects the main trail you're following.

Ride Configurations contributed by Gregg Bromka

TOPOGRAPHIC MAPS

The maps in this book, when used in conjunction with the route directions present in each chapter, will in most instances be sufficient to get you to the trail and keep you on it. However, you will find superior detail and valuable information in the USGS 7.5 minute series topographic maps. Recognizing how indispensable these are to bikers and hikers alike, many bike shops and sporting goods stores now carry topos of the local area.

If you're brand new to mountain biking you might be wondering, "What's a topographic map?" In short, these differ from standard "flat" maps in that they indicate not only linear distance but elevation as well. One glance at a topo will show you the difference, for contour lines are spread across the map like dozens of intricate spider webs. Each contour line represents a particular elevation, and at the base of each topo a particular contour interval designation is given. Yes, it sounds confusing if you're new to the lingo, but it truly is a simple and wonderfully helpful system. Keep reading.

Let's assume that the 7.5 minute series topo before us says "Contour Interval 40 feet," that the short trail we'll be pedaling is two inches in length on the map, and that it crosses five contour lines from its beginning to end. What do we know? Well, because the linear scale of this series is 2,000 feet to the inch (roughly 2 ¼ inches representing 1 mile), we know our trail is approximately ⅘ of a mile long (2 inches × 2,000 feet). But we also know we'll be climbing or descending 200 vertical feet (5 contour lines × 40 feet each) over that distance. And the elevation designations written on occasional contour lines will tell us if we're heading up or down.

The authors of this series warn their readers of upcoming terrain, but only a detailed topo gives you the information you need to pinpoint your position on a map, steer yourself toward optional trails and roads nearby, and see at a glance if you'll be pedaling hard to take them. It's a lot of information for a very low cost. In fact, the only drawback with topos is their size—several feet square. I've tried rolling them into tubes, folding them carefully, even cutting them into blocks and photocopying the pieces. Any of these systems is a pain, but no matter how you pack the maps you'll be happy they're along. And you'll be even happier if you pack a compass as well.

In addition to local bike shops and sporting goods stores, you'll find topos at major universities and some public libraries, where you might try photocopying the ones you need to avoid the cost of buying them. But if you want your own and can't find them locally, contact:

USGS Map Sales, Box 25286, Denver, CO 80225
(888) ASK-USGS (275-8747); http://mapping.usgs.gov/esic/to_order.html/

VISA and MasterCard are accepted. Ask for an index while you're at it, plus a price list and a copy of the booklet *Topographic Maps*. In minutes you'll be reading them like a pro.

A second excellent series of maps available to mountain bikers is that put out by the United States Forest Service. If your trail runs through an area designated as a national forest, look in the phone book (white pages) under the United States Government listings, find the Department of Agriculture heading, and run your finger down that section until you find the Forest Service. Give them a call, and they'll provide the address of the regional Forest Service office, from which you can obtain the appropriate map.

TRAIL ETIQUETTE

Pick up almost any mountain bike magazine these days and you'll find articles and letters to the editor about trail conflict. For example, you'll find hikers' tales of being blindsided by speeding mountain bikers, complaints from mountain bikers about being blamed for trail damage that was really caused by horse or cattle traffic, and cries from bikers about those "kamikaze" riders who through their antics threaten to close even more trails to all of us.

The authors of this series have been very careful to guide you to only those trails that are open to mountain biking (or at least were open at the time of their research), and without exception have warned of the damage done to our sport through injudicious riding. We can all benefit from glancing over the following International Mountain Bicycling Association (IMBA) Rules of the Trail before saddling up.

1. *Ride on open trails only.* Respect trail and road closures (ask if not sure), avoid possible trespass on private land, obtain permits and authorization as may be required. Federal and state wilderness areas are closed to cycling.

2. *Leave no trace.* Be sensitive to the dirt beneath you. Even on open trails, you should not ride under conditions where you will leave evidence of your passing, such as on certain soils shortly after rain. Observe the different types of soils and trail construction; practice low-impact cycling. This also means staying on the trail and not creating any new ones. Be sure to pack out at least as much as you pack in.

3. *Control your bicycle!* Inattention for even a second can cause disaster. Excessive speed can maim and threaten people; there is no excuse for it!

4. *Always yield the trail.* Make known your approach well in advance. A friendly greeting (or a bell) is considerate and works well; startling someone may cause loss of trail access. Show your respect when passing others by slowing to a walk or even stopping. Anticipate that other trail users may be around corners or in blind spots.

5. *Never spook animals.* All animals are startled by an unannounced approach, a sudden movement, or a loud noise. This can be dangerous for you, for others, and for the animals. Give animals extra room and time to adjust to you. In passing, use special care and follow the directions of horseback riders (ask if uncertain). Running cattle and disturbing wild animals is a serious offense. Leave gates as you found them or as marked.

6. *Plan ahead.* Know your equipment, your ability, and the area in which you are riding—and prepare accordingly. Be self-sufficient at all times. Wear a helmet, keep your machine in good condition, and carry necessary supplies for changes in weather or other conditions. A well-executed trip is a satisfaction to you and not a burden or offense to others.

For more information, contact IMBA, P.O. Box 7578, Boulder, CO 80306, (303) 545-9011.

Additionally, the following Code of Ethics by the National Off-Road Biking Association (NORBA) is worthy of your attention.

1. I will yield the right of way to other non-motorized recreationists. I realize that people judge all cyclists by my actions.

2. I will slow down and use caution when approaching or overtaking another and will make my presence known well in advance.

3. I will maintain control of my speed at all times and will approach turns in anticipation of someone around the bend.

4. I will stay on designated trails to avoid trampling native vegetation and minimize potential erosion to trails by not using muddy trails or shortcutting switchbacks.

5. I will not disturb wildlife or livestock.

6. I will not litter. I will pack out what I pack in, and pack out more than my share if possible.

7. I will respect public and private property, including trail use and no trespassing signs; I will leave gates as I found them.

8. I will always be self-sufficient and my destination and travel speed will be determined by my ability, my equipment, the terrain, and present and potential weather conditions.

9. I will not travel solo when bike-packing in remote areas.

10. I will leave word of my destination and when I plan to return.

11. I will practice minimum impact bicycling by "taking only pictures and memories and leaving only waffle prints."

12. I will always wear a helmet when I ride.

Worthy of mention are the following suggestions based on a list by Utah's Wasatch-Cache National Forest and the *Tread Lightly!* program advocated by the U.S. Forest Service and Bureau of Land Management.

1. *Study a forest map before you ride.* Currently, bicycles are permitted on roads and developed trails which are designated bikes permitted. If your route crosses private land, it is your responsibility to obtain right-of-way permission from the landowner.

2. *Stay out of designated wilderness areas.* By law, all vehicles, including mountain bikes are not allowed.

3. *Stay off of roads and trails "put to bed."* These may be resource roads no longer used for logging or mining, or they may be steep trails being replaced by easier ones. So that the path returns to its natural state, they're usually blocked or signed closed to protect new vegetation.

4. *Keep groups small.* Riding in large groups degrades the outdoor experience for others, can disturb wildlife, and usually leads to greater resource damage.

5. *Avoid riding on wet trails.* Bicycle tires leave ruts in wet trails. These ruts concentrate runoff and accelerate erosion. Postponing a ride when the trails are wet will preserve the trails for future use.

6. *Stay on roads and trails.* Riding cross-country destroys vegetation and damages the soil. Resist the urge to pioneer a new road or trail, or to cut across a switchback. Avoid riding through meadows, on steep hillsides, or along stream banks and lakeshores because the terrain is easily scarred by churning wheels.

7. *Always yield to others.* Trails are shared by hikers, horses, and bicycles. Move off the trail to allow horses to pass and stop to allow hikers adequate room to share the trail. Simply yelling "Bicycle!" is not acceptable.

8. *Control your speed.* Excessive speed endangers yourself and other forest users.

9. *Avoid wheel lock-up and spin-out.* Steep terrain is especially vulnerable to trail wear. Locking brakes on steep descents or when stopping needlessly damages trails. If a slope is steep enough to require locking wheels and skidding, dismount and walk your bicycle. Likewise, if an ascent is so steep that your rear wheel slips and spins, dismount and walk your bicycle.

10. *Protect waterbars and switchbacks.* Waterbars, the rock and log drains built to direct water off trails, protect trails from erosion. When you encounter a waterbar, ride directly over the top or dismount and walk your bicycle. Riding around the ends of waterbars destroys their effectiveness and speeds erosion. Skidding around switchback corners shortens trail life. Slow down for switchback corners and keep your wheels rolling.

11. *If you abuse it, you lose it.* Mountain bikers are relative newcomers to the forest and must prove themselves responsible trail users. By following the guidelines above, and by participating in trail maintenance service projects, bicyclists can help avoid closures that would prevent them from using trails.

12. *Know your bicycle handling limitations.*

You get the drift. So that everyone can continue riding our bikes through some of our country's most beautiful places, I urge you to follow the codes above and not be the "one bad apple" that spoils it for the rest of us.

HITTING THE TRAIL

Once again, because this is a "where-to," not a "how-to" guide, the following will be brief. If you're a veteran trail rider, these suggestions might serve to remind you of something you've forgotten to pack. If you're a newcomer, they might convince you to think twice before hitting the backcountry unprepared.

Water: I've heard the questions dozens of times. "How much is enough? One bottle? Two? Three?! But think of all that extra weight!" Well, one simple physiological fact should convince you to err on the side of excess when it comes to deciding how much water to pack: A human working hard in 90-degree temperature needs approximately ten quarts of fluids every day. Ten quarts. That's two and a half gallons—12 large water bottles or 16 small ones. And, with water weighing in at approximately 8 pounds per gallon, a one-day supply comes to a whopping 20 pounds.

In other words, pack along two or three bottles even for short rides. And make sure you can purify the water found along the trail on longer routes. When writing of those routes where this could be of critical importance, each author has provided information on where water can be found near the trail—if it can be found at all. But drink it untreated and you run the risk of disease. (See *giardia* in the Glossary.)

One sure way to kill the protozoans, bacteria, and viruses in water is to boil it. Right. That's just how you want to spend your time on a bike ride. Besides, who wants to carry a stove or denude the countryside stoking bonfires to boil water?

Luckily, there is a better way. Many riders pack along the inexpensive and only slightly distasteful tetraglycine hydroperiodide tablets (sold under the names Potable Aqua, Globaline, and Coughlan's, among others). Some invest in portable, lightweight purifiers that filter out the crud. Unfortunately, both iodine *and* filtering are now required to be absolutely sure you've killed all the nasties you can't see. Tablets or iodine drops by themselves will knock off the well-known *giardia*, once called "beaver fever" for its transmission to the water through the feces of infected beavers. One to four weeks after ingestion, giardia will have you bloated, vomiting, shivering with chills, and living in the bathroom. (Though you won't care while you're suffering, beavers are getting a bum rap, for other animals are carriers also.)

But now there's another parasite we must worry about—*cryptosporidium.* "Crypto" brings on symptoms very similar to *giardia*, but unlike that fellow protozoan it's equipped with a shell sufficiently strong to protect it against the chemical killers that stop giardia cold. This means we're either back to boiling or on to using a water filter to screen out both *giardia* and crypto, plus the iodine to knock off viruses. All of which sounds like a time-consuming pain, but really isn't. Some water filters come equipped with an iodine chamber to guarantee full protection. Or you can simply add a pill or drops to the water you've just filtered (if you aren't allergic to iodine, of course). The pleasures of backcountry biking—and the displeasure of getting sick—make this relatively minor effort worth every one of the few minutes involved.

Tools: Ever since my first cross-country tour in 1965 I've been kidded about the number of tools I pack on the trail. And so I will exit entirely from this discussion by providing a list compiled by two mechanic (and mountain biker) friends of mine. After all, since they make their livings fixing bikes, and get their kicks by riding them, who could be a better source?

These two suggest the following as an absolute minimum:

tire levers	spare tube and patch kit
air pump	Allen wrenches (3, 4, 5, and 6 mm)
spoke wrench	six-inch crescent (adjustable-end) wrench
chain rivet tool	small flat-blade screwdriver

On the trail, their personal tool pouches contain these additional items:

channel locks (small)
air gauge
tire valve cap (the metal kind, with a valve-stem remover)
baling wire (ten or so inches, for temporary repairs)
duct tape (small roll for temporary repairs or tire boot)
boot material (small piece of old tire or a large tube patch)
spare chain link
rear derailleur pulley

spare nuts and bolts
paper towel and tube of waterless hand cleaner

First-Aid kit: My personal kit contains the following, sealed inside double Ziploc bags:

sunscreen
aspirin
butterfly-closure bandages
Band-Aids
snakebite kit
gauze (one roll)
gauze compress pads (a half-dozen 4" × 4")
ace bandages or Spenco joint wraps
Benadryl (an antihistamine, in case of allergic reactions)
water purification tablets/water filter (on long rides)
Moleskin/Spenco "Second Skin"
hydrogen peroxide, iodine, or Mercurochrome (some kind of antiseptic)
matches or pocket cigarette lighter
whistle (more effective in signaling rescuers than your voice)

Final considerations: The authors of this series have done a good job suggesting that specific items be packed for certain trails—rain gear in particular seasons, a hat and gloves for mountain passes, or shades for desert jaunts. Heed their warnings, and think ahead. Good luck.

Dennis Coello

COASTAL VIRGINIA

C oastal Virginia offers a variety of mountain biking opportunities in an area framed by the Atlantic Ocean and Chesapeake Bay to the east and Interstate 95 along the western edge. If you assumed that coastal trails would be flat, you'd be partially correct but possibly very surprised. Although the bike paths at York River State Park and Newport News Park are pretty flat, others in the same area, such as the Marl Ravine Trail at York River State Park and Dogwood Trail at Waller Mill Park, are characterized by short, but very steep ascents and descents.

Starting from sea level along the coast, the land rises to an elevation of approximately 300 feet above sea level at the start of the Piedmont. A less obvious but geologically significant western border between the coastal region and Piedmont is the Fall Line. This line runs roughly along the same path as Interstate 95 and marks the zone where streams over time have created rapids and waterfalls as they flowed from the harder sedimentary rock of the Piedmont across the softer, erosive sedimentary rock of the coastal region.

Many of these streams (including the James River and streams to the north) are tidal, meaning that their water levels rise and fall with the ocean tides. The Falls of the James River is readily apparent at Belle Isle in Richmond, where the river drops 85 feet through the class four Hollywood Rapids. However, this same geologic phenomenon can be seen to greater or lesser extent on other Virginia creeks and rivers along this north-south line from Great Falls in northern Virginia to the Meherrin River in Greensville County.

In its eight years of existence, the Eastern Virginia Mountain Bike Association has taken the mantle of stewardship over a lot of high-quality single-track in coastal Virginia. The club's membership has spent thousands of hours creating and maintaining trails at Harwoods Mill Park, Waller Mill Park, York

River State Park, and Beaverdam Reservoir Park and has developed increased goodwill among municipalities, other trail users, and mountain bikers.

There is more variation among ecological communities within this single region than any other in Virginia. The processes of shaping and reshaping the sea-land interface are ongoing and can be seen at First Landing State Park and False Cape State Park. The accumulation and shifting of sand is the most dynamic of all physiographic processes, and one in which nature is determined to have its way despite the best, and very expensive, efforts of individuals and coastal governing bodies intent on maintaining a status quo among the forces of wind, water, and land.

Moving from east to west you'll find a great deal of difference in plant and animal life from the ocean to the fall line. The sandy soil, salt air, and saltwater create a very specific biological niche for the flora and fauna that not only survive but also succeed. Strictly coastal life-forms include longleaf pine, cypress, live oak, pin oak, and river birch trees. Birds of prey, or raptors, exist at the top of their food chain and are very mobile, yet they can have very specific habitat needs. Along the coast you find the greatest preponderance of southern bald eagles, osprey, and marsh hawks, but these are generally not in other regions of the state. Other raptors such as red-tailed hawks and turkey vultures are less habitat specific and may show up anywhere in Virginia.

And, of course, it was on Virginia's coast at Jamestown that Captain John Smith and company dropped anchor in 1607 and established America's first permanent settlement. Although all of Virginia is ripe with history, it all began on the coast, and many of those early days have been re-created in Colonial Williamsburg, Yorktown, and Jamestown ("The Historic Triangle"); Shirley Plantation, Sherwood Forest, and Berkeley Plantation (site of the country's first Thanksgiving one year before the Pilgrims landed in Massachusetts) in Charles City County; and numerous other historic sites.

As you crisscross coastal Virginia searching for the trail system that best suits your mountain biking interests and abilities, plan to take extra time to better understand this historically significant and biologically diverse region. Much of coastal Virginia has seen considerable change since 1607 when the New World got its start, but it's still possible to ride through natural environments whose morphology and ecological interactions have changed little.

RIDE 1 · False Cape State Park

AT A GLANCE

Length/Configuration: 17-mile loop

Aerobic difficulty: None unless you encounter a head wind

Technical difficulty: Smooth, flat, sandy roads and beach riding; some short pushes through loose sand dunes

Scenery: Secluded marsh ponds and coastal beach with an array of water birds

Special comments: Pedal along the Atlantic Ocean en route to Virginia's most secluded state park

Although mountain biking along the beach might seem like an oxymoron, it's a fitting introduction to one part of the continuum of fat-tire riding options that you'll find throughout Virginia. False Cape State Park has been the state's most secluded and least visited state park, largely because access in the past has been limited to those who are willing to paddle, walk, or bike the requisite five miles through the adjoining Back Bay National Wildlife Refuge to reach Virginia's southernmost state park. Now an electric tram transports visitors through the wildlife refuge, but not bicylces. The tram leases from Little Island City Park between April 1 to October 31. During the winter, a Beach Transporter replaces the tram, because Back Bay Refuge is closed to provide a protective habitat for waterfowl migrating through the area. This requires cyclists ride the five miles along the beach and bypass the interior of Back Bay Refuge. At other times of year, when Back Bay's interior dikes are open, cyclists, as well as hikers, can utilize the beach or pass through the interior of the refuge.

The 17-mile loop described here will guide you through Back Bay and False Cape's pristine coastal paradise and features a seasonally changing display of avian wildlife that seems to have flown straight out of Noah's own collection. This ride includes beach riding along the Atlantic Ocean as well as on flat, sandy roads that traverse the interior of these two adjoining saltwater sanctuaries. Options such as camping at False Cape and sampling various side roads will appeal to those who want to spend more than a day exploring the park.

The 4,321-acre False Cape State Park offers riders with a wide range of abilities the opportunity to pedal through beaches, dunes, wooded swamps—and

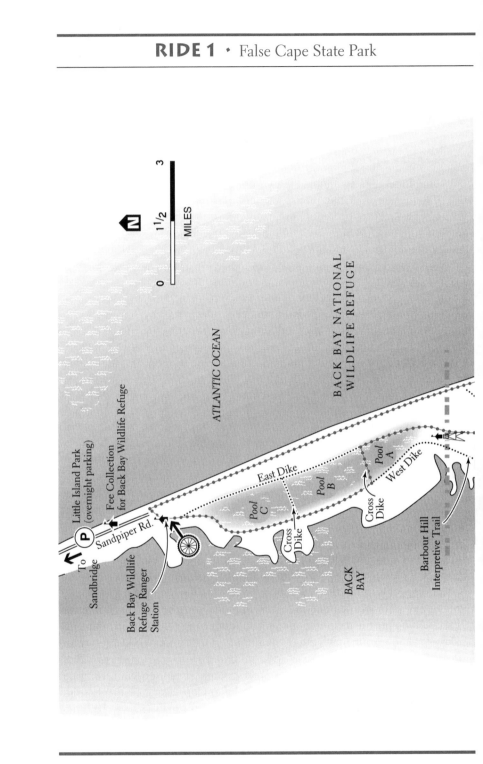

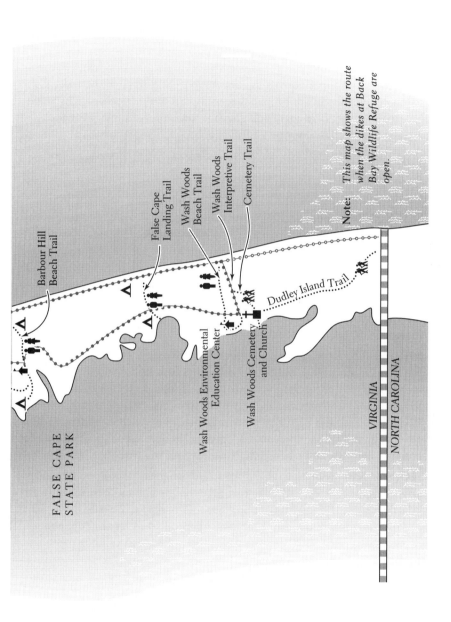

FALSE CAPE STATE PARK

Barbour Hill Beach Trail

False Cape Landing Trail

Wash Woods Beach Trail

Wash Woods Interpretive Trail

Cemetery Trail

Wash Woods Environmental Education Center

Wash Woods Cemetery and Church

Dudley Island Trail

Note: This map shows the route when the dikes at Back Bay Wildlife Refuge are open.

VIRGINIA

NORTH CAROLINA

a bit of Virginia history. Even those with minimal interest in our feathered friends should bring a pair of binoculars and a field guide to look at the birds that hang out along this Atlantic spit of sand.

The former Wash Woods community on False Cape was developed by survivors of one of the many nineteenth-century shipwrecks caused by the resemblance of this landmass to a real cape. These wrecks gave False Cape its name after it gained a reputation as a graveyard for ocean-going traffic. Survivors settled here and built the first structures from cypress that had washed ashore from shipwrecks.

General location: 5 miles South of the Virginia Beach borough of Sandbridge.

Elevation change: None.

Season: Year-round, but check ahead for specific dates of the annual fall "wildlife management time," usually in early October, when the hunting of deer and feral hogs is allowed. Also check on seasonal access through Back Bay National Wildlife Refuge. From November through March, when access through Back Bay Wildlife Refuge is limited to the beach, it's important to schedule your comings and goings with low-tide times. Call Back Bay National Wildlife Refuge or False Cape State Park to find out the times for high and low tide.

Services: There are a limited number of primitive campsites, including beachfront sites, at False Cape State Park, so it's important to reserve a site if you plan to spend the night under the stars. Campers must make reservations by calling (800) 933-7275. There are also environmental education programs at False Cape State Park and Back Bay Wildlife Refuge. A fee is charged to enter Back Bay Wildlife Refuge, although it is possible to purchase an annual pass for entering Back Bay. All other services are available in nearby Virginia Beach.

Hazards: Ravenous mosquitoes, ticks, and chiggers; cottonmouth snakes; and feral pigs (honest!). Plan to cart in an ample amount of drinking water and then some. Bring plenty of bug spray and apply it liberally before starting this ride during the warm months. Plan to cart in an ample amount of drinking water and then some. Water is also available in vending machines.

Rescue index: There are emergency telephones at Barbour Hill and Wash Woods, located in False Cape State Park, as well as at the Back Bay Wildlife Refuge Headquarters.

Land status: Access to False Cape State Park is through Back Bay National Wildlife Refuge. False Cape State Park is managed by the Virginia Department of Conservation and Recreation.

Maps: These are available from the offices of False Cape State Park and Back Bay National Wildlife Refuge or www.dcr.state.va.us/parks.

Finding the trail: Take the Indian River Road East exit from Interstate 64.

Pedal through Back Bay Wildlife Refuge en route to False Cape—Virginia's most secluded state park.

Drive east on Indian River Road, turn left onto Newbridge Road, and then right onto Sandbridge Road (VA 629). Head south onto Sandpiper Road and continue past the entrance station and park next to the office of the Back Bay Wildlife Refuge for day use. If you're planning to camp at False Cape, park at the Little Island Recreation Area Parking lot just before the Back Bay entrance station. From April 1 to the end of October, enter the Back Bay National Wildlife Refuge via a sandy gated road located next to the building for Back Bay's office. If you'll be bypassing the interior of Back Bay Wildlife Refuge, either by choice or due to visiting between November 1 and the end of March when the waterfowl need their privacy, go straight up to the beach from the office building at the refuge.

Sources of additional information:

False Cape State Park
4001 Sandpiper Road
Virginia Beach, Virginia 23456
(757) 426-7128

Back Bay National Wildlife Refuge
4005 Sandpiper Rd.
Virginia Beach, Virginia 23456-4325
(757) 721-2412

Notes on the trail: Since my visit to False Cape, there has been considerable concern about visitors interfering with the nesting cycles of migratory birds in the Back Bay National Wildlife Refuge, which sits between Sandbridge and the state park. The 17-mile loop described here is only passable from April 1 to the end of October. Riders should follows the beach in lieu of the 4-mile trail through Back Bay when the interior dikes are closed from November 1 to the end of March. Both routes are of a similar distance, with the primary difference being that the beach ride is more direct but also more subject to the whimsical effects—sometimes tiring and sometimes magical—of head and tail winds. Those planning to visit should call either False Cape State Park or Back Bay National Wildlife Refuge for current information about access.

This loop ride is based on access through Back Bay Wildlife Refuge, which may not be an option depending on when you schedule your trip. Although beach riding along a narrow strip of hard-packed sand at low tide is fun, riders need to be aware that high tide's return can effectively shut off access.

Starting from the Back Bay Wildlife Refuge office and parking area, you'll pedal along a hard-packed sandy road that's fairly straight, with occasional wide bends, from the eastern to the western side of this spit. The road is flat and mostly out in the open, although there are stretches through the woods where summer insects are bothersome. Continue on this road as it twists and turns past a series of cleared and wooded areas lying between the Atlantic Ocean and Back Bay. The array of birds is incredible.

Shortly after emerging from a woods of live oak and pines, turn right at the sign for False Cape State Park. You'll enter the park past a large, marshy field where a number of the resident feral horses were grazing as I passed by. I was also greeted by a poisonous cottonmouth snake who took advantage of the opportunity to give me a look at his fangs and the white inside of his mouth. If Back Bay's west dike, described above, is closed, take the unwooded east dike and turn left to enter False Cape.

There are numerous trails and sandy roads through False Cape, so you'll have a smorgasbord of opportunities to chose from if you want to do some exploration of your own. However, stop first at the Visitor Contact Station for further information, check in, and continue another 4.5 miles south along the main trail, which runs the length of the park from Barbour Hill to Wash Woods. The 3-mile Dudley Island Trail past Wash Woods continues to the North Carolina line, but its loose, sandy surface makes it impossible to keep riding.

Wash Woods is a good place to head over to the Atlantic Ocean on either the Wash Woods Beach or Interpretive Trail. You'll be slogging less than a mile through the dunes so forget about riding until you get to the beach. After pushing, sweating, and cursing your way across the dunes, turn left just before the water's edge to return to the start. Some riders turn right just before the ocean and head south for 3 miles (one-way) to reach the Virginia/North Carolina border. This will add 6 miles of beach riding to the 17-mile loop, for a total 23 miles.

If you've never ridden on the beach, you're in for quite a surprise. Somewhere between the water and the loose sand is a narrow strip of hard-packed sand that's really nice to ride on in the absence of hurricane surf or a head wind.

If you plan to ride through the interior of Back Bay National Wildlife

Refuge, turn left at the sign for Barbour Hill and make your way through the dunes back to the main road through False Cape State Park. Otherwise, continue along the Atlantic for 7.5 miles of beachfront riding back to the refuge.

RIDE 2 • First Landing State Park

AT A GLANCE

Length/Configuration: 6-mile out-and-back (12 miles round-trip)

Aerobic difficulty: Relatively flat, sandy double-track

Technical difficulty: Easy

Scenery: Exotic lagoons, cypress trees, hanging Spanish moss, and high sand dunes

Special comments: Good family or beginner ride that tends to get crowded, especially in warm weather

First Landing State Park is Virginia's most visited park, and the six-mile out-and-back (12 miles round-trip) Cape Henry Trail gets a lot of use because of the park's location and easy accessibility from the resort city of Virginia Beach. This sandy double-track trail is an easy ride as it winds its way through the 2,888-acre national landmark whose natural features include exotic lagoons, bald cypress, and live oak draped with hanging Spanish moss. The Cape Henry leads to 64th Street before it bends around to end near the boat landing at the Narrows, where soda machines and flush toilets await you.

On April 26, 1607, one hundred English settlers landed at this location and developed the colony's first elective government before ultimately reaching Jamestown, where they established the colony's first permanent settlement. This historic event prompted the park's recent name change from Seashore State Park to First Landing.

The Cape Henry Trail is the only trail within the park open to bicycling. To fully appreciate all of the park's natural beauty and unique environmental features, plan to dismount, lock your bike well, and explore a little on foot along the easily hiked Lagoon, High Dune, Long Creek, or any of the other trails that loop through this coastal Garden of Eden. If a little privacy is more to your liking, plan your trip to First Landing on a weekday, especially outside the busy summer season, or early in the morning before the large crowds of vacationers and residents flock here.

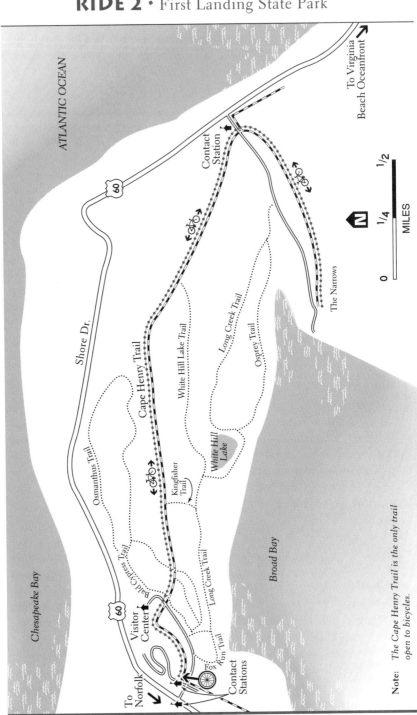

ATLANTIC OCEAN

Chesapeake Bay

To Norfolk

Visitor Center

Bald Cypress Trail

Osmanthus Trail

Shore Dr.

60

60

Cape Henry Trail

White Hill Lake Trail

Long Creek Trail

Osprey Trail

White Hill Lake

Kingfisher Trail

Long Creek Trail

Fox Run Trail

Contact Stations

Broad Bay

Contact Station

The Narrows

To Virginia Beach Oceanfront

N

MILES

0   ¼   ½

Note: *The Cape Henry Trail is the only trail open to bicycles.*

Spanish moss hangs from live oaks in the marshy lagoons at First Landing State Park.

General location: In the city of Virginia Beach on US 60 between Norfolk and the beachfront section of Virginia Beach.

Elevation change: Virtually none.

Season: The park is open year-round, but it tends to be most crowded on warm weekends, especially during the summer. If you're looking for a more solitary ride through First Landing State Park, plan your ride early in the morning on weekends or during the week.

Services: The park offers camping, cabins, a camp store, laundry, and interpretive nature programming. A fee is charged to enter First Landing State Park, though it is reduced in the off-season. Some of these services will be limited outside of the peak season from Memorial Day through Labor Day. All other services are available outside the park in the city of Virginia Beach and nearby Norfolk.

Hazards: Be especially careful of the sheer numbers of other cyclists on the trail.

Rescue index: Park personnel are available to offer assistance at the entrance station and Visitor Center; they drive through the area in easily identifiable vehicles.

Land status: State park.

Maps: Available from park office or www.dcr.state.va.us/parks.

Finding the trail: First Landing State Park is located on US 60 at Cape Henry in the City of Virginia Beach, 4.5 miles east of US 13. You can get onto the Cape Henry Bike Trail after passing the entrance station across US 60 from the campground.

Source of additional information:
First Landing State Park
2500 Shore Drive
Virginia Beach, Virginia 23451
(757) 412-2300

Notes on the trail: First Landing State Park personnel told me that cyclists blazing new trails through the dunes and illegally using some of the other 27 miles of hiking trails here are creating considerable problems and ill will for themselves and other two-wheelers who ride here.

The Cape Henry Trail gets a lot of bicycle traffic during the warm weather of early spring through early fall. This will probably attract some riders and repel others, but it is a fact of life. The trail offers access to a beautiful coastal environment void of hills or obstacles, making a fairly easy 12-mile pedal.

RIDE 3 · Great Dismal Swamp

AT A GLANCE

Length/Configuration: 4.5-mile out-and-back (9 miles round-trip); 140 miles of uncharted logging roads

Aerobic difficulty: Flat, sandy double-track

Technical difficulty: Easy

Scenery: A densely wooded wildlife refuge surrounding Lake Drummond

Special comments: Good beginner ride; visitors from April through September should bring plenty of bug spray to combat the swarms of hungry mosquitoes and chiggers

RIDE 3 · Great Dismal Swamp

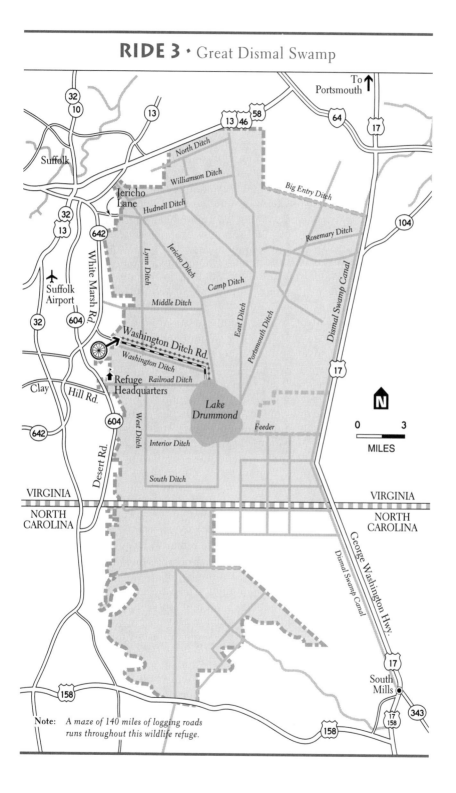

Note: A maze of 140 miles of logging roads runs throughout this wildlife refuge.

History and mystery
intermingle at Lake
Drummond in Great
Dismal Swamp.

The Washington Ditch Road is the designated bike trail at the Great Dismal Swamp National Wildlife Refuge and runs 4.5 miles (nine miles out-and-back) from the western edge of the refuge to Lake Drummond at the center. This hard-packed, sandy double-track parallels one of numerous canals George Washington had dug to drain the swamp for farmland and to connect the Chesapeake Bay and Albemarle Sound via a north-south canal. The ditch itself is thought to be the country's oldest site named for George Washington.

In addition to the Washington Ditch Road, there are more than 140 miles of logging and service roads that crisscross the 107,000-acre dense swamp. However, you should venture off the beaten path with the full knowledge of the variety of resident wildlife to be found here—some beautiful, some quite dangerous—as well as the understanding that these old roads were not designed and are not necessarily maintained for recreational use. The mountain biker in search of challenging terrain may want to pass up riding through Great Dismal Swamp, but the cyclist, nature lover, or historian will find much here to appreciate.

Pedal 4.5 miles into the swamp's interior and plan a picnic lunch along the shore of Lake Drummond. The refuge is open one-half hour before sunrise to one-half hour before sunset.

General location: 6 miles south of Suffolk.

Elevation change: None.

Season: Bikers and birders will want to come during the spring migration from mid-April to mid-May. To avoid ravenous mosquitoes and high marsh grasses, plan to come during the colder months of November through March. Check with refuge officials for specific dates of the various hunting seasons in the Great Dismal Swamp.

Services: All services are available in nearby Suffolk.

Hazards: Getting lost on unmarked former logging roads, falling prey to mosquitoes and chiggers, encountering 3 species of poisonous snakes, and getting between a mother black bear and her cubs are all potential dangers. A large population of resident black bears sometimes ravage neighboring cornfields and then retreat to the refuge.

Rescue index: The office of the Great Dismal Swamp National Wildlife Refuge is located on Desert Road (VA 604) about 5 miles south of the trailhead for the Washington Ditch Road.

Land status: National wildlife refuge.

Maps: There is a map in the brochure available from the refuge office.

Finding the trail: Go south out of Suffolk on US 13 for about 3.5 miles before turning left onto VA 32. After 4.5 miles turn left onto Whitemarsh Road (VA 642), and after going another 5 miles turn left onto the gravel Washington Ditch Road. Park outside the gate at the end of the road.

Source of additional information:
Great Dismal Swamp National Wildlife Refuge
P.O. Box 349
Suffolk, Virginia 23439-0349
(757) 986-3705

Notes on the trail: Much about the 107,000-acre Great Dismal Swamp National Wildlife Refuge is mysterious. The air of mystery is accentuated by a trip on a foggy or rainy weekday morning with no others around. One of the swamp's mysteries concerns William Drummond, the sole survivor of an early expedition for whom Lake Drummond is named. It's unclear how Drummond, North Carolina's first colonial governor (1663–1667), managed to outlive the rest of his hunting party. However, his luck changed in 1676 when he was hanged, drawn, and quartered for his part in Bacon's Rebellion.

Colonel William Byrd II had little good to say about the swamp after his 1728 survey, but he provided the first extensive description in his *Dividing Line Betwixt Virginia and North Carolina*. Byrd is often credited with naming it after his own dismal view of the locale, but others suggest that the name is a derivation of the language spoken by the Nansemond Indians, who are reported to have lived in the swamp as long as 9,000 years ago.

The 3,100-acre Lake Drummond is one of only two natural lakes in Virginia. Local Native American legend and the lake's circular outline have suggested that it was formed by "the fire bird," a meteor. The Nansemond Indians and the early nineteenth-century Irish poet Thomas Moore speak of the Lady of the Lake. This Indian maiden is said to have died just before her marriage and has been paddling across the lake thereafter. Her bereaved brave went into the lake in search of her but was never heard from again. The ill-fated couple was supposedly joined in death, and if you're romantic (or foolhardy) enough to venture out to the lake at the witching hour of midnight, perhaps you'll catch a glimpse of them paddling across Lake Drummond.

Henry Wadsworth Longfellow and Harriet Beecher Stowe also used the swamp as the subject for some of their works. A young American poet, despondent over the rejection of his work by his publisher, Miss Elinor White, traveled from Boston to the Dismal Swamp to use the swamp as a backdrop for his suicide. However, while on his way to the South, Robert Frost devised a better plan to get these 4 poems into print, and he ended up marrying Miss White.

Those who want to learn about the swamp's natural history will be interested to know that 209 species of bird have been spotted here, the best time being during the spring migration from mid-April to mid-May. The refuge also supports a population of black bear that is most active in early June. You may encounter 3 species of poisonous snakes—the cottonmouth, canebrake rattler, and copperhead—18 species of nonpoisonous snakes, and 56 other species of reptiles and amphibians. Visitors from April through September are sure to encounter swarms of hungry mosquitoes and chiggers and should definitely plan to bring plenty of bug spray.

RIDE 4 · Carrollton Nike Park

AT A GLANCE

VA

Length/Configuration: 2.5-mile loop

Aerobic difficulty: Several short, moderate ups and downs—a good workout when done at a fast clip

Technical difficulty: Several man-made log jumps

Scenery: An attractive background of hardwoods surrounding a pond

Special comments: Excellent introduction to single-track riding with minimal ups and downs; bring plenty of bug spray

This 2.5-mile loop was the last of many rides I did to put this guide together. Although last, it certainly was not the least among them. In fact, Carrollton Nike was one of my favorites once I realized that the name derived from its former function as an army missile base and not merely another attempt to influence my choice of athletic shoes. Mae West's reputed remark that sometimes you have to kiss a lot of frogs before finding your prince aptly applies to mountain bike rides as well. After spending the better part of three years riding on trails and rough roads around the state, I'd finally found my princess.

The folks from Mountain Bike Virginia have done a super job designing and maintaining an excellent introductory single-track trail. It will appeal to experienced beginners and intermediate riders who are ready to take the next step into the world of single-track but who may not be up to the challenge of the more technical or steeper sites such as Powhite Park in Richmond or the Marl Ravine Trail outside Williamsburg. Several short climbs and descents, as well as bridges of varied construction from logs to boards, make the loop interesting without unduly taxing novice single-trackers.

The pond forms an attractive background for this ride, but it also serves as a breeding ground for mayflies and mosquitoes from April through September. Pack plenty of bug spray. But don't put this ride off for several years like I did—you'll want to do it sooner rather than later.

General location: Near the town of Smithfield just north of the James River Bridge.

Elevation change: Minimal.

Season: Year-round.

Services: Bathrooms and water at the park are available during the park's operating hours from 8 A.M. until dark.

Hazards: The last leg of the trail is a narrow strip between the edge of a cultivated field and Nike Park Road. If this narrow strip is overgrown, as it was when I visited, it's difficult to see the drainage ditch that also shares this sliver of soil. It's best to ride on the road rather than risk riding into the hidden ditch. Bring plenty of bug spray and use it as needed. Watch for large patches of poison ivy throughout the woods just off the trail.

Rescue index: Help can be found at the parks and recreation department office located at the park during operating hours and in nearby Smithfield at other times. With its ball fields, this is a busy park. You should be able to find help at most times.

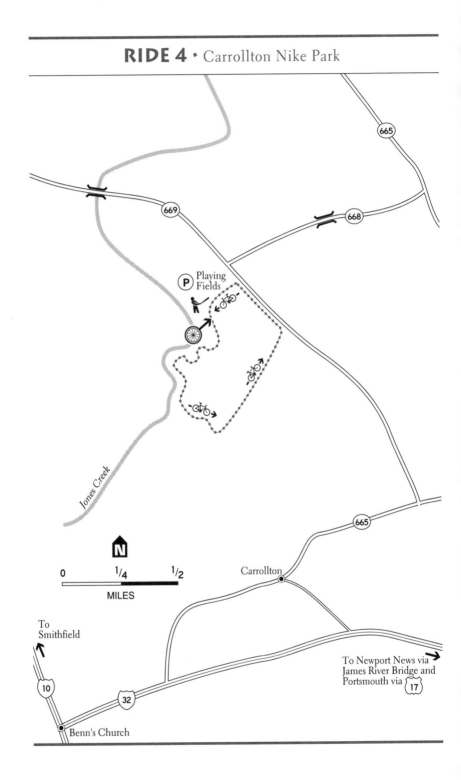

Land status: County park.

Maps: None available at present, but the trail is well blazed and very easy to follow.

Finding the trail: Cross the James River Bridge from Newport News heading toward the town of Smithfield on US 17 south. About 2 miles after crossing the bridge, turn right onto VA 669 and follow the signs to the park's entrance. Enter the driveway and go straight ahead to the last parking loop. The trailhead is on the left and is marked by a small sign listing the IMBA trail rules.

Sources of additional information:

Debra Weir
County of Isle of Wight
Public Recreational Facilities Authority
13036 Nike Park Road
Carrolton, Virginia 23314
(757) 357-2291

Gary Morgan
230 North 32nd Street
Richmond, Virginia 23223
(804) 782-7903 day
(804) 222-8006 evenings

Notes on the trail: Carrollton Nike's mountain bike trail is tucked away at the back of this 150-acre former army Nike missile base and is somewhat hidden by several ball fields. However, this out-of-the-way location in no way reflects the trail's fun factor. This coastal Virginia park has been host to 4 or 5 mountain bike races annually since the trail's opening, and the TREK Freestyle team has even made an appearance.

RIDE 5 · Newport News Park

AT A GLANCE

Length/Configuration: 5-mile loop

Aerobic difficulty: Very flat—ride at a fast clip to get your heart and lungs earning their keep

Technical difficulty: Flat, sandy double-track

Scenery: All wooded

Special comments: Good family ride; the park offers numerous outdoor activities and is near Busch Gardens, Water Country USA, and Colonial Williamsburg

This 8,000-acre park is one of the largest municipal parks in the country and offers some wooded respite from the traffic and ever-growing population

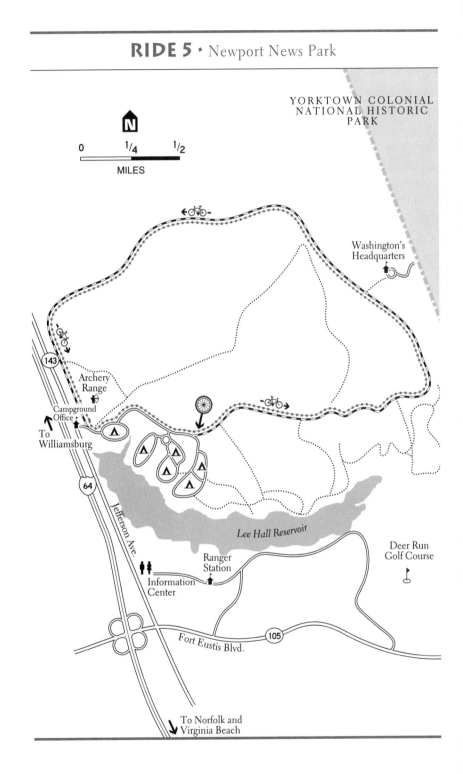

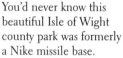

You'd never know this beautiful Isle of Wight county park was formerly a Nike missile base.

of Tidewater Virginia. The five-mile sandy double-track "bike way" is an easy ride through the woods that families and novice mountain bikers will enjoy. The bike trail loops through the largest natural enclave along the coastal region of Virginia, with three dozen mammals and more than 200 species of birds just waiting to say hello. Combined with the camping, golfing, boating, and fishing facilities at this public park, the ride makes a surprisingly nice getaway to the "wilds" of Newport News.

General location: In the city of Newport News just off Interstate 64 via exit 250.

Elevation change: None.

Season: Year-round.

Services: Archery range, camp store and laundry, 188 campsites, 36-hole golf course, arboretum, boat rental, and fishing in reservoir at Newport News Park. All other services are available in Newport News and neighboring areas.

Hazards: None.

Rescue index: Rangers on duty 24 hours. Call (757) 886-7912 or (800) 203-8322.

Land status: City park.

Maps: Available from the park office.

Finding the trail: Take the Fort Eustis Boulevard exit 250 north off I-64. Turn onto Jefferson Avenue (VA 143) going east and follow the signs a short distance to Newport News Park. Upon entering the park, follow the "bike way" signs along the hard-surface road past campgrounds A, B, C, and D; begin pedaling after turning left onto the sandy road just before campgrounds E and F.

Sources of additional information:

Newport News Park
13564 Jefferson Avenue
Newport News, Virginia 23603
(757) 888-3333 or 886-7912

Colonial Historic Park
P.O. Box 210
Yorktown, Virginia 23690
(757) 898-3400

Notes on the trail: Cyclists looking to step back in time have at least two options to choose from. Halfway around the bike way loop you'll see a small sign on the side of the trail for Washington's Headquarters. It was a short distance down this spur trail that George Washington plotted his successful military strategy over Cornwallis's British forces at the Battle of Yorktown, which ended the Revolutionary War. This trail also leads to Yorktown Battlefield.

The 14 miles of paved tour roads wind in and out of the battlefield at the Colonial National Historic Park. Although paved, these are very enjoyable, slightly rolling byways with little traffic that will lead you through a beautiful succession of forests and fields. Any mileage you accumulate on the Washington's Headquarters spur trail or beyond will be in addition to the 5-mile total for the Newport News Park bike way, but those are relatively easy extra miles. Plan to ride through Yorktown, a charming village that sits on a bluff overlooking the York River, and stop by the Yorktown Battlefield Visitor Center.

RIDE 6 · Harwoods Mill Trail

AT A GLANCE

Length/Configuration: 5-mile combination of 3 short loops and an out-and-back section

Aerobic difficulty: Several short, moderate ups and downs—a good workout when done at a fast clip

Technical difficulty: Narrow, twisty single-track with roots and man-made log jumps across trail; loops are designated as Novice, Advanced, and Expert

Scenery: Hardwoods surrounding pond

Special comments: Excellent introduction to single-track riding with minimal ups and downs; bring plenty of bug spray

The Harwoods Mill Trail is one of several routes developed by the Eastern Virginia Mountain Bike Association in coastal Virginia. It is located several miles from Newport News Park and is technically a part of the 6,000-acre municipal outdoor recreation area.

The entire trail system consists of three single-track loops of increasing technical difficulty joined together by a mile-long service road, which is flat, sandy double-track. Together these form a five-mile out-and-back configuration if you've ridden each of the three loops. There are trail markers and posts with colored bands (one white—novice; two yellow—advanced; three orange—expert) to signify the respective difficulty levels of each loop. The novice trail loops along one edge of the Harwoods Mill Reservoir through a forest of holly, oak, and maple. The other trails border a cutover section that is considerably less attractive, although the trails are no less fun to ride.

The idea of having signs that distinguish trails by their level of difficulty is a good one in theory. In this case, however, I wouldn't put much stock in the novice, advanced, and expert designations. I found that each of the three loops has its own share of technical challenges and none is so easy that it should be taken lightly. On the other hand, because of the relatively flat terrain, even the expert trail is not so tough that any intermediate rider with moderate bike handling skills wouldn't be up to the challenge.

General location: In the city of Newport News.

Elevation change: Minimal.

Season: Year-round.

Services: All services are available in the city of Newport News, where this trail is located.

Hazards: Normal hazards associated with twisty and sometimes rooted single-track, although the trail is flat so there are none of the steep ups and downs you find at Waller Mill Park or the Marl Ravine Trail outside Williamsburg.

Rescue index: Assistance can be readily found in the suburban area surrounding the park.

RIDE 6 · Harwoods Mill Trail

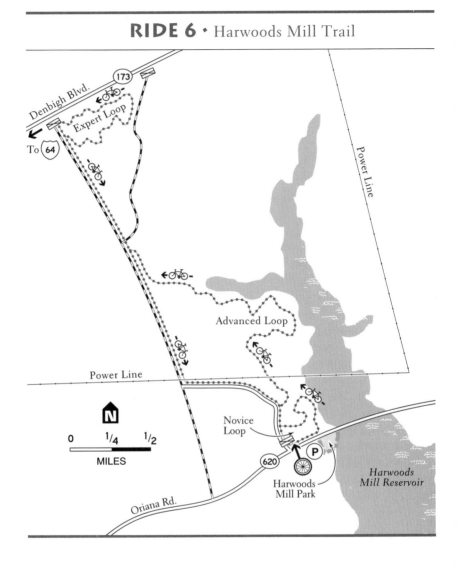

Land status: City park.

Maps: Maps are available from Newport News Park, but this is a well-marked trail that is easy to follow.

Finding the trail: Take exit 258 north off Interstate 64 onto US 17. After 4 miles turn left onto Oriana Road. Cross the Harwoods Mill Reservoir and then turn right into the parking lot. The trailhead is just across Oriana Road from the parking area.

Single-track at Harwoods
Mill winds through
woods around the
edges of the reservoir.

Sources of additional information:

Newport News Park
13564 Jefferson Avenue
Newport News, Virginia 23603
(757) 888-3333

Eastern Virginia
    Mountain Bike Association
P.O. Box 7553
Hampton, Virginia 23666
(757) 722-4609

Notes on the trail: Start riding from the trailhead on Oriana Road along the service road for a short distance until you can turn onto the novice trail, designated by a single white stripe on the signpost on your right. Go ahead and ride each of the 3 single-track loops. I am hard-pressed to say that any of the 3 short loops is considerably more difficult than the others. The last loop (the expert) ends just before Denbigh Boulevard, so turn left here onto the service road and head back to the beginning.

RIDE 7 • Beaverdam Reservoir Park

AT A GLANCE

Length/Configuration: 16-mile total out-and-back with several short loops

Aerobic difficulty: Fairly flat with some hills

Technical difficulty: Relatively smooth with some muddy sections, roots, and log jumps

Scenery: Hardwoods surrounding a large reservoir

Special comments: Excellent introduction to single-track riding a fair numbr of ups and downs, as well as bridges; great birding, including resident bald eagles; bring plenty of bug spray; be mindful of horseback riders

Thanks to a new trail linking both entrances, the five miles of trail snaking along Beaverdam Reservoir's northern edge will soon be part of an eight mile system. Several small loops make this more interesting than usual out-and-back rides. This beginner's single-track has some ups or downs, but none of the technical aspects that would restrict a rider with basic bike handling skills, although it does offer plenty of intricate twists and turns along the wooded edges of the 635-acre body of water.

The reservoir forms a beautiful backdrop for this trail, which never veers too far afield. Coastal waters such as Beaverdam attract readily identifiable water birds like a magnet; a birding guide should be considered standard equipment along with water bottles and food. Nature lovers will want to order a $5 copy of *Critters of Beaverdam* from the park office and be familiar with most of the resident wildlife, from single-celled protozoa to mammals. Or you can be pleasantly surprised, as I was after finishing my ride, when I casually glanced at the upper branches of a lakeside pin oak and spotted a pair of bald eagles. Several beaverdams are visible, as are several small, unique ponds

By the summer of 2001 a 10-mile trail connecting the park's Route 616 and Route 606 entrances will be complete. The addition will only make this good mountain bike ride better.

General location: 5 miles north of Gloucester Courthouse in Gloucester County.

Elevation change: None, but the trail does undulate through ravines.

Season: Riding is possible year-round, but the adjoining private land is often hunted. Call the Virginia Department of Game and Inland Fisheries

The aquatic habitat at Beaverdam Reservoir Park is home to a variety of water birds, including bald eagles.

(804-367-1000) for opening and closing dates of various hunting seasons. Plan to wear bright colors if you ride during those times when hunters are afield. You should also use good judgment if you ride here during periods of wet weather because the trail's low elevation makes it retain water and results in muddy areas.

Services: Fishing, bathrooms, drinks, and candy bars are available at the park office at the main entrance off VA 616. All other services are available on US 17 between the park and Gloucester Point.

Hazards: Low-lying, mud-sucking areas and crowded conditions on a narrow single-track trail.

Rescue index: Help can be summoned from the park office at the main entrance off VA 616 or at any number of commercial establishments along US 17 heading south toward Gloucester Courthouse.

Land status: County park.

Maps: Simple maps available at the trail entrance.

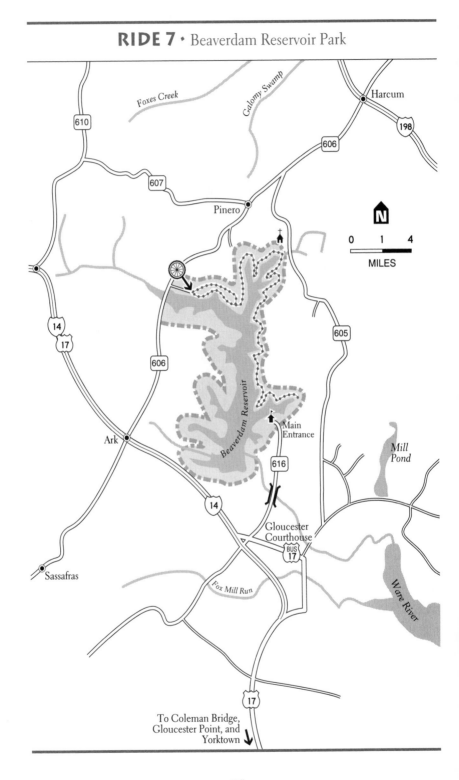

The single-track system at Beaverdam Reservoir Park will eventually stretch 10-miles around the lake.

Finding the trail: Cross the Coleman Bridge from Yorktown to Gloucester Point. Continue on US 17 north to Ark and turn right onto VA 606. After 2.5 miles, turn right into the parking lot at the sign for Beaverdam Reservoir Park. As you enter the parking area from VA 606, the trailhead will be on the opposite side of the lot.

Sources of additional information:

Chris Smith
Park Manager
Beaverdam Park

8687 Roaring Springs Road
Gloucester, Virginia 23061
(804) 693-2107

Notes on the trail: The trail's direction is pretty obvious, and when in doubt there's enough flagging tape along the way to show where the trail is, if not which direction to proceed. It's not too crucial if you go the wrong way at one of the ambiguous turns, as long as you remember that the park boundary is generally 200–300' feet from the water's edge and all land beyond is private property. Eventually, it all leads back to the trailhead. Meandering through the woods instead of being anxious to get from point A to point B is really the fun of a ride like this one.

Be aware of private roads that intersect the trail at some points. These roads are marked as private property and are not for public use. Also, be advised that the Nature Trail at the southernmost end of the multi-use trail is for hikers only. Hence, it is advisable to access the network from the northernmost trailhead.

RIDE 8 • York River State Park

AT A GLANCE

Length/Configuration: 7-mile total out-and-back

Aerobic difficulty: Some moderate ups and downs but pretty flat overall

Technical difficulty: Easy

Scenery: Mature hardwoods lead to a bluff overlooking the York River

Special comments: Good family or beginner ride

York River State Park has two distinctly different sets of trails open to bicycles. The Marl Ravine Trail (Ride 9) is a tough single-track whose technical challenges will delight more advanced riders. The ride described here is a system of trails forming an easy, seven-mile, out-and-back ride from the Visitor Center via the Backbone, Riverview, and White-Tail Trails, with a short loop around Woodstock Pond. The park recently converted the Laurel Glen trail to a beginner mountain bike trail. Approximately 1-mile long, the wooded single-track is primarily flad but is a good training ride for inexperienced bikers.

These wide double-track trails with gradual ups and downs are just the thing for a nice spring or fall day. Bring a picnic lunch and make it a family mountain bike outing for riders of varied abilities. Backbone Trail, as the name implies, is the longest of the trails, and the others shoot away from it like floating ribs. The Riverview and White-Tail Trails spur off the end of the 1.3-mile Backbone and offer two ways to get to a nice bluff in the woods overlooking the York River.

This 2,505-acre state park offers guided environmental canoe tours along Taskinas Creek and its surroundings, which are designated a Chesapeake Bay National Estuarine Research Reserve. The park sits on a beautiful bluff overlooking the York River toward Gloucester County. This piece of land was once the site of a seventeenth- and eighteenth-century public tobacco warehouse where local growers stored their crops before shipment to England.

General location: 11 miles west of Williamsburg.

Elevation change: Gradual but minimal overall.

Season: Year-round, except for those times of year listed below. An especially good time is in the Spring, when the Eastern Virginia Mountain Bike Association (EVMA) and York River State Park host their annual Off Road Duathalon, which combines 20 miles of mountain biking with 5 miles of trail running. Call the park or EVMA for specific dates. The park closes for a week in November and early December for the annual Deer Management Program. Call ahead for specific closure dates.

Services: The park provides facilities for picnicking, fishing, bike and helmet rentals, boating and boat rentals, guided canoe trips, and interpretive nature programs. A fee is charged to enter York River State Park. All other services are available along US 60 heading east toward Williamsburg.

Hazards: Yield the right of way to horses and hikers along the trails.

Rescue index: Personnel are on duty at the Visitor Center, located at the end of the entrance road. They also regularly patrol around the park in marked vehicles.

Land status: State park.

Maps: Available from York River State Park or www.dcr.state.va.us/parks.

Finding the trail: Take exit 231 off Interstate 64 and go east on Croaker Road (VA 607). Turn right onto Riverview Road (VA 606) and then left onto York River Park Road (VA 696). After passing the entrance station, the bike trails will be on your right. You can start by looping around Woodstock Pond, which leads to Backbone Trail.

Sources of additional information:

York River State Park
5526 Riverview Road
Williamsburg, Virginia 23188
(757) 566-3036

Eastern Virginia Mountain
   Bike Association
P.O. Box 7553
Hampton, Virginia 23666
(757) 722-4609

Notes on the trail: Start or end your ride by looping around Woodstock Pond and then heading onto Backbone Trail. The trail is well marked as are the offshoots, onto which bikes are not allowed. At the end of Backbone Trail, you can decide which of the 2 short out-and-back trails—the Riverview (1.5 miles one way) and the White-Tail (.6 mile one way)—you'd like to explore. Both provide nice access into the woods and end on a bluff overlooking the York River. I only wish there was a connection between their ends to create a nice loop rather than 2 separate out-and-backs.

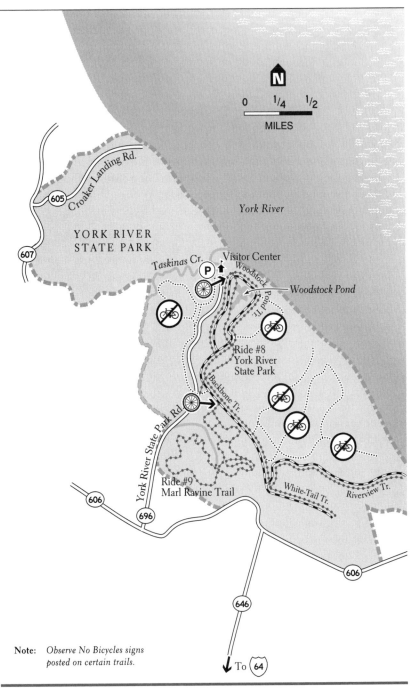

Note: *Observe No Bicycles signs posted on certain trails.*

RIDE 9 • Marl Ravine Trail

AT A GLANCE

Length/Configuration: 6-mile figure eight composed of 2 smaller loops (6 miles total)

Aerobic difficulty: Considerable; many short, steep ups and downs with few flat spots

Technical difficulty: Narrow, twisty single-track

Scenery: Unique, highly fertile coastal plain environment with growths of glade fern, ginseng, and rare native orchids among black walnut, southern sugar maple, and chinquepin oak

Special comments: Challenging course for competitive mountain bikers

The six-mile Marl Ravine Trail at York River State Park was designed by and for riders of intermediate or better mountain biking abilities. (For a less challenging ride at York River State Park, try the fairly level trails described in Ride 8.

The Marl Ravine consists of two loops that form a figure eight of sorts. If you find that the demands of this narrow, twisty single-track with its succession of short, steep uphills and downhills is too much for you, you can use one of the cut-through trails to shorten your ride. As their names imply, the Upper and Lower Trails could be inserted into a familiar tune: "You take the high road, and I'll take the low road"—well, you probably know the rest. You'll stay on the high ground of the Upper Trail before plummeting into the ravine along the Lower Trail, and then you can decide whether or not it's time to head back.

The trail is well marked and easy to follow, but most riders will be too intent on navigating its narrow, twisty—and sometimes rooted—up-and-down single-track to appreciate the "rich shell-marl ravine forest" surroundings of this relatively new addition to York River State Park. Marl is a mixture of clay, sand, and limestone along with some shell fragments.

Marl Ravine was built by members of the Eastern Virginia Mountain Bike Association in cooperation with York River State Park specifically for mountain biking. This sort of partnership is encouraging given the rate at which trails in other areas of the country are being closed to mountain bikers. The club maintains several other mountain biking trails in eastern Virginia, but this was the first to be developed on state property with the blessings from the government folks in Richmond. The relationship between EVMA and York

River State Park has worked so well that plans are under way to develop a second, more challenging loop in the vicinity of Croaker boat landing on the York River. This planned, five-to-seven-mile route will feature longer ups and downs in an area of the 2,500-acre park that consists of deep ravines whose waters drain and replenish the York River.

General location: 11 miles west of Williamsburg off Interstate 64 at the Croaker exit.

Elevation change: Short, steep ascents and descents.

Season: Year-round, except for those times of year listed below. But consider coming for the Off-Road Duathalon in the spring, co-sponsored by the Eastern Virginia Mountain Bike Association (EVMA) and York River State Park. Call the park or EVMA for specific dates. The park closes for a week in late November and/or early December for the annual Deer Management Program. Call ahead for specific closure dates. Avoid Marl Ravine Trail after periods of heavy rain. The trail may be closed during the winter to give it a chance to heal.

Services: The park itself has facilities for picnicking, fishing, boating, guided canoe trips, and interpretive nature programs. There is a fee charged to enter York River State Park. All other services are available along US 60 east going toward Williamsburg.

Hazards: Marl Ravine Trail is a very technical but well-marked single-track with many short, steep ups and downs designed primarily for intermediate to advanced riders. Less experienced bikers should stick to the more level bike paths on the eastern side of the park entrance road.

Rescue index: Personnel are on duty at the park office at end of the main entrance road, and others may be spotted driving around the park in marked vehicles. This is a very popular trail, and you should have no difficulty getting help from other riders when necessary.

Land status: State park.

Maps: Available in the York River State Park brochure. Ask specifically for the Marl Ravine Trail Guide. Or visit www.dcr.state.va.us/parks

Finding the trail: Take exit 231 off I-64 and go east on Croaker Road (VA 607). Turn right onto Riverview Road (VA 606) and then left onto York River Park Road (VA 696). After passing the entrance station, the bike trails will be on your right. Entrance to Marl Ravine Trail is well marked and off Backbone Trail.

Sources of additional information:

York River State Park
5526 Riverview Road
Williamsburg, Virginia 23188
(757) 566-3036

Eastern Virginia Mountain
    Bike Association
P.O. Box 7553
Hampton, Virginia 23666
(757) 722-4609

Notes on the trail: Enter Marl Ravine Upper Trail off of Backbone Trail. The Marl Ravine Upper and Lower Trails form a loop that is actually one-half of the entire Marl Ravine loop. After completing the Upper/Lower Trail loop, you can continue onto Big Loop Trail or bail out onto the flatter Backbone Trail by taking the appropriately named Bail-Out Trail. This is less confusing than it sounds because of well-placed trail signs at critical intersections.

Riders are encouraged to wear helmets and to use common courtesy when encountering other riders on the trail. IMBA's Rules of the Trail are definitely in order on the demanding but very popular Marl Ravine Trail. The Marl Ravine Mountain Bike Trail brochure, available at the York River State Park's Entrance Station as well as at the Marl Ravine trailhead, describes a unique and very fertile coastal habitat that several uncommon and quickly vanishing plants call home. Be sure to stick to the established trails.

RIDE 10 · Waller Mill Park

AT A GLANCE

Length/Configuration: 5.5-mile loop, including several smaller loops, plus 1-mile practice trail

Aerobic difficulty: Considerable; many short, steep ups and downs with few flat spots

Technical difficulty: Narrow, twisty single-track with numerous roots

Scenery: Mature hardwoods surrounding lake

Special comments: Demanding—and popular—single-track in a coastal area where you'd expect flatter, easier riding

The six-mile Dogwood Trail at Waller Mill Park is a good example of how misleading it can be to evaluate the difficulty of a mountain bike route in terms of mileage alone—as road riders are prone to do. This narrow, technical, single-track loop repeatedly switches back as it circles around the eastern section of Waller Mill Pond, so it's easy to get a little disoriented in places. Throw in the short but steep ups and downs, and it's hard to take your eyes off the trail long enough to admire the striking hardwoods and lake that surround you. There is little flat terrain as the trail meanders through the woods, so this ride is strictly for intermediate to advanced riders.

The riding surface itself is very narrow and wends its way around holly and oaks, many of whose roots poke their way across your path, adding to the technical challenge of this loop. The Eastern Virginia Mountain Bike Association

RIDE 10 · Waller Mill Park

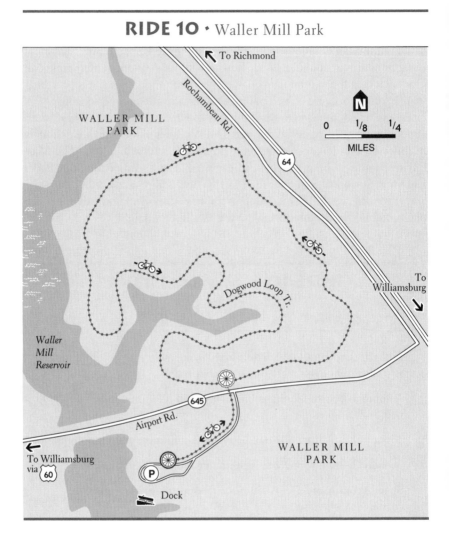

To Richmond

WALLER MILL
PARK

Rochambeau Rd.

64

N

0   1/8   1/4

MILES

To
Williamsburg

Dogwood Loop Tr.

Waller
Mill
Reservoir

645

Airport Rd.

To Williamsburg
via 60

P

WALLER MILL
PARK

Dock

has developed a first-class trail that gives riders the sense they are far from the maddening crowd while actually being in fairly close proximity to the ever-growing Williamsburg–James City–York County area.

General location: 5 miles west of Williamsburg between US 60 and Interstate 64.

Elevation change: Fairly consistent series of short, steep ascents and descents, but little overall change in elevation.

Season: Year-round, but avoid after heavy rains.

Services: Fishing, boat rentals, and soft drinks are available at the park office across Airport Road. All other services are available between the park and downtown Williamsburg on US 60.

Hazards: Sometimes heavy two-way traffic with considerable short, steep ups and downs on very narrow single-track. Unmarked intersections and no signage can also be hazardous.

Rescue index: There is often an attendant on duty at the shelter on the lake, where there are bathrooms and boat rentals. Otherwise, assistance can be summoned from any of the numerous businesses along Richmond Road.

Land status: City park.

Maps: Available from Williamsburg Parks Department, although EVMA's closing of overused trail sections and opening of others, as well as the lack of any straight trail, makes a map unreliable

Finding the trail: Go west out of Williamsburg on Richmond Road (US 60). Turn right at the traffic light and cross the railroad tracks onto Airport Road. Follow the signs to Waller Mill Park where you'll turn right to enter the parking lot. Dogwood Trail starts on the opposite side of Airport Road just across from the park's entrance.

Sources of additional information:

Waller Mill Park
Route 645
Williamsburg, Virginia 23185
(757) 220-6170

Eastern Virginia Mountain
  Bike Association
P.O. Box 7553
Hampton, Virginia 23666
(757) 722-4609

Notes on the trail: The accepted direction of travel on this loop is counterclockwise although there are no signs to designate this. Even if there were, you'd still probably find some riders going in the opposite direction. Be wary of approaching riders at any point along the way and offer right-of-way whenever possible. Due to the narrow width of the trail, there are few places where another rider can get by safely. A little courtesy goes a long way, especially on weekends when trail use is heaviest.

VIRGINIA'S PIEDMONT

While some folks may view Virginia's Piedmont in the central part of the state as merely that area you have to drive through on the way to the mountains or the beach, increasing numbers of central Virginia mountain bikers are riding closer to home instead of packing up to head for the mountains or making the trip to West Virginia to find good spots for fat-tire flying.

Virginia's Piedmont region has seen a considerable amount of new trail construction and increased trail access in the last several years. As I was attempting to put the finishing touches on *Mountain Bike! Virginia*, I continued to learn about newly planned and newly opened trails at various locations throughout this region in particular. This should come as good news to all riders, but especially those whose home turf is Virginia's Piedmont. Increased riding opportunities will not only offer central Virginia bikers some new options but will also ease the considerable pressure older trails have been experiencing.

The Piedmont begins at the base of the Blue Ridge Mountains to the west at an elevation of approximately 1,000 feet above sea level and declines in an eastward direction to Interstate 95 and the fall line at 300 feet above sea level. The Piedmont extends through the northern Virginia region and is about 50 miles wide at the Potomac River. Going south it broadens to 150 miles at the North Carolina border.

The oak-hickory forest is the dominant forest type in the northern part of the Piedmont, but going in a southerly direction the oak-pine forest becomes more predominant, with white and black oak replacing red oak. Virginia and shortleaf pines are most common, but other types, such as the loblolly in the eastern Piedmont, grow in the region.

Virginia's Piedmont has also seen its share of state history. In fact, Civil War memories are probably strongest in this part of Virginia, where Union attempts to cripple the Confederate capital of Richmond were relentless. It was here that the Confederacy's ultimate defeat and surrender took place.

You can ride through the Petersburg National Battlefield, site of a ten-month siege that ultimately led to General Robert E. Lee's abandoning Richmond and retreating west to Sailor's Creek, where the war's last battle was lost by the Confederacy. This was followed by Lee's famous surrender at Appomattox Courthouse. Civil War buffs will surely want to stop at Appomattox Courthouse National Historical Park on the way to Carter Taylor Trail at Holliday Lake State Park.

You can also ride around Belle Isle, an island in the James River located just blocks from the State Capitol Building in Richmond. Belle Isle was the site of a tent city that housed as many as 30,000 Union prisoners during the Civil War. Not too far away is the Visitor Center and focal point for the Richmond Battlefield Park, whose 100-mile battlefield tour takes in nine Civil War battlefields.

Virginia's Piedmont has seen a good bit of recent trail development for mountain bikers. Several years ago I found very few spots in central Virginia that were suitable or legal to ride, but this has changed considerably. One big difference in this region is the work of the various chapters of Mountain Bike Virginia, a young but extremely active statewide organization that works with various governmental land managers to construct and maintain some excellent single-track throughout this region. But keep in mind that nothing is free when it comes to trail access, and the minimum price of our admission is support for local, state, and national mountain bike organizations to help keep these and other trails open.

RIDE 11 · Belle Isle

AT A GLANCE

Length/Configuration: 1-mile loop

Aerobic difficulty: Minimal on this flat route

Technical difficulty: None on island loop, but island interior is challenging and dangerous

Scenery: Views of the Richmond skyline and the James River falls

Special comments: Good family ride on a historic island whose previous tenants included Union POWs during the Civil War

The one-mile flat loop trail around this island in the James River offers a pleasant leg-stretcher with a unique perspective of Richmond's downtown skyline as well as a close look at the often treacherous class four Hollywood Rapids. The perimeter trail is suitable for beginning riders and families, although caution should be exercised by anyone near the water's edge. Other trails that crisscross the center of Belle Isle are steep and rocky in places, and extremely dangerous. They are not officially open to use, and some dare-devils now sport toothless grins for their rule-breaking bravado. The trails at Belle Isle are, however, linked to the trails on the south shore of James River Park via the emergency vehicle bridge. Exit the bridge on the ramp and follow the pipeline west to the 22nd Street entrance. The trail running along the river is flat, however the Buttermilk trail, further from the shoreline, is wooded and hilly.

The recorded history of this "beautiful island" dates back to 1608 when Captain John Smith purchased it from Chief Powhatan. After multiple owners, the Old Dominion Iron and Steel Company operated a factory on the island for 144 years, from 1832 until the city of Richmond purchased this 65-acre granite outcrop. This was not such a beautiful spot for the 30,000 or so Union soldiers who were interred in a squalid tent city on the eastern end of the island during the Civil War. More recently, this section of Richmond riverfront has seen a good bit of development, including the National Park Service Civil War Visitors Center.

General location: Just south of downtown Richmond in the James River beneath the Lee Bridge.

Elevation change: Minimal on trail around the island's perimeter. Short, steep, and often dangerous ups and downs cross the interior of the island.

Season: Year-round.

RIDE 11 · Belle Isle

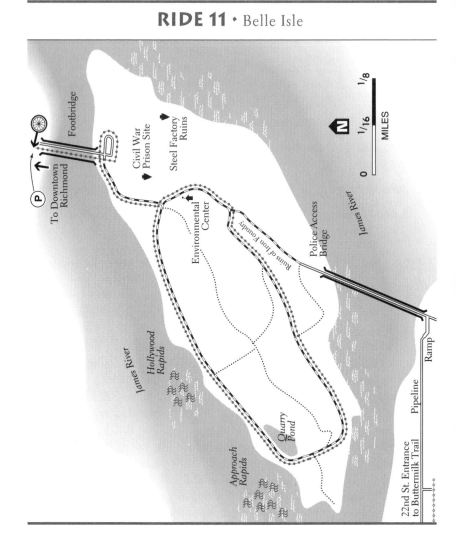

Services: Services are widely available in Richmond and neighboring Chesterfield and Henrico Counties.

Hazards: Strong rapids and currents in James River. Some riders have been injured while using bootleg trails across the island's interior.

Rescue index: This trail gets a lot of use and is located near downtown Richmond, so it should not be difficult to summon assistance if needed.

Land status: City park.

Maps: Available for one dollar from Richmond Department of Recreation and Parks.

Finding the trail: The park is accessible via a long footbridge that runs under the Robert E. Lee Bridge. Access is from Tenth Street onto Tredegar Street and next to the National Park Service Civil War Visitors Center.. Watch for signs near the state capital complex for Belle Isle or the Civil War VisitorsCenter.

Source of additional information:

Park Naturalist/Park Manager

James River Park System

City of Richmond Department of
    Recreation and Parks

4100 Hull Street

Richmond, Virginia 23221

(804) 780-5311

Notes on the trail: Richmond Parks Department Naturalist Ralph White voiced some extreme concerns about the proliferation of illegal trails that irresponsible mountain bikers have created and continue to use across the center of Belle Isle despite the inherent danger and detrimental effects to this unique historic site. Such actions give all of us a bad name and ultimately lead to the kinds of trail closings that have hit many spots outside Virginia, but from which we've thus far been spared. Stay on the main carriage trail— don't use or create new trails across the interior of the island.

Likewise, White has received reports of bikers riding at high speeds while too close to hikers on the island and scaring the bejesus out of them. Be sure to give others on the island a wide berth and don't assume they know you're about to overtake them. If Belle Isle is worthy of our attention as a mountain biking destination, it would behoove us to use it in a responsible manner. We're all in this together, and none of us is an island, especially on the very popular Belle Isle.

RIDE 12 · Chimbarazo Park

AT A GLANCE

Length/Configuration: 1-mile loop

Aerobic difficulty: Considerable; exclusively short, steep ups and downs with few flat or straight spots

Technical difficulty: Narrow, twisty single-track

Scenery: Hillside trail overlooking Richmond's downtown skyline and the James River

Special comments: The trail's short length belies its level of difficulty; despite the amount of energy expended to revitalize this neighborhood, it can be a high-crime area; plan to ride with a friend

himbarazo Park, named for a mountain in the Andes of South America, was the site of one of Richmond's first parks in 1874. Its location above the banks of the James River in the city's Church Hill section offers a 180-degree panorama of the downtown skyline as well as much of the city's former commercial trading district along the river. This park is located in a very historic part of Richmond several blocks from St. John's Church, where Patrick Henry made his famous "Give me liberty or give me death" speech.

A large hospital for Confederate soldiers occupied this site but was demolished after the Civil War. Now residing here is the Visitor Center for the National Battlefield Park whose nine sites surrounding the former Confederate capital figured into the city's defense from 1861 to 1865. Today the Visitor Center serves as the focal point for Richmond's battlefield tour covering over 100 miles.

In regard to the park's mountain biking I suppose there's only so much you can expect from a one-mile trail situated on six acres of parkland. What may surprise you is the amount of huffing and puffing you'll be doing after completing this diminutive loop. The short distance of this tight technical single-track belies its difficulty and the intense demands it places on mountain bikers, as central Virginia riders have seen after racing here as part of a series of Richmond-area races. Plans call for expanding the trail with another mile of somewhat straighter trail.

General location: In the Church Hill area of Richmond.

Elevation change: Short, steep ups and downs.

Season: Year-round.

Services: Services are widely available in Richmond.

Hazards: Tight, technical single-track whose surface is apt to flatten tires. Although there are inherent dangers when riding in any urban environment, you should be especially cautious in this area of Richmond where crime is often still a problem.

Rescue index: Help can easily be summoned from outside this small city park.

Land status: City park.

Maps: None available.

Finding the trail: From Richmond's downtown area go east on Broad Street (US 60) until you reach the National Battlefield Park located in Chimbarazo Park. The trail begins and ends along a gated sidewalk at the edge of the hilltop site overlooking the James River.

Source of additional information:

Gary Morgan
230 North 32nd Street
Richmond, Virginia 23223

(804) 782-7903 day
(804) 222-8006 evenings

RIDE 12 · Chimbarazo Park

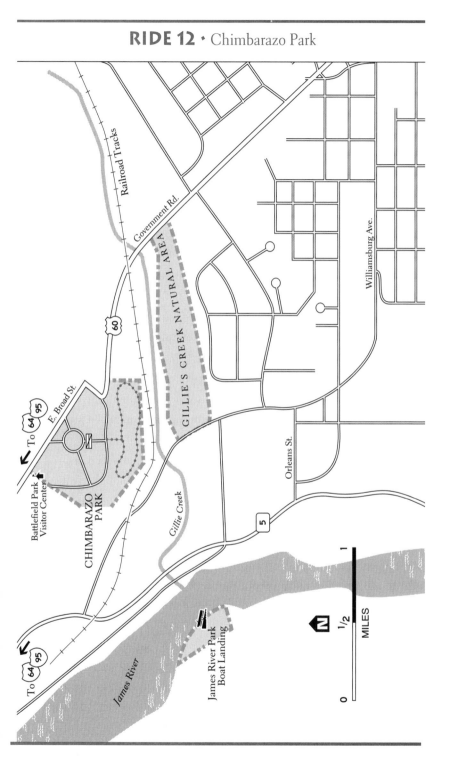

Notes on the trail: Unfortunately a large part of the challenge for riders at Chimbarazo has been to navigate the hillside course without getting a flat tire. Mountain Bike Virginia representative Roger Sattler told me that part of the difficulty in developing the park for mountain biking in conjunction with Richmond's Parks Department has been to reclaim an area that for some time had been used as a local dump site. Sattler strongly suggested that, given the thick vegetative growth and the degree of difficulty of the trail, riders should definitely plan to ride here with a partner and bring extra inner tubes.

RIDE 13 · Dogwood Dell

AT A GLANCE

Length/Configuration: 1- to 6-mile single-tracks

Aerobic difficulty: Considerable; short, steep ups and downs

Technical difficulty: Steep ascents and descents on narrow single-track

Scenery: Dense hardwoods; numerous ravines adjacent to the James River

Special comments: Good single-track for advanced beginners and better riders

On a beautiful, warm (but not hot) Saturday afternoon during Labor Day weekend, I found myself pedaling the system of trails situated among dense woods and ravines behind Richmond's Dogwood Dell and the Carillon. The Carillon, a 240-foot bell tower, pays tribute to Virginians who died in World War I. It stands guard over the southern end of Byrd Park and Dogwood Dell, an open-air amphitheater where as many as 3,000 folks sit on grassy benches during summer to enjoy outdoor concerts.

The trails are tight but smooth single-track that rise and fall in short spurts through creeks and ravines in this area north of the James River and its Nickel Bridge, a name that hasn't kept pace with inflation or the actual cost of using this bridge. Intermediate and better riders will enjoy these trails, which are informally marked by Day-Glo orange arrows to create a route of sorts. However, this is one of those small parks where trails seem to run hither, thither, and yon, creating a patchwork of directional variations. For this reason, it's hard to estimate trail mileage. Let's just say you can spend as much or as little time here as you wish, depending on where you turn and how ambitious you are.

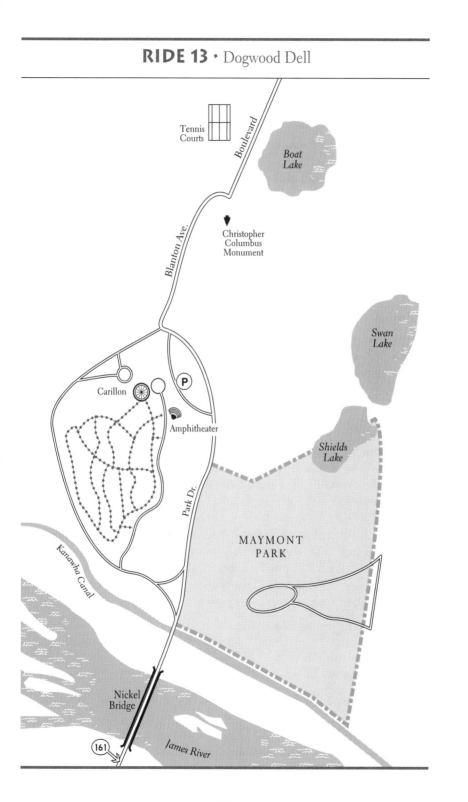

I was so surprised to have the place to myself that nice Saturday afternoon that I wondered if I was in the right place. Two gnarly dudes on bikes, complete with nipple rings, reassured me as I was leaving that this was the place and that those who had opted for more sedentary riding or alternate locations were just a bunch of slackers. Mountain bike routes are increasing in the Richmond area, and those plunking down a dime to cross the Nickel Bridge to ride at Dogwood Dell will definitely get their money's worth.

General location: Just north of the Nickel Bridge in the city of Richmond.

Elevation change: The trail system consists of short, steep ups and downs.

Season: Year-round, although this trail should be skipped when the trail is wet or icy.

Services: All services are available in Richmond and neighboring Chesterfield County.

Hazards: Short, steep ascents and descents on narrow single-track and other riders coming around blind corners.

Rescue index: This trail is located behind a public park in the city of Richmond, so help can be readily found, including toll personnel at the end of the Nickel Bridge across the James River and at nearby Maymont Park.

Land status: Richmond city park.

Maps: None are available at present.

Finding the trail: Go south on the Boulevard through Byrd Park and veer right once the road passes the tennis courts (on the right) and the lake (on the left) and turns into Blanton Road circling the reservoir. Blanton bends back around to the left, and you'll see a large bell tower (the Carillon) in front of you. Pull into the access road to the left of the Carillon and follow it onto one of the dirt roads leading to picnic shelters. Park anywhere around here, but stay off the road. The Dogwood Dell trail system lies behind the Carillon. You can access the trails from a number of points along a hard-surface service road to the left of the wooded area or where the single-track goes into the woods past short traffic barriers.

Source of additional information:

Gary Morgan
230 North 32nd Street
Richmond, Virginia 23223

(804) 782-7903 day
(804) 222-8006 evenings

Notes on the trail: Initially, a large part of the challenge for riders at Chimbarazo was navigating the hillside course without getting a flat tire. Roger Sattler, at the time a Mountain Bike Virgina representative, explained to me that the trail was built on land reclaimed from a local dump. Thick vegetation and the difficulty of the ride also increase the risk of punctured tires. Sattler strongly recommended bringing a partner and spare inner tubes.

RIDE 14 · Powhite Park

AT A GLANCE

Length/Configuration: 8-mile loop with numerous smaller loops

Aerobic difficulty: Considerable; exclusively short, steep ups and downs with few flat or straight spots

Technical difficulty: Narrow, twisty single-track

Scenery: Hillside trails in a natural upland forest with steep marshy ravines; this is an environmentally sensitive habitat for several species of wildflowers

Special comments: Due to the sensitive nature of this park, riders must stick to the established trails and abide by signs denoting private property—no trespassing

It would be easy to overlook this 100-acre park despite its location within Richmond's city limits. But those passing by on the Chippenham and Powhite (pronounced *po-white*) Parkways are traveling at 55 miles per hour or more and are intent on getting to work, home, or one of the innumerable attractions Virginia's capital city and its neighboring suburbs have to offer. However, intermediate and more advanced mountain bikers should slow down so they don't miss the eight-mile loop of steep, technical single-track that Powhite has to offer.

I include no specific trail directions for riding at Powhite since the fragile nature of this area and the trail itself dictates where one should and shouldn't ride. It switches back and loops around to create a maze of single-track running up and down the hillsides adjacent to the swampy bottomland. This trail features challenges like the Doublerock, a very tricky technical descent, and the Buzz, a vertical roller coaster through a deep gully, designed to test and hone advanced bike handling skills of intermediate to expert riders. Future plans call for building a bridge across the swampy area that you must cross to enter into the main trail system.

General location: In the city of Richmond.

Elevation change: The trail system consists of short, steep ups and downs with the occasional flat section thrown in to let you catch your breath.

Season: Year-round, although this trail should be skipped when the trail is extremely wet or icy.

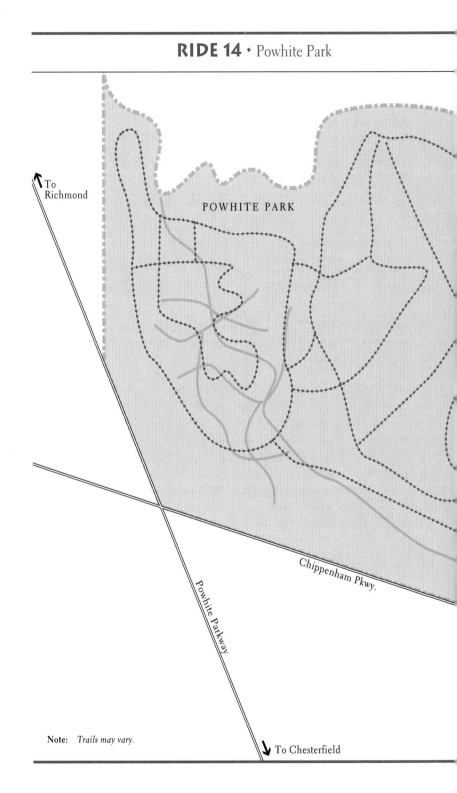

POWHITE PARK

To Richmond

Chippenham Pkwy.

Powhite Parkway

Note: *Trails may vary.*

To Chesterfield

Westover Gardens Blvd.

Jahnke Rd.

Jahnke Rd.

N

0   300   600

FEET

POWHITE PARK

🪑 Picnic
Area

Chippenham Pkwy.

To 95

Services: All services are available in Richmond and neighboring Chesterfield County.

Hazards: Short, steep ascents and descents on narrow single-track.

Rescue index: The park is across the street from Chippenham Hospital. Pretty convenient!

Land status: City park.

Maps: There are none available at present, but the trail is well marked and much easier to follow than it is to ride.

Finding the trail: Powhite Park is located on Jahnke Road across the street from Chippenham Hospital and adjacent to the Powhite Parkway. The trailhead is opposite the end of the parking loop but is not marked as such.

Source of additional information:

Gary Morgan   (804) 782-7903 day
230 North 32nd Street   (804) 222-8006 evenings
Richmond, Virginia 23223

Notes on the trail: The parking areas off Jahnke Road and at the end of Westover Gardens Boulevard are limited, and this is an appropriate indicator of the low-impact nature of this park. The 3 main hills run down into a low-lying swampy area, formerly a beaver pond. This park is a fragile, natural enclave whose off-camber single-track trails have been developed and conditionally opened to mountain bikers. Powhite is an experimental partnership between Richmond Parks and Recreation, Mother Nature, neighboring property owners, and mountain bikers, so riders are *strongly* encouraged to stick to established trails and respect the No Trespassing signs located primarily at the northern edge of the park.

RIDE 15 • Pocahontas State Park

AT A GLANCE

Length/Configuration: 5-mile loop, 4 miles of single-track sbdivided by skill level and 25 miles of forest roads

Aerobic difficulty: Moderate ups and downs; the new single-track circuit has shorter, steeper hills

Technical difficulty: Minimal on Old Mill Trail and forest roads; considerable on new single-track

Scenery: Beaver Lake and Swift Creek to densely and sparsely wooded rolling terrain

Special comments: Old Mill Trail and grassy forest roads are good family rides; the newly developed single-track circuit is a challenging alternative for advanced cyclists

This 7,000-acre park was the Commonwealth's largest when it was donated to Virginia State Parks by the National Park Service in 1946. It was built by Civilian Conservation Corps workers and opened in 1941. My relationship with this crown jewel of the state park system came a few years later. During my two years in the late 1970s as a graduate student at Virginia Commonwealth University in Richmond, I lived just up the road from Pocahontas. This was the pre–mountain bike era so I had to content myself with morning jogs around the five-mile Old Mill Trail loop. This designated bike trail takes a wide circle around Beaver Lake on dirt and gravel forest roads. It's well marked with just a few ups and downs to make things interesting but an easy outing for riders of all ages and ability levels.

In addition to Pocahontas's bike trail around Beaver Lake are 20 miles of grassy forest roads open to mountain biking. I haven't tried to formulate a specific route on these roads, which offer gentle ups and downs, but with the park's bike trail brochures you can put together a variety of loops and out-and-back rides of varying length and minimal difficulty; several of these double-tracks lead down to Swift Creek.

Forest roads are very clearly marked so it would be tough for anyone with an average sense of direction to get lost. Once you're out riding in this thickly wooded oasis it's easy to forget that the fast-growing suburb of Chesterfield County is just around the next bend.

The latest addition for mountain bikers at Pocahontas State Park is four miles of single-track that Chief Ranger Dan Soper developed along with Mountain Bike Virginia. This loop will include a perimeter trail for beginning to intermediate riders with a very technical inner trail section designed for expert riders. Single-track riders are asked to register at the trailhead so that Soper and his staff can get an idea of the amount of use this new trail receives.

Just as the daughter of Chief Powhatan is said to have saved the life of Captain John Smith, this twentieth-century Pocahontas, with its extensive network of off-road, rough-road, and single-track paths, is surely a lifesaver for Richmond-area mountain bikers.

General location: South of Richmond near the old Chesterfield Courthouse complex.

Elevation change: Minimal on the designated bike trail and forest roads. Short, steep ups and downs on the single-track loop.

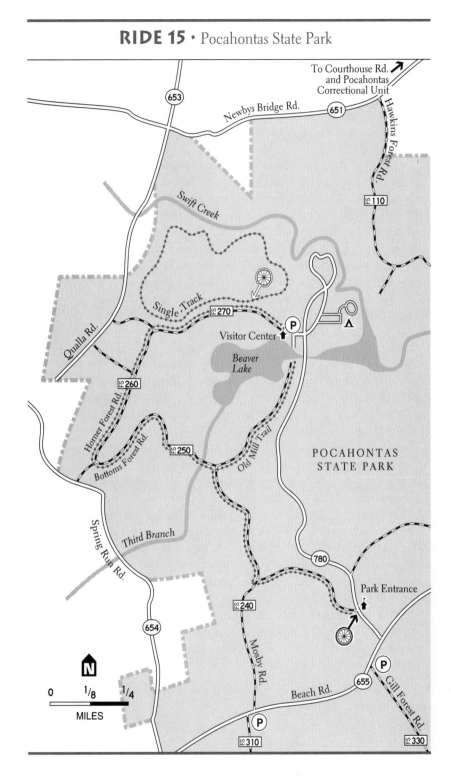

Don't let the superb variety of mountain biking roads and trails at Pocahontas State Park keep you from spending some time at Beaver Lake.

Season: Year-round.

Services: Camping season at the park runs from march through November and swimming is allowed from Memorial Day through Labor Day. All other services are available along Ironbridge Road (VA 10) between the Old Courthouse and Interstate 95. A fee is charged to enter Pocahontas State Park. Call ahead for the availability of campsites.

Hazards: There are several fairly steep downhills that cross wooden bridges at the bottom of their ascent on the 5-mile Old Mill Trail. Be honest about your ability level when using the new single-track loop, especially in regard to the expert inner-trail section.

Rescue index: Park personnel are available throughout the park to offer assistance as needed.

Land status: State park.

Maps: Available from the Pocahontas State Park office.

Finding the trail: Take I-95 south past Richmond and turn off at the Chester exit (61-B). Drive for about 15 miles on Old Hundred Road through the village of Chester, where Old Hundred Road becomes Iron Bridge Road. Turn left at the traffic light onto Beach Road across from the old Chesterfield Courthouse complex. Continue down Beach Road for 5 miles and turn right at the entrance to Pocahontas State Park. Start the 5-mile bike loop from the Visitor Center located a short distance from the entrance station along the park's main road. Parking your vehicle within within park requires a fee, which varies with season., however there is no fee for entrance on a bicycle.

Sources of additional information:

Pocahontas State Park	Gary Morgan
10301 State Park Road	230 North 32nd Street
Chesterfield, Virginia 23838-4713	Richmond, Virginia 23223
(804) 796-4255	(804) 782-7903 day
	(804) 222-8006 evenings

Notes on the trail: The park has incorporated what was formerly Pocahontas State Forest and now encompasses 7,604 acres, as well as the 150-acre Swift Creek Lake and 24-acre Beaver Lake. There are 25 miles of forest roads and 4 miles of single-track available for mountain biking. This is a truly wonderful getaway, especially considering its location just 20 miles from Virginia's state capital. Given the almost infinite possibilities for forming combinations of routes or just exploring, you should plan to camp here at the park and enjoy all it has to offer. Be sure to contact Pocahontas State Park ahead of time to determine the availability of campsites.

RIDE 16 · Poor Farm Park

AT A GLANCE

Length/Configuration: 13-mile single-track network that forms numerous large and small loops

Aerobic difficulty: Guaranteed to make your heart and lungs work overtime

Technical difficulty: Generally smooth, but various sections of rocks, roots, and log jumps keep things interesting

Scenery: Shady hardwoods along the edge of a large suburban park

Special comments: A great introduction to the world of technical single-track for experienced novices; intermediate and expert riders can work to improve speed and technique

RIDE 16 · Poor Farm Park

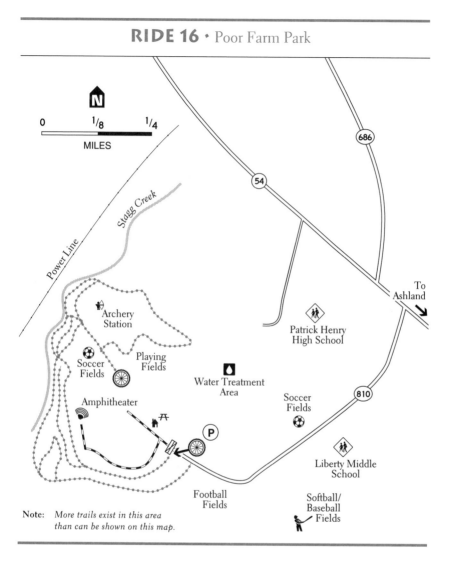

Note: More trails exist in this area
than can be shown on this map.

Poor Farm's approximately 13 miles of single-track are mostly short, steep ups and downs around Stagg Creek, as you'll quickly discover when you start riding. The maze of trails forms a large loop with the possibility of smaller loops depending on the most recent opening and closure of sections of single-track. I've been told that new trail is added almost weekly. Less demanding single-track can be found leading off the parking area behind the amphitheater, but flat, nontechnical riding isn't the reason Richmond-area mountain bikers are flocking here. Mountain Bike Virginia has worked hard to develop and maintain this increasingly popular and difficult trail system.

Its more technical challenges include rocky climbs, log crossings, and some pretty quick ups and downs around Stagg Creek. Poor Farm's trail system offers a good training site for intermediate to advanced riders with an interest in competitive mountain biking.

General location: 4 miles west of Ashland.

Elevation change: Predominantly short, steep ups and downs in the area adjacent to Stagg Creek.

Season: Year-round, although trail may be closed after periods of heavy rain.

Services: All services are available in nearby Ashland.

Hazards: Watch for other riders and yield right-of-way as necessary on this often busy trail system, especially in the more technical section where the challenges increase as the visibility decreases.

Rescue index: This trail has become very popular, so it shouldn't be hard to get help from other riders. Failing that, assistance can be found in nearby Ashland.

Land status: County park.

Maps: None available at present.

Finding the trail: From Ashland go west on VA 54. Turn left after 4 miles onto Liberty School Road. The park is located behind Patrick Henry High School. Park near the picnic shelters and pick up the trail next to the volleyball courts.

Sources of additional information:

Stan Thorne
Hanover County Parks and Recreation
200 Berkley Street
Ashland, Virginia 23005
(804) 365-4695

Gary Morgan
230 North 32nd Street
Richmond, Virginia 23223
(804) 782-7903 day
(804) 222-8006 evenings

A.C. Bruce
Mountain Bike Virginia
(804) 883-6778

Notes on the trail: Trail directions would be superfluous since the nature of this site demands closure of some sections and opening of others as the effects of popularity take their toll. Richmond-area single-track riders have latched onto Poor Farm's trail system and at times it gets downright crowded. Your best chance of having a little handlebar room is at times other than weekends and summer evenings.

RIDE 17 · Petersburg National Battlefield

AT A GLANCE

Length/Configuration: Various gravel double-track trails—each less than 2 miles long—loop off the 4-mile main paved road

Aerobic difficulty: Relatively flat with some incline

Technical difficulty: Smooth paved and unpaved double-track

Scenery: Historic monuments, bunkers, and exhibits that were part of the 10-month siege at Petersburg

Special comments: Good family ride

The Petersburg National Battlefield offers the casual rider the possibility of a pleasant leg-stretcher and some Civil War history by combining the hard-surface, four-mile Siege Road, which runs the length of this 1,500-acre park, with side trips on one or more of the gravel roads and trails—none longer than two miles—that veer off into the woods. These wide, flat trails branch off from the hard-surface road through sites of former fortifications, armed batteries, and the crater formed by a Union mine that exploded under one of the Confederate fortresses.

It is permissible for bicycles to travel both ways on the otherwise one-way Siege Road, but be sure to obey signs that show which trails are off limits to bicycles. In any case, please stay off historical embankments and bunkers. The battlefield road and adjoining trails are most suitable for beginning riders, families, or riders out for some fresh air and a little exercise—especially when done in combination with an educational outing to the site where the Confederacy experienced its bleakest period of the war, between June 1864 and April 1865.

The battlefield tour includes eight numbered points of interest that provide a look back at the siege that was the Civil War's most obvious turning point. Regardless of your political leanings and support for the Confederate cause, we Americans tend to ultimately root for the underdog. It's hard not to feel a great deal of respect for the tenacity of Confederate General Robert E. Lee and his initial army of 65,000 who fought long and hard against a better-equipped Union force of 122,000 men under the command of General Ulysses S. Grant.

General location: In the city of Petersburg.

Elevation change: Minimal.

Season: Year-round.

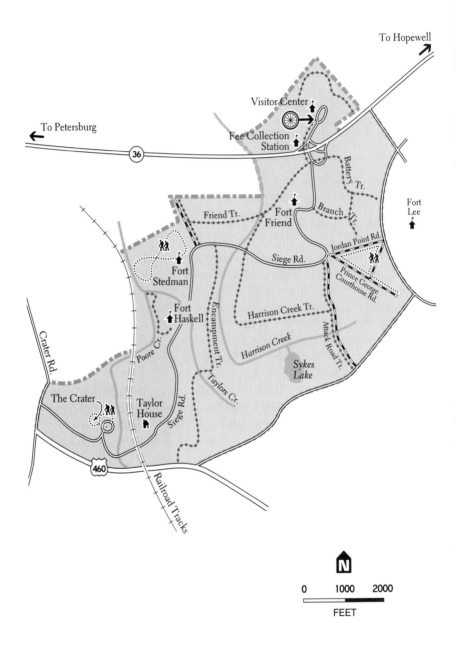

Services: A fee is charged for entrance to Petersburg National Battlefield. All services are widely available in Petersburg and the surrounding area.

Hazards: Most of the trails within the park are relatively flat, although there are some tricky spots along the way.

Rescue index: Park personnel at the entrance station and Visitor Center can provide assistance as needed.

Land status: National park.

Maps: Available at the park's entrance station and Visitor Center.

Finding the trail: Heading south from Richmond on Interstate 95, take the exit for Washington Street East (VA 36). Continue 2.5 miles through Petersburg on VA 36 until you reach the park's entrance. After passing the entrance station, park at the Visitor Center and ride back past the entrance on Siege Road.

Source of additional information:
Petersburg National Battlefield
P.O. Box 549
Petersburg, Virginia 23804
(804) 732-3531

Notes on the trail: The 9-month siege of Petersburg represents the longest battle in America's history as well as the beginning of the end for the Confederate forces. The final victory for the Union Army followed the Rebel departure from Petersburg, the loss of the capital in Richmond, and Robert E. Lee's futile retreat to Appomattox where he surrendered a week later. Take some time to see the map exhibit at the Visitor Center describing this lengthy engagement as well as displays of Civil War artifacts.

RIDE 18 · Occoneechee State Park and Wildlife Management Area

AT A GLANCE

Length/Configuration: 16-mile out-and-back, but it can easily be shortened

Aerobic difficulty: Minimal except in areas of heavy gravel

Technical difficulty: Gravel and grassy double-track with few obstructions

Scenery: Marshy areas and lake views

Special comments: Good family ride; bring plenty of bug spray

The limited trail system at Occoneechee State Park is not open to mountain biking, but the park provides access to the 1,900-acre Occoneechee Wildlife Management Area (WMA), which is open to bicycles, as are 25 other WMAs surrounding Buggs Island Lake and Lake Gaston on this southern border of Virginia. The park is recently debuted a 15-mile multi-use trail, created using existing wildlife management trails. Opened initially to horses only, plans call for white blazes and maps at the trailhead by spring of 2001, as well as biker and hiker access. The route described here,however, is represntative of what area WMA's have to offer.

The nine miles of gravel roads and double-track at Occoneechee WMA stretch onto a narrow peninsula where waterfowl are abundant. These flat out-and-back roads offer the opportunity for some easy riding and bird watching in an area of the state where there are other options for mountain bikers. By piecing together the main gravel road and two spurs, you can put together an easy 16-mile round-trip out-and-back ride.

This 2,690-acre WMA is named for the Occoneechee Indians, who lived on an island nearby in the Roanoke River from 1250 to 1670. In 1676 Virginia Councilman Nathaniel Bacon took it upon himself to lead a group of men to slaughter this tribe, which was so well liked that Bacon's actions were condemned by most Virginians and Governor Sir William Berkeley. Plan to join the Native Americans' annual return to Occoneechee State Park in May for their Heritage Festival and Powwow.

General location: Just above the Virginia–North Carolina border on Buggs Island Lake.

Elevation change: None.

Season: Year-round, although caution should be exercised during fall and winter hunting seasons. Call the Virginia Department of Game and Inland Fisheries (804-367-1000) for the exact opening and closing dates for various game animals.

Services: Camping, showers, boating, and fishing are available within the park. There is also a camp store open during the summer season. A fee is charged to enter Occoneechee State Park. All other services are available in nearby Clarksville.

Hazards: Wear bright colors during hunting seasons.

Rescue index: Park personnel can provide assistance as needed. Help can also readily be found in the nearby town of Clarksville.

Land status: State park and WMA.

Maps: Available from the offices of Occoneechee State Park, the Virginia Department of Game and Inland Fisheries and www.dcr.state.va.us/parks.

Finding the trail: After turning onto the park's entrance road and passing the entrance station at Occoneechee State Park, turn left, staying on the

RIDE 18 • Occoneechee State Park and Wildlife Management Area

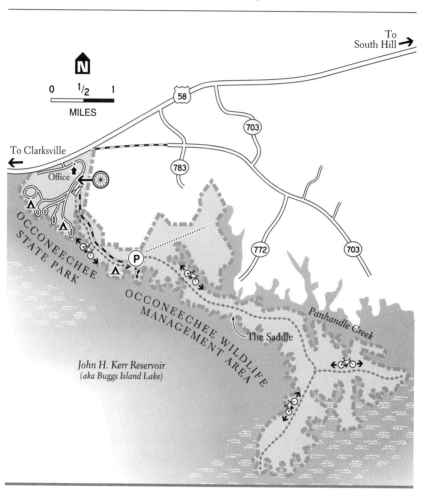

To
South Hill →

N

0   ¹/₂   1

MILES

58

703

To Clarksville
←

Office

783

OCCONEECHEE STATE PARK

772

703

P

OCCONEECHEE MANAGEMENT WILDLIFE AREA

The Saddle

Panhandle Creek

John H. Kerr Reservoir
(aka Buggs Island Lake)

hard-surface main park road. The gravel road leading to the Occoneechee WMA is on the left across from the park office.

Sources of additional information:

Occoneechee State Park
1192 Occoneechee Park Road
Clarksville, Virginia 23927-9449
(804) 374-2210

Department of Game and
  Inland Fisheries
Route 6, Box 410
Forest, Virginia 24551-9806
(804) 367-1000

Notes on the trail: The park and neighboring WMAs offer a very popular vacation spot for families, especially those that include hunters, anglers, and boaters. Plan to bring your bike(s) on your next visit and explore some of these wooded, marshy areas on two wheels. If you plan to explore some of these WMAs, request a copy of *Guide to Wildlife Management Areas*, published by the Army Corps of Engineers, from the Department of Game and Inland Fisheries. But keep in mind that they are managed primarily for hunting. They comprise 50,000 acres of land in an area where I found no other mountain biking destinations. Be sure to bring plenty of bug spray when exploring these marshy areas.

RIDE 19 · Carter Taylor Trail

AT A GLANCE

Length/Configuration: 12-mile loop

Aerobic difficulty: Flat and slightly rolling terrain, Steep hills and a creek crossing on the spur trail from Holiday Lake State Park

Technical difficulty: Gravel and grassy double-track with few obstructions

Scenery: Dense woods, cut-over areas, and open fields in the rolling Piedmont region

Special comments: Good family ride

The 12-mile Carter Taylor Trail is a fairly new addition to the riding options for mountain bikers in the Piedmont. This multi-use loop was dedicated in 1996, and park staff are encouraging its use by mountain bikers while discouraging further use of the five-mile Lakeshore Trail around Holliday Lake. Carter Taylor was a longtime state forester who gave much of himself to the surrounding 19,535-acre Appomattox-Buckingham State Forest, the largest of Virginia's state forests.

The trail has a number of possible starting points where it intersects state roads, although the recommended trailhead is at the forestry center for Appomattox-Buckingham State Forest. The Carter Taylor is well marked as it winds its way through the state forest along single-track, double-track, grassy, overgrown no-track, and gravel roads.

If you're camping at Holliday Lake State Park, you can avail yourself of the trailhead located just across from the campground. A half-mile (one-way)

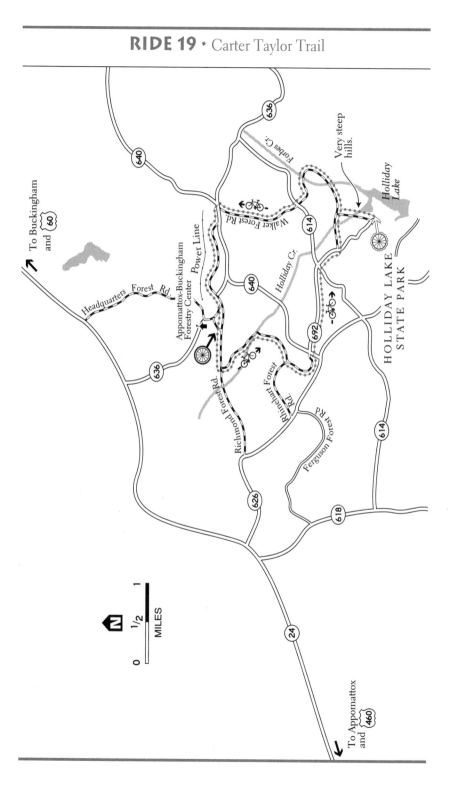

Riders on Carter Taylor Trail through Appomattox-Buckingham State Forest frequently see these CT signs that point the way.

spur from the Carter Taylor to Holliday Lake contains some steep, short uphills and downhills along a section of power line right-of-way that will get all but the most advanced riders walking. Overall the loop is relatively flat, easy to follow, and a trail that riders of all ability levels can enjoy. If time or stamina preclude the entire 12-mile ride, it's also possible to develop a number of shorter loops by using the hard-surface state roads that intermittently intersect with the trail.

Civil War buffs will immediately recall Appomattox Courthouse as the site where Confederate General Robert E. Lee surrendered to Ulysses S. Grant, putting an end to the war. If Civil War history interests you, be sure to plan a trip to the nearby Sailor's Creek Historic State Park, site of the last battle between the Union and Confederate armies, and Appomattox Courthouse National Historical Park.

General location: 40 miles east of Lynchburg and 20 miles north of Farmville.

Elevation change: Typical rolling hills of the Piedmont with some short, steep ups and downs, as well as relatively flat sections of forest roads.

Season: Year-round, although caution should be exercised during fall and winter hunting seasons when riding in the surrounding Appomattox-Buckingham State Forest. Call the Virginia Department of Game and Inland Fisheries (804-367-1000) for the opening and closing dates for various game animals.

Services: Holliday Lake State Park offers facilities for camping, picnicking, swimming, boating, and fishing. A fee is charged to enter the park, although entrance is not necessary to ride the Carter Taylor Trail. All other services are available in nearby Lynchburg.

Hazards: There are some short but very steep sections of trail, especially on the initial power line right-of-way. Yours truly found himself doing an endo along a flat section of muddy trail, so you never know. There are several spots where the trail crosses state roads, and riders should stop and check for oncoming traffic despite the fact that these seem to be little-traveled country roads. Watch for large patches of poison ivy, especially on the last section of power line (it was largely overgrown when I rode the trail). If you're suscep-tible to ticks and poison ivy, you may want to omit this part of overgrown no-track and ride on VA 636, which runs within 40' of the trail.

Rescue index: Summer riders can find assistance at Holliday Lake State Park. Park personnel reside just outside the park entrance, so you should be able to find help at other times pretty readily.

Land status: Virginia state forest and park.

Maps: Available from the offices of Holliday Lake State Park and Appomat-tox-Buckingham State Forest.

Finding the trail: Coming from either the east or west on US 60, turn onto VA 24 at Mount Rush toward Appomattox. (Note: This may appear to be the middle of nowhere, but the historical marker at this spot indicates it's actually the geographic center of Virginia.) After 7 miles turn left onto VA 636 and park next to the forestry center for Appomattox-Buckingham State Forest. You can start on the Carter Taylor Trail by crossing VA 636 and riding down the Richmond Forest Road, located just behind the maintenance buildings opposite the forestry center.

If you're camping at Holliday Lake State Park or plan to swim in the lake, you should start from the well-marked trailhead located across from the campground within the park's boundaries. Instead of turning onto VA 636, continue on VA 24 for 4 additional miles and turn left onto VA 626. Then fol-low the signs for Holliday Lake State Park.

Sources of additional information:

Holliday Lake State Park
Route 2, Box 622
Appomattox, Virginia 24522
(804) 248-6308

Appomattox-Buckingham State Forest
Route 3, Box 7500
Dillwyn, Virginia 23936
(804) 983-2175

Notes on the trail: The trailhead within Holliday Lake State Park is well marked—in keeping with the rest of the trail—but includes a very steep half-mile section of trail along a power line right-of-way. If you'd like to skip this power line section, leave the park on VA 692 past the entrance station and then pick up the trail one-half mile down the road on the right side, where you'll see an information board just into the woods. Follow the obvious double-track from here and continue straight where the spur trail goes right along the power line back to Holliday Lake State Park.

I recommend novice riders, and all riders during particularly wet periods, omit the section of trail between the Holliday Lake State Park spur trail and VA 614. This is a low-lying muddy section with several short, steep ups and downs, and its surface was particularly torn up by hoof prints. A wide but short stream crossing through here makes this area noticeably more difficult than the rest of the trail.

For those starting from the forestry center, pedal or coast downhill a short distance on the Richmond Forest Road and before long you'll see a sign and a dispenser for trail brochures on the left side of this double-track. There's no need for step-by-step directions to navigate this loop since the familiar CT signs have been positioned where you need them. This is not to say there are no ambiguous places where an additional sign or two would have helped, but they are few compared to the confusing trails I often encountered in Virginia's national forests.

On the CT, you only need to look around a little to find the trail's continuation after a short lapse on the edge of a cultivated field or an overgrown section of double-track. Someone finally figured out that you only need trail directions at critical turns, and this is where you will find the unassuming, but welcome, CT signs that point the way. This is very helpful because a large number of county and forest roads intersect the trail along its 12-mile length. For that matter, this almost twenty thousand -acre state forest is laced with numerous unmarked roads that you could, with a map and an adventurous spirit, combine into all kinds of possible rides.

RIDE 20 · Cumberland State Forest

AT A GLANCE

Length/Configuration: 8-mile loop using part of a
fourteen mile loop and a 16 mile out-and-back.

Aerobic difficulty: Short, steep ups and downs on single-track

Technical difficulty: Single-track Willis River Trail features
challenging natural obstacles, while the double-track is easy

Scenery: Dense woods, cut-over areas, and open fields

Special comments: This 16,233-acre state forest has loop combinations to suit all bikers

This loop starts and ends at Winston Lake in Cumberland State Forest
just outside the perimeter of Bear Creek Lake State Park. But keep in
mind that it is only a small sampling of the riding that awaits you in this
16,233-acre state forest. Using all the forest's multi-use trails it is possible to
ride a 14-mile loop. This particular loop, howeve, includes 5.5 miles along
the largely single-track Willis River Trail before returning on gravel roads
back to Winston Lake. Those who live for single-track may want to ride the
entire 16-mile point-to-point (32 miles round-trip if ridden as an out-and-
back) Willis River Trail, which I found surprisingly well blazed and maintained, and quite ridable. The final mile of the trail is unblazed, however.

True to its piedmont surroundings, the Winston Lake loop and, especially,
the Willis River Trail include some climbs that will get your heart-lung
machine earning its keep. Novice riders may find the stretch along Willis
River Trail somewhat difficult, but they can use a map of the Cumberland
State Forest to develop alternate routes using state and forest roads. Despite
the sense of seclusion the Willis River Trail offers, you're never too far from
a secondary or state forest road.

General location: 35 miles west of Richmond and just north of Farmville.

Elevation change: Typical rolling hills of the Piedmont, although the Willis
River Trail has some short, steep ups and downs as well.

Season: Year-round, although caution should be taken during fall and winter
hunting seasons. Call the Virginia Department of Game and Inland Fisheries
(804-367-1000) for the opening and closing dates for various game animals.

Services: Camping, swimming, boating, and toilet facilities are available at
Bear Creek Lake State Park when the park is open.. Swimming is allowed and

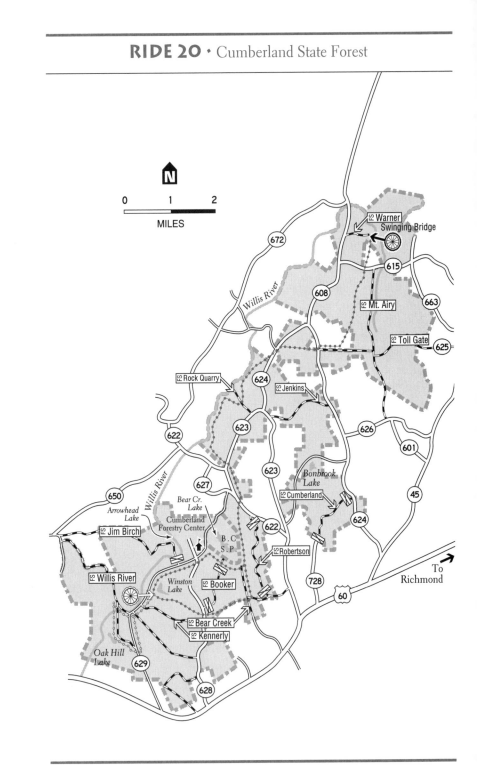

concessions are open from Memorial Day through Labour Day. A fee is charged to enter this park. All other services are available in nearby Farmville.

Hazards: Be alert for hunters during fall and winter seasons.

Rescue index: Summer riders can find assistance at Bear Creek Lake State Park. At other times, help can be found in nearby Farmville.

Land status: Virginia state forest.

Maps: Available from the Cumberland State Forest office.

Finding the trail: Take the Zions Crossroads exit 136 off Interstate 64, heading south on US 15. Turn left onto VA 6 toward Columbia. Cross the James River at Columbia on VA 690. Turn right onto VA 612 next to Lakeside Village and follow this road for several miles before bearing left onto VA 608. Follow the signs for Bear Creek Lake State Park, and then go a little farther south on VA 629 to find Winston Lake on the left.

Sources of additional information:

Cumberland State Forest
Route 3, Box 133
Dillwyn, Virginia 23936
(804) 492-4121

Bear Creek Lake State Park
929 Oak Hill Road
Cumberland, Virginia 23040
(804) 492-4410

Notes on the trail: Cumberland is the second-largest state forest in Virginia and surrounds Bear Creek Lake State Park. It includes 4 lakes and the 16-mile Willis River Trail. Throw in miles of gated and open gravel forest roads and you've got a smorgasbord for mountain bikers of all ability levels. Plan A should involve camping at Bear Creek Lake State Park and spending a few days pedaling around with map in hand while trying out various combinations of trails and roads.

RIDE 21 · James River State Park

AT A GLANCE

Length/Configuration: 3.5-mile loop; a 12-mile trail system

Aerobic difficulty: Terrain is gently rolling with some uphill sections

Technical difficulty: Cabell Trail has few obstructions

Scenery: Dense woods and open fields; the Tye River Overlook offers a great view of the James and Tye Rivers

Special comments: Good family ride

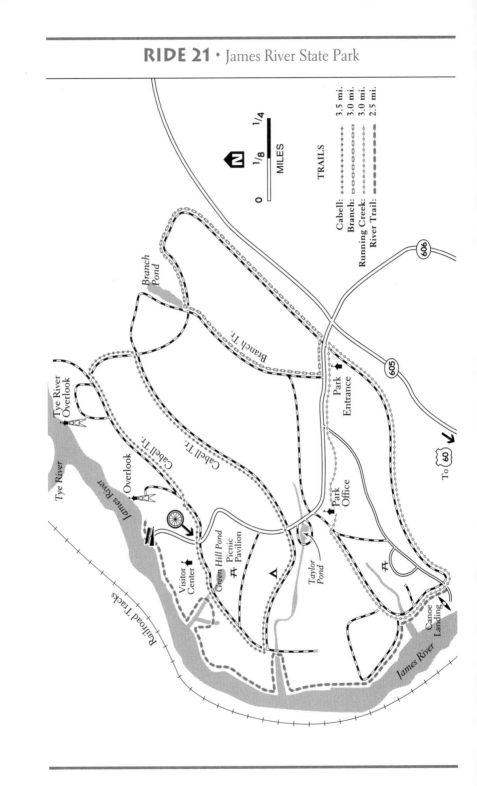

N

0   1/8   1/4
MILES

TRAILS

Cabell: 3.5 mi.
Branch: 3.0 mi.
Running Creek: 3.0 mi.
River Trail: 2.5 mi.

James River State Park (not to be confused with James River Park in the city of Richmond) is Virginia's newest state park. Its 1,500 acres sit on a quiet stretch of the James River, and as I pedaled around, the only sounds were the June breezes whispering through the mixed oak hardwood forest and the far-off wail of a freight train. Although the park's three miles of James River frontage will undoubtedly draw many anglers, 3.5-mile Cabell Trail loop is an exciting addition to the growing number of mountain bike trails that will enable central Virginia fat-tire enthusiasts to ride closer to home and will attract others to the heartland of the Old Dominion.

Cabell Trail is suitable for novice bikers, although parts of it may be a bit difficult for youngsters whose climbing and bike handling skills could be overstressed on some rough sections of trail. It's gravel in some sections and grassy double-track in others, but this orange blazed loop is only the first of a system of multi-use trails that total 12 miles. In addition to a trail along the river there are two loops of three miles each. The Branch trail is blazed green and passes by branch pond. Running Creek Trail is blzed yellow and joins the River Trail along the James for a bit.

The Cabell Trail is named for William Cabell, who spent much of his 68 years in Virginia's early government as a member of the House of Burgesses and the Revolutionary and ratifying conventions of 1788. He was also a signer of the Articles of Association.

General location: On the eastern bank of the James River approximately 25 miles northeast of Lynchburg and southeast of Charlottesville.

Elevation change: Flat and rolling, with manageable hills less than one-half mile long.

Season: Year-round.

Services: When completed, the park will offer camping, fishing, and boat-launching on the James.

Hazards: Short, steep descent to bottomland section about midway along the trail could be hazardous. Until this short descent is more fully developed, it's a good idea to walk your bike down to the bottomland section of the trail.

Rescue index: Park personnel are located at the Visitor Center, the entrance station on VA 606, and are on-duty throughout the park during the summer season. In lieu of those options, head back down VA 605 to the store at the Bent Creek intersection with US 60.

Land status: State park.

Maps: Available from state park office and entrance station.

Finding the trail: The park is accessible from several directions to the east of the James River. The most direct approach is from the intersection of US 60, VA 26, and VA 605, a point on the map labeled as Bent Creek. From Bent Creek drive 8 miles north on VA 605 until you reach the intersection with VA 606. Turn left here to enter the park and follow the signs. Begin riding at Green Hill Pond.

Source of additional information:

James River State Park
Route 1, Box 787
Gladstone, Virginia 24553
(804) 933-4355

Notes on the trail: I'd never had the opportunity to view a state park in the making, but with the well-marked Cabell Trail loop in place, what more could I want? The trailhead is now located uphill from the Green Hill Pond near the Visitor Center. However, I parked and began riding from the Green Hill Pond. The trail starts as gravel double-track heading uphill from VA 606, which runs through the middle of James River State Park. Like the park's other climbs, this first one is less than one-half mile in length and not too steep. Ultimately, climbing difficulty is all a matter of what you're accustomed to riding.

After passing an old cemetery on the left, continue to the Tye River Overlook trail on the left. This spot offers an outstanding view of the Tye-James confluence and is well worth the short walk down this wide, mulched path. Continuing past the overlook, you'll reach the intersection with a short spur trail to Branch Pond (going straight) and a right turn to remain on Cabell Trail. At this point, Cabell Trail becomes a grassy double-track across a ridge of sorts. Keep going until you reach a gate across the trail and its intersection with VA 606. This would be a good spot for small children or others who have had difficulty riding thus far to return to the start via VA 606.

The Cabell Trail picks up on the other side of the main park road; the James River is out of sight but across on the opposite side of an expansive field. You'll pedal a short distance through a natural tunnel of ironwood trees before following the trail through a meadow, and you'll finish the ride at Green Hill Pond.

While the Cabbell trail is a pleasant ride through the woods with little in the way of aerobic or technical challenge, hard-core bikers will want sample the other loops and perhaps the flat ride along the river as well. Park Manager Mark Schuppin told me that he wants Virginia's newest park to meet a wide range of user needs, including those of mountain bikers. He and his staff seem to have done just that.

RIDE 22 · Walnut Creek Park

AT A GLANCE

Length/Configuration: 5-mile single-track loop; 15 miles of trail are still in development

Aerobic difficulty: Considerable

Technical difficulty: Roots, rocks, and logs on this narrow, off-camber single-track

Scenery: Dense woods on hillsides surrounding a 25-acre lake

Special comments: Challenging single-track route for intermediate or expert riders. Less-experienced riders may want to stick to the trail along the water's edge

Doug Wilkins and Craig Griffin, representatives of the Charlottesville chapter of Mountain Bike Virginia, have worked with the Albemarle County Parks Department to develop a nifty five-mile single-track loop through the mature hardwoods surrounding the 23-acre lake at Walnut Creek Park.

The trail presently consists of a single loop with an intersection at the 2.5-mile point where the experts and we mere mortals must temporarily part company. However, the Walnut Creek Trail is still in its early stages of development. Wilkins hopes ultimately to have some 15 miles of trail on this 525-acre site, given adequate manpower and financial resources.

Designed by mountain bikers for mountain bikers, this is nevertheless a multi-use trail system; although with its tight, twisty turns, log jumps, and quick descents, it's hard to believe that this trail wouldn't lose something in the translation from two wheels to two feet. The trail goes up, down, and around the natural contours of this park's hills and ravines. With the exception of the lakeside sections of riding, this is a challenging ride overall that intermediate to advanced riders will really enjoy.

General location: 10 miles southwest of Charlottesville in Albemarle County.

Elevation change: Lots of short, steep ups and downs.

Season: Year-round, although ice and snow make this ride inadvisable during the winter months.

Services: Swimming and drinking water is available at the park when it's open from Memorial Day to Labor Day, during which time a fee is charged to enter. All other services are available in nearby Charlottesville.

Hazards: Short, steep ups and downs with numerous log-crossings on largely off-camber, tight, twisty single-track.

RIDE 22 · Walnut Creek Park

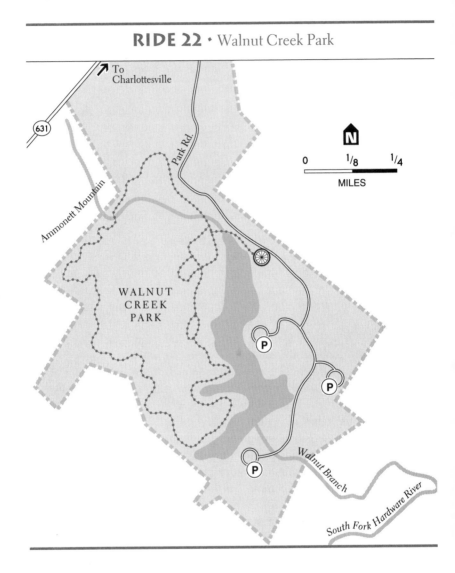

Rescue index: Park personnel can be summoned for assistance from Memorial Day to Labor Day, and at other times help can be found in nearby Charlottesville.

Land status: County park.

Maps: Call ahead for trail maps via mail or obtain one from the park office Memorial Day through Labor Day. You can also download one at www.albemarle.com, but the trail is very well marked so it would be difficult to get lost.

Finding the trail: Take US 29 south from Charlottesville for 7 miles. Turn

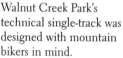

Walnut Creek Park's
technical single-track was
designed with mountain
bikers in mind.

left onto VA 708 at the sign for Walnut Creek Park. Drive for 3 miles and then
turn right onto VA 631. The park is a short distance on the left. The trailhead
is on the right adjacent to a gated road. There is ample parking a little father
down the road at the boat landing.

Sources of additional information:

Albemarle County Parks and
   Recreation Department
401 McIntire Road
Charlottesville, Virginia 22902
(804) 296-5844

Gary Morgan
230 North 32nd Street
Richmond, Virginia 23223
(804) 782-7903 day
(804) 222-8006 evenings

Notes on the trail: Although the trail was designed to be ridden counterclockwise starting at the trailhead going uphill into the woods, there's no
right or wrong way to ride at Walnut Creek. In fact, less experienced riders
would do well to start out in a clockwise direction by heading downhill on
the adjacent dirt road that leads past an abandoned farmhouse and then

along the edge of the lake for a mile or so. This is technically and aerobically much less demanding, and the place where the trail begins to ascend steeply away from the lake is a good spot to turn around to make a relatively easy 4-mile (round-trip) out-and-back ride.

RIDE 23 · Observatory Hill

AT A GLANCE

Length/Configuration: 7-mile maze of single-track loops and trail segments

Aerobic difficulty: Considerable

Technical difficulty: Roots, rocks, and logs on this narrow, off-camber single-track

Scenery: Heavily wooded site

Special comments: Keep in mind that this is private property; it's a privilege to ride on this trail system

Observatory Hill, a.k.a. O-Hill, gets its name from the proximity to the McCormick Observatory on Mount Jefferson. Its wooded location on the University of Virginia campus in the center of Charlottesville makes it easily accessible for a large number of riders as well as day hikers in this university town, which showcases the life and works of Thomas Jefferson.

The trail itself is a maze of steep single-track whose considerable challenges will be more appreciated by intermediate to advanced riders. The trail goes up, down, and around the natural contours of Mount Jefferson. Approximately seven miles of mostly technical single-track are bounded by city and campus roads, so it's pretty difficult to get lost. Newcomers to O-Hill may take a while to get oriented to the way individual trails configure and loop back, but every section of trail will either butt into another trail or dead-end at one of the streets bordering Mount Jefferson. If all else fails, head uphill and you'll eventually hit a road.

The high difficulty level of this trail system lends itself to riders being self-absorbed, but it's important that riders keep an eye out for others and display common courtesy toward all other trail users.

General location: University of Virginia campus in Charlottesville.

Elevation change: Very steep ups and downs.

Season: Year-round.

Services: All services are available in neighboring Charlottesville.

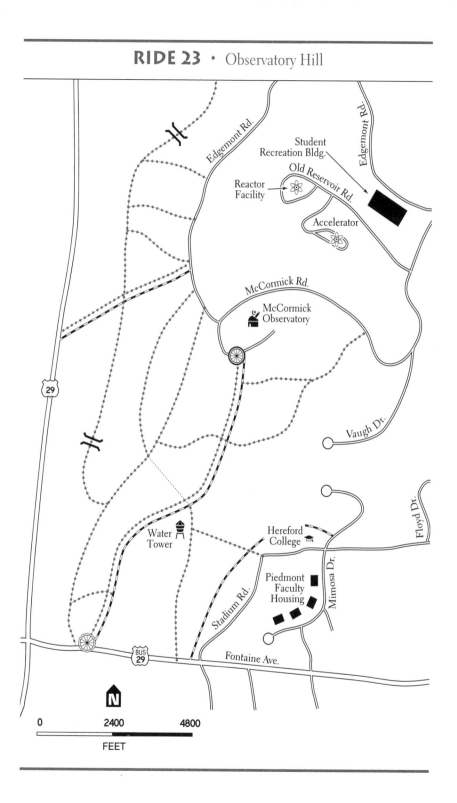

Hazards: Heavy usage on narrow, technical trails as well as short, steep ups and downs. Riders should be aware of and be courteous to hikers on the trail.

Rescue index: O-Hill gets a lot of use from University of Virginia students, both bikers and nonbikers, so it should be no trouble to get assistance if necessary.

Land status: University of Virginia campus.

Maps: Not available.

Finding the trail: Take exit 118 off Interstate 64 onto VA 29 north, toward Charlottesville. Take the Fontaine Avenue exit off this Charlottesville bypass. Turn left onto Maury Avenue, go past Scott Stadium, and turn left onto McCormick Road. Pass the observatory on the left and park nearby off the road. Enter the trail from here.

Sources of additional information:

Mark Gordon
The Bike Factory
198 Zan Roqad
Charlottesville, VA 22901
(804) 975-BIKE

Montain Bike Club at the
University of Virginia
www.student.virginia.edu/~bikeclub

Notes on the trail: Mountain biking at Mount Jefferson is a relatively recent addition to activities at McCormick Observatory which was built in 1880. After several years of informal and sometimes destructive usage by mountain bikers, O-Hill came close to being closed to two-wheel traffic due to complaints of reckless riding, unauthorized cutting of new trails, and subsequent erosion. However, the Mountain Bike Club at the University of Virginia assumed the responsibility of maintaining and policing the trail system and thereby proved to university administrators that mountain bikers could be the solution and not the problem. According to 1 university official, the club has developed a model of interagency and multi-use cooperation that has made them a welcome part of the community. Some of the club's efforts have centered on posting trail signs to educate mountain bikers about what is permissible and what is not.

Kyle Fedler, former president of the Mountain Bike Club at the University of Virginia, filled me in on the annual O-Hill Meltdown race that's been held every spring for the past 10 years. "Without the cooperation of a number of people at UVa., this race as well as the day-to-day riding at O-Hill would be a thing of the past," the doctoral student in religious studies told me. And with its location right on a campus in the center of town, the trail is very convenient, added Mark Gordon, owner/operator of the Bike Factory in Charlottesville.

Given the negative precedent that some mountain bikers set at O-Hill, it's especially important that riders abide by the rules of common sense and common courtesy as well as those posted on trail signs.

NORTHERN VIRGINIA

N orthern Virginia's division from the rest of the state is more socioeconomic than geographic. The Potomac River and Blue Ridge Mountains do form obvious geographic boundaries, but heading south it's a little tougher to agree on a hard and fast line of demarcation. For the purpose of this guide, I've used a line between the cities of Fredericksburg and Culpeper along VA 3 which, if extended, would reach Skyline Drive and Shenandoah National Park near Old Rag Mountain.

This region is, by and large, an outgrowth of its proximity to Washington, D.C.; northern Virginia is very much a cultural melting pot where you're just as likely to hear an East Indian or Vietnamese accent as a southern drawl. Residents of the area learn to accept swarms of traffic and rampant development as the cost of living in an area where restaurants, museums, and other evidence of international culture have few equals throughout the world.

Unfortunately, a place to mountain bike, or for that matter real estate for any purpose, comes at a high price just below the Potomac. Some trails have been paved, such as the 44-mile Washington and Old Dominion Railroad Regional Park (generally referred to simply as the W&OD Trail) running from Washington to Purcellville, while others are in more natural settings, such as the system of dirt and gravel carriage roads at Great Falls Park on the Potomac River. However, the newest and most exciting development in northern Virginia for hardcore single-track riders is the 4.5-mile trail at Fountainhead Regional Park. The Mid-Atlantic Off-Road Enthusiasts (MORE) worked long and hard with the Northern Virginia Regional Park Authority officials to design, develop, and maintain this trail.

Northern Virginia riders would do well to get behind the folks from MORE if they want more places to ride. The club's efforts earned it a 1996

Model Program Award from the International Mountain Bicycling Association (IMBA) for "overall excellence in support of socially responsible and environmentally sound trail cycling in the Mid-Atlantic region," particularly with regard to their educational work with horseback riders and developing creative trail management strategies at Fountainhead.

Northern Virginia's busy thoroughfares are lined with an array of stores, malls, and shopping centers that appear to have no beginning or end. However, don't assume that this seemingly distant relative of the rest of Virginia has entirely given up its family ties while rushing headlong into the world market. You just have to look a little harder for its family tree.

Old Town Alexandria is as good a place as any to find the "Virginia" in northern Virginia. Its tree-lined streets and brick paving are reminiscent of its former function as a small tobacco port on the Potomac River dating back to the 1730s. Now it's hard to imagine George Washington and Robert E. Lee walking these same streets, which today feature a more contemporary array of upscale boutiques, galleries, and craft shops.

Named after the Alexanders who owned the original 60-acre plot, Alexandria prided itself as the "last and best Virginia anchorage for ocean vessels before the Potomac Falls [Great Falls]." Both Washington and Lee called Alexandria home—although not at the same time since Washington's death preceded Lee's birth by several years.

To see northern Virginia's ties with the past, it's necessary to overlook its sometimes overwhelming present and focus on other extant historic locations, such as Washington's Mount Vernon home; Gunston Hall, the eighteenth-century manor called home by Virginia statesman George Mason; and the Manassas National Battlefield Park, where Confederate victories during the Civil War on two occasions took place 13 months apart. Both were named after the small creek named Bull Run that flowed through these green fields and forests. At the First Battle at Bull Run General Thomas J. Jackson received his well-known nickname when Confederate general Barnard Bee called out, "There stands Jackson like a stone wall. Rally behind the Virginians!"

It's fair to say that northern Virginia has shaken off and kept some of its southern culture, but just as its past lies somewhat hidden by its present, so do some very good biking spots lie obscured from view. However, if MORE's start is a good predictor, northern Virginia's residents and visitors should have an increasing number of mountain biking options available in the years to come. Join forces with this group and make sure that additional sites materialize sooner rather than later.

RIDE 24 · Wakefield and Lake Accotink Parks

AT A GLANCE

Length/Configuration: 4-mile loop, with additional single-track figure-8 in developement

Aerobic difficulty: Easy on main loop; short, steep climbs on optional single-track

Technical difficulty: Easy on the loop; rocks, roots, and mud on the optional single-track

Scenery: Woods, suburbs, and a lake

Special comments: One of the most popular off-road destinations in the D.C. area

These two adjacent parks, both within spitting distance of the accursed, traffic-clogged Capital Beltway, are godsends to D.C.-area mountain bikers. Without them there would be virtually no place to ride a mountain bike off-road in these congested, biker-unfriendly suburbs surrounding the nation's capital.

That's not all. The parks provide fun places to spin the cranks for a wide range of fat-tire enthusiasts. Want an easy, scenic ride on a wide dirt trail that circumnavigates a forested lake? You got it: the main loop trail is 3.9 miles long, virtually flat, and a sheer delight to ride.

It's also a great warm-up for the remaining single-track figure-8. Hammerheads, who otherwise drove to the boonies of western Virginia to get their jollies, carved miles of unmarked single-track trails around Lake Accotink in the `90s. However, some local conservationists worried that overly zealous trailblazing compromised the parks' ecosystem. John Bendorites, Park Manager at Lake Accotink was recently charged with delineating the aforementioned figure-8 from the parks' tangle of trails. Riders should be respectful of the new restrictions and mindful that some former trails will be visible, but are off limits.

Despite limitations which exclude riders from the steeper, rougher trails, local enthusiasts will no doubt still flock to the parks. Don't miss the chance to chat it up with some of the hard-core types you'll see unloading their bikes in the parking lot at Wakefield Park. (Look for Saabs with $400 bike racks.) The hammerheads are easy to spot; distinguishing features include shaved legs on men and front *and* rear suspension on bikes.

General location: Just outside the Capital Beltway in Springfield, Virginia, in the suburbs of Washington, D.C.

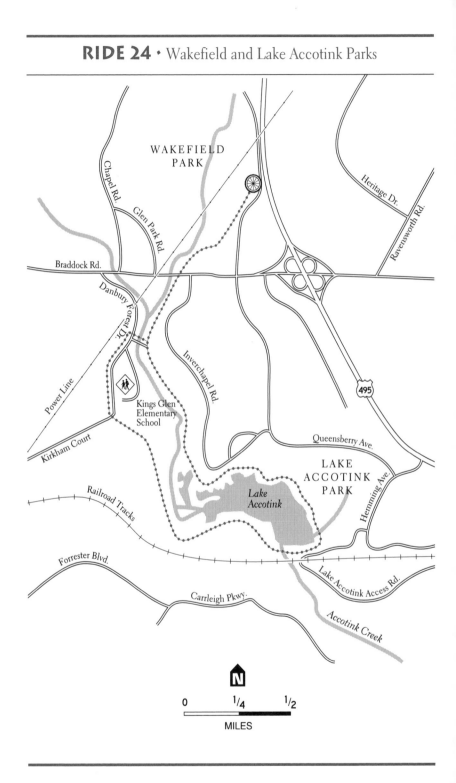

Elevation change: Minimal on the main loop trail; a few climbs on the figure-8.

Season: Year-round.

Services: Rest rooms are located in service buildings in both parks. A snack bar is located in the marina office at Lake Accotink. All services are available in the surrounding suburbs.

Hazards: Lots of pedestrians, joggers, horses, and parents pushing baby buggies on the main loop trail; the single-track offers some mud holes, and Virginia clay that's like ice when wet.

Rescue index: Both parks are surrounded by paved roads and residences.

Land status: Fairfax County Park Authority.

Maps: A trail map is available at the marina office at Lake Accotink, but you really don't need one.

Finding the trail: Mountain bikers in search of a good workout can start at Wakefield Park; it adds a little extra mileage to an otherwise too-short ride and avoids the congestion at Lake Accotink. From the Capital Beltway (Interstate 495), take Braddock Road (exit 5) west, heading outside the Beltway. At the second light, turn right into the park (there's a sign; you can't miss it). Then park in the lot on the left in front of the ball fields. The paved trail to Lake Accotink starts at the left side of the lot as you face the fields. Look for the sign for Wakefield/Accotink Trail.

To reach Lake Accotink Park by car, follow the same directions as above except turn left at the second light onto Queensbury Avenue. Follow it to the end and turn right onto Heming Avenue. The park entrance is a third of a mile on the right.

Source of additional information:

Lake Accotink Park
7500 Accotink Park Road
Springfield, Virginia 22150
(703) 569-3464

Notes on the trail: About 0.7 mile from the parking lot in Wakefield Park (and after passing under Braddock Road), you'll come to an intersection. For an easy 5-mile loop around the lake, turn right here. Cross the creek on the bridge, turn left, and go up the stairs (it will make sense when you get there). At the top of the stairs you enter a residential neighborhood; bear left (more or less continuing straight), ride up the hill (watch for traffic), and descend into a cul-de-sac. Take the paved path and turn left onto the dirt trail, which is the main loop trail in Accotink Park. About 4 miles later you'll end up at the intersection noted above (where you turned right and went over the creek). Continue straight to your car.

Try to hook up with some local riders in the parking lot for more directions and recommendations.

RIDE 25 · Fountainhead Regional Park

AT A GLANCE

Length/Configuration: 5.5-mile (total) series of loops and connecting routes

Aerobic difficulty: You'll get a good workout on the trail's many short, steep climbs

Technical difficulty: Moderate, with lots of deadfall, creek crossings, rocks, and roots

Scenery: Pretty woods and glimpses of Lake Occoquan

Special comments: Designed and built by mountain bikers who love single-track; closed in the winter

Mountain bikers in the Washington, D.C., area are fortunate to have one of the most successful trail advocacy groups in the East working for them: the Mid-Atlantic Off-Road Enthusiasts (MORE). Need proof? Come to this delightful park in Fairfax County and ride this mountain bike trail built and maintained by MORE in an area formerly off-limits to fat-tire bikes. This is what happens when mountain bikers get organized and work with local officials—in this case, the Northern Virginia Regional Park Authority.

No doubt about it: This 5.5-mile single-track trail (a series of loops and connecting routes) was designed by mountain bikers who love challenging riding. With lots of short, steep climbs; stream crossings; plenty of downed trees and deadfall; and twists and turns that will keep your eyes firmly fixed to the trail, it's not a trail for novices. While not especially technical or rocky by Appalachian standards, the trail is still a nonstop succession of climbs, drops, turns, and obstacles that will plant a grin on the faces of intermediate and advanced riders.

The narrow, mostly soft dirt trail passes through a lovely second-growth pine and hardwood forest. When not plunging through small stream valleys, the trail follows narrow ridges leading out to the shores of Lake Occoquan. The lake views are gorgeous—no vacation homes or lodges spoil the shoreline—and the entire trail system is located in a chunk of forest that imparts a feeling of remoteness unusual in D.C.'s suburban sprawl. The trail doesn't pass any paved roads or private residences; the scenery is all woods and water.

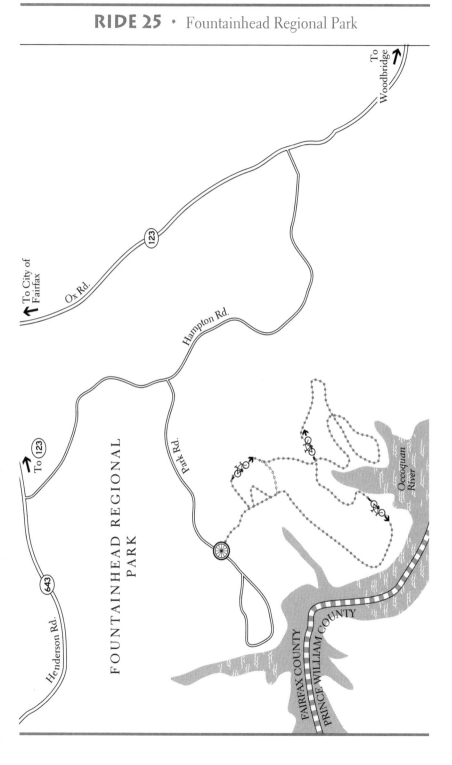

While 4.5 miles isn't a lot of riding, you can extend the ride by going back over some of the loops and riding connecting trails between them. All the trails are marked with red blazes on trees and there are plenty of signs to keep you straight. There's also a good chance that by the time you visit Fountainhead, MORE will have added a few more miles of well-constructed trail to the system.

General location: 10 miles south of Fairfax, Virginia, in the Washington, D.C., suburbs.

Elevation change: Several hundred feet; much of the climbing is short, steep ascents out of creek valleys.

Season: Mid-March to November; the park is closed in the winter.

Services: A snack bar and rest rooms are located at the marina office below the main parking area at Lake Occoquan. All services are available in Fairfax.

Hazards: Use care on the Shock-a-Billy Trail, the final, extremely steep descent. There's an alternative, somewhat less steep, side trai on the right for the less experienced.

Rescue index: The trail system is short, so you're never very far from the main park road. You could also wave down help from anglers in boats.

Land status: Northern Virginia Regional Park Authority.

Maps: A trail map is available at the marina office, but it really isn't necessary on this well-marked trail system.

Finding the trail: To reach Fountainhead Regional Park, take Interstate 95 south from D.C.'s Beltway (I-495) to the Lorton exit. Turn right and head west on VA 642. Next, turn right on Furnace Road, then turn right on Ox Road (VA 123). Finally, turn left on Hampton Road; the park entrance is 3 miles down on the left. After entering the park from Hampton Road, park in the big lot on the right. The signed trail begins across the road (mountain bikes to the left, hikers to the right).

Sources of additional information:

Fountainhead Regional Park
10875 Hampton Road
Fairfax Station, Virginia 22039
(703) 250-9124
(703)250-2473 (for 24-hour trail
  conditions)

Mid-Atlantic Off-Road Enthusiasts
  (MORE)
P.O. Box 2662
Fairfax, Virginia 22031
(703) 502-0359 (ride info line)
www.more-mtb.org

Notes on the trail: After periods of wet weather the trail may be closed. If in doubt, call the park. The park gaits are locked at 6:45 p.m.

RIDE 26 · W&OD Railroad Regional Park

AT A GLANCE

Length/Configuration: 45-mile (one-way) out-and-back

Aerobic difficulty: Easy

Technical difficulty: Paved bike path

Scenery: Suburban D.C., rolling Virginia countryside, horse farms, towns and villages

Special comments: The Leesburg to Purcellville 20-mile (total) out-and-back section is a great ride for first-timers

This trail is known locally as the Virginia Creeper, the nickname of the old railroad that operated along this rail bed from 1859 to 1968. Its official name is the W&OD Railroad Regional Park, a 45-mile-long, 100-foot-wide corridor with a paved bike path stretching from the shadow of the Lincoln Memorial in Washington west to the foothills of the Blue Ridge Mountains of Virginia.

Today the W&OD is spectacularly successful as a recreation and bike commuter trail in the congested Virginia suburbs of Washington. Instead of interurban commuter trains, the trail now serves bike commuters, joggers, equestrians, and people escaping to the scenic, open spaces of the rural Virginia countryside beyond the Capital Beltway. That includes a lot of folks on mountain bikes.

In congested Arlington County the trail links a series of "bubble" parks such as Bonair Rose Garden at Wilson Boulevard and Bluemont Park. Beside the trail, not far from Columbia Pike, is a survey marker placed by George Washington to mark the corner of a 1,200-acre tract of land he owned.

Close to Vienna, the bridge across Piney Branch is a beautiful stone arch that predates the Civil War. In the planned city of Reston, the W&OD connects in several places with the award-winning town's system of trails. In rural Loudoun County, the trail passes by lush horse farms; you may spot horses and hounds setting off on a fox hunt.

Leesburg has an information center open daily; the town has preserved an ambiance of an earlier age. You'll find plenty of restaurants and shops in this popular town (home to many Washington movers and shakers and a few movie stars). At Clarks Gap, the highest point on the trail, the path goes under a stone arch more than 100 years old. Along the westernmost section of the trail leading to its terminus in Purcellville (first settled in 1763), cyclists are treated to views of the rolling hills of the Virginia countryside.

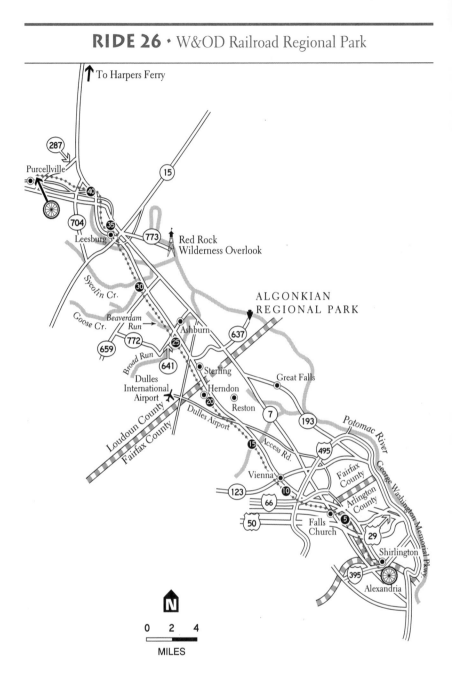

To Harpers Ferry

287

Purcellville

15

40

704

35

Leesburg

773

Red Rock
Wilderness Overlook

Sycolin Cr.

30

ALGONKIAN
REGIONAL PARK

Goose Cr. Beaverdam
Run →

Ashburn

637

659

772

25

Broad Run

641

Sterling

Great Falls

Dulles
International
Airport

20

Herndon

Reston

7

193

Potomac River

Loudoun County
Fairfax County

Dulles Airport

15

Access Rd.

495

Vienna

Fairfax
County

George Washington Memorial Pkwy.

123

10

66

Arlington
County

50

Falls
Church

5

29

Shirlington

395

Alexandria

N

0   2   4

MILES

Note: *This is a paved bicycle trail.*

General location: In the northern Virginia suburbs of Washington, D.C., between Arlington and Purcellville.

Elevation change: Minimal.

Season: Year-round. The Bonair Rose Garden at Wilson Boulevard in Arlington blooms in mid-June. July and August afternoons can get incredibly hot and humid, and there's not much shade along most of the trail.

Services: All services are available along the trail in Shirlington, Falls Church, Vienna, Reston, Herndon, Leesburg, and Purcellville.

Hazards: In some places the road bed is elevated and has steep drop-offs on either side.

Rescue index: The trail parallels and crosses major roads and passes through towns and villages for most of its length; it's very easy to flag down cars.

Land status: Northern Virginia Regional Park Authority.

Maps: A 56-page booklet, *The W&OD Trail Guide*, is sold at bike shops in northern Virginia and at regional parks along the trail for $4.50. You can order it online at www.wofriends.org or send a check for $5.75 to W&OD Railroad Regional Park, 5400 Ox Road, Fairfax Station, Virginia 22039; (703) 352-5900. Include a note requesting a copy of the W&OD guide.

Finding the trail: The eastern terminus of the trail is at the pedestrian overpass over I-395 at Shirlington. That's also where it connects with the Anderson Bikeway, which connects with the Mount Vernon Trail (which follows the Potomac River for 16 miles through Old Town Alexandria to George Washington's plantation). Parking is available all along the trail. For the best scenery (lush Virginia countryside, horse farms, views of the Blue Ridge Mountains), start in Leesburg and head west.

Source of additional information:

Northern Virginia Regional Park
  Authority
5400 Ox Road

Fairfax Station, Virginia 22039
(703) 352-5900
www.nvrpa.org

Notes on the trail: You can start an out-and-back ride virtually anywhere along the length of the 44-mile trail. The most scenic route, however, begins outside the Capital Beltway and heads west. Leesburg is a good starting point; the round-trip distance to Purcellville and back is about 20 easy miles. The trail is slightly uphill as you begin the ride; the return leg will be downhill. Leesburg is located about 35 miles northwest of Washington at the intersection of US 15 and VA 7.

Seventeen rebuilt railroad bridges provide a continuous span of trail along the route's 44-mile length. Some of the spans go over heavily traveled roadways such as the Capital Beltway, Interstate 66, and VA 7, and the trail isn't totally flat. But the climbs are short. A crushed-stone equestrian path parallels the paved bike path from west of Vienna to Purcellville. It's okay to ride your mountain bike on it; just be sure to yield to horses and other users.

RIDE 27 · C&O Canal National Historic Park

AT A GLANCE

Length/Configuration: 184 miles (one-way); short out-and-back options are possible, or set up a shuttle for a one-way trek

Aerobic difficulty: Easy

Technical difficulty: Easy

Scenery: Splendid views of the wide Potomac River, forests, and, farther west, mountains

Special comments: Great Falls, just north of Washington, is one of the most dramatic outdoor scenes east of the Rockies

The C&O Canal Towpath, stretching 184 miles between Washington, D.C., and Cumberland, Maryland, is one of the nation's most historic — and spectacularly scenic — cycling trails. The 12-foot-wide path follows what remains of the Chesapeake and Ohio Canal, a dream of passage envisioned by George Washington and built to link the nation's capital with its resources beyond the Appalachian Mountains.

President John Quincy Adams broke ground for the waterway on July 4, 1828. The canal, built with 74 lift locks to raise mule-pulled barges from nearly sea level to 605 feet of elevation at Cumberland, reached that western Maryland city in 1850.

Alas, the canal was doomed from the start. On the same day it was dedicated, the Baltimore and Ohio Railroad began its push to the west. By the time the canal reached Cumberland, the railroad had been there for eight years and further thoughts of continuing the financially ailing waterway farther west were abandoned.

Operated as a conduit for eastern coal and continually battered by extensive flooding, the canal ceased operation in the 1930s. In 1971 it became a national park and today serves as a recreational mecca for Washingtonians who live inside and outside the Beltway. Hikers, joggers, birders, anglers, mountain bikers, and anyone else in search of a bit of nature flock to the towpath year-round. They're never disappointed.

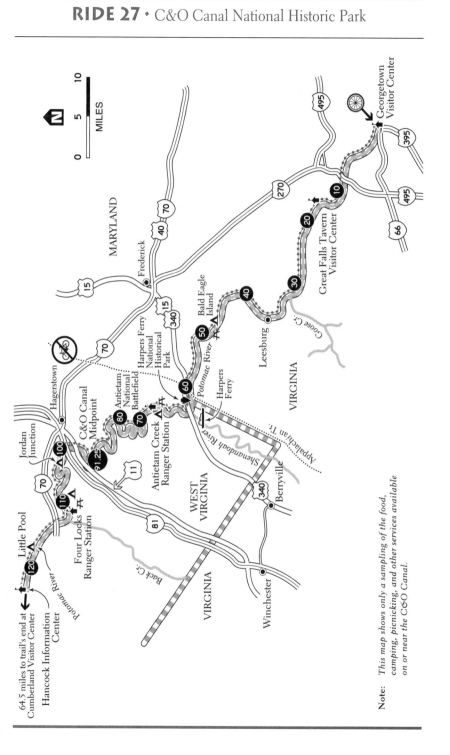

Note: *This map shows only a sampling of the food, camping, picnicking, and other services available on or near the C&O Canal.*

Exploring the towpath by mountain bike is a perfect way to enjoy the park. Two familiar companions are always with you—the wide Potomac River on one side and the canal (or what's left of it) on the other. Sometimes the canal is nothing more than a grassy swamp with trees growing out of it; along some stretches all that remains is a grassy slope where mule-pulled barges once floated. Near Washington, though, sections of the canal are still operational, and in the summer you can take rides on mule-powered barges—just like when the canal was in its heyday 150 years ago.

While the towpath is nearly flat, a wide range of surfaces—packed gravel, sand, wooden boards, and sections of dirt (or mud if it rained recently) littered with rocks and tree roots—greet riders. Flat? yes; always smooth? no.

A lot of American history took place along this route, and the towpath provides curious cyclists with much to explore—especially those with the time and interest to venture away from the towpath. There's also great scenery that greets you at nearly every subtle bend in the trail.

The short list of attractions, starting in Washington: Georgetown, Great Falls Tavern (and a museum), Mather Gorge (where the wide Potomac roars through spectacular Great Falls), Whites Ferry (the last regularly operating ferry on the Potomac River), Harpers Ferry National Historical Park (the site of John Brown's raid, a precursor of the Civil War), Antietam National Battlefield, Fort Frederick State Park (which dates from the French and Indian War), and the Paw Paw Tunnel (near milepost 165; a 3,118-foot, nineteenth-century engineering marvel built to avoid a series of loops in the Potomac River called the Paw Paw Bends; bring a flashlight). Forested islands in the Potomac, rock cliffs rising over the canal, glimpses of wildlife, and fieldstone buildings, locks, and aqueducts are other sights to enjoy along the towpath.

Built during a time when four miles an hour was a blistering pace, the C&O Canal is a place to enjoy nature, soak up some history, and slow down. Pack a lunch, bring some friends, and savor one of the best off-road cycling destinations in the United States.

General location: Between Georgetown in Washington, D.C., and Cumberland, Maryland, along the Potomac River.

Elevation change: 600 feet spread over 184 miles; however, the towpath is essentially flat.

Season: Year-round. Spring rains can turn sections of the towpath into muddy quagmires. In the summer, mosquitos will drive you crazy as soon as you roll to a stop; bring plenty of insect repellent. In July and August, the heat and humidity can be hellish. Mid- to late October brings crisp, cool mornings, warm afternoons, and breathtaking fall colors.

Services: Restaurants, small stores, and bed-and-breakfasts are spread along the entire length of the towpath. Primitive hiker-biker campgrounds are located about every 5 miles. Many are free; equipped with picnic tables, water pumps, and portable toilets; and available on a first-come, first-served basis. Williamsport, at mile marker 100, is a town located right on the canal. It has all services, including a bike shop.

Hazards: The towpath is prone to washouts after heavy winter and spring rains, so it's a good idea (and an absolute necessity for anyone riding the entire length) to call the park ahead of time to find out if any sections are damaged and closed to bikes.

Rescue index: For most of its length, the canal and towpath are close to and occasionally crossed by roads. Many residences line or overlook the canal. The stretch from Paw Paw to Hancock is the most remote part of the trail.

Land status: National park.

Maps: Several publications are invaluable for folks trekking the entire distance. For a free list, call or write Parks and History Association, 4598 MacAurther Blvd. NW, Washington, DC 20007; (202) 472-3083. Basic maps are available online via www.nps.gov. The majority of visitors, however, come only for the day and a map really isn't necessary (although a good road map is invaluable for finding the canal). For general information on the canal and a basic map, call or write Superintendent, C&O Canal National Historical Park, Box 4, Sharpsburg, MD 21782; (301) 739-4200.

Finding the trail: Most folks riding the entire 184 miles (which can be done in 5 or 6 days of easy pedaling) start in Cumberland and follow the Potomac River downstream. You can go the panniers-and-no-hot-shower-for-a-week route or stop at motels and bed-and-breakfasts along the way—or do a combination. For transportation to the start of the ride—or any number of different custom services that either let you ride to your car or that provide sag-wagon support for your gear as you pedal from B&B to B&B—call Catoctin Bike Tours in Mount Airy, Maryland (800-TOUR-CNO).

Daytrippers have virtually unlimited options for shorter explorations of the towpath. Popular starting points close to Washington for out-and-back rides are Georgetown (milepost 0; terrible parking but great bars and restaurants); Great Falls (milepost 14.3; park at Old Angler's Inn on MacArthur Boulevard or Swainn's Lock on River Road); Seneca Creek, where you can see 1 of 11 aqueducts that carried the canal over rivers and creeks (milepost 22.9; off MD 190); and Nolands Ferry, south of Frederick, Maryland (milepost 42; near Dickerson on MD 28). The farther from Washington, the better the scenery (with the exception of Great Falls, which is just north of the Beltway) and the thinner the crowds.

Sources of additional information:

Superintendent
C&O Canal National Historical Park
Box 4

Sharpsburg, Maryland 21782
(301) 739-4200
www.nps.gov/choh

Parks and History Association
4598 MacAurther Blvd. NW
Washington, D.C. 20007
(202) 472-3083

One of the best guidebooks to the towpath is *184 Miles of Adventure: Hiker's Guide to the C&O Canal* by the Mason-Dixon Council of the Boy Scouts of America (48 pages, softcover). It features more than 20 detailed maps and has accurate information for anyone interested in traveling the entire towpath, whether by mountain bike, foot, horse, llama. . . . The cost is $4.00 and the book can be ordered from the Mason-Dixon Council, P.O. Box 2133, Hagerstown, Maryland 21742. It's also widely available at northern Virginia bookstores and outdoor outfitters.

Notes on the trail: While for all intents and purposes the towpath is flat, why make it more difficult than you have to? On any out-and-back ride, pedal the towpath upriver at the start when you're fresh and bursting with energy, then turn around for the slightly downhill return trip.

Another option is to set up a car shuttle so that you only have to ride one-way (downhill, right?). It takes a minimum of 2 vehicles. Drive both vehicles to the end of your ride, park one of them, and pile into the other car (the one with the bikes). Then drive to your starting point, park, and begin the ride. At the finish, pile into the car you stashed earlier and drive back to the start to retrieve the other car. (Note: Not everyone has to go on the car-retrieval trip; if you've parked more than 1 car at the end of the ride, others from your group can proceed to a designated eating establishment and start ordering.)

Sound like an incredible waste of time, energy, and gasoline? It is. Never mind. Just do an out-and-back ride; the scenery looks completely different on the return leg.

RIDE 28 · Mount Vernon Trail

AT A GLANCE

Length/Configuration: 18.5-mile (one-way) out-and-back

Aerobic difficulty: Easy

Technical difficulty: Paved bike path

Scenery: Grand views of the Potomac, downtown Alexandria, and more

Special comments: Watch jetliners take off and land at National Airport

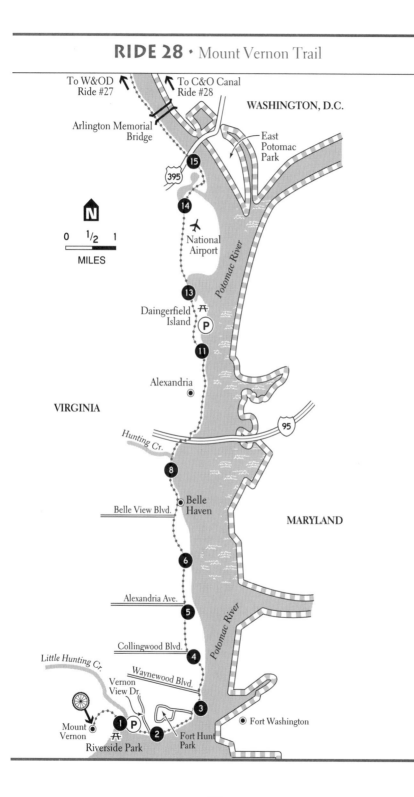

This paved, 18.5-mile-long bike path on the Virginia side of the Potomac River is Washington, D.C.'s premier cycling route. While there's nothing technical about it (except, perhaps, dodging inline skaters as they weave down the path), this trail is incredibly scenic — whether you prefer viewing wildlife on a lush, 240-acre wetland to enjoying stunning views of the river and the skyline of the nation's capital, or watching 727s take off and land at National Airport.

History buffs will find plenty to enjoy. Mount Vernon, George Washington's eighteenth-century plantation, is the southern terminus of the trail and is open to visitors every day of the year. Fort Hunt Park features nineteenth-century fortifications, while Jones Point Lighthouse warned of sandbars in the river from 1836 to 1925. Old Town Alexandria has Christ Church, Robert E. Lee's boyhood home, and Gadsby's Tavern, where the first U.S. president used to stop off on his way to and from his plantation. You can, too.

Closer to Washington, Gravelly Point offers splendid views of the Washington skyline and jetliners screaming overhead as they take off and land at National Airport. The planes are so close it seems you can reach up and touch them. The northern end of the trail at Theodore Roosevelt Island features 2.5 miles of hiking trails (bike racks are provided) and a memorial plaza.

General location: Along the Potomac River in northern Virginia, from Theodore Roosevelt Island south to George Washington's plantation below Alexandria.

Elevation change: Minimal.

Season: Year-round.

Services: All services are available in Alexandria. Rest rooms, phones, and places to eat and picnic are located every couple of miles along the trail.

Hazards: The trail is often crowded with other cyclists, joggers, inline skaters, and people out for a casual stroll. The trail follows city streets through Alexandria, so use normal precautions when dealing with heavy car traffic.

Rescue index: The trail parallels the George Washington Memorial Parkway; public phones are located along the route.

Land status: National park.

Maps: For a free map of the trail, call (703) 289-2500.

Finding the trail: The trail is accessible from many locations, including the northern terminus at Roosevelt Island and the southern end at Mount Vernon. Other popular starting points (all with parking) include Gravelly Point, Daingerfield Island, Belle Haven, and Fort Hunt Park.

Source of additional information:
Superintendent
George Washington Memorial Parkway
Turkey Run Park
McLean, Virginia 22101
(703) 289-2500

Notes on the trail: Bring a bike lock and enjoy a side trip at Dyke Marsh, about 6 miles north of Mount Vernon. More than 250 species of birds have been sighted on the lush, 240-acre wetland that is typical of the Potomac estuary shoreline. Just beyond the northern end of the trail is a connection to the W&OD Trail, another paved bike path that goes west through the Virginia suburbs to the foothills of the Blue Ridge Mountains. You can also cross the Potomac on Arlington Memorial Bridge and follow the river upstream to the C&O Canal Towpath in Georgetown. It's a hard-packed dirt trail that heads northwest for 185 miles to Cumberland, Maryland.

RIDE 29 · Great Falls Park

AT A GLANCE

Length/Configuration: 5.5-mile loop

Aerobic difficulty: Moderate, with a few steep climbs

Technical difficulty: Moderate with short sections of rocky, technical single-track

Scenery: Spectacular as the Potomac crashes through Mather Gorge

Special comments: Stay off trails closed to bikes

One of America's most popular national parks is located just outside Washington, D.C., along the Potomac River. It's a dramatic setting: The wide river builds up speed and force as it falls over a series of steep, jagged rocks and flows through narrow Mather Gorge. It's called Great Falls—and it's one of the most impressive sights this side of the Rockies.

And guess what. You can ride your mountain bike at this 800-acre national park. A 5.5-mile loop on mostly dirt double-track trails offers a good aerobic workout for beginner and intermediate riders. Even racers come here on summer evenings to train. While none of the sections on this loop ride are

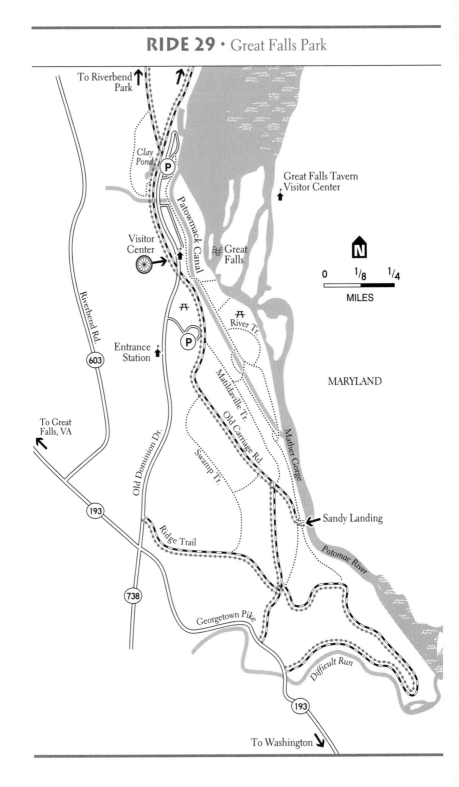

particularly technical or difficult, some of the climbs are steep and there are short sections of rocky single-track and sand. Part of the loop also follows short sections of paved road.

On the ride you'll enjoy many views of Great Falls, steep rock formations, and the fast-moving rapids in the river. The trail is lined with tall oak and maple trees, and, overall, the scenery is often plain spectacular. Before or after your ride, be sure to walk to one of the overlooks near the visitor center. They date from the early twentieth century when the land was a private amusement park and D.C. residents arrived by train.

General location: 14 miles northwest of Washington, D.C., along the Potomac River in suburban Fairfax County, Virginia.

Elevation change: About 250'.

Season: Year-round.

Services: All services are available in McLean, Virginia, and throughout the Washington suburbs.

Hazards: Watch out for the many hikers and mountain bikers that throng this popular park. Swimming and wading in the Potomac River are prohibited because of strong currents and killer hydraulics.

Rescue index: The park is patrolled by national park service rangers.

Land status: National park.

Maps: A trail map is available at the entrance gate and the Visitor Center.

Finding the trail: From Interstate 495 (the Capital Beltway) take VA 193 (Georgetown Pike) west and follow signs to the park. Ride back out of the entrance about a mile and turn left at the gate onto the Ridge Trail.

Sources of additional information:

George Washington Memorial Parkway
Turkey Run Park
McLean Virginia, 22101
(703) 289-2500

Great Falls Park
9200 Old Dominion Drive
McLean, Virginia 22101
(703) 285-2966

Notes on the trail: After getting on the Ridge Trail (see above), turn right at the **T** intersection, which brings you out to the main (paved) road. Turn left and ride about a half-mile and turn right onto the trail opposite a small parking area on the right (this is an alternative starting point; see below). Follow this trail down Difficult Run. Take the first left (uphill; it's a steep climb), then turn left onto the Ridge Trail. Follow it to the Old Carriage Road, bear right, and return to the Visitor Center. You can also start this ride from the gravel parking lot on VA 193 about a half mile from the park. The trail that follows Difficult Run is across the road, behind the gate. Don't give in to the temptation to ride any trails closed to bikes; the park is well patrolled by rangers and you will be ticketed.

RIDE 30 • Prince William Forest Park

AT A GLANCE

Length/Configuration: Numerous gravel roads— all less than 1.5 miles long—can be combined with paved park roads to create longer loops

Aerobic difficulty: Generally minimal

Technical difficulty: None

Scenery: Densely wooded with intermittent streams along trails and roads

Special comments: Good family rides

Prince William Park offers almost ten miles of dirt and gravel roads open to bicyles. By using the hard-surface Scenic Drive in conjunction with unpaved roads and one of the park's free bicycle guides, the beginning biker or family can have a great time pedaling through this 18,622-acre forest.

Many of the rough-road paths open to cycling don't connect to others or dead-end somewhere, so aside from the hard-surface Scenic Drive, it's difficult to put together a loop of any size. What is special about Prince William Forest is its size in proximity to the urban areas of Washington, northern Virginia, and Fredericksburg. Plan a weekend camping trip for you and your family at Prince William Forest Park and bring the bikes along for some easy woods riding.

Prince William Forest offers a natural enclave amid this rapidly developing urban corridor along Interstate 95 to the benefit of Mother Nature as well as those of us who need to hear crickets and hug a tree every so often. With the fall line running north to south through here, you're able to see and enjoy the sound of quite a few streams as they cascade across rocky creek beds. This has also created a varied habitat that beaver, wild turkey, and a vast assortment of threatened and endangered native plants call home.

This is a stark contrast to the tobacco fields that were once in cultivation throughout this area, at least until the soil was depleted and the valuable topsoil was washed away into the nearby harbor at Dumfries. Over time the farms grew smaller and less productive until 1940, when the land was acquired by the National Park System. After being used as a top secret military installation during World War II, it came under its present status in 1948.

General location: 22 miles north of Fredericksburg.

Elevation change: Gentle ups and downs.

Season: Year-round.

Services: The park has group, individual, and backcountry camping and environmental programs in a beautiful wooded habitat, despite its proximity to urban areas of Washington, D.C., and Fredericksburg. There is a fee for entering Prince William Forest Park. All other services are available in towns and cities along US 1 and I-95.

Hazards: None.

Rescue index: Park personnel are on duty at the entrance station, Visitor Center, and are on patrol throughout the park.

Land status: National park.

Maps: Available from park office.

Finding the trail: Take exit 150 off I-95 and follow the signs a short distance to the park entrance. Proceed down the main road to the Visitor Center. You can access the system of double-track bike trails from there.

Sources of additional information:

Prince William Forest Park
18100 Park Headquarters Road
Triangle, Virginia 22172
(703) 221-7181

Friends of Prince William Park
9605 Pierrpont Street
Burke, Virginia 22015

Notes on the trail: Be sure to pick up Prince William Forest Park's *Bicycling Guide* for specifics on what trails are okay to ride, as well as particular park regulations for bicycle use. If you thought northern Virginia was all beltways, malls, and politicians, head down to Prince William Forest Park, the largest national park in the Piedmont and the closest good-sized federal forest to Washingtonians.

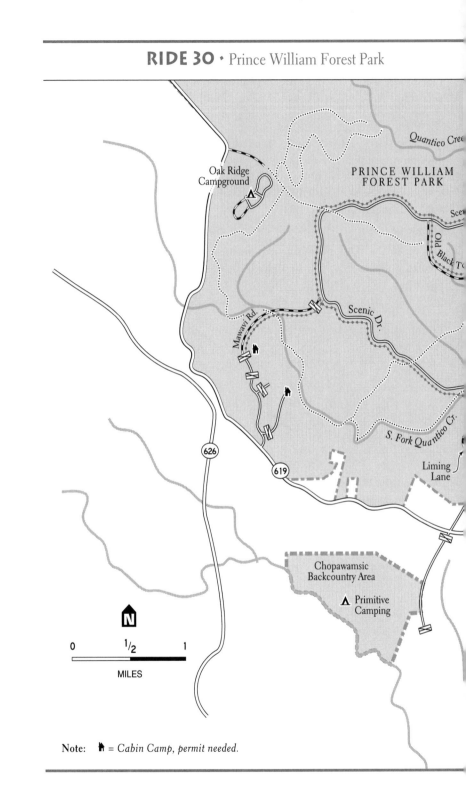

Note: 🖝 = Cabin Camp, permit needed.

To
Washington

Turkey Run
Ridge
Group
Camp

Pyrite Mine Rd.

N. Orenda Rd.

Quantico Cr.

S. Orenda Rd.

Visitor
Center

Park
H.Q.

Quantico National
Cemetery

Entrance

EXIT 150

To
Fredericksburg

THE MOUNTAINS OF
WESTERN VIRGINIA

This section includes rides in an area that runs from the triangular northernmost tip of Virginia and continues southwestward along the backbone of the state before ending at an east-west line formed by the Roanoke River. (Note: Western Virginia's mountains continue through the Blue Ridge Highlands. However, the mountains southwest of the Roanoke River are part of an upland province that's somewhat different and characterized by an overall increase in elevation). The eastern and western parameters are the Blue Ridge Mountains and the West Virginia border, respectively.

This region of Virginia includes 1.7 million acres of George Washington and Jefferson National Forests (although the majority of the Jefferson National Forest is in the Blue Ridge Highlands), representing the state's largest accumulation of mountain bikable public land. While several rides in this section are not in the national forest, most are. You'll notice that more than half of the routes in this book are in the Mountains of Western Virginia and Blue Ridge Highlands sections, largely due to this large parcel of national forest, which features innumerable combinations of single-track, double-track, and gravel roads.

Another bonus is that if you are seeking solitude on your rides, you're sure to find it in the mountains. I continue to be amazed that I can ride for hours in the George Washington or Jefferson without seeing another person, unless I've decided to steer to one of the more popular spots such as Big Levels in George Washington National Forest or the Virginia Creeper Trail in the Mount Rogers National Recreation Area. Although generally not posted, the national forests request that mountain bikers follow the International Mountain Bicycling Association's Rules of the Trail.

After spending very little time west of the Blue Ridge Mountains, you'll soon realize that this region is not a solid mass of mountains but rather a series of ranges punctuated by large and small valleys. The Blue Ridge to the east and Alleghenies to the west frame the well-known Shenandoah Valley while the lesser-known Fort Valley lies in the eye of a needle formed by the 50-mile Massanutten Range. Farther south in the Roanoke area you'll find the New River Valley.

The combination of mountains and valleys creates varied mountain biking opportunities. Some of this terrain has a considerable slope, which will get you using every one of those granny gears, while other locations will be flatter than you would have anticipated. So don't be too quick to dismiss the mountains if you are new to the sport or are looking for a less physically challenging ride.

The elevation range in the mountains of western Virginia varies from 550 feet at the base of the northern end of Massanutten, near Elizabeth Furnace, to 4,463 feet at the top of Elliott Knob, the highest point in George Washington National Forest. This range of elevation is less useful than the change in elevation included on each ride as well as the narrative descriptions of each ride.

As you'd expect, the considerable elevation gradient across this mountainous region produces an equally variable pattern of weather and vegetation. This became clearer to me when I traveled across the southern edge of Virginia from the Virginia-Kentucky border at Breaks Interstate Park to False Cape State Park in the coastal region over several days. While the blooms of spring had come and were waning along the Atlantic Coast at False Cape, the beginnings of spring appeared to be at least three weeks away on the Cumberland Plateau at Breaks. On any given day, you'll find that the temperature is 10 to 15 degrees cooler in the national forests than in Staunton, Harrisonburg, or other more urban areas of the Shenandoah Valley or the New River Valley to the south.

Vegetation changes as you gain elevation from the hemlocks and sycamores growing along moist bottomlands through the oak and chestnuts going up the mountainsides, to the more resilient and tenacious table mountain pines and mountain laurel. The birch, cherry, maple, beech, and red spruce found in the Laurel Fork area of the George Washington National Forest are more typical of the hardwood forests in some northern states than woodlands in any other part of Virginia. However, Laurel Fork is an obvious exception to the Appalachian Cove Forest that covers most of George Washington and Jefferson National Forests. Rather than a forest in transition to becoming another mix of vegetative growth, the Appalachian Cove is a stable climax forest that reached its final mix of trees, shrubs, vines, and plants after millions of years of evolution.

As you bike across the region, you may notice some idiosyncratic place names. Many of these quirks have been passed along from the earliest settlers, who repeated even earlier Native American traditional names.

One of these is the redundant use of "North Mountain" to identify ranges that are not in any way connected besides being located in one of the western Virginia regions. This particular naming of disparate mountains dates back at least as far as Thomas Jefferson's early travels through the mountains. In *Notes on the State of Virginia,* Jefferson's only book despite the voluminous writing he did, the statesman from Charlottesville said, "The ridge of mountains next beyond the Blue ridge [*sic*], called by us the North mountain, is of the greatest extent; for which reason they were named by the Indians the Endless mountains [*sic*]."

And so you'll ride along the top of North Mountain at Dragons Back west of Roanoke, and another North Mountain west of Lexington, and still another as you pedal your way up to Elliott Knob, the tallest peak in George Washington National Forest. And yet another North Mountain can be seen across the Shenandoah Valley from the Massanutten Mountain range just northeast of Harrisonburg.

Virginia's territory to the west of the Blue Ridge Mountains followed a different course of settlement than to the east. Despite early forays by Englishmen from the eastern settlements—John Lederer in 1669 and Governor Alexander Spotswood and the Knights of the Golden Horseshoe in 1716—a combination of Scotch-Irish and German settlers from Pennsylvania largely settled the Great Valley of Virginia. From the days of its first European settlements in the early 1700s, the fabric of western Virginia was woven of threads from different values, traditions, languages, and, of course, geography than those of coastal Virginia.

But even before Lederer's expedition, the bluish haze of accumulated water vapor from the heavily wooded slopes provided the blue mountains with a name given by the Native Americans. We know them as the Blue Ridge Mountains, the leading edge of succeeding ranges of the "Apalataei" (Appalachians) that run from south-central Pennsylvania to northwestern Georgia.

The fertile Valley of Virginia amid the western Virginia mountains was the breadbasket for an entire growing nation and then for the Confederacy while neighboring slopes provided high-grade iron ore for weapons and ammunition during the 1800s. Unfortunately for the southern cause, this source of food and munitions located just 120 miles or so from the Confederate capital of Richmond made the valley an equally important target for the Union army.

Massanutten Mountain figured heavily into Confederate General Stonewall Jackson's highly successful and well-known Civil War Valley Campaign. During the spring and summer of 1862, the former Virginia Military Institute professor used an intimate knowledge of the Massanutten range, gained largely from the intricate maps drawn by Staunton mapmaker Jedediah Hotchkiss, to repeatedly foil a much larger northern army during a protracted game of cat and mouse.

Now Massanutten is increasingly figuring into the lives of today's mountain bikers, and the routes in this guide only scratch the surface of possibility on this 50-mile range. Massanutten's appeal is not limited to recreational riders, however. Located at the southern end of this range, the Massanutten Ski Resort hosted the 1997 World Cup Downhill Championship over July Fourth weekend. Over the years Massanutten has also been the site of the annual Hoo-Ha and Yee-Ha races. I have not included any routes for this private resort because, aside from the races named, their policies regarding recreational riding on the resort property have been inconsistent. You can call Great Eastern Resort Management (800-207-MASS) for the most up-to-date riding and racing information at this very popular resort.

There is a great deal of mountain biking territory to explore in the region. In addition to the rides described here, new routes can be explored; grab a map of any given national forest district and head out on some interesting roads and trails. Many of the rides I've shared utilize gravel Forest Service roads because these are consistently maintained to a ridable standard. Unfortunately, the same can't be said for gated forest roads and hiking trails.

The recently published "Guidelines for Mountain Biking in the George Washington and Jefferson National Forests" brochure offers the following:

"Expect to carry and walk your bike for considerable distances on almost all of the trails in the national forests. No trails are maintained for continuous mountain bike riding. Trails are narrow and sometimes steep and are always pretty rough due to rock."

However, the good news is: "You may ride your bike on any forest road or trail unless it is specifically closed to mountain bike use. The closed routes are very few and are well signed." (Note: I didn't cover all 1.7 million acres of national forest land in Virginia, but I never saw a trail closure sign, except at designated wilderness areas.)

The pamphlet adds, "You may ride behind the gates and tanktraps (mounds of earth used to block roads). These roads may have signs that say 'Road Closed.' The closure applies to motorized vehicles, not to horses, hikers, and pedal-powered bikes."

As a result, the end of a day spent riding, walking, and bushwhacking often brought the refrain, "Gee, it looked a lot different on paper." I found that it was difficult to reliably predict what was really *out there* until getting *out there* to find out, much to the chagrin of different riding partners who generally didn't sign any long-term contracts with me. I grew to appreciate the difficulties that John Lederer and Governor Spotswood must have had in trying to round up companions for their explorations.

RIDE 31 • Elizabeth Furnace

AT A GLANCE

Length/Configuration: 11.5-mile loop

Aerobic difficulty: Considerable, especially on the tortuous climb to the top of Green Mountain

Technical difficulty: Varies from unobstructed double-track to technical single-track

Scenery: Great views of the neighboring Massanutten range, especially from Signal Knob

Special comments: You'll encounter varied terrain, from the ascent through verdant Mudhole Gap to mountaintop riding

This 11.5-mile loop covers a little bit of everything from hard-packed gravel forest road to technical single-track, so it's not for the wary or those with amateur bike-handling skills. Fortunately, the first seven miles, going as far as the Strasburg Reservoir, lend themselves to an easier 14-mile out-and-back alternative that skips the single-track ascent and descent across the top of Green Mountain, the toughest part of the ride.

Before the Civil War broke out in 1862, a number of area furnaces processed iron and manganese ore mined in Fort Valley. Elizabeth Furnace turned out approximately 250 tons of pig iron each year during its peak production in the 1840s. Despite the use of Signal Knob at the northern end of Massanutten as a lookout post for the Confederate army, Fort Valley and its iron-producing furnaces were a consistent target for the Union army. This location came to be known as the "valley of death" because of the rampant destruction Union troops wreaked on its mines, furnaces, and farmland. For more information on iron production, plan to hike the short interpretive Pig Iron and Charcoal Trails.

Fort Valley, sometimes called Powell's Fort Valley, is named for a mysterious counterfeiter. It's said that local Indians showed Powell where on Massanutten to dig for the gold he turned into counterfeit dollars. These same Indians supposedly hid Powell when the authorities caught on to him. Little is known about his death, and local legend has it that he buried a good bit of unspent gold on top of Signal Mountain. I can't vouch for such tales, but this ride will offer you a golden opportunity to explore the beautiful northern end of Massanutten Mountain.

RIDE 31 · Elizabeth Furnace

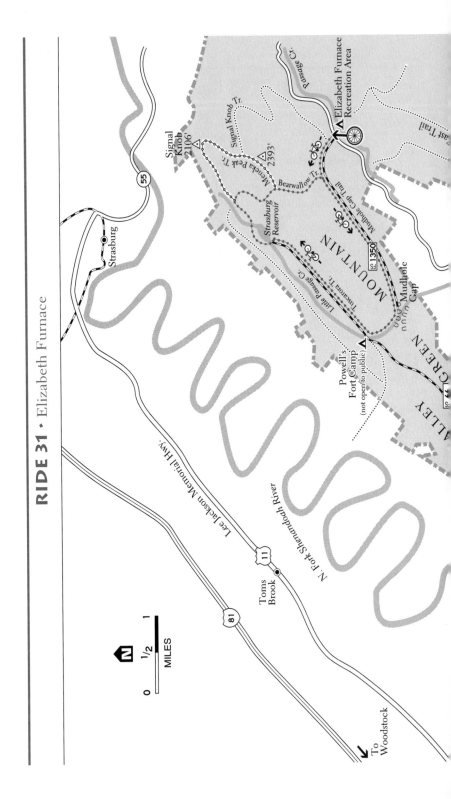

Strasburg

Signal Knob 2106'

Signal Knob Tr.

Meneka Peak Tr.

2393'

Bearwallow Tr.

Strasburg Reservoir

Elizabeth Furnace Recreation Area

Tuscarora East Trail

Mudhole Gap Trail

Passage Cr.

MOUNTAIN

GREEN

VALLEY

Little Passage Cr.

Tuscarora Tr.

Mudhole Gap

Powell's Fort Camp
(not open to public)

55

N. Fork Shenandoah River

Lee Jackson Memorial Hwy.

11

Toms Brook

81

To Woodstock

N

0   1/2   1
MILES

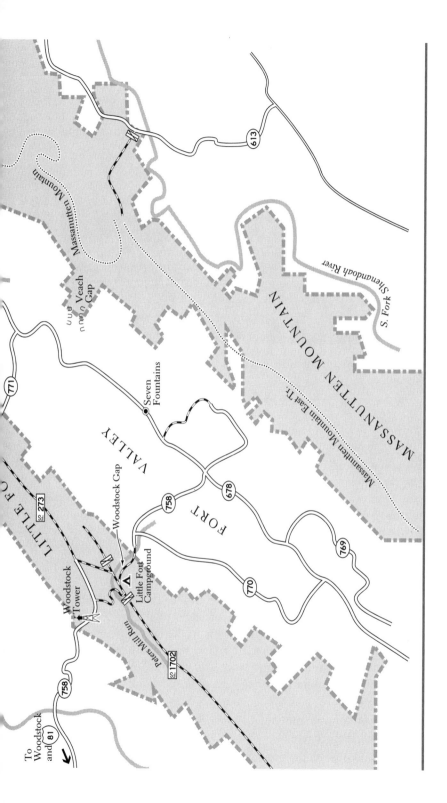

Signal Knob was a Confederate lookout at the northern end of Massanutten Mountain.

General location: 10 miles west of Front Royal.

Elevation change: Starting at 785', the initial climb has mostly ups with a few short descents thrown in until the road ends at 1,050'. It feels like a greater ascent than just 265 vertical feet in the first 3.5 miles, but the intermittent descents nullify the overall climb along here. You'll gain another 170' in the mile through Mudhole Gap. By far the greatest climb is going to be the 1.2-mile gain of 360' to the top of Green Mountain. The ride ends on a downhill note with a 3.3-mile, mostly downhill run, losing 1,096' before ending across from the campground.

Season: Year-round, although not when frozen ice and snow at high elevations make the ride dangerous. Be especially careful when riding during the succession of hunting seasons that begin in the fall; wear bright colors and avaid combinations of brown, black and white, which make you resemble a deer. Call the Virginia Department of Game and Inland Fisheries (540-248-9360) for the opening and closing dates of hunting seasons for various game animals.

Services: Water and camping are available when the Elizabeth Furnace Recreation Area is open.

Hazards: The ascent and descent of Green Mountain on rocky single-track can be pretty tricky. Little Passage Creek running through Mudhole Gap can become treacherous to cross when the water level is above normal levels.

Rescue index: Assistance can be summoned by the campground volunteers when the recreation area is open. At other times, head toward Strasburg or Front Royal.

Land status: George Washington National Forest—Lee Ranger District.

Maps: George Washington National Forest map of the Lee Ranger District; USGS 7.5 minute quads: Strasburg and Toms Brook; PATC's map G. A National Geographic Trails Illustrated map of the Lee District is set to debut in 2001 and will replace the Forest Service map.

Finding the trail: From Strasburg go 5 miles east on US 55 to Waterlick. Take a right onto VA 678 and drive 5 miles to the recreation area. The ride starts on Mudhole Gap Trail, a purple-blazed trail that runs on gravel Forest Service Road 1350 and starts directly opposite the entrance to Elizabeth Furnace Recreation Area campground.

Sources of additional information:

Lee Ranger District of the George Washington National Forest
109 Molineu Road
Edinburg, Virginia 22824
(540) 984-4101 or 984-4102

Those interested in doing trail maintenance in the Lee Ranger District can contact:

Wil Kohlbrenner
1717 Georgetown Road
Mount Jackson, Virginia 22842
(540) 477-2971

Notes on the trail: Starting on Mudhole Gap Trail, follow the purple blazes at two forks in the road and passa gate before starting a long, gradual climb up the gravel road. Climb until the road ends after approximately 3.5 miles. Keep riding on a well-worn single-track that continues past the end of the road. This is the start of a rocky 1-mile section of trail through Mudhole Gap, a name that belies the natural beauty through the gap on a slight uphill along Little Passage Creek. There are several creek crossings, so either plan to get your feet wet or turn back when the prospect of having wet feet in colder weather is not so appealing.

You'll see the last of Mudhole Gap's wild rhododendrons and hemlocks as you cross Passage Creek, pass a gate, and emerge onto the gravel FS 66. Turn right onto this road just across from Powell's Fort Camp. You'll pick up the orange blazes signifying the Massanutten Mountain West Trail. As you ride here and throughout other sections of the Massanutten range, you're bound to notice how well blazed and well maintained most of the trails are. This is due in no small way to volunteers from the Potomac Appalachian Trail Club (PATC) and their long-standing interest in this area.

I put on my best smile and yielded the right of way to a large group of runners/hikers who were involved in the Dogwood Half Hundred Race/Hike, despite the fact that I was really itching to try my skills on the Green Mountain descent. Given the enormous investment of time and energy the PATC has put into this trail system, other mountain bikers can also acknowledge those efforts through courteous, responsible bike-handling.

Continue on this road until you reach the Strasburg Reservoir. If you're not up for the .8-mile steep ascent of Green Mountain on rocky single-track, turn around at the reservoir and trace your way back to the start. Otherwise, to continue the 11.5-mile loop as described, veer left into the woods on the orange-blazed trail heading toward Signal Knob.

The trail begins to climb steeply along the edge of the reservoir, but it drops fairly soon. The Massanutten Mountain Trail West widens and levels off, and then you'll need to decide whether you're going to go out to Signal Knob at the well-marked intersection with the blue-blazed Bear Wallow Trail or start the climb to the top of Green Mountain. (The ride to Signal Knob offers strenuous climbing on the way out and descending on the way back on what ends up as a 2.4-mile out-and-back, making the entire Elizabeth Furnace ride a 14-mile ride.)

To start up Green Mountain, turn right onto the blue-blazed Bear Wallow Trail on what becomes a fairly steep climb on rocky single-track before cresting at the intersection with the white-blazed Meneka Trail. Stay on Bear Wallow for a great descent, but try to maintain continuous control over your bike and be considerate of others on the trail.

There are some great views from the top of Green Mountain as well as along the descent, so take time to enjoy these vistas of Fort Valley and the neighboring peaks. Ignore a pink-blazed trail on the right. Just before a very noticeable creek crossing, turn right onto the white-blazed Spur Trail and shortly thereafter turn left onto Mudhole Gap Trail to finish the downhill back to the start.

RIDE 32 · Massanutten Campout

AT A GLANCE

VA

Length/Configuration: 3-day point-to-point; daily riding totals are 9.5, 17, and 8 miles

Aerobic difficulty: Moderate on first day; considerably more difficult on second and third days

Technical difficulty: Generally follows unobstructed double-track

Scenery: Roadside trout streams, dense woods, and mountaintop views from the crest of Massanutten; don't miss the panoramic views from Massanutten Story Trail and Woodstock Tower

Special comments: A great introduction to mountain bike camping

George Washington's surveying jaunts for Lord Fairfax across the sewing needle–shaped Massanutten Mountain before the Revolutionary War must have left quite an impact on him. It's said that years later while commanding the colonial forces against the British in New Jersey his backup plan was to beat a hasty retreat to western Virginia and hide out in the natural fortifications of Fort Valley—the eye of the Massanutten needle. Had he known about mountain bikes, he would have undoubtedly planned to bring his fat-tire flyer along.

Unlike George Washington, you will be able to combine your explorations of this mountain range by two-wheeler with camping along the way. The relatively short mileages will give you time to jettison your gear after setting up camp; you'll be able to do some exploring on an unencumbered bike.

The first leg of this 35-mile point-to-point journey is a scant 9.5 miles from the Massanutten Visitor Center to the Camp Roosevelt Recreation Area on a well-maintained, sometimes gated national forest road. This will offer an opportunity to get accustomed to the handling of a fully laden bike with a relatively short mileage requirement, set up your campsite, and then do some riding on the Duncan Hollow Trail, which has some of the better single-track I've seen.

From there you'll continue northward for 17 miles past Edinburg Gap, across the top of Powell Mountain, and on to Woodstock Gap, where you'll spend the night at the Little Fort Recreation Area the second day. Powell Mountain is named for the illusive counterfeiter of the same name who is said to have mined a considerable amount of gold from Massanutten Mountain and to have left his treasure buried somewhere around here upon his death.

The third and final day of riding will lead you for eight miles through Little Fort Valley and on to the Elizabeth Furnace Recreation Area. This low-mileage day will enable you to learn more about the history of Elizabeth Furnace and the role this and other Shenandoah Valley producers played in the growth of a nation. You can also leave your gear at the Elizabeth Furnace Campground and ride single-track to Signal Knob, a former Confederate lookout post, or drop a fishing line into Passage Creek and see if fresh trout will be on tonight's dinner menu.

DAY 1: MASSANUTTEN VISITOR CENTER TO CAMP ROOSEVELT

This is a great ride for those looking to try their hand at mountain bike camping. Forest Service roads are more forgiving of mistakes you may make on a

RIDE 32 • Massanutten Campout Day One

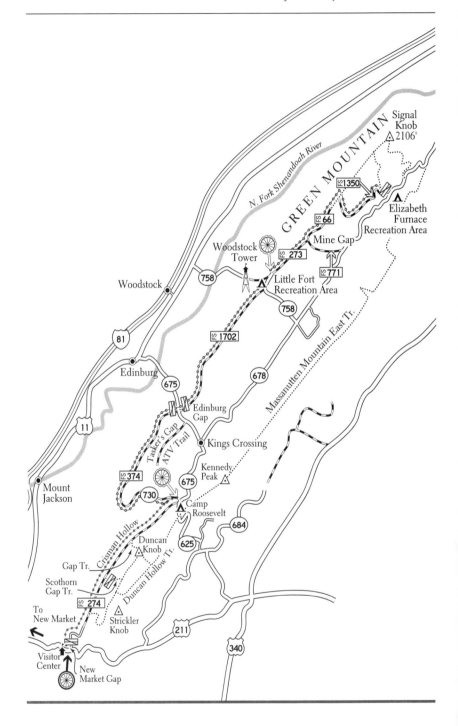

fully laden bike than are narrow, tortuous trails. Since these gated roads are seasonally locked, you may not have to contend with any traffic, depending on when you plan your adventure. However, once you've set up camp in any of the Forest Service campgrounds along the way, you're set to do some exploring sans luggage on any number of marked and unmarked trails and roads that crisscross Massanutten. Although I've set this up as a point-to-point odyssey, you could also double the distance and turn it into a long out-and-back by returning on the same or even a slightly different route.

General location: New Market Gap is 5 miles east of New Market.

Elevation change: Starting out from New Market Gap, the first 2 miles are a steady climb, gaining 500'. The next 7 miles of roller coaster are generally downhill, losing about 1,100' before reaching Camp Roosevelt.

Season: Year-round, although not when the snow and ice of winter are covering the top of Massanutten Mountain. Be especially careful when riding during the succession of hunting seasons that begin in the fall; at those times, wear bright clothes and avoid brown, black, and flashes of white. Call the Virginia Department of Game and Inland Fisheries (540-248-9360) for the opening and closing dates of hunting seasons for various game animals.

Services: Services are available in the towns of New Market, Woodstock, Edinburg, and Strasburg along US 11 just west of Massanutten.

Hazards: The rider with moderate bike handling skills will find little on this national forest road to cause a problem, but expect a fully laden mountain bike to behave differently than a stripped-down one.

Rescue index: Help can be found at the Visitor Center at New Market Gap when open or in the town of New Market at other times.

Land status: George Washington National Forest—Lee Ranger District.

Maps: George Washington National Forest map of the Lee Ranger District; USGS 7.5 minute quad: Hamburg.

Finding the trail: This ride starts at the Massanutten Visitor Center at New Market Gap on US 211, approximately 5 miles east of New Market.

Sources of additional information:

Lee Ranger District of the George Washington National Forest
109 Molineu Road
Edinburg, Virginia 22824
(540) 984-4101 or 984-4102

Those interested in doing trail maintenance in the Lee Ranger District can contact:

Wil Kohlbrenner
1717 Georgetown Road

Mount Jackson, Virginia 22842
(540) 477-2971

Notes on the trail: Cross US 211 with caution and head north on hard-surface Forest Service Road 274. The road turns to gravel when you reach the Massanutten Story Trail on the right. Stop here to read the informational signs and learn how this 50-mile mountain range emerged from an ocean that covered this area 400 million years ago. At the end of this .3-mile boardwalk trail is a view across Page Valley that will have you snapping shots with your camera.

Continue down the road and follow Passage Creek. Anglers should plan to get the proper fishing licenses and bring some ultralight gear to test the trout in these mountain streams. You'll find both natives and introduced rainbows lying in wait. At the end of a 6-mile descent you'll pass a gate and come to the intersection with VA 730. Turn right here to reach the Camp Roosevelt Recreation Area, your home for the night.

The first group of Civilian Conservation Corps enrollees arrived here on April 3, 1933, just a month after the CCC program began, to set up the nation's first CCC camp in time for President Franklin D. Roosevelt's planned visit a week later. The president didn't show up, but over the next 4 months Camp Roosevelt was followed by 1,500 others across the nation with the intent of training this "army with shovels" as well as the construction of projects oriented toward the country's natural resources.

The CCC and the Depression were a blessing in disguise as far as Virginia outdoor recreational use was concerned. Trails, roads, and campgrounds were constructed on a scale we will never see again. They are testimonials to the future that, despite the economic woes that beset the country, these men maintained their pride and sent part of their slim wages home to their families.

DAY 2: CAMP ROOSEVELT TO LITTLE FORT RECREATION AREA

This 17-mile ride includes a rougher riding surface than that of Day 1. The Peters Mill ATV Trail heading north from Edinburg Gap will test your bike handling skills and endurance as you huff and puff your way up the first mile north of the gap. However, the next six miles are a real sweet downhill to the campground near Woodstock Tower. Plan to check out the views across the Shenandoah Valley from the tower. Note: ATV's tear this road up regularly and it is regraded annually, so surface conditions vary widely.

General location: Edinburg Gap is 8 miles southeast of the town of Edinburg. The Little Fort Recreation Area at Woodstock Gap is 5 miles east of the town of Woodstock.

Elevation change: From Camp Roosevelt at 1,200', you'll climb steadily through Moreland Gap and more sharply on FS 374 before cresting at 2,300'. You'll descend to 1,691' at Edinburg Gap, then resume climbing on Peters Mill Run ATV Trail, which tops out at 2,400' to the east of Waoneze

Passage Creek accompanies you on your journey across Massanutten Mountain.

Peak. From here, it's a long downhill to Little Fort Recreation Area at Woodstock Gap at 1,340'.

Season: Year-round, although not when the snow and ice of winter are covering the top of Massanutten Mountain. Be especially careful when riding during the succession of hunting seasons that begin in the fall; wear bright clothes and avoid any colors that might make you look like a deer at a distance. Call the Virginia Department of Game and Inland Fisheries (540-248-9360) for the opening and closing dates of hunting seasons for various game animals.

Services: Services are available in the towns of New Market, Woodstock, Edinburg, and Strasburg along US 11 just west of Massanutten.

Hazards: Although still a gravel forest road, the initial climb is on a rougher, rocky ATV trail than that of the first day's ride.

Rescue index: Help can be found in the towns of Edinburg and Woodstock. The Lee Ranger District office is also located in Edinburg.

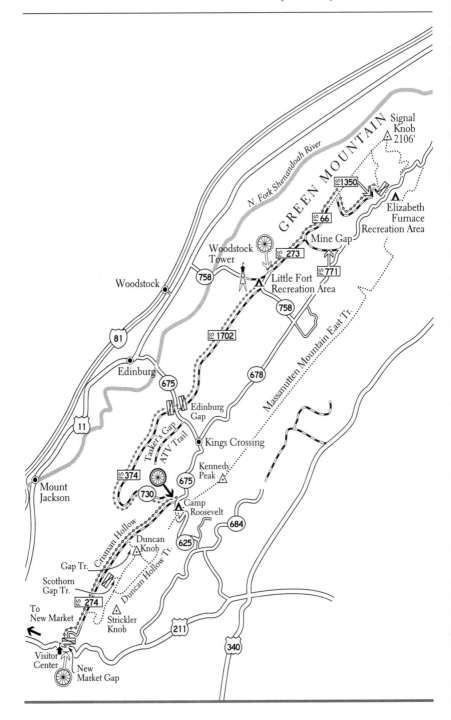

Land status: George Washington National Forest—Lee Ranger District.

Maps: George Washington National Forest map of the Lee Ranger District; USGS 7.5 minute quads: Hamburg, Rileyville, and Edinburg.

Finding the trail: This section of the ride starts at Camp Roosevelt, approximately 5 miles east of Mount Jackson.

Sources of additional information:

Lee Ranger District of the George Washington National Forest
109 Molineu Road
Edinburg, Virginia 22824
(540) 984-4101 or 984-4102

Those interested in doing trail maintenance in the Lee Ranger District can contact:

Wil Kohlbrenner
1717 Georgetown Road
Mount Jackson, Virginia 22842
(540) 477-2971

Notes on the trail: Starting from Camp Roosevelt, ride west on VA 730. Cross the bridge over the sharp bend in the road at Carolyn Furnace Lutheran Camp and start to climb. The road quickly turns to gravel and continues to climb for the next 7 miles. Turn right at Moreland Gap onto FS 374 and continue climbing. As you approach Edinburg Gap, The Peters Mill ATV Trail runs through the woods on the right and continues across VA 675; don't be too surprised by the sudden presence of ATVs. At the intersection with VA 675 continue across this sometimes busy hard-surface road and begin a steep uphill on FS 1702 on a rougher section of road that does double duty as a section of the ATV trail. This road is reputedly a favorite for ATV-riders, especially on muddy weekends. However, I didn't see any riders on my several visits here—just lucky I guess.

This initial steep climb levels off to a small wildlife clearing and starts a series of 1-mile ascents and descents. Before you've gone 2 miles you'll come to 2 unmarked gravel road intersections. Take the left fork at each place and hope that more unmarked intersections have not been added in the meantime.

A regular problem I had riding unfamiliar roads and trails in the national forests was the lack of directions at intersections that didn't show up on Forest Service maps, and topographic maps that hadn't been changed in 10 years or more. While the natural features generally haven't changed, the process of building roads and returning them to seed after timber harvests is ongoing, so you can reasonably expect road-building efforts and timbering to mask roads and trails in many areas of the forest.

After descending for several miles, turn right just beyond an intersection with Peters Mill Run onto an unmarked gravel road leading to the loop in the

Little Fort Recreation Area at Woodstock Gap. A trail within the campground goes up to the Woodstock Tower. After setting up your campsite, be sure to walk up to the tower for a panoramic view of the lower Shenandoah Valley and the well-known bends of the Shenandoah River. An interesting semantic/geographic quirk is that the Shenandoah River flows from south to north before joining the Potomac River at Harpers Ferry. Therefore it is correct when people refer to going "down the valley" while proceeding in a northerly direction. Strange but true!

DAY 3: LITTLE FORT RECREATION AREA TO ELIZABETH FURNACE RECREATION AREA

The final day of the campout will offer some great views from atop the western flank of Massanutten looking east across Fort Valley to Massanutten East. Enjoy these last eight miles of more gradual climbs and descents. Plan to set up camp at Elizabeth Furnace, do some fishing in Passage Creek, and explore the northern end of Massanutten, whose historical significance and natural beauty make it a fascinating end of the line.

Single-track enthusiasts should set up camp and then explore the Elizabeth Furnace trail system, which is very well maintained due largely to the ongoing efforts of the Potomac Appalachian Trail Club. Signal Knob is the northernmost point of Massanutten and was used by the Confederate army to watch for Union troops trying to make their way into the Shenandoah Valley.

General location: The Little Fort Recreation Area at Woodstock Gap is 5 miles east of the town of Woodstock. Signal Knob is 4 miles southeast of Strasburg.

Elevation change: Start at 1,340' at Little Fort Recreation Area. Ascend slightly on FS 66 before dropping back through Mudhole Gap at 1,200'. After leaving the gap, head uphill a short distance before merging onto FS 1350. End the ride with a quick descent to Elizabeth Furnace Recreation Area at 785'.

Season: Year-round, although not when the snow and ice of winter are covering the top of Massanutten Mountain. Be especially careful when riding during the succession of hunting seasons that begin in the fall; wear bright clothes and avoid any colors that might resemble a deer at a distance. Call the Virginia Department of Game and Inland Fisheries (540-248-9360) for the opening and closing dates of hunting seasons for various game animals.

Services: Services are available in the towns of New Market, Woodstock, Edinburg, and Strasburg along US 11 just west of Massanutten.

Hazards: Riding through the rocky and beautiful Mudhole Gap can be tricky with a fully loaded bicycle, especially if Little Passage Creek is running high.

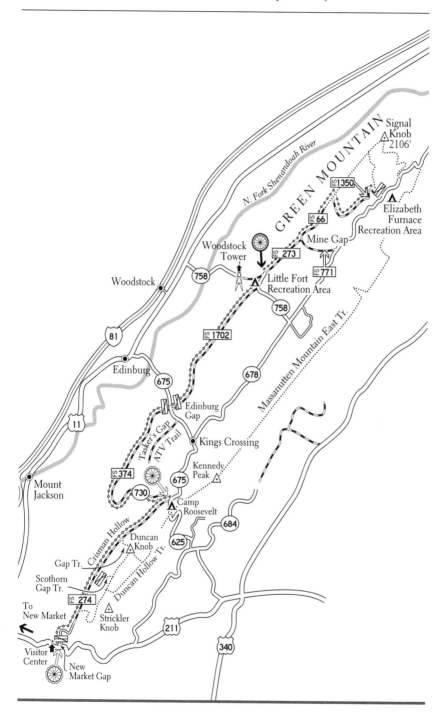

Rescue index: Help can be found in the town of Woodstock and in the summer at the Elizabeth Furnace Recreation Area.

Land status: George Washington National Forest—Lee Ranger District.

Maps: George Washington National Forest map of the Lee Ranger District; USGS 7.5 minute quads: Rileyville, Strasburg, and Toms Brook.

Finding the trail: This section of the ride starts at Little Fort Recreation Area at Woodstock Gap, 5 miles east of Woodstock.

Sources of additional information:

Lee Ranger District of the George Washington National Forest
109 Molineu Road
Edinburg, Virginia 22824
(540) 984-4101 or 984-4102

Those interested in doing trail maintenance in the Lee Ranger District can contact:

Wil Kohlbrenner
1717 Georgetown Road
Mount Jackson, Virginia 22842
(540) 477-2971

Notes on the trail: From the Little Fort Recreation Area, it's a straight shot north on FS 273 through Little Fort Valley. At Mine Gap you'll turn left onto FS 66 after passing a gate and sign that reads Maintenance Ends 2.3 Miles. But since you're on a mountain bike, the prospect of riding on the unmaintained section up ahead should not be daunting.

After passing the entrance to the Powell's Fort Camp on the left, you'll notice the orange blazes for the trail. Follow these for a short distance before turning right onto the purple-blazed Mudhole Gap Trail, which begins in a small parking lot. This is the unobtrusive entrance to Mudhole Gap through which Little Passage Creek flows. This 1-mile section of rocky single-track is beautiful but can be slick, so plan on walking your bike or at least taking it very slowly on this short downhill with several creek crossings.

The rocky trail through the gap is an old wagon road. Note the blazes and be alert for a left turn up a short, steep single-track, which returns to FS 1350. Enjoy a very sweet 3.5-mile downhill to the Elizabeth Furnace Recreation Area to complete this 3-day camping trip.

RIDE 33 · Duncan Hollow

AT A GLANCE

Length/Configuration: 17-mile loop

Aerobic difficulty: Considerable on the ascent of Duncan Hollow to Scothorn Gap

Technical difficulty: Unobstructed double-track for the first half; rocky, technical single-track on the return trip

Scenery: Roadside trout streams, dense woods, mountaintop views from the crest of Massanutten, and a spectacular panorama of Page Valley

Special comments: Experienced riders will enjoy the technical single-track ascent of Duncan Hollow, while novices may want to ride to Camp Roosevelt and then return along the same Forest Service roads

The 50-mile-long Massanutten Mountain offers many opportunities for single- and double-track mountain biking from its southern end just east of Harrisonburg to its northern terminus southeast of Strasburg. This 17-mile loop covers half its distance on a well-maintained national forest road. The other half is a combination of rough jeep trail and some of the finest single-track you're likely to find in these parts.

The suitability for riders of different ability levels will vary with the terrain. The first part of the ride offers no technical obstacles, and the ups and downs tend to be very gradual, so any novice who feels comfortable with a 20-mile out-and-back on hard-packed road could handle this part. The 17-mile loop as described here includes a good bit of scrambling along rocky single- and double-track and should be reserved for riders whose fitness and bike handling skills are intermediate or better.

Be sure to stop at the one-quarter-mile Massanutten Story Trail near the start of the ride to learn how Massanutten Mountain evolved out of Massanutten Ocean. Be prepared for panoramic views from the end of this trail looking out across Page Valley. Farther along you'll turn to come back onto the Duncan Hollow Trail at Camp Roosevelt. Now a national forest recreation area, this was the site of the country's first Civilian Conservation Corps work camp when its tent flaps opened on April 17, 1933. For mountain bikers it marks the point at which you'll head off into the woods on orange-blazed Duncan Hollow Trail on some of the best single-track east of the Blue Ridge Mountains.

General location: 5 miles east of New Market.

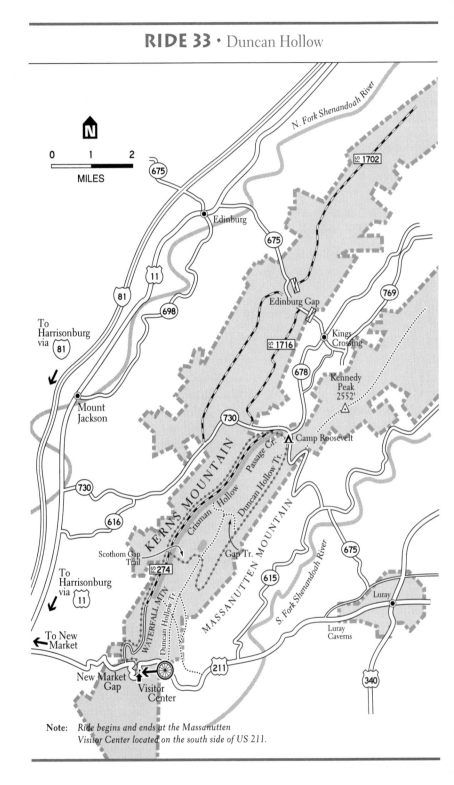

Note: Ride begins and ends at the Massanutten
Visitor Center located on the south side of US 211.

Elevation change: Starting from New Market Gap, the first 2 miles are a steady climb of 500'. The next 7 miles of roller coaster are generally downhill, losing about 1,100'. Turning off into the woods on the Duncan Hollow, you'll climb up to Middle Mountain (2,700') and cross Waterfall Mountain at Scothorn Gap (2,429') before dropping back down to FS 274 (1,940'). After a short climb, you'll finish on a nice 2-mile downhill.

Season: Ice and snow will make this ride inadvisable during the winter months, especially on the Duncan Hollow section. Be careful during the succession of hunting seasons that begin in the fall; wear bright clothes at those times, avoiding black, brown and flashes of white. Call the Virginia Department of Game and Inland Fisheries (540-248-9360) for the opening and closing dates of hunting seasons for various game animals.

Services: Water is available at the Massanutten Visitor Center (when open). All other services are available in nearby New Market.

Hazards: The usual hazards associated with narrow single-track, but be especially careful of loose, rocky sections of trail near Scothorn Gap.

Rescue index: Help can be found at the Massanutten Visitor Center when open and in the town of New Market at other times.

Land status: George Washington National Forest—Lee Ranger District.

Maps: George Washington National Forest map of the Lee Ranger District; USGS 7.5 minute quad: Hamburg.

Finding the trail: This ride starts at the Massanutten Visitor Center at New Market Gap on US 211, approximately 5 miles east of New Market.

Sources of additional information:

Lee Ranger District of the George Washington National Forest
109 Molineu Road
Edinburg, Virginia 22824
(540) 984-4101 or 984-4102

Those interested in doing trail maintenance in the Lee Ranger District can contact:

Wil Kohlbrenner
1717 Georgetown Road
Mount Jackson, Virginia 22842
(540) 477-2971

Notes on the trail: This ride starts from the Massanutten Visitor Center, crosses US 211, and then goes north on FS 274. The initial climb will warm you up so you can savor a long roller-coaster downhill through Crisman Hollow along Passage Creek. After the gate where the forest road ends, turn right onto VA 675 toward the Camp Roosevelt Recreation Area.

It's said that a young surveyor named George Washington surveyed much of Massanutten Mountain for Lord Fairfax.

Just up the road from Camp Roosevelt, you'll turn right onto the orange-blazed Duncan Hollow Trail to start the second half of this loop (or pitch a tent at Camp Roosevelt to serve as your base camp for this and other Massanutten area rides.) The Potomac Appalachian Trail Club does a great job of blazing and maintaining trails along Massanutten Mountain.

The Duncan Hollow Trail descends gradually to cross the creek in teh hollow, then ascends along an old wagon road paralleling the creek. The trail gets steeper and rockier until you crest Middle Mountain and descend to intersect the Scothorn Gap Trail, blazed yellow. Go straight across this intersection and follow Scothorn Gap, which is rather technical for a short stretch. Then, ride around a dried beaver pond to reach a clearing.

It's all downhill from here, as they say, and rather steeply, too. After passing a gate and then crossing through Passage Creek, turn left onto FS 274. Follow this road the way you came or take a little more time to explore the numerous trails and dirt roads that enter and depart Crisman Hollow.

In the aftermath of riding Duncan Hollow, PATC Massanutten Trail Crew Leader Wil Kohlbrenner was kind enough to inform me that a number of changes are taking place on Lee District trails. Riders should always keep in mind that any trail is subject to change, either by natural or man-made forces.

RIDE 34 · Brandywine Lake Overnighter

AT A GLANCE

Length/Configuration: 26-mile out-and-back (52 miles total)

Aerobic difficulty: Considerable, even without a fully loaded bike

Technical difficulty: Generally minimal on this double-track route

Scenery: From lush riparian areas at low elevations to clear views from Shenandoah Mountain ridge tops

Special comments: Challenging mileage for this 2-day camping trip between national forest campgrounds

This 26-mile out-and-back (52 miles round-trip) will offer you an opportunity to try some mountain bike camping while riding entirely on dirt and gravel Forest Service roads—albeit ones that are pretty rough in spots. These roads tend to be more forgiving of the mistakes that easily occur while piloting a fully laden bike across rough terrain. You'll start at Brandywine Recreation Area and pedal to spend the night at Camp Run, with only the sounds of the winds whispering through the pines and sugar maples and the rushing waters of Camp Run to keep you awake before your return the next day.

Shenandoah Mountain forms an obvious but not insurmountable boundary between Virginia and West Virginia. This overnighter traverses the West Virginia side just below Shenandoah Mountain's 3,600-foot elevation along the ridge top. The additional weight and handling demands of a mountain bike loaded for touring, as well as the considerable climbing and distance on this route, make it suitable for riders of intermediate and better fitness and skill levels.

General location: 25 miles west of Harrisonburg on US 33.

Elevation change: This ride starts at Brandywine Recreation Area at 1,850' and climbs to just under 2,200' before turning onto FS 151. The ride rises and falls in stretches that may continue for 3-mile sections, but it averages out to an elevation of 2,000'.

Season: The best time to ride here is spring through fall. The effects of seasonal and unseasonal cold spells are more pronounced along this route near

RIDE 34 · Brandywine Lake Overnighter

Note: This is a two-day ride that returns on the same route the second day after an overnight at Camp Run.

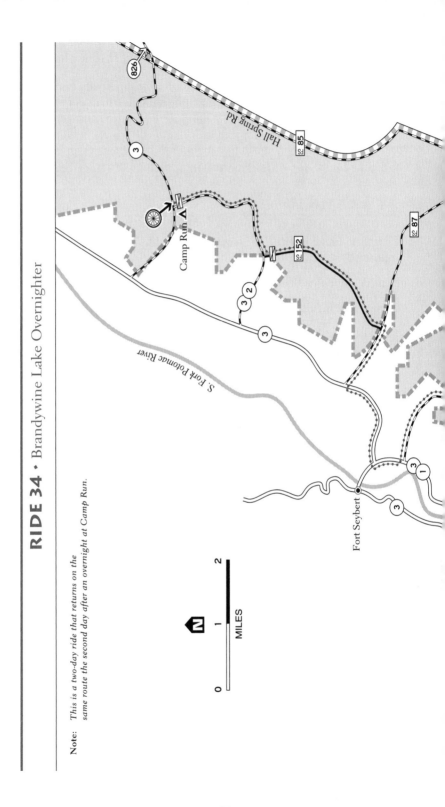

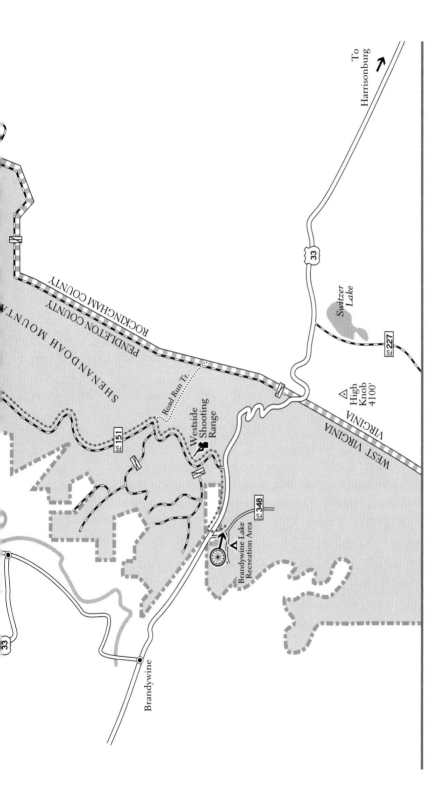

To
Harrisonburg

33

Switzer
Lake

FS 227

ROCKINGHAM COUNTY
PENDLETON COUNTY

SHENANDOAH MOUNT

Road Run Tr.

FS 151

Westside
Shooting
Range

High
Knob
4100'

WEST VIRGINIA
VIRGINIA

CR 348

Brandywine Lake
Recreation Area

33

Brandywine

the top of Shenandoah Mountain. Winter snowfall is greater and tends to remain longer on this ridge along the West Virginia border than in the nearby city of Harrisonburg. Temperatures on any given day may be as much as 20 degrees colder than in Harrisonburg.

Services: Brandywine Recreation Area is a national forest fee area and includes a 10-acre lake with sand beach for swimming and fishing, 34 campsites, and flush toilets. Water is turned off in the early fall before the first freeze. Camp Run Campground is more primitive and has 9 campsites, a single vault toilet, and no water. All other services are available in Franklin, West Virginia, west on US 33, and in Harrisonburg, east on US 33.

Hazards: Be sure to wear brightly colored clothing if you choose to ride during the succession of hunting seasons beginning in the fall. Call the Virginia Department of Game and Inland Fisheries (540-248-9360) for the opening and closing dates of hunting seasons for various game animals.

Don't underestimate the effects of a full-load bike on your bike's handling.

Rescue index: Help can be found at Brandywine Recreation Area during the summer. At other times you can ride a short distance down to Sugar Grove, West Virginia, for assistance.

Land status: George Washington National Forest—Dry River Ranger District.

Maps: George Washington National Forest map of the Dry River Ranger District; USGS 7.5 minute quads: Brandywine and Fort Seybert.

Finding the trail: Go west from Harrisonburg on US 33 for approximately 25 miles. After you crest Shenandoah Mountain at High Knob and descend into West Virginia, turn left into the Brandywine Recreation Area near the bottom of the mountain.

Source of additional information:
Dry River Ranger District of the George Washington National Forest
112 North River Road
Bridgewater, Virginia 22812
(540) 828-2591

Notes on the trail: From the entrance to Brandywine Recreation Area, head back toward the Virginia side of Shenandoah Mountain on VA 33. However, before starting the climb up the mountain, turn left onto FS 151 at the sign for the National Forest Shooting Range at Westside. The next 12 miles offer some fantastic views of the neighboring mountains as the road rises and falls in 1-to-2-mile sections dropping through mountain streams at the bottom of many downhill runs. After a short drop through Dice Run you'll leave the national forest temporarily at a small lake on the left clearly marked by No Trespassing signs.

In the shadow of
High Knob, Brandy-
wine Lake is the starting
point for a long climb
to Flagpole Knob.

After crossing a cattleguard continue straight though some open fields. A
mile or so later FS 151 intersects WV 3/4. Turn right here and then take the
next right turn onto hard-surface WV 3. You'll stay on this road through Fort
Seybert and then turn right onto gravel FS 87 at the sign for Rough Run. As
the sign indicates, the going gets somewhat rougher from here on. Shortly
thereafter, turn left and pass the gated entrance to the Mitchell Knob Hunter
Access Road. Continue to climb for 3 miles and enjoy the downhills that follow. At the end of one particularly nice descent (are there really any bad
ones?), pass the gated end of the road and bear to the right. You'll pass 2 more
gates in the next several miles before turning left onto WV S/1 and arriving
at Camp Run, your lodging for the night. Roll out your sleeping bag, put a
mint on the pillow, and enjoy your stay. Return to Brandywine Lake following the same route in reverse.

RIDE 35 • Lake to Lake

AT A GLANCE

Length/Configuration: 17-mile out-and-back (34 miles total)

Aerobic difficulty: Considerable; the first 10 miles ascend steeply

Technical difficulty: Considerable; you'll climb rough, rocky double-track and then descend rocky single-track

Scenery: Low-elevation lush riparian areas and clear views from Shenandoah Mountain ridge tops

Special comments: A physically and technically challenging ride

The Dry River Ranger District between Reddish Knob and Briery Branch is a favorite destination for many of Harrisonburg's large contingent of mountain bikers. An annual Super Bowl Sunday ride through this part of the George Washington National Forest provides alternate recreation for non–couch potatoes regardless of the weather or trail conditions. Although not etched in stone, the ride usually starts at the Briery Branch eatery at the intersection of VA 257 and 731. From there it's a long climb to Briery Branch Gap on hard-surface VA 924, followed by one of several routes back to the bottom via Hone Quarry and Hone Quarry Lake. I honestly don't know if there really is more than one way to skin a cat, but I do know plenty of ways to enjoy mountain biking in this part of the Dry River District. And here's a good one!

This 17-mile out-and-back (34 miles round-trip) starts from Switzer Lake, lying in the shadow of High Knob atop Shenandoah Mountain. You'll climb steadily for more than ten miles along rocky, rutted double-track before you reach the Shenandoah Mountain ridge top just below Reddish Knob. From there you'll fly down to the Hone Quarry Campground and Recreation Area. This descent is a hairy one, so much so that it left one of IMBA's cross-country trail maintenance ambassadors with a broken clavicle.

If interest and safety permit, keep an eye toward the sky during the spring and fall periods of migration, when birds of prey use this as a thoroughfare to and from their wintering grounds. In spring, those of you with a keen eye for raptors may be able to pick out the peregrine falcons who were reared and released here several years ago from High Knob in a cooperative program between the national forest, the Virginia Department of Game and Inland Fisheries, and the Peregrine Fund.

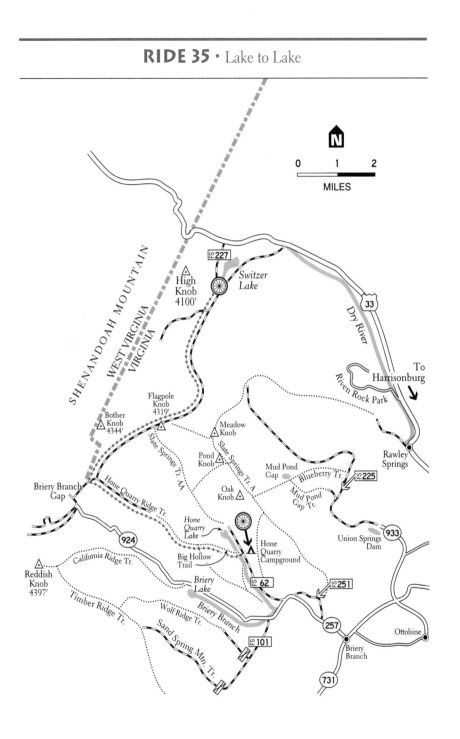

N

0   1   2
MILES

SHENANDOAH MOUNTAIN

WEST VIRGINIA
VIRGINIA

FS 227

High Knob 4100'

Switzer Lake

Dry River

33

To Harrisonburg

Riven Rock Park

Flagpole Knob 4319'

Bother Knob 4344'

Meadow Knob

Slate Springs Tr. AA

Pond Knob

Slate Springs Tr. A

Mud Pond Gap

Blueberry Tr.

FS 225

Rawley Springs

Briery Branch Gap

Hone Quarry Ridge Tr.

Oak Knob

Mud Pond Gap Tr.

Union Springs Dam

933

Hone Quarry Lake

California Ridge Tr.

924

Big Hollow Trail

Hone Quarry Campground

Reddish Knob 4397'

Briery Lake

FS 62

FS 251

Timber Ridge Tr.

Wolf Ridge Tr.

Briery Branch

257

Ottobine

Sand Spring Mtn. Tr.

FS 101

Briery Branch

731

General location: 10 miles west of Harrisonburg.

Elevation change: The ride starts at Switzer Lake at 2,400'. The steep, rocky forest road peaks by Flagpole Knob at 4,302'. After coming down off the top, start your descent on the Hone Quarry jeep road at 3,869' and keep dropping until you reach 1,920' at the campground.

Season: Some of the Harrisonburg riders do an annual Super Bowl Sunday ride in the Reddish Knob area, so it's possible to ride here in the winter. However, a safer and more consistently enjoyable time to ride is from spring through fall. Caution should be taken during fall and winter hunting seasons. Call the Virginia Department of Game and Inland Fisheries (540-248-9360) for the opening and closing dates for the various game animals and plan to ride in brightly colored attire at those times.

Services: All services are available in nearby Harrisonburg.

Hazards: Steep, rocky, and 10 miles long—what more would you ask for to start a ride? The descent is also rocky and narrow for most of the way. This could be a pretty tough ride depending on your level of fitness and bike handling skills.

Rescue index: From Brandywine Lake, head east on VA 33 toward Harrisonburg and stop at a house or business along the way. From Hone Quarry, try the convenience store at Briery Branch.

Land status: George Washington National Forest—Dry River Ranger District.

Maps: George Washington National Forest map of the Dry River Ranger District; USGS 7.5 minute quads: Brandywine, West Virginia, and Reddish Knob.

Finding the trail: Drive west on US 33 out of Harrisonburg. As the road starts to climb Shenandoah Mountain, watch for a sharp bend to the right where a third traffic lane appears. At this point turn left onto unmarked Forest Service Road 227. Follow the road until you pass Switzer Lake on the left and find a place to pull your car far enough off the road to avoid blocking other traffic.

Source of additional information:

Dry River Ranger District of the George Washington National Forest
112 North River Road
Bridgewater, Virginia 22812
(540) 828-2591

Notes on the trail: I can't think of a prettier sight than a lake situated at the base of mountains. Whenever I head down toward Switzer Lake from US 33, the landscape at the foot of Shenandoah Mountain and High Knob makes me think I've died and gone to heaven. However, after a few miles of pedaling up FS 227 with its rocky, steep attributes and almost endless climb, I realize that I must not have made it to heaven after all; instead I'm at that other place. This climb is the real thing; it just keeps going and going.

At the unmarked intersection of several Forest Service roads near the top of Shenandoah Mountain, turn right onto the dirt and gravel forest road and continue to climb toward Flagpole Knob at the top of Slate Springs Mountain. (After a quarter mile, a left turn will take you downhill on the Slate Springs Trail AA. It will also lead you past a small structure of stacked, rock slabs said to have been built and used as impromptu housing by Confederate deserters. For this ride, continue straight.)

Follow this road until you see a gated dirt road below you to the left. Take this sharp switchback turn to the left and follow what is initially the Hone Quarry Road. The road dissolved into single-track until a 1999 fire prompted its bulldozing. Turn left when you reach the yellow-blazed Big Hollow Trail, also widened, which drops more steeply and ends just above the Hone Quarry Campground.

You can do this ride with a shuttle vehicle left at Hone Quarry or as a 2-day camping trip by spending the night at Hone Quarry.

RIDE 36 • Slate Lick Lake

AT A GLANCE

Length/Configuration: 19-mile loop

Aerobic difficulty: Considerable; several healthy climbs

Technical difficulty: Minimal; primarily hard-packed Forest Service roads

Scenery: From lush riparian areas at low elevations to clear mountaintop vistas

Special comments: Long exhilarating descents more than compensate for physically challenging climbs

I'm not sure which is tougher: saying the name of this 19-mile loop five times really fast or finding the first five miles of abandoned double-track from Slate Lick Lake and Gauley Ridge Road that begin this ride. The trail, such as it is, appears and disappears intermittently as it meanders along the course of Slate Branch. However, as long as you stay in the flat bottomland, you can't go too far off course. As a postscript to the old adage about dog being man's best friend, I was able to successfully navigate this small overgrown valley by following several sets of hoof prints left by horses.

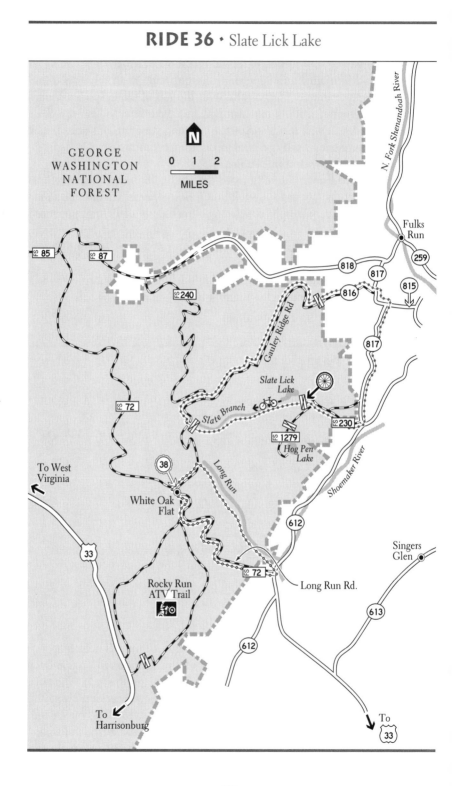

The rest of the ride includes some healthy climbing on hard-packed forest roads before you reach the top of Gauley Ridge. However, you will have forgotten the grueling climb long before you reach the bottom of a four-mile descent, which seems to keep going and going before emptying onto hard-surface county roads that take you back to the start. This ride offers little technical challenge; the toughest parts are the two-mile steep ascent up to Gauley Ridge and the sheer length of the ride. However, keep in mind that four to six miles are downhill, and anybody with moderate stamina and a good internal compass can handle it.

General location: 20 miles northwest of Harrisonburg.

Elevation change: This ride starts at 1,400' and stays fairly level for the first 5 miles, and then it climbs steeply for the next mile. The middle of the ride is a 7-mile series of short climbs and long descents from the Knobs that will take you out of the national forest and onto paved and gravel county roads. Catch your breath before finishing up on a few short steep ups and downs.

Season: Year-round, although snow and ice in winter may preclude riding. Call the Virginia Department of Game and Inland Fisheries (540-248-9360) for the hunting season opening and closing dates. If riding during hunting season, plan to wear brightly colored attire.

Services: All services are available in nearby Harrisonburg.

Hazards: The first 5 miles adjacent to Buck Lick Run are difficult to follow and should not be attempted after periods of heavy rain due to the possibility of flooding; you need to cross the stream in several places without bridges.

Rescue index: Head back toward US 33 and get help from any of the stores along the way.

Land status: Mostly George Washington National Forest—Dry River Ranger District, with some state-maintained roads.

Maps: George Washington National Forest map of the Dry River Ranger District; USGS 7.5 minute quads: Fulks Run, Rawley Springs, and Singers Glen.

Finding the trail: Leave Harrisonburg on US 33, heading west for about 5 miles. After passing through the town of Hinton, turn right onto VA 613 and go a few miles before turning left onto VA 612. Continue on VA 612 for 8 miles before turning left onto FS 230. This hard-packed road will lead you through the creek, whose fording could be dangerous after periods of heavy rainfall or during the spring thaw. Follow the road to the end and park just before the gate.

Source of additional information:

Dry River Ranger District of the George Washington National Forest
112 North River Road
Bridgewater, Virginia 22812
(540) 828-2591

Many rocky streambeds are ridable as long as the water level is down.

Notes on the trail: Park your vehicle just outside the gate at the end of FS 230 and ride past the gate, heading west on this gravel road. After this double-track passes the lake, it becomes much less discernible. I ended up using a combination of intermittent double-track, single-track, the occasional light blue blaze, and—when all else failed (which happened more often than not)—some very obvious hoof prints from horses. Let that be a lesson for those of you who feel that equestrians and mountain bikers can't benefit from each others' trail use. The other option is to stay near Buck Lick Run, which courses through this riparian area close to where the trail is or should be.

Ironically, there's a very obvious double blue blaze just before the gated intersection with Gauley Ridge Road where you'll turn right. The good news is that from here on out, you'll have no trouble following the combination of forest and county roads that loop back to the start. On the other hand, you'll see precious few sections as flat as what you've ridden so far. However, the toughest climb is the initial mile or so up to Gauley Ridge followed by a less severe ascent to the Knobs. Along the way are some really outstanding views of the neighboring peaks and ridges. Your other reward is the 7 or so miles of downhill that seem to go on and on but never long enough.

After flying past the national forest boundary, you'll come out into a rural Rockingham County neighborhood on VA 816. When the road turns to hard surface, turn right at the stop sign onto VA 817. After that take another right

Slate Lick Lake is one of many mountain lakes that riders will find in the George Washington National Forest.

turn onto gravel VA 817. After reentering the boundaries of the national forest, the unmarked dirt road (FS 230) that you entered to get to the start should be familiar. Turn left onto FS 230 to return.

RIDE 37 • Long Run

AT A GLANCE

Length/Configuration: 10-mile loop

Aerobic difficulty: Considerable on the 6-mile ascent of Long Run Road

Technical difficulty: Several slickrock creek bed crossings on the 4-mile descent through Long Run

Scenery: From lush riparian areas at low elevations to clear mountaintop vistas

Special comments: A straightforward ride—a hellacious climb followed by an awesome downhill

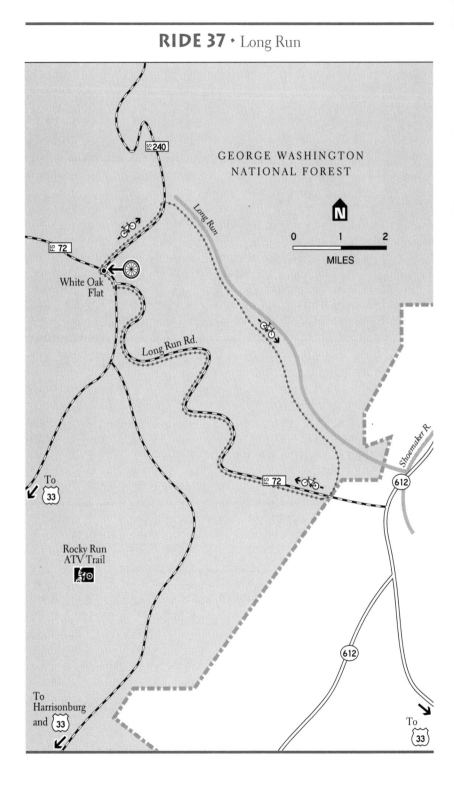

Mark Nissley and his shop are a Harrisonburg fixture and seem to have resided in this college town forever. So Mark's Bike Shop seemed like a logical place to begin my quest to uncover the favorite rides for local mountain bikers. In the course of writing this guide, I've found most people to be quite willing to share the names and locations of rides that draw a lot of thumbs-up. At the time Mark had put together a notebook of local favorites, and the Long Run Ride was first on the list.

This is a very straightforward, albeit tough ride even for those who drink their coffee black and eat their frozen yogurt without any toppings. It involves a steady six-mile climb to White Oak Flat and then a four-mile descent or vice versa, depending on whether you like to eat your desert or your meal first. The climb offers some of the finest views of the neighboring peaks and ridges as a diversion from the eternal nature of this ascent, while the descent is a pretty tricky drop through rocky and possibly slick sections of Long Run. It goes back and forth through Long Run and doesn't last nearly long enough for a climb, despite the creek's name. Consider this a ride for intermediate or better riders who don't mind getting wet.

General location: 20 miles northwest of Harrisonburg.

Elevation change: The 6-mile climb gains and the 4-mile descent loses 1,500'.

Season: Avoid this ride in winter when snow and ice will impede travel on the downhill section, which includes quite a few stream crossings. Ride carefully and wear bright colors during the fall hunting seasons. Call the Virginia Department of Game and Inland Fisheries (540-248-9360) for the opening and closing dates.

Services: Services are widely available in Harrisonburg.

Hazards: The Long Run jeep trail through the woods is pretty rutted and could be treacherous on a high-speed descent, especially after particularly rainy periods.

Rescue index: There are numerous homes along VA 612 at the bottom of Long Run Road where one could go to get assistance.

Land status: George Washington National Forest—Dry River Ranger District.

Maps: George Washington National Forest map of the Dry River Ranger District; USGS 7.5 minute quads: Rawley Springs and Singers Glen.

Finding the trail: Leave Harrisonburg on US 33, heading west for about 5 miles. Turn right onto VA 613 and make the next left turn after a few miles onto VA 612. Follow VA 612 to the intersection with Forest Service Road 72, Long Run Road. Drive up FS 72 and enter the national forest. Park your car well off the road where possible if you want to start with a climb. Drive all the way to the top and park if you plan to start with the descent.

Sources of additional information:

Dry River Ranger District of the
 George Washington National Forest
112 North River Road
Bridgewater, Virginia 22812
(540) 828-2591

Blue Ridge Cycle Works
774 East Market Street
Harrisonburg, Virginia 22801
(540) 432-0280

Mark's Bike Shop
1570 South Main Street
Harrisonburg, Virginia 22801
(540) 434-5151

Notes on the trail: Some riders park at the bottom of the road on or near property owned by the Gospel Hill Church either with or without permission. I obviously can't suggest trespassing and there are quite a few No Parking signs implying that you also might consider another approach.

Numerous pulloffs are large enough for a single car along FS 72. Another option is to park at White Oak Flat, near either the intersection with Second Mountain road or the intersection with Gauley Ridge Road. The latter was my choice, so I started by riding past the gate to the north on Gauley Ridge Road. The road climbs slightly and you'll be treated to some outstanding mountain views to the left as well as the "snap, crackle, pop" of overhead high voltage lines. The right turn for Long Run jeep road is unmarked except for the tread marks of previous riders. Long Run is the second rough road on the right—less than a mile from White Oak Flat—just across from the high-voltage towers.

This is a great downhill with numerous creek crossings and some other technical stuff thrown in just to keep you from dozing off. Those with full suspension bikes will soon forget the additional expense by the end of this 4-mile downhill, and those without will surely be in the market for one or at least for a new kidney. You can also expect to get a little muddy unless you've come during a drought. As the jeep road levels out, it bends right into the "other" Long Run Road—you know, the one that goes uphill.

Now for some riders this sequence may be like eating desert before the main course. But for other mountain bikers, a climb that seems to stretch on forever is just their thing. One rider's drudgery is another's delight. So gear down, sit back, and think some happy thoughts as you prepare to assault Hogpen Mountain for the next 6 miles. It's not a particularly steep climb, except in isolated spots, but it seems to keep going. As you look ahead to the next, seemingly final peak, another will loom ominously ahead of you—and so it goes.

RIDE 38 · Blueberry Trail

AT A GLANCE

Length/Configuration: 4-mile loop

Aerobic difficulty: Considerable on the 2-mile climb to Mud Pond Gap

Technical difficulty: The initial ascent is a good introduction to technical riding

Scenery: Super views of neighboring peaks on the climb to Mud Pond

Special comments: A fun ride for all

This is the potato chip of rides: a single four-mile spin around this loop is sure to leave you craving more. The two-mile climb from the start to Mud Pond—a name that pretty well describes the wildlife puddle at the top—is a nice gradual introduction to technical single-track along a somewhat rocky path. This ride accommodates everyone—novices will rally to the challenge of the climb and go nuts over the smooth, fast downhill, while more experienced riders will want to take more than one trip around this loop.

The initial ascent is gradual, but the descent from Mud Pond back to the forest road is a real downhill roller coaster guaranteed to make a mountain bike lover out of anyone. Along the way you'll see how the Blueberry Trail got its name, especially if you ride in the summer when the trailside bushes are in bloom. There are some nice views of Narrow Back Mountain on the ascent, but on the way down you'll be too busy looking at your front wheel and the trail in front of you to notice anything else.

Although I wouldn't send someone with a brand new bike and little mountain biking experience on this ride, it's not so tough that a novice with basic bike-handling skills wouldn't be up to the challenge and have a great time in the process. There are some terrific views of neighboring peaks on the climb to Mud Pond Gap.

General location: 10 miles west of Harrisonburg.

Elevation change: The climb from the starting point at Forest Service Road 225 to Mud Pond gains 540', followed by a fantastic 700-foot descent back to FS 225. It ends with a short climb back to the start.

Season: Year-round, although the presence of snow and ice will make this ride inadvisable in winter. Riders should also use caution during fall and winter hunting seasons and dress in highly visible attire. Call the Virginia Department of Game and Inland Fisheries (540-248-9360) for the opening and closing dates of hunting seasons for the various game animals.

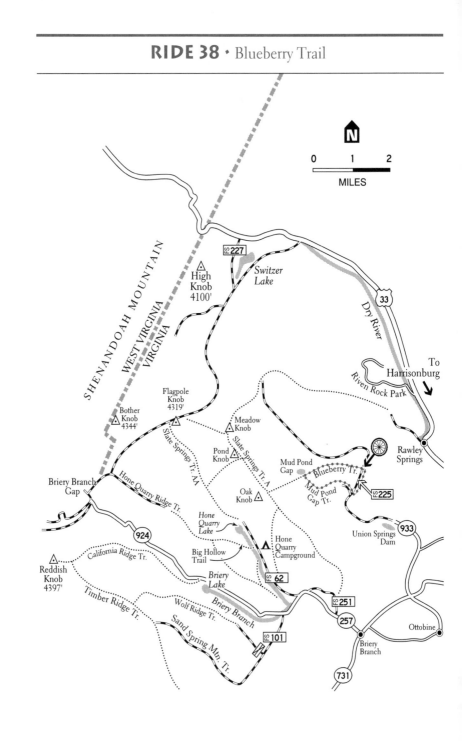

N

0   1   2

MILES

FS 227

△ High Knob 4100'

Switzer Lake

33

Dry River

SHENANDOAH MOUNTAIN

WEST VIRGINIA
VIRGINIA

To
Harrisonburg

River Rock Park

Flagpole Knob 4319'

Bother △ Knob 4344'

△

Meadow △ Knob

Slate Springs Tr. A

Slate Springs Tr. A

Pond △ Knob

Mud Pond Gap

Blueberry Tr.

Rawley Springs

Briery Branch Gap

Hone Quarry Ridge Tr.

Oak △ Knob

Mud Pond Gap Tr.

FS 225

Hone Quarry Lake

924

Big Hollow Trail

△ Hone Quarry Campground

Union Springs Dam

933

△ ... Reddish Knob 4397'

California Ridge Tr.

Briery Lake

FS 62

Timber Ridge Tr.

Wolf Ridge Tr.

Briery Branch

FS 251

257

Ottobine

Sand Spring Mtn. Tr.

FS 101

Briery Branch

731

Shaded, grassy double-track provides seclusion and outstanding two-wheel travel in Jefferson National Forest (photo by Larry E. Grossman).

Services: All services are available in Harrisonburg.

Hazards: The initial climb is a good introduction to technical riding with rocks and roots to challenge you. Try to maintain good control on the descent.

Rescue index: A gas station/market and restaurant at Briery Branch has a phone from which you can summon help.

Land status: George Washington National Forest—Dry River Ranger District.

Maps: George Washington National Forest map of the Dry River Ranger District; USGS 7.5 minute quad: Briery Branch.

Finding the trail: Leave Harrisonburg, heading south toward Dayton on VA 42. After passing the traffic light, take the next right onto VA 257 heading west. Continue straight at Ottobine onto VA 742. Veer left onto VA 933 toward Union Springs Dam, which you'll pass on the left. VA 933 turns into FS 225. Go several miles past the dam and at the crest of the road with a gated forest road on your left, pull off onto the parking enlargement on the right. Through the gate across the road is Blueberry Trail, which may or may not be marked.

Source of additional information:
Dry River Ranger District of the George Washington National Forest
112 North River Road
Bridgewater, Virginia 22812
(540) 828-2591

Notes on the trail: At the crest of FS 225 is a wide spot to the right of the road that makes a good place to park. Blueberry Trail starts on the other side of FS 225 just past a gate. It's quite possible that the trail sign will be gone by the time you get out here, so the crest in FS 225 adjacent to the gate on the left side may be the best indication of the location of the trailhead. The trail starts as single-track meandering uphill on a rocky stretch. The ascent and rocky surface combine to offer a very reasonable challenge for advanced novices and intermediate riders. Blueberry Trail continues uphill for several miles, gathering better and better views of neighboring peaks until it reaches a flat spot, with Mud Pond on the right.

After taking a break for a snack or lunch at the top, take the unmarked trail to the left, Mud Pond Gap Trail, where it intersects with Blueberry Trail. The following 1.5-mile descent along a smooth stretch of double-track is sure to bring a wide smile. But like most downhills, it ends way too soon. Just after splashing through a narrow branch of Union Springs Run at the bottom of the descent, you'll hit FS 225. From there, turn left onto the road and finish with a short but steep climb back to the start. If the Blueberry Trail to Mud Pond Gap ride left you hungry for more, wash down a few potato chips with some cold water and do it again. But remember, I warned you that this ride can be habit forming.

RIDE 39 · Sandspring Mountain Trail

AT A GLANCE

Length/Configuration: 9.5-mile loop

Aerobic difficulty: The initial climb up Sandspring Mountain Trail is steep

Technical difficulty: The descent on Wolf Ridge Trail is rife with rocks and logs

Scenery: Super views of neighboring peaks on the ascent of Sandspring Mountain

Special comments: A good ride for intermediate to advanced riders to alternately test their climbing and downhill skills

In my quest to find the most desirable mountain biking routes in an area where the effects of mountain biking have been largely unfelt, I went into numerous shops asking about local favorites. Gerald Knicely, owner/operator of Mole Hill Bikes near Harrisonburg, was one of my early contacts and, like most, was willing to share his favorites. Gerald puts in long hours at his shop, serving customers who seem constantly to find their way to his location on the outskirts of Dayton, right in the middle of the Shenandoah Valley Mennonite community. I knew Gerald's favorite route would be a good one since he tries to make those days when he's able to go riding really count.

I learned a couple of things from this 9.5-mile loop he described. The first was the Mennonite gift for understatement. And the second was that one rider's heaven may be another's hell. This is especially true when it comes to mountain biking, a lesson I've relearned countless times in the past several years.

The three-mile climb up Forest Service Trail 423, a.k.a. Sand Spring Mountain Trail, was described to me by Knicely as "a long pull." This is a good example of Mennonite understatement. Most of us would call it one hell of a climb and no piece of cake. Intermediate and better riders or novices with very good stamina should give this one a try.

General location: 15 miles west of Harrisonburg.

Elevation change: The ride starts at 1,948' on Tilman Road and climbs for the first 3 miles to the top of Sand Spring Mountain at 3,700'. From this point, the trail continues a short distance to the neighboring Timber Ridge peak and then descends to Tilman Road.

Season: Year-round, although snow and ice will make this loop impassable. Riders should also use caution during fall and winter hunting seasons and dress in highly visible attire. Call the Virginia Department of Game and Inland Fisheries (540-248-9360) for the opening and closing dates of hunting seasons for the various game animals.

Services: All services are available in nearby Harrisonburg.

Hazards: Tough climb followed by a technical descent with numerous blowdowns on a rocky surface.

Rescue index: Help can be found in the nearby town of Bridgewater, which has a rescue squad and a tactical rescue team.

Land status: George Washington National Forest—Dry River Ranger District.

Maps: George Washington National map of the Dry River Ranger District; USGS 7.5 minute quad: Reddish Knob.

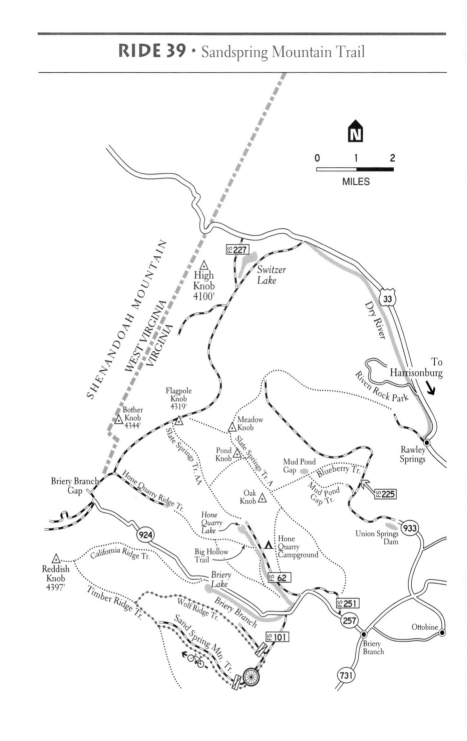

Harrisonburg mountain bikers take a break from a rocky, single-track climb near Reddish Knob in western Virginia (photo by Larry E. Grossman).

Finding the trail: Go south from Harrisonburg on VA 42. Turn onto VA 257 at Dayton and head west for about 15 miles. Stay on VA 257 past Ottobine and Briery Branch. After passing Hone Quarry Campground on the right, take the next left onto Tilman Road (FS 101). The gated Sand Spring Mountain Trail, actually a rocky double-track marked on the gate as Trail 423, is on the right. Its location is about half the distance along this road to Hearthstone Lake, so if you pass Hearthstone Lake on the right, you've gone too far.

Sources of additional information:

Dry River Ranger District of the
 George Washington National Forest
112 North River Road
Bridgewater, Virginia 22812
(540) 828-2591

Mole Hill Bikes
440 Main Street
Dayton, Virginia 22821
(540) 879-2011

Notes on the trail: This rocky double-track starts as a steep ascent and only gets steeper. It gains roughly 1,800' in elevation in 3 miles before hitting the crest of Sand Spring Mountain and Wolf Ridge shortly thereafter. While I could only imagine the Mole Hill mountain bikers jumping on their mounts and pedaling to the top, breaking nary a bead of sweat nor getting off to take a breather, yours truly did a whole lot of pushing, huffing, and puffing to get there.

Although the Timber Ridge Trail, veering off to the left from the top of Sand Spring Mountain, looked like an appealing way to drop back down to Tilman Road (FS 101), I opted to avoid taking any journalistic license and to do the ride the way Gerald had described it. I continued to the top of Wolf Ridge. You should then turn right and start descending on Wolf Ridge Trail.

Just as the ride to the top was not for the faint of limb, neither is the ride back to the bottom for the faint of heart. It starts as a narrow single-track on a loose, rocky surface with a number of blowdowns thrown in just to make things interesting. The trail veers right at an intersection with the Lynn Trail, which leads to Briery Lake. Judging by the chainring marks across the top of the trees stretched across the trail, the riders from Mole Hill (which, by the way, is 1 of 2 inactive volcanoes in Virginia) must have had a great time bunny-hopping across those massive oaks and hickories.

I've learned that the best way to cope with a ride that's over my head is to get philosophical and gut it out, and so I did. The Wolf Ridge descent eventually turned into a very manageable grassy double-track about 4 miles from Tilman Road, so I had plenty of time to change my opinion of Gerald Knicely and his favorite ride. In fact, after finally turning right onto FS 101 for the last mile back to my truck, I tried my best to remember the other rides that Gerald Knicely had offered and wondered if they would be as good as this one.

RIDE 40 · The Long Way to Reddish Knob

AT A GLANCE

Length/Configuration: 26-mile loop

VA

Aerobic difficulty: This ride has its share of climbs, and the final 6-mile assault on Reddish Knob is the climax

Technical difficulty: Minimal

Scenery: Dense, wooded roadside areas and super views of neighboring peaks

Special comments: This isn't the quickest route to this Shenandoah Mountain peak, but the views and final 7.5-mile downhill make it well worth the effort

If you ask any of the Harrisonburg riders how to get to the 4,397-foot summit of Reddish Knob, chances are they'll to steer you up VA 924 from Briery Branch, resulting in a tough ten-mile climb on a hard-surface road.

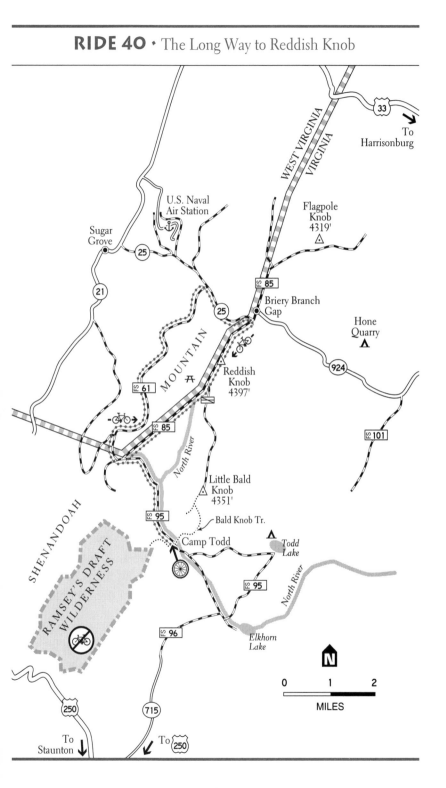

There's no doubt that it's a good workout—for a road cyclist. However, if you want to do Reddish Knob the longer, harder way, keep reading and plan your assault from the West Virginia side.

This 26-mile loop on lightly traveled national forest roads has its share of ups and downs, including a six-mile thigh-buster from West Virginia up to Reddish Knob. At the end of day you'll know that you've done some real climbing, but the 7.5-mile descent back to the start will probably make you forget the tough parts of the ride. Although entirely on hard-packed dirt and gravel Forest Service roads, rides such as this one lack nothing when it comes to leaving the crowds behind. I didn't see any cars for the first 13 miles. This ride provides a good workout in terms of required climbing but little technical skill. If the prospect of a 26-mile ride with a 6-mile climb thrown in does not intimidate you, have at it.

General location: The ride starts 20 miles west of Staunton.

Elevation change: After a gradual rise from the start of the ride at Camp Todd to the Virginia–West Virginia boundary, the ride drops rapidly for 1.6 miles, losing 1,104' in elevation right off the bat. The next 11.5 or so miles are a roller coaster of ups and downs until the climb to Reddish Knob begins at the intersection of FS 61 and 25. This 6-mile ascent gains 1,860' before reaching Reddish Knob at 4,397'. It's nice to end any ride on a downhill, and this one is a 7.5-miler dropping 2,037' from Reddish Knob back to the beginning.

Season: Year-round, although not when snow and ice remain on the roads in this part of the national forest. Be cautious during fall and winter hunting seasons and plan to wear brightly colored attire if riding during those times. Call the Virginia Department of Game and Inland Fisheries (540-248-9360) for the opening and closing dates for various game animals.

Services: The convenience store at West Augusta is the closest market to the start of the ride. Staunton and Harrisonburg have all other necessary services.

Hazards: Presence of ice and snow at high elevations would preclude attempting this ride. I've seen times in winter when all traces of snow had melted in the valley, but there were still several feet on the ground around Reddish Knob.

Rescue index: Sugar Grove, West Virginia, is the closest town where you could summon help. Although these Forest Service roads are open to vehicular traffic, I didn't see any cars for several hours, until I began the final approach to Reddish Knob.

Land status: George Washington National Forest—Dry River Ranger District.

Maps: George Washington National Forest map of the Dry River Ranger District; USGS 7.5 minute quads: Palo Alto, Reddish Knob, and West Augusta.

A little snow and ice doesn't deter local mountain bikers from the annual Super Bowl Sunday Ride near Reddish Knob.

Finding the trail: Head west on US 250 from Staunton. After 14.5 miles, cross a small bridge over Calfpasture River and immediately turn right onto VA 715. Pass the entrance for Braley Pond on the left and continue on FS 96 after the hard surface turns to gravel. At the first intersection, turn left onto FS 95 and go 3 miles to the sign on the left for Camp Todd. Park and start riding from here.

Source of additional information:

Dry River Ranger District of the George Washington National Forest
112 North River Road
Bridgewater, Virginia 22812
(540) 828-2591

Notes on the trail: Starting from Camp Todd on FS 95, begin riding west, away from the direction you entered this area. A very gradual uphill will bring you to the West Virginia border. However, you'll have little time to consider visiting another state as you descend quickly for the first mile and a half. Turn right onto FS 61 just before the end of this initial downhill. You'll enjoy a roller coaster of 1- to 2-mile ups and downs on this road. The scenery changes from open vistas to closed woods. Hemlock, maples, pines, and others will alternately dominate the nearby landscape.

Don't be too quick to pooh-pooh this ride simply because it's not single-track. The views to the east of the Shenandoah Mountain are really impressive, and in the course of 26 miles you'll have ample opportunities to show your stuff on long uphills and downhills. You'll know that you've developed an attraction for this sort of mountain bike touring when you find yourself looking curiously at unmarked roads that veer off into the woods and wonder where they go. Just make a mental note to return to find out. Should you make good on this pledge, you're definitely hooked.

Eventually you'll come to the intersection with FS 25, which goes west to Sugar Grove, West Virginia, and east toward the string of Shenandoah Mountains you've been eyeing for the last couple of hours. There's no delaying any longer. It's time to start climbing Reddish Knob. The views toward the top can keep you preoccupied as you pedal slowly but ever upward.

After reaching Briery Branch Gap, turn right onto hard-surface FS 85 and continue for two miles until you reach the parking lot atop Reddish Knob. When I finally reached the top, I felt that I'd accomplished something pretty special. However, the only greeting I got was from a timber rattlesnake lying across the road. He was none too pleased to see me and made that quite clear. However, Reddish Knob offers a panoramic view that few others in the area can touch, and maybe that's special enough. After you've had enough time in the clouds, turn back down the hardtop for a quarter mile, then take a left on the dirt surfaced FS 85. The fun starts when you begin a descent that will keep going for the next 7 miles back to the start.

When you arrive back at Mark's, Mole Hill, or Blue Ridge Cycleworks and someone questions you about your day's ride, look them in the eye and proudly announce, "I took a 26-mile ride up to Reddish Knob." Before anyone asks how you managed to turn a 10-mile climb into a muddy 26-mile affair, you can assure them, "Anyone can handle a 10-mile climb on a hard-surface road. When I climb Reddish Knob, I like to go the long way."

RIDE 41 • North River Gorge Trail

AT A GLANCE

Length/Configuration: 8-mile out-and-back

Aerobic difficulty: Minimal

North River Gorge
Trail includes a number
of creek crossings and
rocky sections.

Technical difficulty: Considerable; the trail crosses the rocky North River a dozen times in each direction

Scenery: Dense woods and rock outcroppings in the gorge formed by this beautiful mountain stream

Special comments: Good family ride when the stream is low—plan to get your feet wet

I stumbled onto this easy four-mile out-and-back (eight miles round-trip) trail quite by accident and have referred many others to it as a good beginners trail. It is marked intermittently by yellow blazes, but even in their absence it is not too tough to follow. North River Gorge Trail expands and contracts between single- and double-track as it roughly follows North River through the woods in this small valley, which lies between Lookout and Trimble Mountains. Anglers should pack some lightweight gear and pit their skills against native and introduced trout. Even when the water level is low in the summer,

The cool waters of North River slow down and provide a welcome mid-summer retreat in George Washington National Forest.

there are usually some deep pools where the trout lie in wait. Nonanglers may enjoy wading these same pools during the warm summer months.

Although this is a fairly easy ride, several rocky sections in addition to the dozen river crossings might offer a good technical challenge even for advanced riders. This is also a great spot for seeing wildlife. In over two and a half decades of rambling through the outdoors, this is the only place I've ever seen a black bear in the wild.

General location: 25 miles northwest of Staunton and about the same distance southwest of Harrisonburg.

Elevation change: None.

Season: Late spring through early fall is the best time to ride this route; caution should be taken during fall and winter hunting seasons. Call the Virginia Department of Game and Inland Fisheries (540-248-9360) for the opening and closing dates for various game animals. Plan to wear brightly colored attire if riding during those times. With its numerous creek crossings, this ride is best when the water level is low or the air temperature is high—plan to get your feet wet one way or the other.

Services: Camping and water are available in the North River Campground at the south end of the trail. There is a small store just outside the national forest near Natural Chimneys at the intersection of VA 718 and VA 730. All other services are available in Harrisonburg, Bridgewater, and Staunton.

Hazards: The 12 water crossings are troubling when the North River is high and moving fast, especially when air and water temperatures are cold.

Rescue index: Go to the store at Natural Chimneys or contact a ranger at Natural Chimneys.

Land status: George Washington National Forest—Dry River Ranger District.

Maps: George Washington National Forest map of the Dry River Ranger District; USGS 7.5 minute quad: Stokesville.

Finding the trail: To get to the North River Campground at the southern end of the trail, follow VA 42 from Bridgewater. Just outside the town's limits over the bridge at the south end of Bridgewater, turn onto VA 727 heading west. Go about 3 miles to the intersection with VA 613. Turn left, staying on VA 727, and continue 2.5 miles to the intersection with VA 730 at Sangerville. Turn left onto VA 730 and go 6 miles to the intersection with VA 718, the community of Stokesville. Turn right onto VA 718, and after 1 mile enter the national forest. Turn left onto Forest Service Road 95 and stay on the hard-surface road. Continue for 4.5 miles, going straight on the hard-surface road just below the entrance to Todd Lake. Turn left onto FS 95B and go 1 mile before reaching the North River Campground on the left. Unless you're planning to stay at this campground, park off the road outside the campground. The unmarked North River Gorge Trail is located just beyond the gate across the North River at the back of the campground loop road. You can also start this ride where the North River Gorge Trail intersects FS 95 just west of the community of Stokesville.

Source of additional information:
Dry River Ranger District of the George Washington National Forest
112 North River Road
Bridgewater, Virginia 22812
(540) 828-2591

Notes on the trail: Although it makes little difference which end of the trail you start at, I prefer the south end by the North River Campground. This especially makes sense if you're camping in the area. Although lacking any amenities, this campground is open year-round and offers access to a number of different rides in this part of the George Washington National Forest.

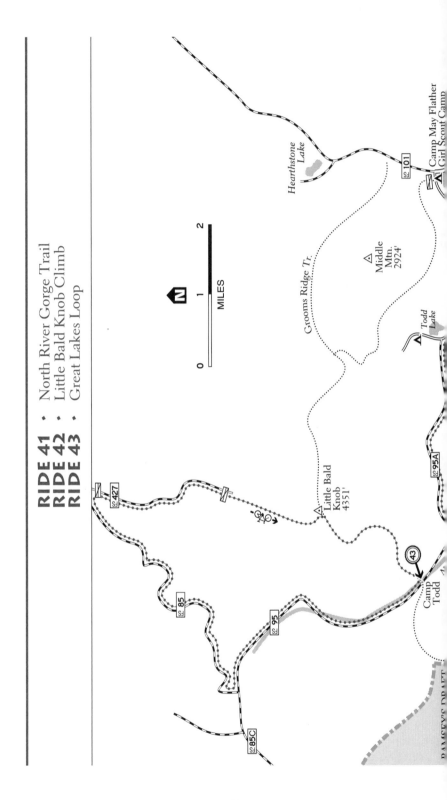

RIDE 41 : North River Gorge Trail
RIDE 42 : Little Bald Knob Climb
RIDE 43 : Great Lakes Loop

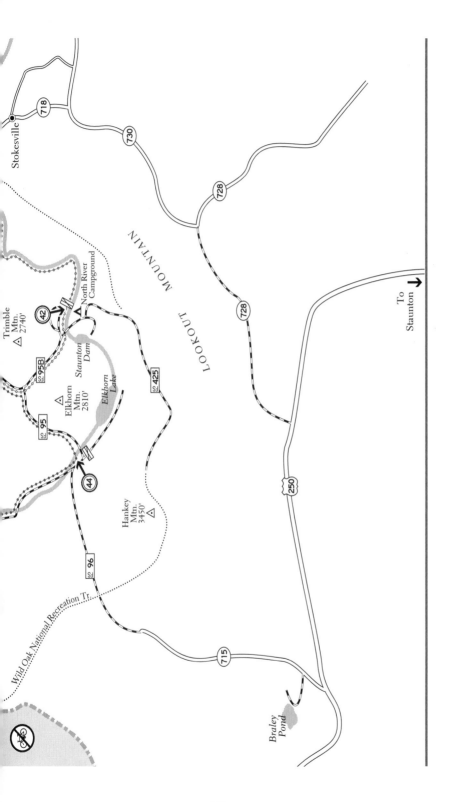

Stokesville

718

730

728

728

To Staunton →

LOOKOUT MOUNTAIN

North River Campground

Trimble Mtn. 2740'

42

Staunton Dam

95B

Elkhorn Mtn. 2810'

Elkhorn Lake

425

95

44

Hankey Mtn. 3450'

96

Wild Oak National Recreation Tr.

715

250

Braley Pond

This trail is marked with yellow diamond at North River Campground and a grey diamond at an intersection with Fire Road 95. It is not difficult to find, regardless. The campground loop is horseshoe shaped, and the North River Gorge Trail starts just beyond a gate at the far end of the loop opposite the entrance from FS 95B. At several places along the trail neither yellow blazes nor obvious human traffic point the way. However, continue in the direction of the North River and don't move up the side of surrounding mountains; you shouldn't stray too far from the trail.

At one spot toward the end of the ride it's easy to take a wrong turn. Look for the yellow diamonds. As you come to the ed of the trail, after th eeleventh river crossing, you wil lnotice a very large suspension foot bridge, cross the bridge and follow the trail for .8 mile to Fire Road 95. The trail ends just west of Camp May Flather, which is off-limits to public travel. From this point you should turn around and return to the North River Campground via the North River Gorge Trail. However, you can also turn this into an 8.5-mile loop by turning left onto hard-surface FS 95 and following the "Finding the trail" directions above to North River Campground.

RIDE 42 • Little Bald Knob Climb

AT A GLANCE

Length/Configuration: 17.4-mile loop

Aerobic difficulty: Considerable during the initial 12.8-mile climb

Technical difficulty: Tough single-track descent

Scenery: Superb top-of-the-world views of neighboring peaks as you near Little Bald Knob

Special comments: Extremely demanding climb followed by a tough, tortuous descent

This 17.4-mile loop will probably reveal things about your climbing abilities you may not already know—for better or worse. The ride starts with a 9.8-mile climb on hard-packed forest road and continues to climb rougher double-track to the top of Little Bald Knob across what appears to be the top of the world. A hairy single-track descent will lead you back through Horse Trough Hollow and the North River to end the ride.

The physical demands on the ascent and technical demands on the descent make this ride suitable for intermediate to advanced riders with good stamina and the good sense to hop off the bike and walk when necessary. Climbing FS 85, you'll meander across the border between Virginia and West Virginia. You can decide when you finally make it to the top whether this one was almost heaven or more reminiscent of the other place. Just be happy if you don't wind up like Martha Moats Baker, who stopped to rest near the top of Little Bald Knob but never left.

General location: 15 miles west of Staunton.

Elevation change: You'll gain 2,000' in the first 12.8 miles from Camp Todd to the top of Little Bald Knob. The 3-mile descent will take you back to Camp Todd, losing the same 2,000'.

Season: You can expect to ride this route year-round, but pick another ride when the possibility of snow and ice may be present on the Forest Service roads or at higher elevations. Caution should be taken during fall and winter hunting seasons; plan to wear brightly colored attire during those times. Call the Virginia Department of Game and Inland Fisheries (540-248-9360) for the opening and closing dates for various game animals.

Services: There is a convenience store in West Augusta at the intersection of Deerfield Road and Parkersburg Turnpike. All other services are available in nearby Staunton.

Hazards: Very rough on the 3-mile descent on technical single-track from Little Bald Knob back to Camp Todd. You'll descend almost 2,000'.

Rescue index: The closest public phone is at the convenience store at West Augusta.

Land status: George Washington National Forest—Dry River Ranger District.

Maps: George Washington National Forest map of the Dry River Ranger District; USGS 7.5 minute quads: Palo Alto and West Augusta.

Finding the trail: Head west on US 250 out of Staunton. After 14.5 miles, cross a small bridge over the Calfpasture River and immediately turn right onto VA 715. Pass the entrance for Braley Pond on the left and continue on FS 96 after the hard surface turns to gravel and dirt. At the first intersection, turn left onto FS 95 and go 3 miles to the sign on the left for Camp Todd. Park and start riding here.

Source of additional information:

Dry River Ranger District of the
George Washington National Forest
112 North River Road

Bridgewater, Virginia 22812
(540) 828-2591

Notes on the trail: Starting from the Camp Todd information sign, head west on FS 95. There is a slight uphill grade, but that will seem like nothing once you turn right onto FS 85 and start to climb in earnest. Continue for the next 9.8 miles and turn right onto the unmarked, gated Little Bald Knob Road—a.k.a. FS 427—located at a sharp bend in FS 85 .7 mile from the Shenandoah Picnic Area. You should start watching for this turn after passing a small picnic area on the left side of the road.

Little Bald Knob Road continues to climb on a somewhat rocky jeep road past a series of clearings, called "balds" in these parts. My favorite part of this ride was the climb across the top on the Little Bald Knob Road. With few neighboring peaks visible at this part of the ride, it was the first of many that I refer to as "top of the world rides." The road ends at its intersection with the 25.6-mile wild Oak Recreational Trail. Before long, you'll notice a spot on the left with magnificent views of the neighboring peaks to the north. Continue straight ahead, following the blazes onto narrow single-track through Horse Trough Hollow. Unless you're an extremely experienced rider with an excellent set of brakes, don't be too proud to walk down these last 3 miles, which are rocky, narrow, and steep. An alternative is to head back along FS 427, FS 85, and then FS 95 for what amounts to a hellacious descent.

Here is a bit of local lore that may be of interest should you notice the granite marker lying under the shade of an ageless oak to the left of Little Bald Knob Road. It reads:

Martha Moats Baker: Born 1880, Froze to Death Near This Spot On Brushy Mt. January 1925, Found Aug. 30, 1925

It seems that Martha Moats had taken off in January to cross the mountain over to her homeplace at Brushy Fork. Charlie Howdyshell was ranging his cattle on the mountain that spring, and his dogs alerted him to her remains. They were able to identify her by a pasteboard suitcase she had. When her husband was informed that her body had been found, his first question was, "Did you find the 75 cents and that pocketknife of mine that she took with her?" Like Mrs. Moats, you might find one of the numerous balds an inviting place to lie down and stay for a night or longer. Be sure to pack some warm camping gear so you don't make this *your* final resting place.

RIDE 43 · Great Lakes Loop

AT A GLANCE

Length/Configuration: 14-mile loop

VA

Aerobic difficulty: Several climbs from 1 to 3 miles long

Technical difficulty: Minimal; route is on gravel and hard-packed Forest Service roads

Scenery: Majestic lakes set against a mountainous backdrop

Special comments: Good introduction to continuous uphills and downhills—ending with a 4-mile downhill!

B eginning mountain bikers generally spend a lot of time cultivating one particular area in which to ride. It may not offer the area's best riding possibilities but in an activity that seems a little awkward at first, there's some security in developing familiarity with the bike and a specific locale at the same time. Such is the case with this 14-mile loop of gravel Forest Service roads where I did a lot of my earliest mountain biking. The Great Lakes Loop is also dear to me because my description of it was published in the August 1991 issue of *Mountain Bike* magazine.

Water is an obvious draw to this loop, and there's no more appealing sight for me than mountains framing a body of water. I hope you take advantage of the postcard-like landscapes the Allegheny Mountains paint behind these man-made lakes. And trout anglers should take note of the one-mile, trout-stocked section of the North River that runs out of the dam and past the North River Picnic Area. In addition to enjoying the expansive waters of Braley Pond, Elkhorn Lake, and the North River Reservoir nestled against backgrounds of mountain scenery, I've used the three-mile climb as an indication of what kind of shape I was in at the beginning of the spring riding season.

A beginner with some ability to use granny gears or a willingness to get off and walk will have no problem on this ride, nor will a rider of greater ability or experience, for that matter. As you pedal past Todd Lake on the first part of the climb, you can take in some great views of Chestnut Ridge off to the right.

General location: 15 miles west of Staunton.

Elevation change: Starting from Elkhorn Lake, you'll ride several 1-plus mile ascents and descents. However, these are just to get you warmed up for the 3-mile ascent past Todd Lake and up to 2,400' at the top of the climb along Leading Ridge Road (FS 95A). Check your brakes, sit back, and enjoy that long downhill back to Elkhorn Lake at 2,060'. This downhill seems like a longer vertical drop than 350' over 4 miles.

Season: The best time to ride is from spring through fall, although riders should use caution during fall hunting seasons and dress in highly visible attire. Call the Virginia Department of Game and Inland Fisheries (540-248-9360) for the opening and closing dates of hunting seasons for various game animals.

Services: Todd Lake Recreation Area offers developed campsites, bathrooms, sandy beach, and a swimming lake in the summer when open. North River Campground is a primitive setting, although it does have an SST

Unmarked double-tracks beckon you to follow the lesser-traveled path as you cycle through George Washington National Forest in the mountains of western Virginia.

(sweet-smellin' toilet) available. A fee is charged to enter Todd Lake and stay at the North River Campground. The closest stores are a convenience store at West Augusta and a grocery store in Churchville. All other services are available in nearby Bridgewater, Harrisonburg, and Staunton.

Hazards: There's little to worry about on this route, which utilizes gravel forest roads, although some rough parts of the steep downhill section of FS 95A are subject to erosion. There is also a very tight hairpin left turn where FS 95A runs into FS 95 on the long downhill section.

Rescue index: Help can be summoned from the convenience store at West Augusta where US 250 and VA 629 intersect.

Land status: George Washington National Forest—Dry River Ranger District.

Maps: George Washington National Forest map of the Dry River Ranger District; USGS 7.5 minute quads: Stokesville and West Augusta.

Finding the trail: Head west on US 250 out of Staunton. After 14.5 miles, cross a small bridge over the Calfpasture River and immediately turn right onto VA 715. Pass the entrance for Braley Pond on the left and continue on FS 96 past where the hard surface turns into gravel and dirt. At the first intersection, turn right and then after one-half mile again turn right at the entrance to Elkhorn Lake. Leave your vehicle at either of the parking areas near the lake and begin riding back toward the entrance.

Source of additional information:
Dry River Ranger District of the George Washington National Forest
112 North River Road
Bridgewater, Virginia 22812
(540) 828-2591

Notes on the trail: Camping abounds in the national forest, but if you're partial to the company of others, Todd Lake has a developed campground. The North River Campground is a small, flat clearing with a US Forest Service toilet and picnic tables. Campers at either of these sites can alter their starting point to begin the ride just outside their tent flap. I've always parked and started riding from Elkhorn Lake, which is how I describe this route.

Park near the lake and ride back to the intersection with FS 95. Turn right onto FS 95 at the stop sign and continue until you reach the well-marked intersection with FS 95B. Continue straight on FS 95B, which dead-ends after a mile at the Staunton Dam and North River Picnic Area. This is a great place to picnic or spend some quiet time looking out over the 17,000-acre watershed that provides water for the city of Staunton 16 miles away. A beautiful trout-stocked section of the North River runs along the road, and whether you're an angler or not this is a great spot to sit and ponder the meaning of life.

If you don't want to ride the additional 4 miles (2 miles each way) to the North River Dam, turn left onto FS 95 at the aforementioned intersection with FS 95B and ride to the intersection with hard-surface FS 523. Turn left here and begin a short but steep quarter-mile climb to Todd Lake. This turn begins a climb that will continue, after you turn left onto gravel FS 95A, for 3 miles before the road crests after you pass Barger Wildlife Pond on the right.

The 4-mile descent that follows is guaranteed to make you forget the effort you gave to get to the top. A word of caution for those who use a light touch on their brakes: You'll literally fly on this descent, but keep in mind that this rutted gravel road takes a very sharp left onto FS 95 on the descent back to Elkhorn Lake.

RIDE 44 · West Augusta Trail

AT A GLANCE

Length/Configuration: 7.5-mile loop

Aerobic difficulty: Minimal; climbs are gradual

Technical difficulty: None

Scenery: Hardwoods in various states of growth

Special comments: Good family ride if done as an out-and-back, omitting the stretch on busy highway; plan a picnic at Braley Pond

This relatively easy 7.5-mile loop offers little in the way of killer climbs or technical riding. It's a good route for the family wanting to have a picnic and/or fish at Braley Pond and then cycle on a double-track trail winding through mature hardwoods. The downside is the 3.5-mile section along heavily traveled US 250, but there's no reason not to turn around just before the gate and avoid riding this stretch of busy highway. Mileage remains about the same for each option.

Braley Pond offers a great getaway, with facilities for cooking out, picnicking, and fishing for trout, stocked throughout the spring and summer. You'll encounter few other riders on West Augusta Trail, located at the back of the pond. If you go during the week, chances are you'll have this beautiful spot, framed by the Alleghenies, all to yourself. Park Rangers recently added a new option to this ride. The 2-mile Johnson Trail circles Braley Pond, and adds a little more than a mile to aforementioned 7.5 miles.

More advanced riders looking for technical single-track with much more climbing can follow a set of double blazes on the right side of the trail just after the first creek crossing after Braley Pond. This other route leads to the Bridge Hollow Trail outside Ramseys Draft Wilderness. If you take this alternate you'll have to ride back along US 250 or do an out-and-back along the same route. Keep in mind that riding a bicycle within this or any other wilderness area is forbidden.

General location: 15 miles west of Staunton.

Elevation change: The ride starts at 1,986' by Braley Pond, and the trail climbs gradually to a high point of 2,200' before dropping back down to 2,068', where it intersects US 250. US 250 continues slightly downhill to the intersection of VA 629 and rises gradually back to the start. This is pretty minimal change in elevation for trails and roads in this region.

RIDE 44 · West Augusta Trail

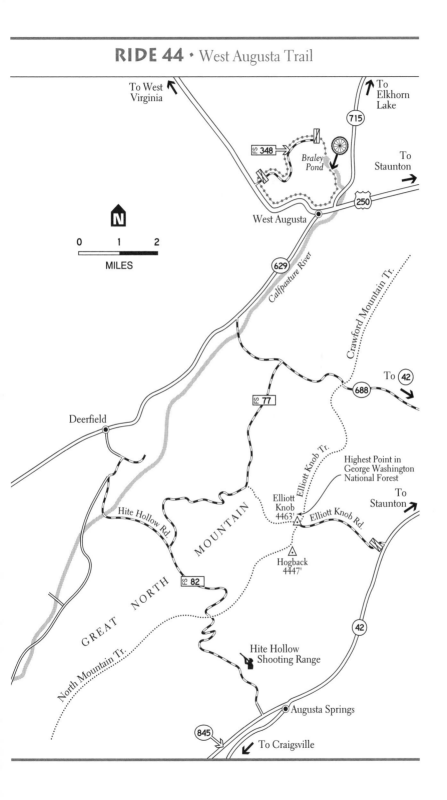

To West Virginia

To Elkhorn Lake

715

FS 348

Braley Pond

To Staunton

250

West Augusta

N

0   1   2

MILES

629

Calfpasture River

Crawford Mountain Tr.

To 42

688

FS 77

Deerfield

Elliott Knob Tr.

Highest Point in George Washington National Forest

Elliott Knob 4463'

To Staunton

Elliott Knob Rd.

Hite Hollow Rd.

MOUNTAIN

Hogback 4447'

GREAT   NORTH

FS 82

42

North Mountain Tr.

Hite Hollow Shooting Range

Augusta Springs

845

To Craigsville

West Augusta Trail is a popular getaway for mountain biking families in George Washington National Forest (photo by Dennis Coello).

Season: Year-round, but wear brightly colored attire during the succession of fall and winter hunting seasons beginning in October. Call the Virginia Department of Game and Inland Fisheries (540-248-9360) for the opening and closing dates for various game animals.

Services: Services are widely available in Staunton, and food and drinks can be purchased at the convenience store west of the turnoff for Braley Pond on US 250.

Hazards: Be very careful riding the 3.5-mile stretch along often heavily traveled US 250.

Rescue index: Assistance can be summoned from the convenience store at the intersection of US 250 and VA 629.

Land status: State-maintained roads and George Washington National Forest—Deerfield Ranger District.

Maps: George Washington National Forest map of the Deerfield Ranger District; USGS 7.5 minute quad: West Augusta.

Finding the trail: Go west of Staunton for 14.5 miles on US 250 and pass through the village of Churchville. After cresting a hill with a sign for North Mountain, take the next right turn onto VA 715 just after a small bridge over the Calfpasture River. Drive a short distance and turn left into the entrance for Braley Pond. Park out of the way along the loop parking area. You'll cross the bridge over to the reservoir, climb up to the dam, and carefully ride along the right side of the pond. The trail starts at the back of the pond.

Source of additional information:
Deerfield Ranger District of the George Washington National Forest
148 Parkersburg Turnpike
Staunton, Virginia 24401
(540) 885-8028

Notes on the trail: Depending on your interests and abilities, you can either ride or walk your bike along the trail on the right side of Braley Pond. When you've reached the flat area at the back of the pond, cross the small wooden bridge and start on the gravel double-track leading away from the pond. You'll follow it as it winds its way up and over small hills until it finally ends at the gate just before US 250. At this point, you can either return the way you came or pass the gate and begin riding downhill with caution along US 250. Turn left onto VA 715 and left again to enter the Braley Pond area and end the ride.

RIDE 45 · Deerfield Horse Trail

AT A GLANCE

Length/Configuration: 18-mile loop

Aerobic difficulty: Some tough climbs

Technical difficulty: Moderate

Scenery: Spectacular views from the Breastworks and along the ridge

Special comments: Remember to yield to equestrians on this loop

The name *Shenandoah* conjures various images—some real and some aided by the romance of song and print material. The name is generally translated from a long-forgotten Native American language to mean "Daughter of the Stars," but this is by no means the definitive meaning, only the most popular. This 18-mile loop lies on the western edge of Shenandoah Valley at the top and base of Shenandoah Mountain with the Augusta–Highland County boundary running through it.

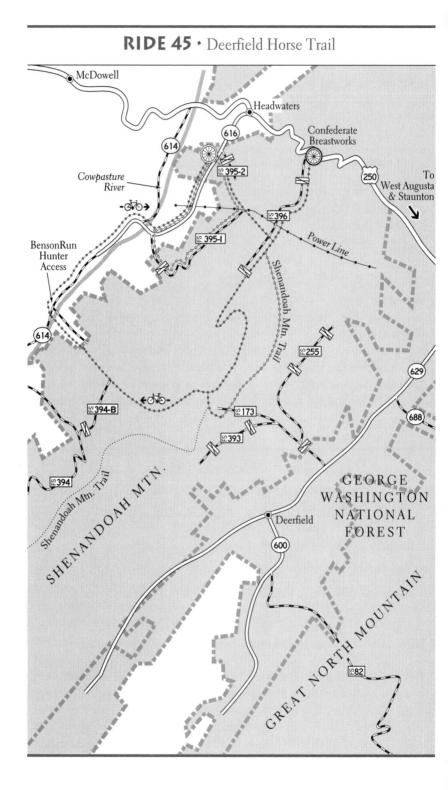

As the name implies, this route has been developed as a 25-mile system of trails and forest roads for horse travel by the Buffalo Trail Riders, but this does not mean horses and mountain bikes can't share the same trail. I found that horse travel can be an advantage on those national forest trails that otherwise tend to get overgrown and hard to follow. Just remember this rule of thumb: Bikers should yield to equestrians, especially when the going gets rough and narrow as it does on this loop.

The ride starts on US 250 (formerly known as the Staunton-Parkersburg Turnpike). This was the main thoroughfare across Virginia, and Civil War rebel troops used this vantage point to dig chest-high embankments to guard the Shenandoah Valley and its resources of iron and grain from Union troops. The ride features some tough climbs with a moderate amount of rough trail and road surface, which makes it most suitable for better-than-average riders.

General location: 25 miles west of Staunton.

Elevation change: The Shenandoah Mountain Trail climbs to 3,687'. From there you'll drop along Benson Run before reaching VA 616 at 1,800'. This road remains fairly level, but you'll turn onto Forest Service Road 395-2 to ascend Shenandoah Mountain to an elevation of 3,200'. The ride ends on a 2-mile downhill back to the Confederate Breastworks.

Season: Snow and ice at high elevations make this ride inadvisable. Also, riders should be aware of hunting seasons and wear bright colors as appropriate. Call the Virginia Department of Game and Inland Fisheries (540-248-9360) for the opening and closing dates for various game animals.

Services: All services are available in Staunton.

Hazards: Overgrown sections may hide large rocks and uneven trail surface. Also, be carefull not to startle the horses with whom you share the trail.

Rescue index: You can contact help from a pay phone at the West Augusta convenience store at the intersection of VA 629 and US 250.

Land status: George Washington National Forest—Deerfield Ranger District.

Maps: George Washington National Forest map of the Deerfield Ranger District; USGS 7.5 minute quads: Deerfield and McDowell.

Finding the trail: Travel west from Staunton on US 250 and pass the West Augusta Post Office. Climb past Ramsey's Draft and park at the top of Shenandoah Mountain in the parking area for the Confederate Breastworks on the right. To find the trail, ride a short distance downhill on US 250 going east. Turn right onto FS 396 and continue past the gate.

Source of additional information:

Deerfield Ranger District of the George Washington National Forest
148 Parkersburg Turnpike
Staunton, Virginia 24401
(540) 885-8028

Notes on the trail: The Trailriders and Forest Service have successfully marked this trail system with yellow plastic blazes, flagging tape, and paint blazes. This is a good thing, since this western flank of Shenandoah Mountain is a veritable maze of otherwise unmarked logging roads. A short option (actually one of many) is a 10-miler that starts from the horse camp on SR 616 and offers outstanding views from FS 365 (a.k.a. Liberty Road). Best of all, however, is to look at this slope as an area that's ripe for exploring and adventure. Remember to be courteous of other trail users as you explore these woods.

RIDE 46 · Elliott Knob

AT A GLANCE

Length/Configuration: Possibilities include a 2.9-mile out-and-back (5.8 miles total), and a 9-mile point-to-point (which can be ridden as an 18-mile out-and-back)

Aerobic difficulty: There's no easy way to get to Elliott Knob (4,463'), the highest point in George Washington National Forest

Technical difficulty: Ascending Elliott Knob via North Mountain Trail includes rock riding

Scenery: Panoramic views of the Shenandoah Valley

Special comments: Good for advanced mountain bikers who are into bagging peaks

Elliott Knob (at 4,463 feet) is the tallest peak in the George Washington National Forest, although that might be a moot point with the consolidation of Virginia's two national forests and the presence of Mount Rogers (5,729 feet) in Jefferson Forest. Be that as it may, it's still a heck of a climb, particularly if you make the frontal assault from VA 42 straight up the east side. This is a steep, 2.9-mile, one-way climb that riders do to test their stamina, just to say they did it, and because it's there. As a 5.8-mile out-and-back, the descent is just as challenging as the ascent— although obviously in different ways—and should only be undertaken by riders with a high degree of climbing and downhill abilities.

A more manageable alternative is the nine-mile point-to-point from Dry Branch Gap on VA 688, across the North Mountain ridge line past Elliott Knob, with a wonderful descent on grassy double-track before the finish at Hite Hollow Road (Forest Service Road 82). This option offers a pretty tough

RIDE 46 • Elliott Knob

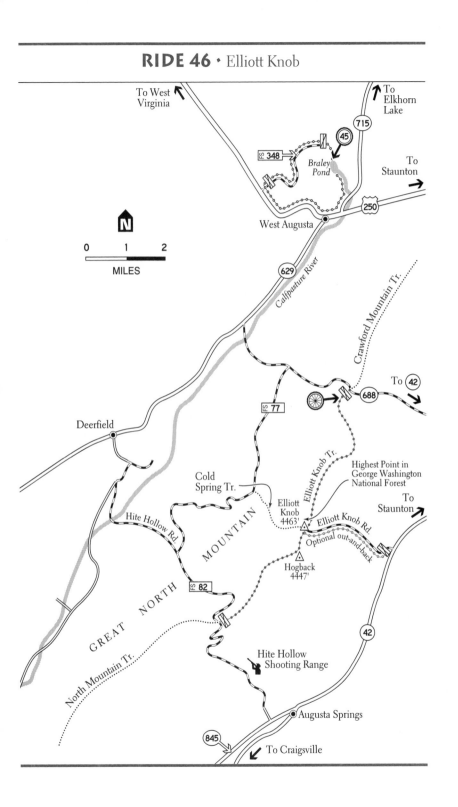

To West Virginia

To Elkhorn Lake

715

45

FS 348

Braley Pond

To Staunton

250

West Augusta

N

0 1 2

MILES

629

Calfpasture River

Crawford Mountain Tr.

To 42

688

FS 77

Deerfield

Elliott Knob Tr.

Cold Spring Tr.

Highest Point in George Washington National Forest

Elliott Knob 4463'

Elliott Knob Rd.

To Staunton

Hite Hollow Rd.

MOUNTAIN

Optional out-and-back

Hogback 4447'

FS 82

GREAT NORTH

North Mountain Tr.

Hite Hollow Shooting Range

42

Augusta Springs

845

To Craigsville

Signs such as this don't deter mountain bikers intent on completing the climb to Elliott Knob, the highest point in George Washington National Forest.

climb on rocky single-track and should be undertaken by riders in decent shape who can also handle some technical rock riding. It's best done as a one-way by using shuttle vehicles at either end, but riders who just can't get enough of the George Washington's highest peak can turn around and go back for a very grueling 18-mile out-and-back.

However you reach the top—and plan to get back down—you'll find some great views across the Shenandoah Valley from Elliott Knob. That is, if you don't mind sharing them with a large radio tower. The fire lookout tower at the peak was built in 1948 and remained in use through the early 1960s. It was placed on the National Historic Lookout Register in 1994.

General location: 15 miles west of Staunton.

Elevation change: Elliott Knob Road gains 2,338' in 2.9 miles. From Dry Branch Gap, North Mountain Trail to Elliott Knob gains 1,882' over 4.4 miles and then loses 1,281' before reaching its intersection with Hite Hollow Road.

Season: Year-round, but the presence of winter snow and ice will make this ride inadvisable. Also riders should beware of riding during hunting season and wear bright colors as appropriate. Call the Virginia Department of Game and Inland Fisheries (540-248-9360) for the opening and closing dates for various game animals.

Services: All services are available in Staunton.

Hazards: Killer uphill and downhill on the frontal assault via the Elliott Knob Road. Technical, rocky ascent from Dry Branch Road to Elliott Knob.

Rescue index: Help can be contacted from Our Place, a local restaurant just east on US 42 at Buffalo Gap. If the restaurant is closed, continue back toward Staunton on VA 254 to get assistance.

Land status: George Washington National Forest—Deerfield Ranger District.

Maps: George Washington National Forest map of the Deerfield Ranger District; USGS 7.5 minute quad: Elliott Knob.

Finding the trail: Travel west from Staunton on West Beverley Street (VA 254) through Buffalo Gap, continuing south to VA 42. To reach the North Mountain Trail, turn right onto VA 688 by the small white church and park at the gap between Crawford and North Mountains. North Mountain Trail to Elliott Knob heads south from this trailhead. To get to Elliott Knob Road, continue on VA 42 South past VA 688. After you pass the gated entrance to Falls Hollow Trail, the next gated road on the right will be the (unmarked) Elliott Knob Road. Note that this road starts out running south and parallel to the railroad tracks across the road and VA 42.

Source of additional information:

Deerfield Ranger District of the   Staunton, Virginia 24401
   George Washington National Forest   (540) 885-8028
148 Parkersburg Turnpike

Notes on the trail: A more interesting ride that still offers plenty of technical and aerobic challenge is the 4.4-mile ride along North Mountain Trail from Dry Branch Gap. There are some outstanding views of Deerfield Valley. The yellow blazes along this largely single-track trail do a good job of pointing the way, which is primarily uphill with the occasional short downhill thrown in to keep things interesting. Upon reaching the top of Elliott Knob Road and after a respite to enjoy views of the Shenandoah Valley, there are several options for completing your ride.

   If you're riding solo and looking for a relatively short ride, turn around and head back on North Mountain Trail for a pretty technical downhill and an 8.8-mile out-and-back. However, if you really can't resist the notion of a 2.9-mile descent on almost vertical Elliott Knob Road, check your brakes, close your mouth, and have at it.

A far more appealing one-way option—albeit longer—is to continue across on North Mountain Trail, which turns south a short distance down Elliott Knob Road. The trail descends in the saddle between Elliott Knob and Hogback, which at 4,447' is of respectable height for these parts and offers a panoramic view east across the Shenandoah Valley. The trail widens to a grassy double-track at this spot, which was cleared during WW II as a potential radar site. The double-track gets a bit ambiguous on top of Hogback, but just keep going downhill in a southerly direction for what I found to be the most enjoyable part of the ride, a 3-mile gradual descent to FS 82, Hite Hollow Road. The full point-to-point ride from VA 688 to FS 82 across North Mountain Trail is 9 miles long; you'll need to position shuttle vehicles in advance or have a great set of climbing legs to turn around for an 18-mile out-and-back.

RIDE 47 • Walker Mountain

AT A GLANCE

Length/Configuration: 13-mile loop

Aerobic difficulty: The 6-mile gradual ascent will work your cardiovascular system

Technical difficulty: Moderate on short single-track descent

Scenery: Great views of neighboring peaks as you reach the top of Walker Mountain

Special comments: Leave the crowds behind on this moderate ride in a quiet part of the national forest

The 13-mile Walker Mountain loop combines a lot of forest road through a cool, hemlock-shaded gorge adjacent to Clayton Mill Creek with a 1.2-mile stretch of single-track. I've grown to love the area for its beauty, solitude, and proximity to some of my favorite out-of-the-way places, like Goshen Pass and Williamsville. The initial six-mile climb on hard-packed forest road is not easy, but for a rider with a moderate amount of stamina it makes a challenging introduction to the kinds of lengthy ascents you're likely to find in Virginia's national forests. The good thing about climbs such as this is they take you to an elevation where you can get a good view of the neighboring ridges and Marble Valley.

General location: 25 miles west of Staunton.

RIDE 47 · Walker Mountain

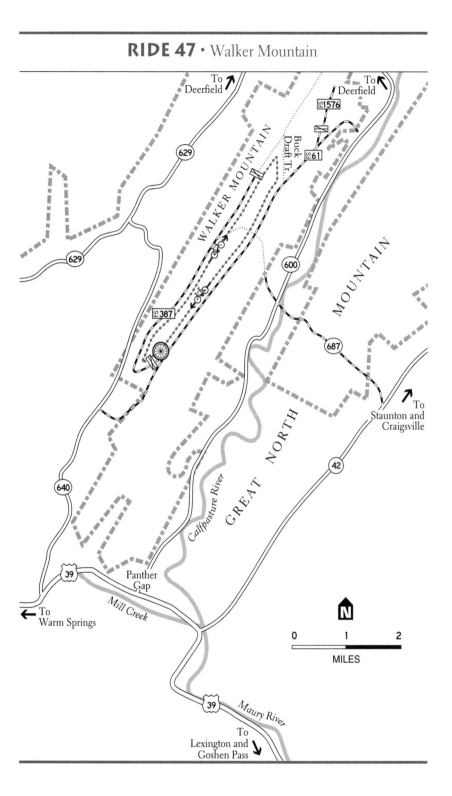

The climb to the top of Walker Mountain is long and tough—but worth it.

Elevation change: The ride begins just before the gate at 1,948' and climbs rather steeply around 2 sharp bends. Once Walker Mountain Jeep Trail straightens, it continues to climb before reaching the ridge at 3,100' and peaking at 3,115'. It intersects the trail from the west and drops down the eastern side of Walker Mountain to Clayton Mill Road at 2,320'. The hard-packed forest road has a short uphill and then heads downhill for 3.5 miles to the start.

Season: Year-round, although snow and ice in winter make this ride inadvisable. A good example of the unpredictability of weather at the beginning of spring and end of fall in the mountains of western Virginia is my encounter with snow flurries when I rode this loop in early April. Riders should use caution during fall and winter hunting seasons and dress in highly visible attire. Call the Virginia Department of Game and Inland Fisheries (540-248-9360) for the opening and closing dates of hunting seasons for various game animals.

Services: All services are available in nearby Staunton.

Hazards: Watch for hunters during the succession of seasons beginning in the fall.

Rescue index: Assistance can be summoned in the town of Craigsville, which has a volunteer rescue squad.

Land status: George Washington National Forest—Deerfield Ranger District.

Maps: George Washington National Forest map of the Deerfield Ranger District; USGS 7.5 minute quads: Craigsville, Deerfield, and Green Valley.

Finding the trail: Leave Staunton, heading west on US 250 for approximately 25 miles. Turn left onto VA 629 at the convenience store at West Augusta. After 10 miles, turn left onto VA 600 in the village of Deerfield and then turn right at Marble Valley onto Forest Service Road 61. Follow this road to FS 387 on the right and park just before the gated entrance.

Source of additional information:
Deerfield Ranger District of the George Washington National Forest
148 Parkersburg Turnpike
Staunton, Virginia 24401
(540) 885-8028

Notes on the trail: The ride begins with a gradual climb up to the ridge line at the top of Walker Mountain that crests where the gated Walker Mountain Road ends and the Walker Mountain Jeep Road/Trail begins. Although the road is largely overgrown with crown vetch, it's not hard to "break trail." The jeep road past the gate has some blowdowns blocking the way, but the 1.5 miles before turning east (right) onto Back Creek Trail is still quite ridable.

The intersection of these 2 trails is easy to miss, so keep an eye out for yellow-blazed Back Creek Trail, which runs east and west across the top of Walker Mountain. Turn right onto the trail, which is initially a little tough to follow. After a short stretch of overgrown vegetation and blowdowns, other yellow blazes become apparent on this 1.2-mile single-track down to FS 61.

At one point on the descent I encountered a garter snake trying to make a meal of a toad. The toad was half in and half out, and still very much alive. The snake backed away from me as if I was going to try to wrestle Kermit away from him. I had definitely worked up an appetite by that point, but I wasn't quite ready to devour one of the Muppets. After turning right onto FS 61, you'll pedal a short uphill before finishing the ride on a super 3.5-mile downhill run, always a great way to end a ride.

RIDE 48 · Williamsville Loop

AT A GLANCE

Length/Configuration: 21-mile loop

Aerobic difficulty: Generally flat; 1 tough climb to Bullpasture Mountain

Technical difficulty: Easy

Scenery: Expansive pastures at the foot of mountain ridges with rushing streams

Special comments: Plan your trip in conjunction with the area's annual Maple Festival

This 21-mile loop on gravel and hard-surface roads offers an interesting look at Highland County, also called Little Switzerland, on some of the flattest terrain you're likely to find in this county of some 2,500 souls. As well as being the least populated county east of the Mississippi River, Highland boasts a sheep population that outnumbers its *Homo sapiens*. Whether the exact figures are true or not I can't say, but on a weekday in July I saw fewer people than sheep, or even deer for that matter, while out on this fairly easy ride. Besides the 21-mile distance, the only feature that would impede any rider is the 1.5-mile climb across Bullpasture Mountain.

You'll encircle Bullpasture Mountain on little-traveled hard surface and dirt state roads that hug low-lying farms at the foot of the mountain. Besides herds of sheep and the occasional white-tail deer, Cowpasture and Bullpasture Rivers will accompany you as you pedal along at a leisurely pace. Anglers should take note that these two rivers are excellent trout streams. Summer tubing and swimming in the Bullpasture just below the swinging bridge are also popular, although the water is chilly at any time of year.

McDowell and all of Highland County comes alive during the two Maple Festival weekends in March. Weather in Highland is hard to predict at that time, and in my two decades of going to eat buckwheat cakes, homemade sausage, and local maple syrup, I've seen everything from a foot of snow to T-shirt weather. If you're coming from out of the area, dress for the extremes. Also noteworthy are the annual Hands and Harvest Festival, held on Columbus Day weekend, and the annual Mountain Mama Bicycle Tour held on the first weekend of August. Civil War buffs may recall that McDowell was the site of Stonewall Jackson's first victory over the Yanks in his famous Valley Campaign in the spring of 1864.

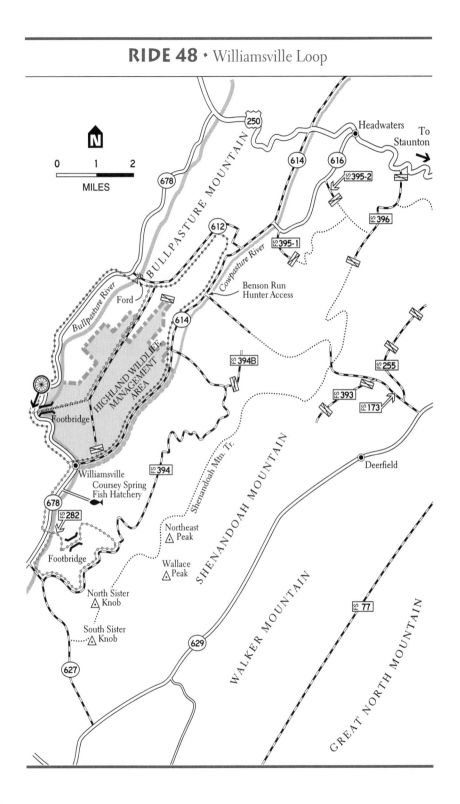

Those who enjoy "real" mountain rides will find their way to Virginia's Highland County—also known as Little Switzerland.

General location: 40 miles west of Staunton straddling the Bath and Highland County boundary.

Elevation change: This ride consists primarily of gentle ups and downs along the east and west flanks of Bullpasture Mountain. The only real climb is the 1.5-mile traverse of Bullpasture Mountain on gravel VA 612, gaining some 670', followed by a welcome descent on the other side to the Bullpasture River.

Season: Year-round, although snow and ice in winter make this ride inadvisable. Riders should also use caution during fall and winter hunting seasons and dress in highly visible attire. Call the Virginia Department of Game and Inland Fisheries (804-367-1000) for the opening and closing dates of hunting seasons for various game animals. You might plan this ride in conjunction with 1 of 2 Highland County Maple Festival weekends in March.

Services: There is a small convenience store just south of "downtown" Williamsville on VA 678. Otherwise all services are available in Staunton.

Hazards: Fording the Bullpasture River on VA 612 when the water is high in the spring and after periods of heavy rain is inadvisable.

Rescue index: Although these roads are lightly traveled, they are nevertheless county roads, so flagging down a passing motorist is your best chance to get help. There is a pay telephone outside the convenience store on VA 678 just south of Williamsville.

Land status: Gravel and hard-surface county roads.

Maps: USGS 7.5 minute quads: McDowell, Monterey SE, and Williamsville; Highland and Bath county maps from the Virginia Department of Transportation.

Finding the trail: Head west out of Staunton on US 250 for approximately 30 miles. After entering Highland County and cresting the mountains, turn left onto hard-surface VA 678 at the village of McDowell. Continue on VA 678 until reaching the Virginia Department of Game and Inland Fisheries parking area on the left by the swinging bridge across the Bullpasture River. Park and begin this ride from there.

Source of additional information:
Highland County Chamber of Commerce
P.O. Box 223
Monterey, Virginia 24465
(540) 468-2550

Notes on the trail: Leave the Game and Inland Fisheries parking area, heading south on VA 678. The initial climb through beautiful Bullpasture Gorge will give way to a descent through the village of Williamsville. Take the first left turn across the bridge over Bullpasture River onto VA 614. The hard surface becomes a fairly flat gravel road, and you'll now pick up Cowpasture River as it flows south toward its confluence with the Bullpasture just below Williamsville. About halfway into the ride you'll take a left onto VA 612 and begin a 1.5-mile climb to the top of Bullpasture Mountain. The 3-mile descent down the western side of the mountain will allow you to catch your breath before fording Bullpasture River at the bottom.

This crossing can be anything from refreshing to downright dangerous, depending on the depth of the river. At any rate, plan to get your feet wet before reaching the other side. After periods of heavy rain and during the spring thaw, this crossing is inadvisable. An alternate route for heartier riders who come outside of hunting seasons is to ride as far as the point where VA 612 crests Bullpasture Mountain and take a left across the top of the mountain on Hupman Valley Trail through the Highland Wildlife Management Area. This avoids fording the river but, as you'd expect, is tougher than riding down hard-surface VA 678. However, both will get you back to your starting point in due time.

Assuming you've been able to cross Bullpasture River unscathed, continue and turn left onto hard-surface VA 678. The last 6 miles are pretty easy going, although 678 is more traveled than the gravel road on the eastern flank of Bullpasture Mountain. Once you rejoin Bullpasture River in the homestretch, you'll probably be tempted to dip your feet or cast a line into this section of trout water, which beckons anglers and white-water boaters from far and wide.

RIDE 49 • Wallace Tract

AT A GLANCE

Length/Configuration: 20-mile loop

Aerobic difficulty: Steady 5-mile climb with intermittent downhills

Technical difficulty: Largely overgrown

Scenery: Bullpasture and Cowpasture Rivers, dense woods, and views of neighboring peaks

Special comments: A great out-of-the-way destination for biking, camping, trout fishing, white-water tubing, and caving

Before Virginia's Department of Game and Inland Fisheries went to a year-round trout season, throngs of anglers would line the banks of Bullpasture and Cowpasture Rivers every spring to cast a line and catch their limit on opening day. There are more accessible places to catch a few trout than the remote hamlet of Williamsville, situated a stone's throw into Bath County from Highland County, but these rivers have carved an attractive setting out of the expansive open fields and rocky crags that line this secluded western Virginia landscape. Just as this setting has continued to draw anglers and white-water boating enthusiasts, so has it repeatedly drawn this mountain biker like the swallows to San Juan Capistrano.

As the Bullpasture River disappears into the Cowpasture just south of Williamsville, the ominous cliffs that form well-known Bullpasture Gorge disappear into grasslands dotted with sheep and the occasional clutch of whitetail deer. This 20-mile loop takes in all of the above features and includes a 5-mile climb into the clouds, the subsequent descent along single-track Wallace Tract Trail, and a glimpse of the antebellum Wallace House before crossing a swinging cable and wooden footbridge over Cowpasture River. From there you climb back through Williamsville before returning to the start.

One draw of this ride is its remote setting against Shenandoah Mountain; it's as if Mother Nature had an artistic epiphany and then destroyed her palette. Another enticement is that you can navigate the 2.5-mile Wallace Tract Trail without getting lost, scratched, or drenched while fording Cowpasture River. In short, this trail is the Aegean Stable I've decided to clean

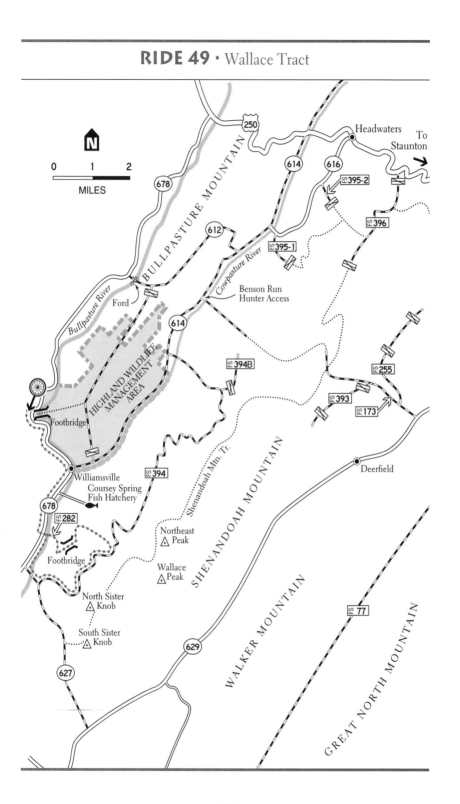

before moving on to life's next labor. Others may not share my enthusiasm for bushwhacking through overgrown fields, nor will more technically inclined riders want to spend their time pedaling hard-surface county roads and hard-packed Forest Service roads, but this ride certainly has a charm all its own.

General location: 45 miles west of Staunton near Williamsville.

Elevation change: This route starts by the swinging bridge over Cowpasture River at 1,600'. You'll climb slightly to the intersection with VA 678, staying just under 1,600' before turning onto FS 394. The route ascends to the trailhead at 2,400' and drops back to start. North (3,292') and South Sister (3,088') Mountains on the Shenandoah Mountain Trail would increase the challenge.

Season: Spring through late fall, although traffic picks up during deer season in November. It would be fun to combine this ride with 1 of 2 Highland County Maple Festival weekends in March, although it can be pretty chilly then. Riders should also use caution during fall and winter hunting seasons and dress in highly visible attire. Call the Virginia Department of Game and Inland Fisheries (540-248-9360) for the opening and closing dates of hunting seasons for various game animals.

Services: Camping is allowed along the grassy edges surrounding this Virginia Department of Game and Inland Fisheries parking area. There is a small convenience store just south of "downtown" Williamsville on VA 678. Otherwise all services are available in Staunton.

Hazards: The trail is overgrown and can be hard to follow as it wends through open fields lying between the base of Wallace Peak and Cowpasture River.

Rescue index: There is a pay telephone outside the Williamsville store on VA 678. Although these roads are lightly traveled, they are nevertheless county roads, so flagging down a passing motorist is your best chance to get help.

Land status: State-maintained roads and George Washington National Forest—Deerfield Ranger District.

Maps: George Washington National Forest map of the Deerfield Ranger District; USGS 7.5 minute quads: McDowell, Monterey SE, and Williamsville.

Finding the trail: Head west out of Staunton on US 250 for approximately 35 miles. After entering Highland County and cresting mountains, turn left onto hard-surface VA 678 at the village of McDowell. Continue on VA 678 for 10 miles until Bullpasture River, to the left of the road, edges its way next to the road and together they wind through a high, rocky gorge. Turn left into the unmarked Virginia Department of Game and Inland Fisheries parking area next to a swinging bridge. You'll begin the ride here.

Sources of additional information:

Highland County
  Chamber of Commerce
P.O. Box 223
Monterey, Virginia 24465
(540) 468-2550

Virginia Department of Game and
  Inland Fisheries
P.O. Box 996
Verona, Virginia 24482
(540) 248-9360

Deerfield Ranger District of the
  George Washington National Forest
148 Parkersburg Turnpike
Staunton, Virginia 24401
(540) 885-8028

Notes on the trail: Leave the parking area and turn left, heading uphill on VA 678. After a short warm-up climb, you'll ride a 2-mile roller-coaster descent through Williamsville. Pass the bridge on the left over Bullpasture River and begin to climb.

If you've never seen mammoth rainbow and brown trout, on which many a fish story is loosely based, be sure to stop by the Coursey Spring Fish Hatchery on the left side of VA 678 from 8 A.M. to 3:30 P.M. Here fish are raised for subsequent release into Virginia's stocked trout waters. Otherwise, continue pedaling and turn left onto FS 627 and cross Cowpasture River. Just south of Williamsville, the Bullpasture lost its identity as it flowed into the Cowpasture, which followed a parallel course on the east side of Bullpasture Mountain.

After a short, flat mile, turn left onto FS 394. A sign at this intersection identifies the distance to VA 614 as 18 miles, but you won't go that far—although the next several miles of climbing will feel longer than 5 miles. Fortunately the 1- to 2-mile climbs are punctuated by downhills, as well as some great views of neighboring ridges to the east and west. After 6 of these combined ups and downs, watch for a sign on the left with a picture of a hiker and the descriptive word *Trail.* Turn left here and pass a gate onto unidentified 2.5-mile Wallace Tract Trail.

Start downhill on this single-track section of old road and follow the yellow plastic diamonds posted prominently on trailside trees. After meandering through the woods, the trail empties into an area of cultivated farmland, don't assume you're home free. The trail actually becomes more difficult to follow through these expansive agricultural fields, depending on how high they've grown. I can only suggest that you follow a combination of track or trail left by humans, deer, and/or tractors. Make your way to Cowpasture River within eyeshot of a suspended bridge across the river.

From here, cross the bridge and continue up unmarked FS 282 gravel road to VA 678. Turn right onto a somewhat familiar hard-surface road and pedal the final 6 miles back to the start.

RIDE 50 · Hidden Valley

AT A GLANCE

Length/Configuration: 12-mile loop

Aerobic difficulty: Some respectable ascents

Technical difficulty: None, except minimal on the initial stretch along and through Jackson River

Scenery: World-class lodging, trout fishing, and a restored antebellum mansion

Special comments: Pamper yourself with a night at Hidden Valley Bed and Breakfast after looping around this quiet Bath County retreat

Exploring the large expanses of Virginia's national forests for good places to mountain bike was sometimes a crapshoot for me. It seemed that despite the amount of pretrip preparation with trail guides, topo maps, and suggestions from knowledgeable riders, I was still at a loss to accurately predict what was really there until I got out and rode. The 12-mile loop described through Hidden Valley in the far reaches of Bath County was one of those pleasant surprises. Everything worked as I'd hoped it would in terms of single-track, double-track, and national forest roads connecting, with no guesswork involved in an area of outstanding natural beauty. Who could ask for more?

Starting with an easy flat stretch along and through the Jackson River, you'll ride on double-track and forest roads that circle Little Mountain before you return to the start on a 2.5-mile downhill. Some ups and downs will get your heart and lungs working, but it's nothing that even novice riders with a moderate level of fitness can't handle.

The appeal of this locale is long-standing—in fact, ongoing archeological excavations at Hidden Valley have traced a Native American presence back 9,000 years. The present Warwickton mansion, an antebellum home built by Judge James Woods Warwick in the late 1840s, was the filming site of *Sommersby*, a Civil War movie released in 1993 starring Richard Gere and Jodie Foster.

General location: 5 miles west of Warm Springs.

Elevation change: This ride begins at 1,750' and remains fairly level before crossing the Jackson River for the third time. Shortly after leaving the river, you'll start climbing on Forest Service Road 481 and will reach the highest

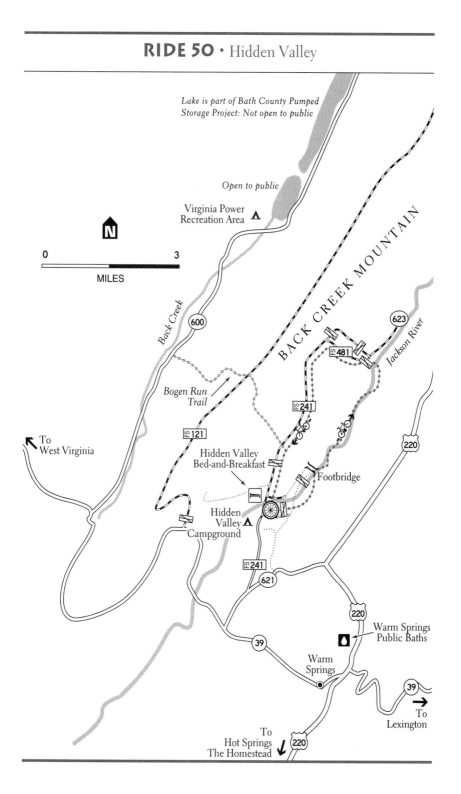

Lake is part of Bath County Pumped
Storage Project: Not open to public

Open to public

Virginia Power
Recreation Area

N

0   3

MILES

Back Creek

BACK CREEK MOUNTAIN

600

623

481

Jackson River

Bogen Run
Trail

241

220

121

To
West Virginia

Hidden Valley
Bed-and-Breakfast

Footbridge

Hidden
Valley
Campground

241

621

220

39

220

Warm Springs
Public Baths

Warm
Springs

39

To
Lexington

To
Hot Springs
The Homestead

Civil War reenactors at Hidden Valley feel at home next to one of the dependencies of the antebellum Warwick mansion, where the movie *Sommersby* was filmed.

point of the ride at 2,400'. The climb is steady but not steep, and you'll finish with a 2.5-mile downhill.

Season: Warmer weather offers the best time to ride, given the definite possibility of getting wet feet while fording the Jackson River. Riders should use caution during fall and winter hunting seasons and dress in highly visible attire. Call the Virginia Department of Game and Inland Fisheries (540-248-9360) for the opening and closing dates of hunting seasons for the various game animals.

Services: Lodging is available at the Hidden Valley Bed and Breakfast. Camping is available at the Hidden Valley Campground, a clean, no-frills campground managed by the Warm Springs Ranger District. Other services are available in nearby Hot Springs and Warm Springs, including the renowned Homestead Resort.

Hazards: River crossings when the Jackson River is high.

Rescue index: Emergency calls can be made from the Hidden Valley Bed and Breakfast.

Land status: George Washington National Forest—Warm Springs Ranger District.

Maps: George Washington National Forest map of the Warm Springs Ranger District; USGS 7.5 minute quad: Sunrise and Warm Springs.

Finding the trail: From Warm Springs, take US 39 west for 1.4 miles. Turn right onto VA 621 just after you pass the sign for Hidden Valley. Go 2 miles down the road past the Hidden Valley Campground and park just before you cross the Jackson River. The trail begins as a double-track through the meadow on the right.

Sources of additional information:

Warm Springs Ranger District of the
  George Washington National Forest
Highway 220 South–Route 2, Box 30
Hot Springs, Virginia 24445
(540) 839-2521

Hidden Valley Bed and Breakfast
P.O. Box 53
Warm Springs, Virginia 24484
(540) 839-3178

Notes on the trail: The route described here starts as a flat double-track that runs through the meadow for the first mile before entering a wooded area along the Jackson River. Arrows initially point the way and are replaced by painted blue blazes, but even without markings it's easy to follow this wide path through the woods. You'll come to a well-marked intersection with Muddy Run and Muddy Run Trail. Follow the blue blazes to the left and cross a small wooden bridge over Muddy Run.

Continue riding along Jackson River, a mountain stream with a reputation for monster trout. This ride works best in the summer or fall, when the river is relatively low and getting wet feet is more refreshing than endangering. Pack a picnic lunch and stop along the way to test your angling skills against wary native browns or more gullible rainbows. But be sure to heed the following special regulations:

- Only single hook artificial lures can be used.
- Creel limit of 2 fish, both of which must be larger than 16 inches.
- A Virginia fishing license is required, as well as trout and national forest stamps.

You'll soon come to a narrow swinging bridge that spans the Jackson. This would have been a nice place for some trail directions, but I'll save you the guesswork that temporarily confounded me. Instead of crossing the bridge, follow what is now Gorge Road to the right of the bridge and cross through the river. A brown and white Forest Service arrow on the other side of the river points left, but ignore this and go right. If the river is too high, too cold, or otherwise uninviting, go ahead and cross the bridge and then turn right at the end. Keep going until you intersect with Gorge Road. (At the end of the bridge to the left is blue-blazed Rock Shelter Trail, which includes a nice section of single-track on a ledge above the river. This 2.3-mile trail goes back to the Hidden

Valley Bed and Breakfast. However, the presence of this trail with its freshly painted blazes but no trail signs only confused the issue.) Continue along Gorge Road, stopping to fish, picnic, wade, or just enjoy this beautiful stretch of western Virginia mountain stream. There are no blazes or trail markings of any kind, but even as the road gets overgrown in spots it's pretty easy to follow.

Along the way you'll encounter 2 more river crossings without bridges. The river is wide here, so if you opt not to get cold wet feet, turn around at the second crossing and head back. However, if you're able to press on, cross the river and pass a gate across the road. Very shortly after leaving the woods you'll see a fresh gravel road (VA 623) that goes right.

Take the gated road to the left (unmarked FS 241). Over the next couple of miles, you'll ascend and descend on an overgrown gravel road with no real killer hills. If you're lucky, you might see a bunch of wild turkeys, deer, or any of the other wildlife that leave their mark in the soft road surface. You'll reach a ridge and enjoy some spectacular views of Back Creek Mountain to the west. Pass several gates—one of the perks of riding a mountain bike—and eventually pass the Hidden Valley Bed and Breakfast on the right. This ride ends back at your vehicle after a 2.5-mile downhill.

Mountain bikers looking for a more vigorous workout can add a 12-mile (one-way) out-and-back spinoff onto Bogan Run Trail on the right, along the final downhill stretch on FS 241. You'll immediately start the 1-mile climb to the top of Back Creek Mountain at 3,460', but continue across FS 121 at the top of Back Creek Mountain. Stay on Bogan Run Trail for another tortuous 5 miles before turning around to return to Hidden Valley for a tough 24-miler.

RIDE 51 · Laurel Fork

AT A GLANCE

Length/Configuration: 18-mile loop

Aerobic difficulty: Considerable; the ride ascends for 14 miles

Technical difficulty: Ranges from rocky double-track to rocky creek bed

Scenery: Towering mountain laurel, snowshoe hare, northern flying squirrels, and assorted flora and fauna generally found in more northern climes

Special comments: Prepare for an expedition into one of Virginia's unique ecological niches

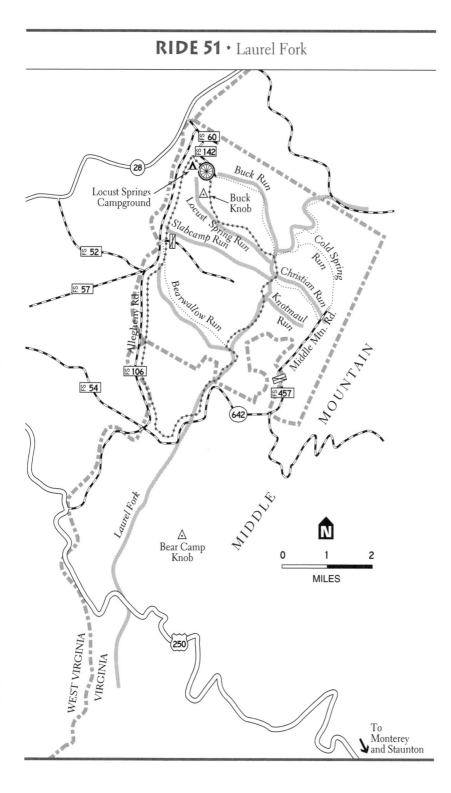

FS 60
FS 142
28
Locust Springs Campground
Buck Run
Buck Knob
Locust Spring Run
Slabcamp Run
Cold Spring Run
Christian Run
Krotmaul Run
FS 52
FS 57
Bearwallow Run
Allegheny Rd.
Middle Mtn. Rd.
FS 106
FS 54
FS 457
642
MOUNTAIN
Laurel Fork
MIDDLE
Bear Camp Knob
N
0   1   2
MILES
WEST VIRGINIA
VIRGINIA
250
To Monterey and Staunton

Riding this 18-mile loop on a combination of single-track, hard-packed Forest Service roads, and creek bed should not be taken as a casual experience. First of all, Laurel Fork Special Management Area is not on the way to anywhere, so if you're going to take the time and trouble to get out here, you'd best be alert to this area's unique qualities. A high level of alertness is also necessary as you pedal or push your way upstream on Laurel Fork Trail, which appears and disappears as rapidly as some of the rare wildlife tucked away in this corner of Highland County.

When I rode this loop, the trail was washed out in some spots and had disappeared in others, so I ended up using the fork itself as my guide. This wasn't bad in July, but keep in mind that the temperatures at this altitude are going to be considerably cooler than at lower elevations. This is definitely a fair-weather ride for those who are in very good shape and feel comfortable being disoriented at times in a remote semiwilderness area. Come to think of it, Laurel Fork in the winter may be just the place to train for Alaska's Iditibike.

Laurel Fork is a 9,900-acre special management area because of its unique flora and fauna, much of which Virginians can see only in this corner of the state. Although a part of George Washington National Forest in name and management, Laurel Fork is contiguous with West Virginia's Monongahela National Forest, of which it was once a part. Elevations of 2,700 feet to over 4,000 feet result in a forest of northern hardwoods and montane red spruce unlike the Appalachian oak forest you'll see throughout the rest of George Washington National Forest. The animal life in these parts is also quite unique, including the northern flying squirrel, snowshoe hare, fisher, and water shrew. Although not on anyone's endangered or threatened list, the mountain laurel reaches heights of 40-plus feet.

Laurel Fork runs south to north on its way to the Potomac River. The fork divides this isolated 9,900-acre area into two sides. Much controversy has surrounded this spot and how to tap its underground natural gas deposits, so periodically you'll see wells along the roads. There are more than 28 miles of trails, many of which were used by trams in the early 1900s to remove native spruce, hemlock, and other indigenous hardwoods. These include Bear-wallow and Slabcamp Run Trails, which are roughly parallel and connect the western edge of Laurel Fork with Laurel Fork Trail. Because of Laurel Fork's unique qualities and the distance from much of Virginia, it makes sense to spend some extra time exploring.

General location: 30 miles north of Monterey, Virginia.

Elevation change: Start at Locust Springs Campground where the elevation is approximately 3,700'. From there you'll descend to Laurel Fork at 2,900'. Going upstream to the intersection of Laurel Fork with VA 642 will take on a very gradual ascent to 3,216'. You'll have a pretty decent climb to 3,654' before turning right onto Allegheny Road (FS 106) and continuing to climb to 3,800'

Laurel Fork's unique northern boreal community is home to over 25 indigenous species of flora and fauna found nowhere else in Virginia.

just outside Locust Springs Recreation Area. A short descent will take you back to the start of the ride. The climb from 2,900' to 3,800' covers 14 miles.

Season: Late spring through early fall. Winter comes early and stays late in the Potomac Highlands, and it takes few prisoners. Riders should also use caution during fall and winter hunting seasons and dress in highly visible attire. Call the Virginia Department of Game and Inland Fisheries (540-248-9360) for the opening and closing dates of hunting seasons for various game animals.

Services: There are several sources for lodging and food in Monterey. Primitive camping and water are available at Locust Spring Recreation Area at the start of the ride, and there's good trout fishing in Laurel Fork. Rustic lodgings are available at the Endless Mountain Retreat Center.

Hazards: Laurel Fork Trail and the body of water of the same name merge in places; this is more than unpleasant when the water level is high and temperatures are low.

You may see snowshoe hare, northern flying squirrels, and the occasional mountain biker in remote Laurel Fork Special Management Area.

Rescue index: This is a pretty remote spot, so the best chance of getting help is to backtrack toward Monterey.

Land status: George Washington National Forest—Warm Springs Ranger District.

Maps: George Washington National Forest map of the Warm Springs Ranger District; USGS 7.5 minute quads: Thornwood and Snowy Mountain.

Finding the trail: Take US 250 west out of Staunton and continue across the mountain ranges of Highland County. Pass through Monterey on US 250 and into West Virginia. Monterey is approximately 55 miles west of Staunton, but the series of mountain ranges in Highland County will add considerably to your travel time. Turn right onto WV 28, heading north for about 6 miles. Then turn right onto FS 106 and follow the signs to the Locust Springs Recreation Area, where you'll park to begin this ride.

Sources of additional information:

Warm Springs Ranger District of the
George Washington National Forest
Highway 220 South/Route 2, Box 30
Hot Springs, Virginia 24445
(540) 839-2521

Rick Lambert
Highland Adventures
P.O. Box 151
Monterey, Virginia 24465
(540) 468-2722

Highland County Chamber
of Commerce
P.O. Box 223
Monterey, Virginia 24465
(540) 468-2550

Tom Brody
Endless Mountain Retreat Center
HC 2, Box 141
Hightown, Virginia 24465
(540) 468-2700
e-mail: endless@mountainretreat.com
www.mountain-retreat.com

Notes on the trail: Start riding downhill away from the Locust Springs shelter on the grassy, double-track Locust Spring Run Trail, marked by blue blazes. One-half mile later, the grassy double-track becomes a more challenging, rocky single-track, crossing Locust Spring Run repeatedly before joining Laurel Fork. Native mountain laurel reaching heights of 20–30' grow here, but try to keep at least one eye on the slick, rocky trail as it continues downhill—the last downhill you're going to see for the entire ride, in fact.

Once you reach Laurel Fork, turn right and head upstream. You'll be going more or less uphill for the next 14 miles, but a larger concern should be staying on top of—or at least in the vicinity of—Laurel Fork Trail, which is as illusive as the snowshoe hare and northern flying squirrel that call this area home. There's no avoiding the fact that you'll be hiking, slogging, or swimming your way up the fork, so make sure weather conditions afford some margin of comfort for getting wet. However, if you come during a dry stretch in July, you need not worry about getting wet, contracting hypothermia, and the like. In early spring or late fall, your margin of error gets smaller.

Continue up Laurel Fork, passing the Bearwallow and Slabcamp Run Trails, two of the many former tram beds for removing timber. Both trails intersect Allegheny Road, which you'll be joining in a more roundabout fashion. However, if weather, trail condition, or physical factors require that you do a shorter ride (or cut the 14-mile climb somewhat), you can turn right onto one of these two trails. This changes the total ride mileage to 8.6 miles via Slabcamp Trail and 13.2 miles via Bearwallow Trail.

For those of you going the full distance, continue along Laurel Fork as it changes from the flat, grassy tram bed it once was to the rocky creek bed of Laurel Fork.

Eventually, after you pass a small cabin on the left, you'll turn right onto VA 642 where Laurel Fork intersects this secondary road. Several miles later, you'll again turn right at a well-marked intersection with Allegheny Road

(FS 106). The climbing begins in earnest on this 8-mile homestretch. Continue to the intersection with FS 60, which may look familiar from your previous entrance into Locust Spring Recreation Area. Turn right onto FS 60 to finish the ride on a short downhill back at the Locust Spring shelter.

RIDE 52 · Lake Robertson

AT A GLANCE

Length/Configuration: Several combinations of out-and-back and loop rides can be created from trails less than 2 miles long

Aerobic difficulty: Minimal to moderate

Technical difficulty: Minimal, depending on the trail chosen

Scenery: Wooded setting surrounding a 31-acre lake at the foot of North Mountain

Special comments: Good for family rides; the public campground offers swimming, boating, and fishing, among other outdoor recreational activities

The 581-acre Lake A. Willis Robertson recreation area is somewhat overshadowed by neighboring George Washington and Jefferson National Forests, which are not only much larger but also named for Virginia statesmen more prominent than former Senator A. Willis Robertson, father of TV evangelist Pat Robertson. Be that as it may, this beautiful spot at the base of North Mountain west of Lexington is truly an undiscovered gem in western Virginia. It's so undiscovered that several communiqués between myself, the park superintendent, and park personnel were necessary to ascertain that mountain bikes were indeed allowed on their trail system.

I don't describe a specific ride, for you should look at this recreational complex as a system of trails (all less than two miles in length) from which to develop your own particular route. The trails range from single-track to woods roads and a combination thereof, running uphill away from the 31-acre lake. As the trails get farther away from the lake, they tend to get less defined.

Given the range of outdoor recreational facilities, the relative short length of the trails, and the ease of riding, this is an excellent destination for families and less experienced mountain bikers. Lake Robertson also makes a great base camp from which to explore some of the rides located in nearby George Washington and Jefferson forests.

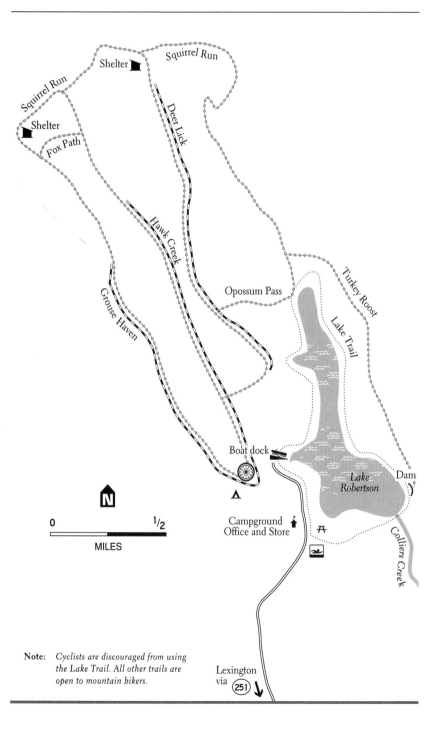

Shelter

Squirrel Run

Squirrel Run

Shelter

Fox Path

Deer Lick

Hawk Creek

Grouse Haven

Opossum Pass

Turkey Roost

Lake Trail

Boat dock

Lake Robertson

Dam

Colliers Creek

N

0   1/2

MILES

Campground
Office and Store

Note: Cyclists are discouraged from using
the Lake Trail. All other trails are
open to mountain bikers.

Lexington
via (251)

213

The leaf-covered trails around Lake Robertson at the foot of North Mountain are a great place to ride on a brisk autumn day.

General location: 14 miles west of Lexington.

Elevation change: Changes from 1,400–2,200' from east to west, away from the lake.

Season: Summer is the best time for families to visit because all facilities are open, although for riding the only limiting factors would be winter snow and ice, and pressure during hunting seasons. Call the Virginia Department of Game and Inland Fisheries (540-248-9360) for the opening and closing dates of hunting seasons for various game animals. Be sure to wear brightly colored attire if riding during any of the fall and winter hunting seasons.

Services: This recreation area offers 53 campsites, a 31-acre lake for fishing and boating, a swimming pool, a picnic area, drinking water, and a camp store. All other services are available in Lexington.

Hazards: Trail blazes become scarce as you get farther from the lake. Trails are not necessarily maintained for mountain bike use, so don't be surprised by nature's obstacles in your path.

Rescue index: Assistance can be solicited from the office or camp store.

Land status: Public land administered by Rockbridge County Parks.

Maps: A brochure with a map is available from the camp store at Lake Robertson; USGS 7.5 minute quads: Collierstown and Longdale Furnace

Finding the trail: From Intersate 81 or I-64, take US 11 to the south side of Lexington. Follow the signs to Lake Robertson near Collierstown. The recreation area is located approximately 14 miles west of Lexington near Collierstown on VA 770.

Source of additional information:

Superintendent   Lexington, Virginia 24450
Lake A. Willis Robertson   (540) 463-4164
RFD 2, Box 251

Notes on the trail: Park personnel have requested that riders stay off the narrow Lake Trail that hugs the edge of Lake Robertson. However, that leaves a number of possible biking options ranging from one-half-mile-long (one-way distance) Opossum Pass and Squirrel Run Trails to the 1.75-mile (one-way distance) Turkey Roost Trail. The hard-core mountain biker probably isn't going to beat a path to Western Rockbridge County to try out a combination of sub-2-mile trails. For the novice or family wanting to go to the mountains with the relative comforts of a well-equipped campground and a number of other outdoor pursuits close at hand, Lake Robertson might be just the right place.

RIDE 53 · Longdale Recreation Area

AT A GLANCE

Length/Configuration: 11-mile loop

Aerobic difficulty: The initial 2-mile climb will make you huff and puff

Technical difficulty: Some natural obstacles and creek crossings on the 3-mile single-track section

Scenery: Pedal in the shadow of North Mountain, then through a densely wooded riparian area along Sinking Creek

Special comments: Combine this novice ride with swimming at Longdale Recreation Area

This 11-mile loop is a good beginner's alternative to the tough climb that is part of the North Mountain Ridge route (Ride 54) that also starts at the Longdale Recreation Area. The majority of the ride follows moderate ups and downs on gravel Forest Service roads, but undoubtedly the best part is a three-mile section of logging road and single-track that carves its way through a wooded section of Boggs Hollow and crisscrosses Sinking Creek. The woods section is the only part that might cause any problem for novice bikers, but it's just a matter of dismounting and walking through questionable areas.

This local community grew up around the Longdale Furnace, one of the many western Virginia furnaces that developed around the region's abundance of high-grade iron ore. These dotted the immediate area from 1822 until 1922, when the last furnace closed its doors for good.

General location: 20 miles west of Lexington; 20 miles east of Covington.

Elevation change: The ride starts at 1,335' and ascends gradually to 1,980' on FS 271 before descending through the woods along Sinking Creek.

Season: Those looking forward to a swim in the lake will want to schedule their visit during the summer, when all of the facilities at Longdale Recreation Area are open. However, those interested in mountain biking only can ride year-round when the snow and ice of winter don't impede travel on the hard-packed forest roads or single-track through the woods. Be especially careful during the succession of hunting seasons that begin in the fall; wear bright clothes, preferably blaze orange, at those times. Call the Virginia Department of Game and Inland Fisheries (540-248-9360) for the opening and closing dates of hunting seasons for various game animals.

Services: The Longdale Recreation Area was built by the Dolly Ann CCC Camp in 1939 and was originally called Green Pastures Forest Camp. It has a small swimming lake with a sandy beach, a bathhouse with flush toilets, and picnic sites. It is a fee-charged area. Services are widely available in Lexington or Covington.

Hazards: Creek crossings and single-track section through woods.

Rescue index: Help can be summoned from other park visitors and some of the commercial establishments on US 60.

Land status: George Washington National Forest—James River Ranger District.

Maps: George Washington National Forest map of the James River Ranger District; USGS 7.5 minute quads: Clifton Forge, Longdale Furnace, and Sugarloaf Mountain.

Finding the trail: From Lexington, take Interstate 64 west and get off at the Longdale Furnace exit. Continue west on US 60 and turn left at the sign for Longdale Recreation Area. Continue on the left fork (FS 271) past the driveway entering the recreation area. Leave your vehicle at the small parking area on the left just after you pass the sign and intersection of North Mountain Trail.

Source of additional information:

James River Ranger District of the George Washington National Forest
810-A Madison Avenue
Covington, Virginia 24426
(540) 962-2214

Notes on the trail: Start at the small parking area on FS 271 adjacent to the sign for North Mountain Trail. Begin riding gradually uphill on FS 271 and turn left onto 271-B. Although this road is not marked, there is a stop sign for traffic on 271-B located at a sharp bend in FS 271. Stay on this road and continue past the gate at the end of the road. The subsequent trail is an unblazed, old logging road that is relatively easy to follow around a number of small ravines and runoffs that find their way into Sinking Creek.

You'll near the end of the wooded section as you cross a series of earthen berms before the double-track becomes seriously rutted, although it's flat and still quite ridable. Notice the rock ledge/waterfall on the left of the trail partially obscured by a dense grove of hemlocks. A little way after this waterfall you'll turn left onto an unmarked dirt road (FS 271-C). Shortly after this intersection, FS 271-A heads left toward the Longdale Recreation Area. Go that direction if you're ready for a swim. Otherwise, continue the gradual climb on a long straight section of forest road before careening on a 2-mile downhill back to the beginning.

RIDE 54 · North Mountain Ridge

AT A GLANCE

Length/Configuration: 17-mile loop

Aerobic difficulty: Considerable on the initial 5-mile climb

Technical difficulty: Considerable as you tiptoe across the rocky North Mountain ridge

Scenery: Breathtaking panoramic views of the Shenandoah Valley

Special comments: This ride combines a tough 5-mile climb, views from the top of the world, and a delicious 4-mile descent

E arly European settlers used "North Mountain" to refer to many mountains on the western side of Virginia's Great Valley. Once you reach the ridge line of this ride, you'll see why the Native American term *endless mountains* seems to fit much better. Semantics aside, you're sure to flip (not literally, I hope) over the endless views from atop this particular North Mountain.

Andy Hunter, longtime proprietor of the Lexington Bike Shop, shared this 17-mile loop with me, and you'll have to stop by his shop to thank him after crossing the top of North Mountain and marveling at the awesome views east toward Lake Robertson and Lexington. Note that I don't use the word *awesome* in the current adolescent vernacular but in the sense that the views "inspire an emotion that combines dread, veneration, and wonder." I definitely felt all three, although the dread didn't occur until I met up with a skunk on the trail.

Take plenty of time to look out from the rock outcroppings atop this ridge line at 3,200 feet. The orange-blazed trail is relatively easy to follow, but in tricky places you can also look for the faded blue blazes that previously marked this route to the top of North Mountain. The loop combines grassy double-track, single-track, and gravel forest roads to create a really awesome ride. And this time I do mean it in the adolescent vernacular. Intermediate and better riders will love every aspect of this ride, but the climb may be too demanding for those with less ability or experience.

General location: 20 miles west of Lexington; 20 miles east of Covington.

Elevation change: The ride starts at 1,335' and climbs steadily for 5 miles before reaching the top of North Mountain at 3,200'. The trail rises and falls gradually over the next 3 miles as it follows the top of the ridge. After joining VA 770, the ride takes you on a 4-mile descent, dropping 1,300'.

Season: Year-round, although snow and ice at higher elevations in winter make this ride inadvisable. Riders should also use caution during fall and winter hunting seasons and wear highly visible attire, preferably blaze orange. Call the Virginia Department of Game and Inland Fisheries (540-248-9360) for the opening and closing dates of hunting seasons for various game animals.

Services: Available in Lexington or Covington.

Hazards: Steep drop-offs to the east from the top of North Mountain. North Mountain Trail can be a little tricky to find from the end of Forest Service Road 334.

Rescue index: Assistance can be summoned from fellow visitors, commercial establishments or the Sheriff's Department.

Land status: George Washington National Forest—James River Ranger District.

Maps: George Washington National Forest map of the James River Ranger

District; USGS 7.5 minute quad: Longdale Furnace.

Finding the trail: From Lexington, take Interstate 64 west and get off at the Longdale Furnace exit. Continue west on US 60 and turn left into Longdale Recreation Area. Continue on the left fork (FS 271) past the driveway into the recreation area. Leave your vehicle at the small parking area on the left just after you pass the sign and intersection of North Mountain Trail.

Sources of additional information:

James River Ranger District of the
  George Washington National Forest
810-A Madison Avenue
Covington, Virginia 24426
(540) 962-2214

Lexington Bike Shop
130 South Main Street
Lexington, Virginia 24450
(540) 463-7969

Notes on the trail: The trail begins as an overgrown woods road and climbs for the first 5 miles, starting off moderately and becoming steeper before reaching the ridge line. After crossing a second set of earthen berms, you'll descend briefly and climb again before arriving at the intersection where the Simmons Road ends by abutting North Mountain Trail. At this point you'll turn right and head uphill just before crossing Piney Mountain Branch. Toward the end of the ride you'll come in the opposite direction to this point from Simmons Road.

You'll be riding and walking on single-track through a dense riparian area shaded by towering hemlocks and hardwoods with an understory of moss, thick lush ferns, and beautiful rock formations. There is a series of marked and not so well marked creek crossings, but keep in mind that you're ascending this creek bed ravine and guide yourself accordingly. Finally you'll reach a saddle between 2 small peaks near the boundary between George Washington and Jefferson National Forests.

North Mountain Trail takes a sharp ascent up the peak on the left while the other fork of the trail heads across Blacks Gap and onto an isolated section of Jefferson's Glenwood District across Green Hill. When the trail finally reaches the summit after 5 miles, there will be no doubt that your efforts have been rewarded with views that on a clear day stretch across the valley to the Blue Ridge Mountains.

You'll see few blazes across the top of the mountain, but follow the obvious single-track as it circumvents rock outcroppings, cuts through a deep thicket of rhododendron, and maneuvers a rock passageway that looks like something out of an Indiana Jones movie. Before reaching VA 770, the trail across the top narrows and it's a sheer rock face on the right side, so be sure to stop and admire those great views. On one section of this trail I narrowly avoided a close encounter with Peppi La Pew, but I gave this black and white critter a wide berth and plenty of time to make his way across. Snakes have

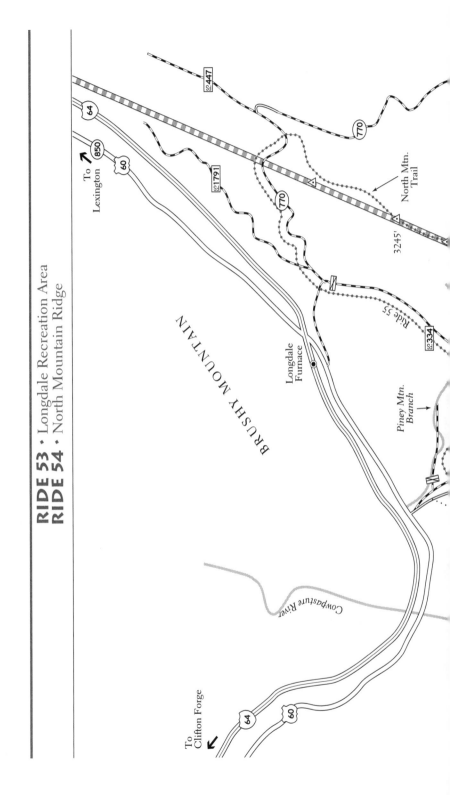

RIDE 53 · Longdale Recreation Area
RIDE 54 · North Mountain Ridge

To
Lexington

FS447

770

770

FS1791

North Mtn.
Trail

3245'

Ride 55

FS334

BRUSHY MOUNTAIN

Longdale
Furnace

Piney Mtn.
Branch

Cowpasture River

To
Clifton Forge

64

60

64

850

60

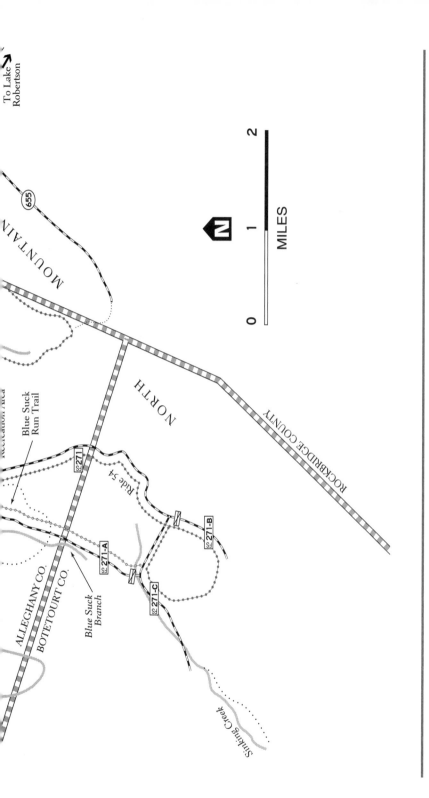

To Lake Robertson

655

MOUNTAIN

Blue Suck Run Trail

NORTH

FR 271

Ride 54

FR 271-A

FR 271-B

FR 271-C

Blue Suck Branch

ALLEGHANY CO.
BOTETOURT CO.

ROCKBRIDGE COUNTY

Sinking Creek

N

MILES

0   1   2

A chance to overlook the rest of the world is the payoff for the long climb up North Mountain.

long gotten a bad rap, but I'd much prefer to encounter a rattler at close quarters to sharing the trail with a skunk.

North Mountain Trail eventually intersects with VA 770, and at this point you'll bid adieu to the ridge line and begin a very exciting 4-mile descent down the left side of North Mountain on this gravel road. Then take another left onto FS 334 (also called Simmons Road). Pass the gate at the beginning of the road and continue until the road ends. At this point you're not far from the intersection you previously encountered just before Piney Mountain Branch, but it is a little tricky.

Continue past the earthen berms where the road ends and through the thick undergrowth of crown vetch. Look for a high road to the left and a low road to the right. Take the high road slightly uphill and continue until you see a trail emerge through the vegetation on a roadside surface. After a narrow creek crossing, the road will again appear to fork; this time go straight over another set of bunkers before you arrive on North Mountain Trail. At this point you'll backtrack 2.5 miles downhill on the section that started this ride.

A good alternative to this ride's considerable climbing is to start from the intersection of North Mountain Trail and VA 770 and do a down-and-back ride across the top of North Mountain.

RIDE 55 · Dry Run

AT A GLANCE

Length/Configuration: 10-mile point-to-point, or 20-mile round-trip for hardier riders

Aerobic difficulty: Considerable for the 4-mile climb on rocky single- and double-track

Technical difficulty: Ample rocky, obstructed single-track, especially on the steep, rutted descent of Bald Knob

Scenery: Beautiful stands of mountain laurel along Dry Run and views of neighboring peaks

Special comments: This ride makes you ponder the coexistence of industry and Mother Nature

As you begin pedaling on this ten-mile point-to-point (or tough, 20-mile round-trip ride) from the end of Cypress Street in Covington onto Dry Run Road (FS 339), you'll find it hard to believe that Dry Run's rushing waters and lush growths of mountain laurel and sassafras will quickly replace the sulfurous smells emanating from Westvaco's smokestacks; but after a mile and a half of climbing on a Forest Service road, that's exactly what happens. It amazed me how rapidly I was thrust into a verdant setting that resembled some of the wilderness areas I've hiked through over the years.

This is a great route, and I plan to return to ride it with a better supply of spare tubes. This was not the case on my first trip, so I ended up doing a good bit of C & C (carrying and coasting.) The two-and-a-half-mile, technical, double-track descent on Dry Run Trail is guaranteed to keep you grinning for weeks. I completed this ride with the assistance of a second vehicle, which worked out well since I dragged my one-wheeled bike for a good bit of this ten-mile point-to-point outing. Most riders of average fitness levels and bike handling skills could do this as a one-way trip, but anyone planning to do a 20-mile round-trip should be intermediate or better—and have a more-than-adequate supply of spare tubes.

General location: Northern end of Covington.

Elevation change: The ride starts at 1,440' and climbs to a saddle between Peter's Ridge (3,610') and one of the peaks of Bald Knob (3,840') at 3,640' before dropping down to FS 125 at an elevation of 2,454'.

Season: Ice and snow make this ride inadvisable during the winter months. Be especially careful during the succession of hunting seasons that begin in the fall; wear bright clothes, preferably blaze orange, at those times. Call the Virginia Department of Game and Inland Fisheries (540-248-9360) for the opening and closing dates of hunting seasons for various game animals.

Services: All services are available in the city of Covington, which adjoins both ends of this ride.

Hazards: Crossing Dry Run can be treacherous when the water level is high, and the final 2.5-mile descent on loose rocky surface could pose some difficulties.

Rescue index: Although while you're on the trail you'll have the impression that you're in the middle of nowhere, the ends of this point-to-point are only minutes from civilization and assistance if needed.

Land status: George Washington National Forest—James River Ranger District.

Maps: George Washington National Forest map of the James River Ranger District; USGS 7.5 minute quad: Covington.

Finding the trail: Begin the ride at the end of Cypress Street in Covington. The gravel road on the other side of the gate is FS 339 although it is not marked as such.

Sources of additional information:

James River Ranger District of the
George Washington National Forest
810-A Madison Avenue
Covington, Virginia 24426
(540) 962-2214

Allegheny Highlands Chamber of
Commerce
241 West Main Street
Covington, Virginia 24426
(540) 962-2178

Notes on the trail: Continue up FS 339 until it ends abruptly. From there follow the orange diamonds through the woods onto the otherwise unmarked Dry Run single-track trail. After a short descent, you'll come to a lush area where Dry Run cascades across some beautiful rock formations. This is a great place to stop, have lunch, or fix a flat tire (as was the case for me).

Unfortunately, it's also a good place to lose the trail. Dry Run (the creek) and the trail of the same name become intermingled here, and someone missed a good opportunity to put some of those orange plastic blazes to good use and clarify things. The best advice I can offer is that you'll cross the stream twice and start climbing this ravine in a northeasterly direction before you pick up some blazes and the trail itself. Eventually you'll leave Dry Run behind and climb through a profuse stand of mountain laurel and wild blueberries growing at the trail's edge.

The trail levels off somewhat and begins to follow the shoulder of Big Knob's twin peaks which, at more than 4,000', are the higher points in the Allegheny Mountains.

RIDE 55 ⋆ Dry Run
RIDE 56 ⋆ Fore Mountain Trail

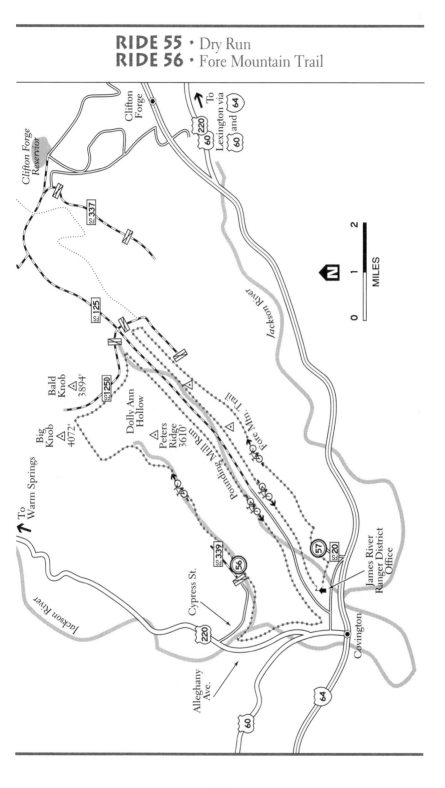

Shortly thereafter, the trail becomes more ridable double-track. Continue and eventually you'll start to drop after reaching nearby Bald Knob (3,894'). With the trees bare, you'll have some great views to the east of Piney Ridge and Fore Mountain. Dry Run Trail (actually a road at this point) gets rocky after starting to descend radically, so check your brakes and sit back to enjoy a hairy 2.5-mile drop, losing 1,346' before the intersection with FS 125.

RIDE 56 • Fore Mountain Trail

AT A GLANCE

Length/Configuration: 15-mile loop

Aerobic difficulty: Considerable on the 4-mile climb on rocky single- and double-track

Technical difficulty: Ample rocky, obstructed single-track—especially on the steep, rutted descent of Bald Knob

Scenery: Beautiful stands of mountain laurel along Dry Run and views of neighboring peaks

Special comments: A ride through this beautiful, verdant area may change your ideas about the coexistence of industry and Mother Nature

If the sum of your knowledge about Covington is that it's a mill town largely dependent on the tree-chewing efforts of the Westvaco paper corporation, this 15-mile loop on single-track, double-track, forest road, and hard-surface roads should offer a pleasant surprise. Fore Mountain Trail quickly leaves the sounds and smells of the city behind for some breathtaking views from atop Fore Mountain, towering growths of mountain laurel growing along Pounding Mill Run as it crashes over its rocky bed, and a six-mile descent to end the ride.

Fore Mountain Trail is one of those rare single-track hiking trails that's also very suitable for mountain biking. However, its rocky surface makes it more suitable for intermediate and better riders, especially on the climbs. The four-mile downhill stretch on hard-packed Forest Service Road 125 is suitable for riders of any ability level, especially on the downhill toward US 60. The huge stands of mountain laurel and massive hemlocks growing along the banks of Pounding Mill Creek create a natural beauty that seems incongruous with Covington's industrial base.

General location: Just east of Covington on US 60.

Elevation change: The trail starts at 1,400' and ascends steeply on narrow single-track before reaching the ridge line near 2,700'. The trail rises and falls with the top of Fore Mountain before beginning a nice 6-mile descent from Fore Mountain Trail on Dry Run Trail, to intersect with FS 125 at 2,454'. FS 125 continues to follow the downhill course of Pounding Mill Creek back to the start of the ride.

Season: Ice and snow make this ride inadvisable during winter months. Be especially careful during the succession of hunting seasons that begin in the fall; wear bright clothes at those times. Call the Virginia Department of Game and Inland Fisheries (540-248-9360) for the opening and closing dates of hunting seasons for various game animals.

Services: All services can be found in Covington.

Hazards: The trail is blocked in several places by downed trees. Getting around these infrequent obstacles is doable but tricky.

Rescue index: Help can be found at any number of businesses on US 60 near the trailhead.

Land status: George Washington National Forest—James River Ranger District.

Maps: George Washington National Forest map of the James River Ranger District; USGS 7.5 minute quad: Covington.

Finding the trail: The trailhead is well marked and begins next to the Dolly Anne Work Center on US 60 east of Covington.

Sources of additional information:

James River Ranger District of the
  George Washington National Forest
810-A Madison Avenue
Covington, Virginia 24426
(540) 962-2214

Allegheny Highlands Chamber of
  Commerce
241 West Main Street
Covington, Virginia 24426
(540) 962-2178

Notes on the trail: Start this ride near the Dolly Ann Work Center on Smoky Bear Lane (FS 125) located off US 60 just east of Covington. Leave your vehicle in the parking area on the left just before the gate and the Dolly Anne Work Center. Follow the orange blazes and ascend steeply on the single-track Fore Mountain Trail. The trail levels off after the initial 2-mile climb, following a ridge just below the peak of Fore Mountain.

Interstate 64 and Westvaco's smokestacks will become a distant memory as the towering hardwoods cool you off and trailside wild blueberries are yours for the picking. Although in several spots the trail is blocked or intersected by woods roads, the orange blazes are well placed and Fore Mountain Trail is not hard to follow.

After passing a gate across the trail while descending, turn left onto Dry

Run Trail and go through another gate before the intersection with FS 125. You'll continue to descend on this forest road, which is accompanied by the trout-stocked waters of Pounding Mill Creek and some impressive stands of 25-foot native mountain laurel.

This last descent starts on Fore Mountain Trail and ends where gravel FS 125 turns into hard-surface Dolly Anne Drive. You've rejoined civilization, so start watching for vehicular traffic. When you reach well-traveled US 60, carefully cross the median and turn left. Continue through several busy intersections before turning left at the Western Sizzlin' Steak House, where Smoky Bear Lane leads back to your vehicle.

RIDE 57 • Blue Suck Falls

AT A GLANCE

Length/Configuration: 4.5-mile loop

Aerobic difficulty: Moderately tough climbs; don't let the short length of this ride deceive you

Technical difficulty: Trails are generally smooth, but watch out for rocks and blowdowns

Scenery: Lake Douthat, waterfalls, and dense hemlock woods with wild blueberries

Special comments: Good ride for advanced novices and better cyclists

Let's face it, the name of this 4.5-mile loop at Douthat State Park is enough to pique the curiosity of most riders and entice them to western Virginia. However, the additional attraction of one of the area's finest downhill single-track sections is no turnoff either. Intermediates and advanced beginners will find this a memorable mountain biking experience.

It would be relatively easy to overlook this 4,493-acre state park because of its proximity to over one million acres of national forest. However, Douthat can easily stand on its own merits: the charm of its facility, the beauty of its site, and, of course, the quality of mountain biking experience on its trails. Opened as one of Virginia's six original state parks in the early 1930s, Douthat and its future generations of users were the fortunate recipients of the pride and perseverance of the country's Civilian Conservation Corps workers. Between 1923 and 1942 the workers cleared trails and built a dam, cabins, a restaurant, a guest lodge, picnic areas, a swimming beach, and other recreational facilities that remain ours to enjoy. In 1986 on the fiftieth anniversary of this park and the entire Virginia State Park System, Douthat State Park was recognized as a Registered Historic Landmark.

General location: 40 miles southwest of Lexington.

Elevation change: The ride begins at an elevation of 1,367' and climbs to 2,160'. It then drops back to the start after a fantastic downhill stretch.

Season: Ice and snow make this ride inadvisable during the winter months. Be especially careful during the succession of hunting seasons that begin in the fall; wear bright clothes at those times. Call the Virginia Department of Game and Inland Fisheries (540-248-9360) for the opening and closing dates of hunting seasons for various game animals.

Services: Douthat State Park offers camping, cabin rentals, picnic shelters, swimming from a sand beach, boating, and fishing. A fee is charged for area usage. Other services are available in nearby Clifton Forge.

Hazards: Ascents and descents on semitechnical single-track. Watch for other trail users.

Rescue index: The park office is located 1 mile from the Stony Run trail-head on VA 629.

Land status: Douthat State Park.

Maps: A trail map is available from Douthat State Park; www.dcr.state.va.us/parks; USGS 7.5 minute quad: Healing Springs.

Finding the trail: From Interstate 64, take VA 629 north for 9 miles until you enter the park. Park at the Stony Run trailhead on the left side of VA 629.

Source of additional information:
Douthat State Park
Route 1, Box 212
Millboro, Virginia 24460
(540) 862-8100

Notes on the trail: You'll begin the ride with a steep climb up Tobacco Ridge Trail, after which you'll drop down to intersect with Blue Suck Falls Trail. Go left, heading toward the falls. This section of trail is pretty rocky since it follows the creek bed draining the falls. Bear right at the falls, but be sure not to go any higher up the trail than the falls. The next intersection will be with Pine Tree Trail. Turn right here and after a short climb you'll begin one of my favorite downhill sections in the national forest. Enjoy yourself, but watch out for other trail users ahead of you. Turn right onto Salt Stump Trail and take another right onto Backway Hollow Trail at the next junction.

This trail carries you down to Douthat Lake. There's nothing more spec-tacular than a mountain lake, and this one is no exception. Follow the lake trail in a counterclockwise direction around the 50-acre body of water, and at the south end pedal left onto Blue Suck Trail. This leads to a gravel road and

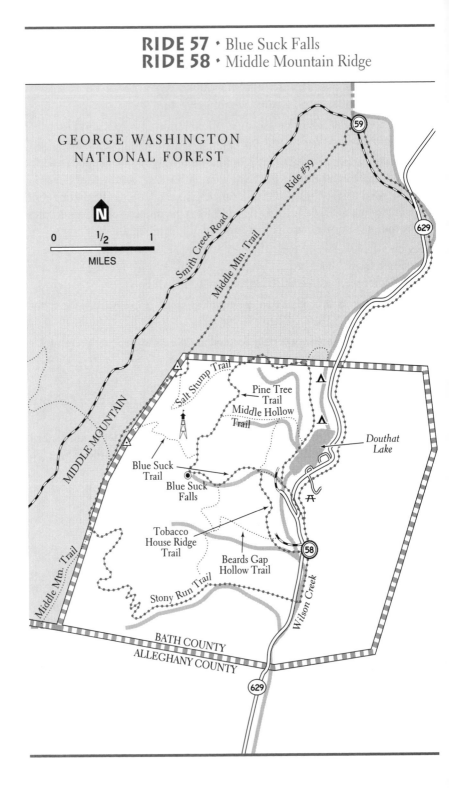

GEORGE WASHINGTON
NATIONAL FOREST

N

0   ½   1

MILES

Smith Creek Road

Middle Mtn. Trail

Ride #59

59

629

Salt Stump Trail

Pine Tree Trail

Middle Hollow Trail

Douthat Lake

MIDDLE MOUNTAIN

Blue Suck Trail

Blue Suck Falls

Tobacco House Ridge Trail

Beards Gap Hollow Trail

58

Middle Mtn. Trail

Stony Run Trail

Wilson Creek

BATH COUNTY
ALLEGHANY COUNTY

629

then out to VA 629, the main road through the park. Turn right onto this road and finish the ride. If anyone asks about this ride, go ahead and tell them "It sucked" and save that downhill for yourself.

RIDE 58 · Middle Mountain Ridge

AT A GLANCE

Length/Configuration: 11-mile loop

Aerobic difficulty: Includes some tough single-track climbs; don't let the short length deceive you

Technical difficulty: Plenty of rocks and blowdowns

Scenery: Lake Douthat and neighboring peaks from atop the ridge

Special comments: The dangerously fast 3.5-mile downhill at the end of the ride will give you a permanent grin

This single-track ride across the top of Middle Mountain is a longer and more challenging ride than Blue Suck Trail at Douthat State Park and others in this guide. You can set it up as a 6.5-mile point-to-point by using a shuttle vehicle or an 11-mile loop with the additional mileage on hard-surface and gravel roads. Either way you'll test your abilities on demanding single-track climbs as well as a 3.5-mile descent that's guaranteed to have you clenching your teeth together for some time to come. Regardless of how you decide to do this ride, you'll get a good workout and a good test of your bike handling skills. Mountain bikers attempting either option should have intermediate or better fitness and bike handling skills.

Douthat State Park is notable for the charm of its facility, the beauty of its site, and, of course, the quality of its mountain biking experience. Opened as one of Virginia's six original state parks in 1936, Douthat and we, the users, were the fortunate recipients of the pride and perseverance of the country's Civilian Conservation Corps workers. Between 1923 and 1942 these workers cleared trails and built a dam, cabins, a restaurant, a guest lodge, picnic areas, a swimming beach, and other recreational facilities that remain ours to enjoy. In 1986 on the fiftieth anniversary of this 4,493-acre park and the entire Virginia State Park System, Douthat State Park was recognized as a Registered Historic Landmark.

General location: 40 miles southwest of Lexington.

Elevation change: Middle Mountain's trailhead sits at 1,840' and immediately climbs via a series of tortuous switchbacks before hitting the Middle Mountain Ridge. The trail continues to rise and fall between peaks and saddles until it intersects Stony Run Trail at a low-lying saddle (3,100'). Stony Run descends in a series of switchbacks and intersects with VA 629 at 1,333'.

Season: Ice and snow make this ride inadvisable during winter months. Be especially careful when riding during the succession of hunting seasons that begin in the fall; wear bright clothes at those times. Call the Virginia Department of Game and Inland Fisheries (540-248-9360) for the opening and closing dates of hunting seasons for various game animals.

Services: Douthat State Park offers campsites, cabin rentals, picnic shelters, swimming from a sand beach, nonmotorized boating, and fishing. A fee is charged for area usage. Additional services are available in nearby Clifton Forge.

Hazards: Very steep ascents and descents on technical single-track.

Rescue index: The park office is located one quarter mile from the Stony Run trailhead on VA 629.

Land status: Douthat State Park.

Maps: A trail map is available from Douthat State Park; USGS 7.5 minute quad: Healing Springs.

Finding the trail: From Interstate 64, take VA 629 north for 9 miles and enter the park. Continue north on VA 629, leave the park's boundaries, and turn left onto Smith Creek Road. Continue to the Middle Mountain trailhead on the left side of the road.

Source of additional information:
Douthat State Park
Route 1, Box 212
Millboro, Virginia 24460
(540) 862-8100

Notes on the trail: Start this ride by pedaling, pushing, or dragging your way up the series of 6 switchbacks on Middle Mountain Trail. Rest assured, the ridge smoothes out over the next 6 miles as you cross the top of this mountain. At a saddle between 2 peaks you'll eventually arrive at the trailhead for Stony Run Trail on the left. Check your brakes, sign your last will and testament, and start to descend one of the hairiest downhills you're likely to encounter (and survive). This 1,700-foot drop twists and turns across a series of switchbacks with relatively few rocks along the way, despite the trail's name. Plan a stop about two-thirds of the way to the bottom at Stony Run Falls, if for no reason other than to let your rims and brake pads cool down. Finish this downhill on VA 629 at Stony Run trailhead for the 6.5-mile point-to-point ride, or pedal down VA 629 for 4.5 miles to finish the 11-mile loop.

RIDE 59 • Big Levels Reservoir Loop

AT A GLANCE

Length/Configuration: 6-mile loop with a maze of overgrown single- and double-track

Aerobic difficulty: Minimal on gently sloping inclines

Technical difficulty: Creek crossings and rocky no-track can be tricky

Scenery: You'll encircle this mountain lake on a densely wooded path

Special comments: After you've completed this relatively easy route, try exploring on your own

Developed in 1930 as a wildlife management area, Big Levels has acquired recent notoriety among Virginia's rapidly growing number of mountain bikers. And deservedly so, since there's something for everyone in this 32,000-acre parcel located at the base of the famed Blue Ridge Mountains. Coal Road (Forest Service Road 42) through Big Levels offers access to numerous fat-tire possibilities in the form of trails and logging roads, most of which are unmarked. Some of the more popular sections of this area are well trodden, so you can easily follow the bike tracks of others and see where they come out.

The Big Levels Reservoir Loop is a good six-mile loop to introduce riders of varied ability levels to the bottomland section of Big Levels. Its ups and downs are minimal, and it is the shorter of the two Big Levels routes presented here. (For a longer and more challenging alternative, take a look at Big Levels to the Blue Ridge.) This loop around the Mills Creek Reservoir offers a sampling of single-track, double-track, and rocky no-track along the reservoir. All in all, it's a good way to get acquainted with this wonderful area. Pack a picnic lunch and plan to eat on the dam overlooking the reservoir with panoramic mountain views as far north as Massanutten.

Big Levels is the destination of choice for a lot of riders who are new either to mountain biking or the area. It's best to think of this area of largely unmarked trails and logging roads as one that is ripe for exploration. The best Big Levels riding results from setting out with map in hand on a sunny day and getting adventurous.

General location: 10 miles south of Waynesboro.

Elevation change: Minimal change in elevation.

Season: Ice and snow make this ride inadvisable during winter months. Be especially careful during the succession of hunting seasons that begin in the fall; wear bright clothes at those times. Call the Virginia Department of

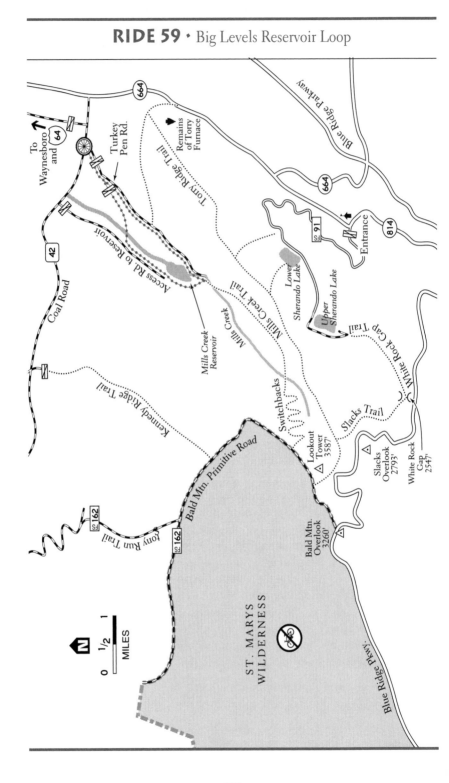

Big Levels' trails and roads attract riders of all ages and ability levels.

Game and Inland Fisheries (540-248-9360) for the opening and closing dates of hunting seasons for various game animals.

Services: There are several gas and food stores along VA 664 near Big Levels. All other services are available in nearby Waynesboro.

Hazards: Riding along the bottom section of Big Levels adjacent to Coal Road involves few risks besides watching out for other riders. Stream crossings can become difficult after periods of heavy rain and in winter.

Rescue index: Assistance can be found at Sherando Lake during the summer when the Sherando Lake Recreation Area is open. At other times, you can summon help from one of the stores along VA 664 between the Coal Road and Waynesboro.

Land status: George Washington National Forest—Pedlar Ranger District.

Maps: George Washington National Forest map of the Pedlar Ranger District; USGS 7.5 minute quads: Big Levels and Sherando.

From above Big Levels Reservoir you can see all the way to Massanutten Mountain on a clear day.

Finding the trail: Take exit 96 (Waynesboro/Lyndhurst) off Interstate 64 and head south on VA 664 toward Sherando Lake. Turn right onto FS 42 and drive three-quarters of a mile on this gravel road. Park on the left at the first well-worn parking area just past a gated road on the right side of Coal Road. The sometimes gated Turkey Pen Road starts here.

Sources of additional information:

Glenwood and Pedlar Ranger Districts
of the George Washington
and Jefferson National Forest
P.O. Box 10, 27 Ranger Lane
Natural Bridge Station, Virginia 24579
(540) 291-2188

Cycle-Recycle
320 West Main Street

Waynesboro, Virginia 22980
(540) 949-8973

Rockfish Gap Outfitters
US 250 East
Waynesboro, Virginia 22980
(540) 943-1461

Notes on the trail: Start riding from the parking area, heading away from Coal Road on unmarked and sometimes gated Turkey Pen Road. Continue on a slight but steady uphill grade before reaching the end of the road. Ride straight across several large berms on what becomes Mills Creek Trail. After pedaling through a thicket of autumn olive crowding the trail on both sides, you'll drop quickly to Mills Creek and cross it.

At this point, approximately 3 miles into the ride, bear to the right onto a visible but unmarked trail that leads behind Turkey Pen Ridge to the back of the reservoir. The trail, such as it is, is not hard to follow, although there are several drops through streams without bridges, so this might not be an advisable ride after heavy rains or when winter would make cold, wet feet no fun.

After arriving at the marshy end of the reservoir, navigate your way to the left side of the reservoir and make your way along the rocky bank where the only thing that resembles a trail is a narrow swath with minimal vegetation. When you pass the reservoir, bear right into a cleared area (as opposed to going left into the woods). Crest the hill even with the dam on the right and be sure to walk over to check out some really great panoramic mountain and water views from atop the dam. Then go downhill on the gravel road, and within one-half mile you should notice an unmarked trail on the right leading into the woods.

Take this trail and traverse a flat section of single-track that leads back to Turkey Pen Road. Although not marked, this trail is generally easy to follow, with the exception of several places where other unmarked trails and old logging roads intersect. There's one good-sized creek crossing, but the rest is pretty smooth sailing until you reach a gate just before Turkey Pen Road. Turn left onto the road and coast back to the beginning.

It should be noted that swimming in the Mills Creek Reservoir is not allowed, nor is camping within 200 feet of the water.

RIDE 60 • Big Levels to the Blue Ridge

AT A GLANCE

Length/Configuration: 21-mile loop with a maze of overgrown single- and double-track

Aerobic difficulty: Local riders use the tortuous climb up Bald Mountain to test their climbing and aerobic capacity

Technical difficulty: Look out for a steep switchback climb, narrow and rocky Mills Creek Trail, and descents along single-track Slacks and White Rock Gap Trails

Scenery: Dense woods with trailside streams and breathtaking views of the Upper and Lower lakes of Sherando

Special comments: Big Levels draws a wide audience of mountain bikers, but the challenge of the switchback ascent separates their abilities

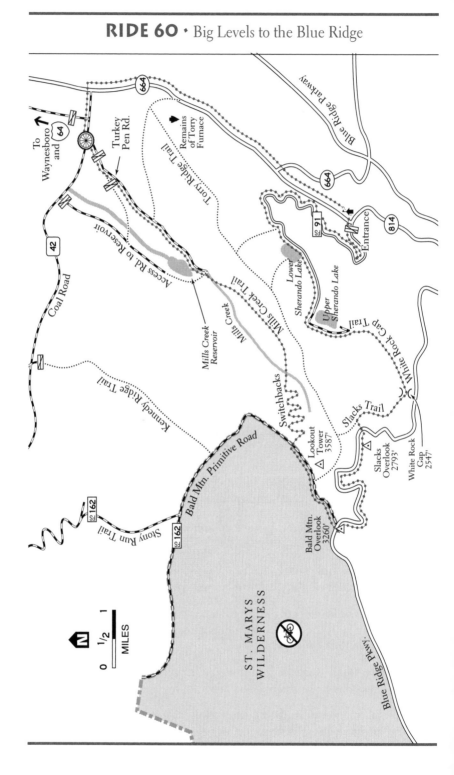

Although Big Levels Reservoir Loop is a nice six-mile introduction to the Big Levels region, those of you looking for the greatest challenges in your mountain biking destinations will want to try something with a little more grit. The heartier will continue pedaling higher up the Blue Mountains, so called by hunting parties of Native Americans who passed through the Shenandoah Valley.

This 21-mile loop will challenge your climbing and aerobic abilities along a tortuous section of barely single-track, known locally as "the Switchbacks," leading up to the Blue Ridge Mountains; recharge your batteries with endless views from the Blue Ridge Parkway; and then delight you with a four-mile single-track descent into the Sherando Lake Recreation Area, where you can swim in the lake before finishing up at Big Levels. Wow, what a ride! Needless to say, this ride should only be attempted by very competent, fit mountain bikers who can handle the tough single-track ascent and descent as well as the total distance.

General location: 10 miles south of Waynesboro.

Elevation change: The most extreme changes in elevation are from Coal Road at the end of Turkey Pen Road (1,595') to the site of Bald Mountain fire tower (3,587') near the parkway via the Switchbacks. The 1.5-mile climb up Bald Mountain gains over 1,000' and is pretty grueling. The 2.8-mile single-track descent from the Blue Ridge Parkway to Sherando Lake drops 1,677'. I've done the descent several times by itself as a point-to-point with vehicles at each end.

Season: Ice and snow make this ride inadvisable during winter months. Be especially careful when riding during the succession of hunting seasons that begin in the fall; wear bright clothes at those times. Call the Virginia Department of Game and Inland Fisheries (540-248-9360) for the opening and closing dates of hunting seasons for various game animals.

Services: You can pick up drinks and snack items at several convenience stores along VA 664. All other services are available south on VA 664 in Waynesboro. Camping and swimming are available at nearby Sherando Lake Recreation Area (April throughOctober only; a fee is charged).

Hazards: Watch for slippery, moss-covered rocks at creek crossings. Heading up to Bald Mountain Road and the Blue Ridge Parkway via the Switchbacks presents its own share of hazards; this is a very steep climb along a very narrow single-track carved out of the side of the mountain. The same is true for the descent from the Blue Ridge Parkway down to Sherando Lake. Be sure to watch out for others on these narrow ascents and descents.

Rescue index: Help can be found near the trailhead at one of the convenience stores along VA 664. You can also flag down a car along the Blue Ridge Parkway or one of the national park service vehicles that regularly

Intrepid mountain bikers take off from Big Levels Reservoir before attempting the tortuous switchback climb up Bald Mountain.

patrol this road. As you near Sherando Lake, you can find help from Forest Service staff at this national forest recreation area.

Land status: George Washington National Forest—Pedlar Ranger District.

Maps: George Washington National Forest map of the Pedlar Ranger District; USGS 7.5 minute quads: Big Levels and Sherando.

Finding the trail: Take exit 96 (Waynesboro/Lyndhurst) off Interstate 64 and head south on VA 664 toward Sherando Lake. Turn right onto FS 42 and drive .75 mile on this gravel road. Park on the left at the first well-worn parking area just past a gated road on the right side of Coal Road. Turkey Pen Road starts here. It is typically gated off January through March.

Sources of additional information:

Cycle-Recycle
320 West Main Street
Waynesboro, Virginia 22980
(540) 949-8973

Rockfish Gap Outfitters
US 250 East
Waynesboro, Virginia 22980
(540) 943-1461

Glenwood and Pedlar Ranger Districts
of the George Washington
and Jefferson National Forest
P.O. Box 10, 27 Ranger Lane
Natural Bridge Station, Virginia 24579
(540) 291-2188

Notes on the trail: Start riding from the parking area, heading away from Coal Road on the unmarked and sometimes gated Turkey Pen Road. Continue on a slight, steady uphill grade before you reach the end of the road. Ride straight across several large berms on what is now Mills Creek Trail. After pedaling through a thicket of autumn olive that crowds the trail on both sides, you'll drop quickly to Mills Creek and cross it.

Follow the blue-blazed Mills Creek Trail to the left at the point where the Big Levels Reservoir Ride turned right onto the unnamed, unmarked trail around the reservoir. However, to ascend the Blue Ridge you'll stay on Mills Creek Trail as it bends to the left. It suddenly gets very steep as it creeps up Bald Mountain via a series of switchbacks over the next mile and a half. This section of the trail is very narrow, and riders I've encountered are more intent on speed than concern for their fellow mountain bikers. A word to the wise: keep an eye out for downhill riders and yield the right-of-way.

When you finally reach the top, be sure to treat yourself to a big drink of water and some gooey, sugary treat. You earned it! Here you'll turn left onto Bald Mountain Road and head to the Blue Ridge Parkway, whose appeal need not be limited to road riders. Turn left onto the parkway and savor the vistas and wide riding surface for a few miles before turning at Slacks Overlook on the left and following Slacks Trail to the right, just behind the picnic table at the edge of the small parking area. You'll start on blue-blazed Slacks Trail and descend for several miles before continuing downhill on orange-blazed White Rocks Trail. This entire descent is a single-track lover's nirvana. Enjoy it, but watch for others coming uphill.

After a wide creek crossing, the trail starts to level off and you'll arrive at the upper Sherando Lake. Turn onto the hard-surface road to the right and continue past the lower lake on the left before a steep climb above the lake. The lower lake is open for swimming during summer and offers a sandy beach and a modern bathhouse. Continue on the road past the entrance station and turn left onto VA 664. After a mile or so you'll arrive at Coal Road on the left. Finish the ride back to your vehicle and start planning your next Big Levels route.

Big Levels is the destination of choice for a lot of riders who are new either to mountain biking or to the area. However, try to think of this area of mostly unmarked trails and logging roads as one that is prime for exploration. The best Big Levels riding results from going out with map in hand on a sunny day and getting adventurous.

RIDE 61 · Pedlar River Loop

AT A GLANCE

Length/Configuration: 23-mile loop with shorter routes possible

Aerobic difficulty: The 3.5-mile climb will separate the mountain folk from the flatlanders

Technical difficulty: None

Scenery: Lush greenery along Pedlar River; some mountain views from Shady Mountain Trail

Special comments: A nice combination of long uphills and downhills with a little single-track thrown in for variety

This 23-mile, figure-eight loop lies on the eastern edge of the Blue Ridge Mountains and combines some decent uphills and downhills on Forest Service roads with single-track through forests of hardwoods, pines, and hemlocks. It takes in Panther Falls and a couple of really nice downhills on the Shady and Taylor Mountain Trails. This is a nice ride for a warm day since the whole ride seems to takes its lead from Shady Mountain Trail, which is overshadowed by an assortment of evergreens and deciduous trees that keep most of this 23-miler pretty cool.

Starting from a primitive campground on the banks of Pedlar River, you'll also find yourself in the shadow of Coleman Mountain, Brown Mountain, and the Blue Ridge Parkway as you loop back and forth across the lower Pedlar River and Little Irish Creek. You'll even cross the Appalachian Trail at one point.

There is little in the way of technical abilities required on this ride, so the total distance and the 3.5-mile climb gaining 1,000' will be the deciding factors regarding whether you ought to give it a try.

General location: 10 miles east of Buena Vista.

A look at Virginia's Shenandoah Valley from atop the Blue Ridge Mountains.

Elevation change: This ride has its definite ups and downs. From the Pedlar River Campground where the ride begins at an elevation of 1,058', you'll climb to 1,890' at the turn onto Taylor Mountain Trail. The trail drops to 1,400' where it crosses the river and gains 200 feet on the other side. The 3.5-mile climb on FS 311/315 and VA 607 ascends to 2,410' where it runs adjacent to the Blue Ridge Parkway. From there Shady Mountain Trail continues upward to 2,640', the highest point on the ride, before dropping to 1,840' where it intersects with FS 315. And then it's all downhill back to the start.

Season: Ice and snow make this ride inadvisable during winter months. Be especially careful during the succession of hunting seasons that begin in the fall; wear bright clothes at those times. Call the Virginia Department of Game and Inland Fisheries (804-525-7522) for the opening and closing dates of hunting seasons for various game animals. The Shady Mountain Trail is open to vehicle use by disabled hunters during hunting season.

Services: All services are available in Buena Vista. The Pedlar River Campground offers an outhouse and wooded sites, but little else.

Hazards: Crossing Pedlar River at the end of Taylor Mountain Trail when the water temperature is low or the water level is high could be very hazardous.

Rescue index: Help can be found in Buena Vista.

Land status: George Washington National Forest—Pedlar Ranger District.

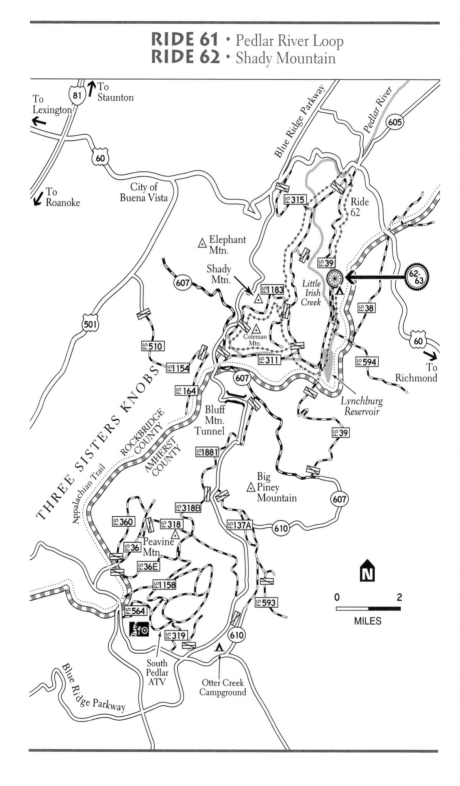

Little Irish Creek runs
down the eastern slope
of the Blue Ridge
Mountains before
spilling into Pedlar River.

Maps: George Washington National Forest map of the Pedlar Ranger District; USGS 7.5 minute quad: Beuna Vista.

Finding the trail: Heading east from Buena Vista on US 60, pass the Blue Ridge Parkway and enter Amherst County. Turn right onto FS 39 and cross Pedlar River after several miles. Park along the road at Pedlar River Campground just past the bridge.

Source of additional information:
Glenwood and Pedlar Ranger Districts of the George Washington and
    Jefferson National Forest
P.O. Box 10, 27 Ranger Lane
Natural Bridge Station, Virginia 24579
(540) 291-2188

Notes on the trail: Start at Pedlar River Campground and head north on FS 39. Make a sharp switchback turn onto the last gated and unmarked woods road on the left before US 60. Descend into the woods and cross a small wooden bridge before the trail ends at Pedlar River. There is no bridge across the Pedlar so cross the river as safely as you can. An unmarked but well-used trail ascends from the river on the opposite side and leads into a parking area.

Leave the parking area and turn left onto FS 315. You'll climb a bit and drop down to Panther Falls on the right. Panthers, or mountain lions, were obviously common around here at some point, but sightings now are rare and generally unsubstantiated. The falls are very slippery, but this is a beautiful spot. Stop here and take a breather.

Start up again and, after some steady climbing, begin downhill and pass one end of the gated Forest Developement Road 1183 (a.k.a. Hico Road) on the right. Turn right onto FS 311 and take another right onto VA 607, continuing a 3.5-mile climb until you're up to the Blue Ridge Parkway. Just before passing under the parkway, turn right onto unmarked, gated Shady Mountain Trail. The trail continues to climb before a sweet downhill run with some magnificent views. After passing the gated opposite end you passed before, turn right onto FS 315, continuing straight past FS 311, and make a left onto FS 39 to finish up at Pedlar River Campground.

RIDE 62 · Shady Mountain

AT A GLANCE

Length/Configuration: 13.5-mile loop with longer routes possible

Aerobic difficulty: The 3.5-mile climb will separate the mountain folk from the flatlanders

Technical difficulty: None, although overgrown crown vetch on Shady Mountain Trail can hide natural obstacles

Scenery: Lush greenery along Pedlar River; some mountain views from Shady Mountain Trail

Special comments: A shorter alternative to the Pedlar River Loop with some healthy climbing and a 7-mile descent

I thoroughly enjoyed checking out rides along Pedlar River on the eastern slope of the Blue Ridge Mountains. The area had a different feel to it compared to rides west of the Blue Ridge Mountains, and the squiggles and lines on the Forest Service maps readily translated into some nice mountain bike loops.

This 13.5-mile loop begins and ends at Pedlar River Campground on FS 39, using primarily gravel forest roads. The low-lying location of this primitive campground makes it vulnerable to washout when the river outgrows its banks. If this is the case when you plan to sleep out, there are plenty of other beautiful spots to pitch a tent amid this quiet forest of towering oaks and pine trees.

This loop is a shortened version of the Pedlar River Loop and eliminates the need to ford the Pedlar. Although it entails some healthy climbing, it ends with a seven-mile downhill that, for most of us, is a darn good tradeoff. Riders of most ability levels should be able to handle this ride and will have a good time.

General location: East of the city of Buena Vista and the Blue Ridge Parkway.

Elevation change: There are a couple of substantial climbs on this loop, which starts at of 1,058'. After some short climbs, you'll take on several real thigh-burners, including a 4-miler that gains 1,535' before cresting on Shady Mountain Trail at 2,640'. The ride finishes with a 7-mile downhill back to the start.

Season: Ice and snow make this ride inadvisable during winter months. Be especially careful during the succession of hunting seasons that begin in the fall; wear bright clothes at those times. Call the Virginia Department of Game and Inland Fisheries (804-525-7522) for the opening and closing dates of hunting seasons for various game animals. Shady Mountain Trail is open to vehicle use by disabled hunters as requested.

Services: All services are available west of the Blue Ridge Parkway in the city of Buena Vista.

Hazards: Hunter use and vehicles on Shady Mountain Trail during hunting seasons. This trail tends to be overgrown, and this may mask hazards such as small animals and large boulders.

Rescue index: Help can be found in Buena Vista.

Land status: George Washington National Forest—Pedlar Ranger District.

Maps: George Washington National Forest map for the Pedlar Ranger District; USGS 7.5 minute quad: Buena Vista.

Finding the trail: Heading east from Buena Vista on US 60, pass the Blue Ridge Parkway and enter Amherst County. Turn right onto FS 39 and cross Pedlar River after several miles. Park along the road near Pedlar River Campground just past the bridge.

Source of additional information:

Glenwood and Pedlar Ranger Districts of the George Washington
    and Jefferson National Forest
P.O. Box 10, 27 Ranger Lane
Natural Bridge Station, Virginia 24579
(540) 291-2188

Notes on the trail: Head south from the campground on FS 39. A gradual uphill and downhill will take you along the northern end of Lynchburg Reservoir. As the road begins to straighten, turn right onto FS 315 (it's obvious but not marked as such). Make a second right on FS 311, or Little Fish Creek Road. After climbing, the road drops to Little Irish Creek above a neat little rocky section where the creek cascades into a hollow beneath the road. Take a breather here, but be wary about venturing too far onto the slippery rocks.

Continuing uphill, you'll cross the Appalachian Trail and turn right onto VA 607 at the stop sign. The road twists and parallels the Blue Ridge Parkway for a short ways. You'll reach what appears to be the end of this long climb, but it's only a brief respite. Just before VA 607 tunnels under the parkway after a sharp bend to the left, turn right onto an unmarked dirt road. Pass the gate and, after a short downhill stretch, you'll resume climbing on unmarked Hico Road. This road is intermittently covered by crown vetch; it will soon turn to single-track. It's easy to follow and offers some nice views of Coleman Mountain and beyond on the right of the trail.

Don't get so focused on the scenery that you miss the huge boulder lying smack-dab in the middle of the way. For a bike it's no problem to get by, but this will stop any four-wheelers on the trail during hunting season, when disabled hunters are allowed to drive up the road. Eventually you'll come to an unmarked intersection with a gravel road on the right. Make a sharp left here and shortly afterward pass a gate and sign for Shady Mountain Trail. Turn right onto FS 315 and continue downhill until you reach the intersection with FS 39. Turn left and coast back to the beginning of the ride. Shady Mountain Trail is well named, and in the absence of shade in a few spots, you'll find some spectacular views of neighboring Blue Ridge peaks.

RIDE 63 · Cave Mountain Lake

AT A GLANCE

Length/Configuration: 13.5-mile loop with other options possible on hard-packed Forest Service roads

Aerobic difficulty: Considerable on the 6.3-mile climb

Technical difficulty: Minimal even on the single-track descent of Wildcat Mountain Trail

Scenery: Densely wooded forestland en route to excellent views of neighboring peaks

Special comments: Finish your ride with a dip in the lake and a good night's sleep under the stars

This 13.5-mile loop ascends and descends Wildcat Mountain via gravel forest roads, single-track, and a short stretch of hard-surface road. Climbers will enjoy the 6.3-mile ascent, which is not unduly steep but seems to go on forever. Many more riders will enjoy the four-mile descent from the crest of the climb, and everyone will savor a swim at Cave Mountain Lake after the ride. A nice feature of the climb is the terrific views of neighboring peaks as you gain altitude. This ride offers no technical challenges aside from the single-track descent on the Wildcat Mountain Trail, but riders should be fit enough to handle the 6.3-mile climb on Forest Service roads starting just outside Cave Mountain Lake Recreation Area.

This region is full of limestone deposits, the main ingredient of caves and associated underground limestone foundations. Plan to visit the caverns at Natural Bridge, the bridge for which Rockbridge County is named. Purchased by Thomas Jefferson in 1774, this 215-foot arch is one of the Seven Natural Wonders of the World and is thought to be the remains of a former cavern whose roof has long since collapsed.

In addition to the well-documented limestone deposits underlying this area are two quarries where jasper has been found. This multicolored mineral—red, brown, and yellow—formed over hundreds of thousands of years from a mixture of iron ore, quartzite, and heated water. Archaeological excavations and summer field schools sponsored by George Washington and Jefferson National Forests have uncovered tools and artifacts of jasper that Native Americans fashioned as far back as 10,000 and as recently as 400 years ago.

General location: 5 miles south of Natural Bridge.

Elevation change: The ride starts along FS 765 in Possum Hollow at an elevation of about 1,400' and climbs steadily to 2,000'. The descent along Wildcat Mountain Trail into and out of the Cave Mountain Recreation Area will drop you to 1,200'. The next part of the ride is a 6.3-mile climb that gains 1,487'. From there, it's a welcome 3.7-mile downhill back to the start.

Season: Ice and snow make this ride inadvisable during winter months. Be especially careful during the succession of hunting seasons that begin in the fall; wear bright clothes at those times. Call the Virginia Department of Game and Inland Fisheries (540-248-9360) for the opening and closing dates of hunting seasons for various game animals.

Services: Most services are available in the village of Natural Bridge Station. Cave Mountain Lake Recreation Area offers camping, a picnic area, and a lake for swimming complete with sand beach. There is a fee to use this national forest recreation area, which is open May through October.

Hazards: The single-track descent can be tricky, especially at the waterbars and creek crossings.

Rescue index: Assistance can be obtained at Cave Mountain Lake Campground during the summer. At other times head toward the village of Natural Bridge Station for help.

Land status: Jefferson National Forest—Glenwood Ranger District.

Maps: Jefferson National Forest map of the Glenwood Ranger District; USGS 7.5 minute quad: Arnold Valley.

Finding the trail: Take exit 180 off I-81 and follow US 11 to Natural Bridge. Take US 130 south from Natural Bridge Station and turn right onto VA 759. Follow signs past Hopper Creek Group Campground until the road turns to gravel and becomes FS 765. Park off the edge of the road just before the gate and begin riding on FS 765 on the other side of the gate.

Source of additional information:

Glenwood and Pedlar Ranger Districts of the George Washington
  and Jefferson National Forest
P.O. Box 10, 27 Ranger Lane
Natural Bridge Station, Virginia 24579
(540) 291-2188

Notes on the trail: Follow FS 765, an overgrown but very ridable gravel forest road. After the initial climb, the road levels off somewhat, followed by a sharp bend to the left. FS 765 starts downhill for a short distance; here you should notice the orange-blazed Wildcat Mountain Trail crossing the road. Turn right and drop quickly on steep single-track. Try not to disturb the waterbars in the trail as you approach and make several creek crossings before entering the Cave Mountain Recreation Area Campground. At present, Wildcat Mountain Trail is overgrown in some spots. Be prepared to dismount and navigate past brush and snags. When you reach the gravel campground loop, turn right and bear right at the information board onto hard-surface FS 780, which will lead you out of the recreation area.

Turn left onto VA 781 when you exit the Cave Mountain Recreation Area and, after a short distance,take a left on FS 812 to start climbing. Those who like uphills should savor the next 6 miles. Take a left at Hoop Pole Gap, staying on FS 812, you are now in Batetourt (*bod-a-tot*) county. As you approach the ridge line, to the left you may notice the cable systems used to harvest timber from steep terrains. This minimizes the need for habitat destruction from skid trails and logging roads.

Continuing to climb, you'll again turn left onto FS 812 a mile or so beyond Hoop Pole Gap, at an intersection with FS 768 that goes to North Creek Campground. Some wonderful views of the neighboring peaks open up as you near the crest of the climb on Pine Mountain. Just after the road peaks and begins to drop, turn left onto unmarked, double-track FS 765. Largely overgrown by crown vetch, the underlying gravel surface makes this a nice downhill after you pass a gate across the road. At one point, you'll coast through a carpet of wildflowers covering the surface. Continue on this 4-mile descent, turning right onto a more familiar section of FS 765, until you reach the gate where you started.

RIDE 64 • Thomas Mountain

AT A GLANCE

Length/Configuration: 5.3-mile loop with other options possible on Forest Service roads

Aerobic difficulty: Minimal climbing by local standards

Technical difficulty: None

Scenery: Densely wooded forestland en route to excellent views of neighboring peaks

Special comments: A good leg-stretcher before tackling other rides near North Creek Campground

This 5.3-mile loop climbs Thomas Mountain on gravel forest roads and some grassy double-track. It's a pretty straightforward up-and-down affair, but that's not to say a wide range of bikers won't enjoy some interesting riding with great views. It involves a healthy climb but no technical challenges. For a longer ride over more challenging terrain, try the 12-mile Pine Mountain Trail (Ride 66), which also leaves from North Creek Campground.

North Creek Campground offers 14 primitive sites, drinking water, and little else besides a beautiful, quiet, secluded base from which to explore the surrounding woods on charted and uncharted double-track, some of which was formerly a rail bed used to remove timber from the mountains in the early 1900s. North Creek is a beautiful little mountain stream that follows FS 59 before emptying into the James River.

General location: 5 miles off Interstate 81 and east of the town of Buchanan.

Elevation change: You'll start at the North Creek Campground (1,125') and climb steadily during the first part of the ride until you reach an elevation of 1,600' along FS 782. You'll descend through Colon Hollow before returning to the start of the ride.

Season: Year-round, although the presence of snow and ice at higher elevations in winter will make this ride inadvisable. Riders should also use

RIDE 63 • Cave Mountain Lake
RIDE 64 • Thomas Mountain
RIDE 65 • Pine Mountain Trail

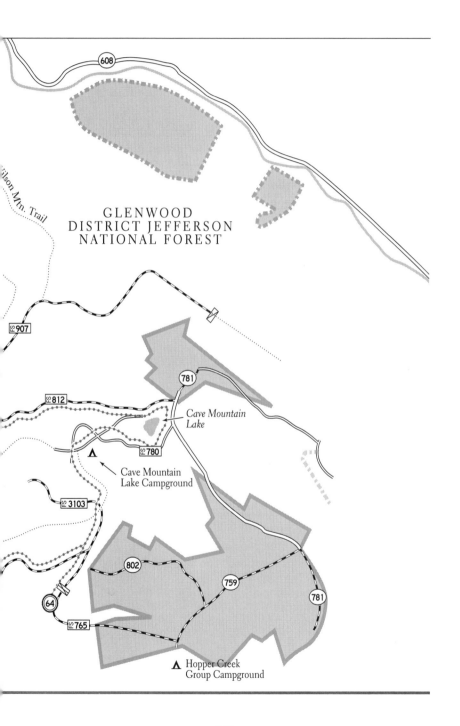

608

Wilson Mtn. Trail

GLENWOOD
DISTRICT JEFFERSON
NATIONAL FOREST

FS 907

781

FS 812

Cave Mountain
Lake

FS 780

Λ

Cave Mountain
Lake Campground

FS 3103

802

759

64

781

FS 765

Λ Hopper Creek
Group Campground

caution during fall and winter hunting seasons and dress in highly visible attire. Call the Virginia Department of Game and Inland Fisheries (804-525-7522) for the opening and closing dates of hunting seasons for various game animals.

Services: North Creek Campground has primitive sites and seasonal water. Arcadia and Buchanan offer the basics, and all other services are available in the nearby village of Natural Bridge Station.

Hazards: None for a rider of moderate ability and stamina.

Rescue index: Assistance can be summoned from the store at Arcadia when it's open and in the nearby town of Buchanan at other times.

Land status: Jefferson National Forest—Glenwood Ranger District.

Maps: Jefferson National Forest map of the Glenwood Ranger District; USGS 7.5 minute quad: Arnold Valley.

Finding the trail: Take exit 168 from I-81 and head south on VA 614. Cross the James River and turn left onto FS 59 following signs for North Creek Campground. This loop starts from the campground 2.5 miles ahead on the right side of FS 59.

Source of additional information:

Glenwood and Pedlar Ranger Districts of the George Washington
    and Jefferson National Forest
P.O. Box 10, 27 Ranger Lane
Natural Bridge Station, Virginia 24579
(540) 291-2188

Notes on the trail: From North Creek Campground on FS 59, head east toward Apple Orchard Falls, take the first left turn onto gravel FS 768, and start pedaling uphill. Don't try to spin too fast or you'll run out of steam. Continue past the gated end of the road (ignoring a second gated road off to the right). After you pass this gate, you'll notice that the road is overgrown but continues uphill until it temporarily crests at almost 3 miles into the ride. A series of relatively short up and downhill stretches will twist its way around the sides of Thomas and Pine Mountains as it resumes, ascending before a left onto FS 782, Colon Hollow Road. The ride ends on a happy note—a 1.5-mile downhill back to the start.

RIDE 65 • Pine Mountain Trail

AT A GLANCE

Length/Configuration: 12-mile loop with other options possible on Forest Service roads

Aerobic difficulty: A lot of climbing, although not steep

Technical difficulty: This trail is a log jumper's dream come true

Scenery: Densely wooded forest en route to views of neighboring peaks before descending toward the James River

Special comments: A longer and more challenging alternative to the Thomas Mountain Trail from North Creek Campground

This 12-mile loop climbs Thomas and Pine Mountains on gravel forest roads and grassy double-track and ends with a stretch on hard-surface road back to North Creek Campground. It offers some interesting riding with great views and a large degree of solitude. As you descend on Pine Ridge Trail, there will be little doubt as to how this mountain got its name. Unfortunately, this otherwise great downhill is littered with large pines that have blown down across the trail, as if a giant had spilled a box of toothpicks.

Pine Ridge Trail saw relatively little use compared to other recreational trails in the district, so it was removed from the Forest Service list of maintained trails in the district. It looked to me like a great opportunity for a mountain bike group or other trail organization to get involved and clear out this section of double-track.

General location: 5 miles off Interstate 81 and east of the town of Buchanan.

Elevation change: The ride begins at an elevation of 1,125' and climbs steadily on forest roads across Thomas and Pine Mountains until it peaks at around 2,200'. Pine Mountain Trail drops near the James River at 814 feet. The rest of the ride is a gradual uphill back to the start.

Season: Spring through fall, although autumn riders should be aware of hunting seasons and ride and dress accordingly in bright colors. Call the Virginia Department of Game and Inland Fisheries (804-525-7522) for the opening and closing dates of hunting seasons for various game animals.

Services: North Creek Campground has primitive sites and seasonal water. All other services are available in the nearby town of Natural Bridge.

Hazards: Numerous blowdowns on the Pine Mountain Trail descent can make this part of the ride difficult.

Rescue index: Assistance can be summoned from the store at Arcadia when it's open, and in the nearby town of Buchanan at other times.

Land status: Jefferson National Forest—Glenwood Ranger District.

Maps: Jefferson National Forest map of the Glenwood District; USGS 7.5 minute quad: Arnold Valley.

Finding the trail: Take exit 168 from I-81 and head south on VA 614. Cross the James River and turn left onto FS 59, following signs for North Creek Campground.

Source of additional information:

Glenwood and Pedlar Ranger Districts
of the George Washington
and Jefferson National Forest

P.O. Box 10, 27 Ranger Lane
Natural Bridge Station, Virginia 24579
(540) 291-2188

Notes on the trail: This loop starts at North Creek Campground on FS 59. Heading east toward Apple Orchard Falls, take the first left onto gravel FS 768 and start a pretty steep uphill. Don't try to spin too fast or you'll run out of steam before the climb ends. The 12-mile loop from North Creek Campground offers some real perks in the form of outstanding views onto neighboring peaks and across the James River. Heading east (away from Arcadia) on FS 59, turn left onto FS 768 and begin to climb immediately. Continue uphill past FS 782, the turn for the short loop, and you'll pass an unmarked, gated woods road on the right at a sharp bend to the right. Shortly thereafter, near the crest of the climb, turn left onto FS 3027 and pass a gate across this grassy double-track. At an unmarked grassy intersection, follow the left fork on a fairly steep, but short-lived, ascent of Thomas Mountain.

Continuing to pedal toward the top of Thomas and then Pine Mountain, you'll ride a succession of ups and downs ranging from one-quarter to almost a mile. There are some very nice views from the ridge atop Pine Mountain about 5 miles into the ride. There's a series of peaks across the top, but it will become very obvious at which point you begin to descend Pine Mountain. If you're luckier than I was, the piles of pines blocking the 2-mile trail descent will have been cleared and you'll be treated to a memorable downhill section approaching the James River. Otherwise, just grin and bear it.

When you do reach the end of the trail, turn left onto gravel VA 622, which veers away from the railroad tracks before crossing a small bridge and intersecting VA 614 across from Arcadia Mercantile. Turn left onto this hardsurface road and pass the remains of 1 of the many iron furnaces that dotted the Shenandoah Valley until well into the Civil War. You'll cross a bridge where North Creek flows into Jennings Creek and turn left onto FS 59. Continue up the road, admire North Creek as it wends its way through the rocky passage, and eventually reach the starting point of this ride.

RIDE 66 • Otter Creek Outing

AT A GLANCE

Length/Configuration: 17-mile loop with other options possible on a maze of unmarked double-track

Aerobic difficulty: A good bit of climbing

Technical difficulty: A considerable amount of rocky double-track, no-track, and creek crossings (all rocky)

Scenery: Lush, densely wooded creeks and awesome views from the Blue Ridge Parkway

Special comments: This is not just a ride—it's an adventure

This 17-mile loop combines riding on hard-packed service roads, through creek beds, and along the hard-surface Blue Ridge Parkway, arguably the finest cycling road you'll ever find. Million-dollar views from the 470-mile Blue Ridge Parkway are a dime a dozen.

This ride doesn't require as much in the way of extraordinary physical or bike handling abilities as it does adventurous spirit. It typifies what I've come to enjoy most about mountain biking and, at the same time, what made me hesitate to write a guidebook of this sort. This is a roundabout way of saying that this ride can be somewhat tough to follow in places, due largely to obscure, unmarked intersections in the woods for which yours truly can only provide rather vague directions.

I guess *Mountain Bike! Virginia* or any guide of this ilk would not be complete without at least one ride in which the author honestly states, "This is a great ride, but you're pretty lucky if you don't get disoriented, if not downright lost, at times." However, before you conjure up survival scenarios that include subsisting on swamp cabbage and pine needle sandwiches for months, I should add that on no part of this ride will you be more than three-fourths of a mile from the Blue Ridge Parkway, which carries a steady stream of cars during its peak seasons from spring through fall. So we're not exactly talking about the middle of nowhere.

The other editorial disclaimer is that you should expect to get wet feet on this ride, which includes creek crossings through Otter Creek, Cashaw Creek, Dancing Creek, and Terrapin Creek. You'll also use Browns Creek as your path *under* the Blue Ridge Parkway.

I'm not sure how appealing this ride sounds. But a lot of discomfort can

RIDE 66 • Otter Creek Outing

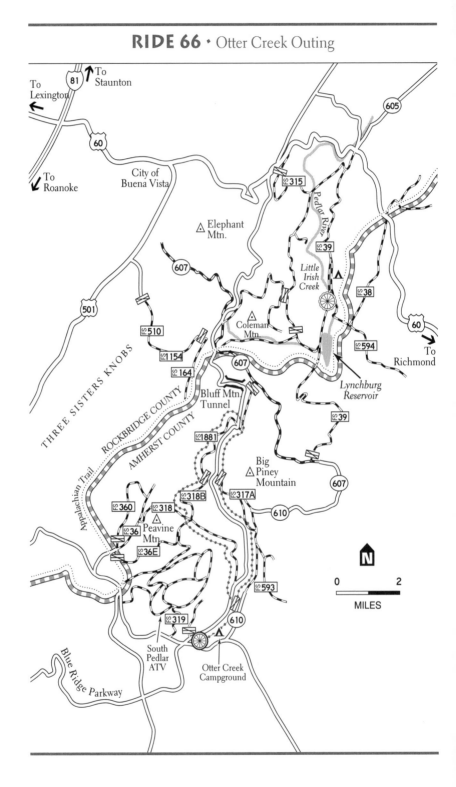

To Lexington

81

To Staunton

To Roanoke

60

605

City of Buena Vista

FS 315

Pedlar River

△ Elephant Mtn.

FS 39

607

Little Irish Creek

△

FS 38

501

FS 510

Coleman Mtn. △

60

To Richmond

FS 1154

FS 594

FS 164

607

Lynchburg Reservoir

THREE SISTERS KNOBS

ROCKBRIDGE COUNTY

AMHERST COUNTY

Bluff Mtn. Tunnel

FS 39

FS 1881

Appalachian Trail

Big △ Piney Mountain

607

FS 318B

FS 317A

FS 360

FS 318

610

△

FS 36

Peavine Mtn.

FS 36E

N

FS 593

0   2

MILES

FS 319

610

△

South Pedlar ATV

Otter Creek Campground

Blue Ridge Parkway

be forgiven when a ride ends on a nice downhill, as Otter Creek Outing does. This final descent, in particular, on the Blue Ridge Parkway keeps dropping for five miles. The spectacular views and the opportunity to reach speeds approaching the legal limit on this ridge-top road help you forget the less desirable parts of this outing. Fat-tire enthusiasts with an adventurous spirit and willingness to take time to smell the abundant mountain laurel and pedal on Robert Frost's lesser-traveled road will love this ride. I know I did.

General location: On the Blue Ridge Parkway just north of the James River and approximately 10 miles southeast of the town of Glasgow.

Elevation change: The Blue Ridge Parkway crosses the James River just south of the start of this ride at an elevation of 649', the lowest point on the entire parkway. The elevation at Otter Creek Campground, the start and end of this loop, is 804'. After leaving the Blue Ridge Parkway on unmarked Forest Service Road 318, you'll ascend to the top of Peavine Mountain at Peavine Gap, which peaks at approximately 1,800'. You'll descend on a maze of unmarked roads and creek beds until you pass under the Blue Ridge Parkway for the second time at an elevation of 1,550'. Then it's back up to the Blue Ridge Parkway just south of Rice Mountain Overlook, elevation 1,746'. The last leg of your journey includes a few ups and downs on the parkway, but you'll finish a 5-mile descent back at Otter Creek Campground, elevation 804'.

Season: Year-round, although snow and ice at higher elevations in winter make this ride inadvisable. Riders should also use caution during fall and winter hunting seasons and dress in highly visible attire. Call the Virginia Department of Game and Inland Fisheries (804-225-3867) for the opening and closing dates of hunting seasons for various game animals.

Services: Camping and food are available at the Otter Creek Campground, restaurant, and Visitor Center. A larger selection of services is available in Glasgow and Buena Vista by going north on US 501.

Hazards: Watch for hunters when you leave the narrow strip of park service land adjoining the Blue Ridge Parkway and enter George Washington National Forest, where hunting is allowed in season. Creek crossings can be difficult, depending on recent rainfalls and ambient temperatures.

Rescue index: Help can be found at the Otter Creek Campground and Restaurant where this ride begins. Those who ride with cellular phones can call 800-727-5928 to report emergencies to the U.S. Park Service.

Land status: National park service and George Washington National Forest—Pedlar Ranger District.

Maps: George Washington National Forest map for the Pedlar Ranger District; Potomac Appalachian Trail Club map #13; USGS 7.5 minute quads: Big Island and Buena Vista.

Finding the trail: From Lynchburg go west approximately 20 miles on VA 130 until you reach the Blue Ridge Parkway. Take the ramp onto the Blue Ridge Parkway going north. The Otter Creek Campground complex will be just ahead near milepost 61 on the right side of the parkway. Park at the southern end of the parking lot and begin riding from here.

Sources of additional information:

Glenwood and Pedlar Ranger Districts
of the George Washington
and Jefferson National Forest
P.O. Box 10, 27 Ranger Lane
Natural Bridge Station, Virginia 24579
(540) 291-2188

Superintendent
Blue Ridge Parkway
700 Northwestern Plaza
Asheville, North Carolina 28801
(704) 298-0398

Notes on the trail: Starting from the Otter Creek Campground parking area, head north on the Blue Ridge Parkway. You'll pass a number of signed overlooks. Since this ride is meant as an adventure, not a race, you might stop and read the signs to learn as much as you can about this area. At the crest of a gradual ascent about 5 miles into the ride, you'll notice an unmarked dirt road (FS 317 A) that's gated on both sides of the parkway.

Pass the gate after turning onto the road on the left and start a short climb as you enter the more heavily wooded national forest and leave the narrow boundary of national park service land that surrounds the Blue Ridge Parkway. As you drop down to a small mountain stream, you see your first unmarked intersection. One gravel double-track fords the creek and goes left; one fords the creek and goes straight; and the third doesn't cross at all as it starts uphill. You can pose the question to yourself, "How adventurous do I feel?" If the answer is "Not very adventurous," then cross through the stream, take a right on FS 1881 and get ready to climb Peavine Mountain.

After a short ascent, stay on the main road past an unmarked gated road on the left, blocking a bunkered road that comes down off Peavine Mountain. This road is rough and rocky in spots, especially in proximity to those spots where you'll have to ford several seasonal streams. You may hear the occasional sound of traffic along the Blue Ridge Parkway as you leave the national forest and cross the boundary onto park service land.

The rocky road merges with Browns Creek—which was fairly dry when I did this route—and you'll follow this under the parkway. Shortly after this short tunnel under the parkway, the creek bed becomes a rocky but ridable road ascending fairly quickly. The going gets steeper before you pass a gate. Turn left onto the parkway just south of Bluff Mountain Tunnel and enjoy riding along this ridge-top road for the next 7 miles.

Perhaps most important is that you're careful to avoid damaging your *pedals* while traversing the numerous rocky sections of creek bed, or you might find yourself up the creek without a . . . I'll let you finish the sentence.

RIDE 67 • Spec Mines

AT A GLANCE

Length/Configuration: 21-mile loop

Aerobic difficulty: One sustained climb to the Blue Ridge Parkway

Technical difficulty: Minimal

Scenery: Forest roads surrounded by dense woods and awesome views from the Blue Ridge Parkway

Special comments: A good workout with no technical aspects

This 21-mile loop will take you across the Blue Ridge Parkway on Old Sweet Springs Road at Black Horse Gap, where the former Black Horse Tavern served the needs of nineteenth-century travelers. Unlike many other mountainous locations of early iron mines surrounding the Shenandoah Valley, Spec Mines was relatively difficult to access, so its iron ore was not mined until the early 1900s by the Pulaski Iron Company. More cost-efficient iron-ore mines in Pennsylvania resulted in Spec Mines's closure in the 1920s. The 88,000-acre Pulaski Tract was acquired by the U.S. Forest Service in the early 1940s, and there are still some open mines in the Spec Mines Branch drainage area.

Almost half of this ride follows the gravel and hard-packed, wide Glenwood Horse Trail, and the rest traverses the Blue Ridge Parkway, whose 470 miles are the delight of many road bikers. However, there's no reason mountain bikers can't also coast along this interstate ridge-top ride. Be sure to yield the right-of-way to horses on this section of the 85-mile Glenwood Horse Trail. Jerry Jacobsen, then recreation ranger for the Glenwood District, told me that he had not heard of any user conflicts along Glenwood Horse Trail, and courtesy and common sense go a long way toward keeping everybody happy.

Those with even a passing interest in birding should carry binoculars and a field guide during fall and spring rides so they can stop at one of several scenic overlooks on the parkway and spot various birds of prey along their annual migration route.

The Spec Mines loop offers little in the way of technical challenge. Although there are some decent ups and downs, the 21-mile distance is the only limiting factor for less-experienced riders. Factor in several downhills, including the final two-mile drop on old Sweet Springs Road (FS 186), and you've got a ride that most of you should be able to handle—and certainly enjoy.

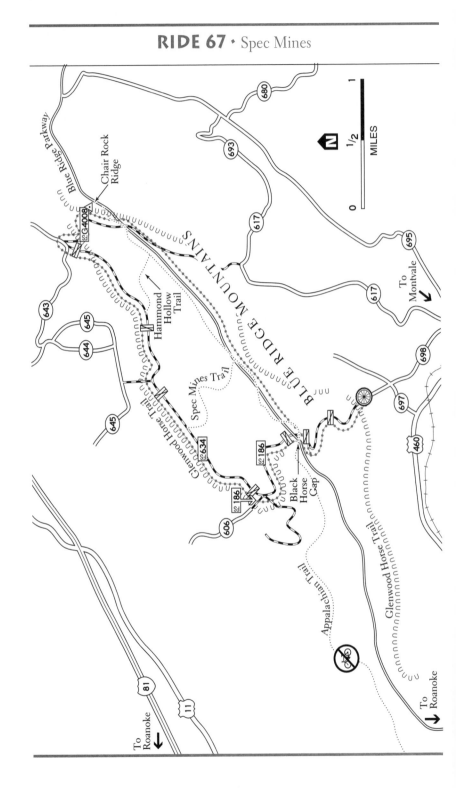

General location: 15 miles southwest of Buchanan and just south of Black Horse Gap on the Blue Ridge Parkway.

Elevation change: From the equestrian parking lot at 1,220', you'll begin with a healthy climb to 2,404' at Black Horse Gap. You'll quickly descend the other side of the mountain to 1,500'. As you ride across the northeast flank of this mountain range, you'll rise and fall in gradients between 1,300' and 1,500' until you reach Chair Rock Hollow and FS G4008. You'll climb to Bobbletts Gap at 2,111' on the parkway and continue ascending to 2,527' at Harveys Knob Overlook. The rest is all downhill. Be sure to turn off at Black Horse Gap, where you'll quickly descend back to the equestrian parking lot.

Season: Year-round, although snow and ice in winter make this ride inadvisable. Riders should also use caution during fall and winter hunting seasons and dress in highly visible attire. Call the Virginia Department of Game and Inland Fisheries (804-525-7522) for the exact opening and closing dates of hunting seasons for various game animals.

Services: Many services are available in the nearby towns of Troutville and Buchanan.

Hazards: Watch for and yield right-of-way to equestrians on this route.

Rescue index: Assistance can be found in Troutville and Buchanan or in extreme emergencies from traffic along the heavily traveled Blue Ridge Parkway.

Land status: Blue Ridge Parkway and Jefferson National Forest—Glenwood Ranger District.

Maps: Jefferson National Forest map of the Glenwood Ranger District; USGS 7.5 minute quads: Montvale and Villamont.

Finding the trail: Take exit 167 off Interstate 81 toward Buchanan. After crossing the James River, turn left onto VA 43 and follow this road until it joins the Blue Ridge Parkway. Turn right onto the parkway and make a quick left onto VA 695 at Bearwallow Gap. Follow VA 695 for 9 miles to VA 617. Turn left onto VA 617 and right onto VA 698 just before the railroad tracks. Follow VA 698 It becomes FS 186 when it enters the national forest and later FS 3078. Park in the Day Creek Horse Trail parking area and begin the ride.

Source of additional information:

Glenwood and Pedlar Ranger Districts
  of the George Washington
  and Jefferson National Forest

P.O. Box 10, 27 Ranger Lane
Natural Bridge Station, Virginia 24579
(540) 291-2188

Notes on the trail: From the Day Creek Horse Trail parking area, turn left onto FS 186 before you pass the gate; begin a 2-mile climb toward Black Horse Gap. You'll pass an interesting rock formation and another gate before cresting this initial climb at the Blue Ridge Parkway. This is a heck of a way to start a ride, but keep in mind that it will be a great way to end your outing after 21 miles of pedaling.

Continue straight across the parkway onto FS 186 on the other side after passing still another gate. One of the perks of riding in a national forest is being able to traverse gated roads that are seasonally closed to vehicular traffic. Many mountain bikers like the extra room of a wide road and the seclusion of carless areas in the forest. After a descent that doesn't last nearly long enough, turn right onto FS 634-2 going past—you guessed it—another gate. I've visited maximum security prisons that had fewer gates than this ride, but at least you won't be frisked by burly correctional officers or asked to put your possessions in a manila envelope while looping around this section of the Blue Ridge Mountains—plus the views are a whole lot better.

Keep riding up and down this hard-packed road along the base of the mountain. Pass several more gates and a sign for Spec Mines Trail on the right. Just before passing the third gate along the road, turn onto an unmarked dirt road that veers off to the right. You're now on FS 634-3, or Pulaski Tract Road, but you'd never know it from the lack of directions at this intersection.

After some stretches of downhill that ford a couple of mountain streams, you'll encounter and pass another gate. The road bends sharply to the left, drops through another creek bed, and then begins to climb steeply uphill. It passes a pair of gateless gate posts—for a change—and then reaches another gate. After passing this gate, turn right onto the unmarked gravel road, and shortly thereafter come to an intersection. Go right onto hard-packed Bob-blett's Gap Road, FS 4008, and continue climbing toward the parkway. There are some great views of the surrounding countryside off to the right, so don't be timid about stopping as you near the parkway.

Shortly after passing the Appalachian Trail on the left, you'll reach a stone bridge carrying the parkway. Push or ride your way up the bank to the parkway and head south (a right turn). Wonderful vistas are plentiful, so try to stop along the way from this perch at 2,500' or so. After Taylors Mountain Overlook, you'll notice a horse-crossing sign and then Blackhorse Gap. Turn left onto FS 186, pass the next-to-last gate of the ride, and enjoy a 2-mile descent back to the start.

RIDE 68 · Carvins Cove Reservoir

AT A GLANCE

Length/Configuration: 7.3-mile out-and-back (14.6 miles total) plus 30 miles of single-track options

Aerobic difficulty: A mild climb

Technical difficulty: Minimal

Scenery: Dense woods and lakeside picnic area

Special comments: Good family ride when shortened to a 10-mile (round-trip) out-and-back to the picnic area

Located just outside Roanoke's city limits surrounding the Carvins Cove Reservoir is a system of fire roads and trails that many New River Valley mountain bikers have taken a liking to. In fact, the area has become so popular that I was able to pick up a free copy of the "Carvins Cove Trail Map" from the counter at East Coasters bike shop in Roanoke. I began with a loop called the New Year's Ride, which appeared to encompass a good bit of the eastern side of the trail system surrounding Carvins Cove. Since that ride, the web of trails in the area has grown even more intricate.

I learned several things in the aftermath of getting lost using the aforementioned trail map. I got lost because I didn't know which mailbox on Timberview Road marked the point at which to turn onto the Green Ridge Trail. I later learned the significance of the city's No Trespassing signs on the 1,000-foot climb. I also learned that the Wateredge Trail, the final link in the New Years Day Ride's chain, was off limits to bikes.

But most importantly I learned that, according to Mr. Larry Creasy from the City of Roanoke's Public Utilities Department, the only section of Carvins Cove on which it is legal to ride bicycles is the 7.3-mile out-and-back (14.6 miles round-trip) Carvins Cove Trail, a well-maintained gravel service road that runs from the boat dock past the picnic area and meets hard-surface Carvins Cove Road at the Bennett Springs entrance. Therefore, in deference to what is legal, I'm offering this single route as the available ride.

This ride is devoid of any killer hills that would make it too great a challenge for riders besides young children or others who are aerobically challenged. Pack a nice lunch and eat at the waterfront picnic area located about two-thirds of the way from the boat dock to the end of Carvins Cove Trail. With

RIDE 68 • Carvins Cove Reservoir

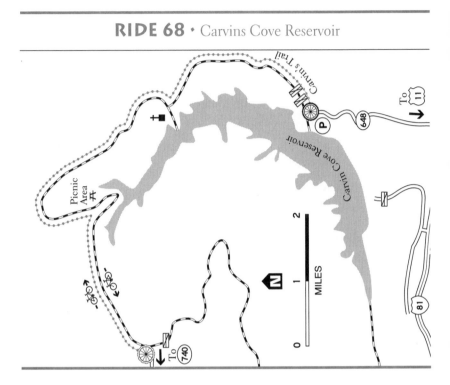

ample rest and sustenance, this should be a good time for the average rider. I even ran into one biker and his golden retriever who were making a go of it. The cyclist was doing okay, but his pooch was—you guessed it—dog-tired.

General location: Just outside the city of Roanoke in Botetourt County.

Elevation change: Moderate ups and downs with no killer hills.

Season: Spring through fall is the best time to ride here, although year-round riding is possible in the absence of ice and snow.

Services: All services are available in nearby Salem and Roanoke.

Hazards: None.

Rescue index: The boat dock and parking lot are located 4 miles up Reservoir Road from Peters Creek Road, one of Roanoke's main thoroughfares, so help is never too far away.

Land status: City of Roanoke Reservoir.

Maps: A trail map is available from East Coasters in Roanoke, although I'd be cautious about using the routes as described since some involve trespassing and others are difficult to follow.

A number of small creeks
empty into Carvins Cove
Reservoir near Roanoke.

Finding the trail: Follow Peter's Creek Road east past Hollins College. Just before the next traffic light, turn left onto Reservoir Road and follow this road up to the parking area for Carvins Cove's boat dock. Stop here and begin riding on the gated gravel road on the right side of the entrance to the parking area.

Source of additional information:

East Coasters Cycling and Fitness
4341 Starkey Road
Roanoke, Virginia 24014
(540) 774-7933

Notes on the trail: The Carvins Cove system of trails and gravel roads has been marked on trail maps available in Roanoke-area bike shops. I found these maps fine for those who already know the trails, but pretty ambiguous for those who are unfamiliar with details such as which Timberview Road mailbox to turn at or any specific trail markings that would correspond to what was shown on paper. More important, however, I learned that these maps will lead you across private property and sections of city-controlled land posted "no trespassing."

RIDE 69 · Dragon's Back

AT A GLANCE

Length/Configuration: 10.5-mile loop with numerous single-track configurations to duplicate the annual race held here

Aerobic difficulty: Race-quality single-track climbs

Technical difficulty: Ascents and descents on rocky single-track are challenging, but the rocky traverse of Dragon's Back (at 3,000') keeps racers coming back

Scenery: Great views from the top of North Mountain; however, riders who rubberneck don't last too long on the Dragon

Special comments: Though relatively short, this ride will test your fitness and technical skills

"Beware the lair of the dragon. Rising like a monolith to form one wall of the pristine Catawba Valley, North Mountain, a.k.a. Dragon's Back, is a technical bike knight's delight, traversing a ridge narrow as a broadsword's blade, with rocks and rises to challenge the noblest of all riders," or so sayeth the announcement for the 1997 East Coasters Virginia Championship Mountain Bike Series.

Whether you're a racer or not, you're bound to savor the challenge of the trails and forest roads that comprise the Dragon's Back course, a perennial favorite in the Virginia Championship Mountain Bike series. The beginner and expert races use different combinations of Forest Service Road 224, the 1.6-mile Deer Trail, the 1.5-mile Grouse Trail, the 1.7-mile Turkey Trail, and, of course, the most outstanding feature of this ride, the rocky stretch along the Dragon's Back—the most southwestern of the five North Mountain trails in Virginia. Its rocky upcroppings across the top give the course its name.

I've laid out this particular ride as a loop starting from the intersection of FS 224, ascending Turkey Trail, traversing the ridge, and descending Deer Trail instead of attempting to duplicate the race course for any given year or any particular class of racer. This 10.5-mile loop will get your legs and lungs

RIDE 69 • Dragon's Back

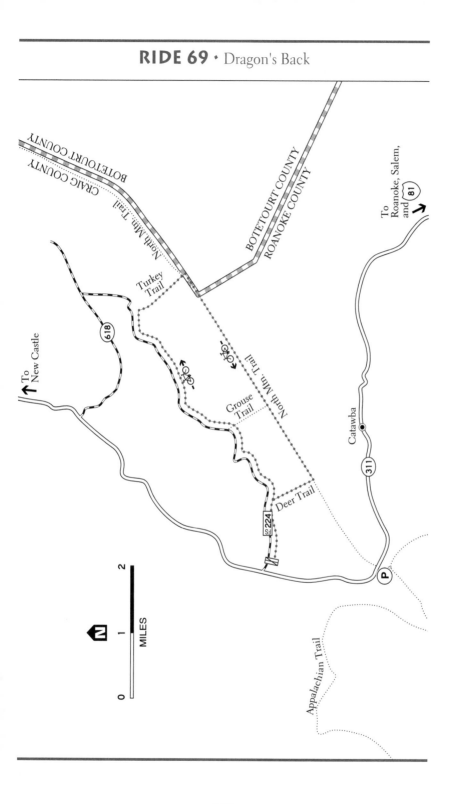

working at full capacity. And if one lap doesn't do it for you, take another spin around in the opposite direction.

If you crave more of a challenge, show up next time with a number pinned to the back of your suit of armor and test your mettle against some of Virginia's finest knights. This is a technically and physically challenging loop despite its modest length, and only lords and ladies of intermediate abilities or better should attempt this one. Suits of armor are optional.

General location: 13 miles north of Salem.

Elevation change: Wildlife Road (FS 224) rises and falls, staying around 1,600', and North Mountain Trail, the fearsome Dragon's Back, stays at around 3,000'. The ascent on Turkey Trail is 1.7 miles while the descent on Deer Trail is 1.6 miles, making for some pretty steep ups and downs.

Season: Year-round, although the presence of snow and ice at higher elevations in winter will make this ride inadvisable. Riders should also use caution during fall and winter hunting seasons and dress in highly visible attire. Call the Virginia Department of Game and Inland Fisheries (540-782-9051) for the opening and closing dates of hunting seasons for various game animals.

Services: All services are available in nearby Salem and Roanoke.

Hazards: Ascents and descents on rocky single-track. Dragons Back is narrow across the top of North Mountain. It doesn't leave much room for error and doesn't take prisoners.

Rescue index: There are numerous commercial establishments between the trailhead and Interstate 81 where you can summon assistance.

Land status: Jefferson National Forest—New Castle Ranger District.

Maps: Jefferson National Forest map of the New Castle Ranger District; USGS 7.5 minute quads: Catawba and Looney.

Finding the trail: Take exit 141 off I-81 and follow US 311 toward New Castle. After about 13 miles, turn right onto FS 224 at the sign for Wildlife Road. Go to the trailhead for Deer Trail on the right side, park, and start your ride there.

Sources of additional information:

New Castle Ranger District
  of the Jefferson National Forest
Box 246
New Castle, Virginia 24127
(540) 864-5195

East Coasters Cycling and Fitness
4341 Starkey Road
Roanoke, Virginia 24014
(540) 774-7933

Notes on the trail: From the intersection of FS 224 and Deer Trail, ride east (away from US 311) on this rolling Forest Service road. Turn right onto Turkey Trail and head up the side of North Mountain on rocky single-track until you reach the ridge. Turn right onto North Mountain Trail and, unless you've got Tinker Juarez or Missy Glove hot on your wheel, be sure to take some time to admire the great views from atop North Mountain. Then continue to Deer Trail, where you'll turn right to descend back to the start. Watch for other riders and yield right-of-way as necessary.

While pedaling through this neck of the woods, my curiosity was piqued by the number of unmarked, gated woods roads that veered off FS 224. I made a mental note to come back and do some exploring. However, I was more surprised that there were so few others out pedaling on such a beautiful, warm Saturday afternoon at the end of March. I guess it just wasn't the right kind of day for knights such as these.

RIDE 70 · Barbours Creek Wilderness

AT A GLANCE

Length/Configuration: 18-mile loop with the option to duplicate a longer race route

Aerobic difficulty: Includes a 5-mile climb

Technical difficulty: Traversing Potts Mountain and the final rocky, rutted descent will keep you on your toes

Scenery: Densely wooded

Special comments: A tough ride and a taste of the even longer Trek Escape race that's been held here since 1987

The notion of mountain biking in wilderness areas raises all kinds of sentiments, so it wouldn't surprise me if the title of this ride raised some interest, ire, or confusion among readers. I can assure you that I'm not advocating a mass illegal mountain bike ride in federally designated wilderness areas, nor did I find some pro–mountain biking loophole within the parameters of the Wilderness Act of 1964.

What I did find is a really neat 18-mile loop that completely encircles 5,700-acre Barbours Creek Wilderness Area on a combination of gravel forest roads, double-track, and single-track, none of which enter the wilderness area. This ride offers a combination of stiff climbs, technical stuff, and a downhill at ride's end that's guaranteed to paint a permanent grin on your face. The physical and technical demands of this loop will be appreciated by intermediate and more experienced riders.

The Trek Escape at Potts Mountain has been part of the East Coasters Virginia Championship Mountain Bike Series since 1987, making it one of

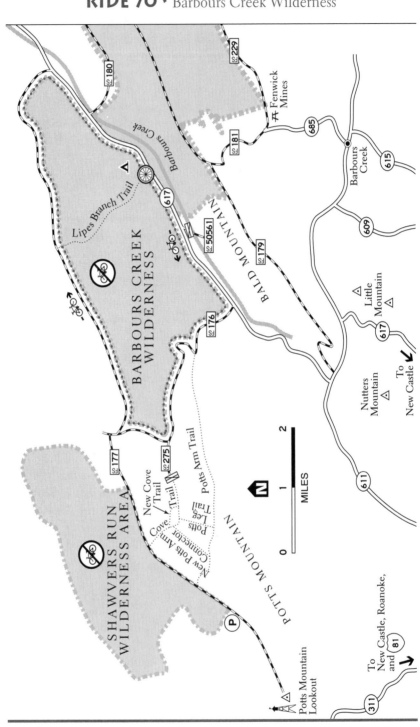

This grassy double-track provides great mountain biking on Potts Mountain just outside Barbours Creek Wilderness.

the older continuous races in the state. This ride follows part of the route of the Trek Escape, although the actual race route is longer and includes roads and trails on the west side of Forest Service Road 176 leading toward Potts Mountain Lookout. Call East Coasters to get the specific race route for the current year.

General location: 30 miles north of Roanoke.

Elevation change: The ride starts at 1,840' and drops to 1,612' at the turnoff onto Sweet Springs Turnpike, a.k.a. FS 176. The 5-mile climb up Potts Mountain gains 1,700' before steering across the northern edge of Barbours Creek Wilderness, which peaks at 3,804'. The ride ends by dropping back down to VA 617 at 2,360' and returning to the Pines Campground.

Season: Year-round, although snow and ice at higher elevations in winter make this ride inadvisable. Riders should also use caution during fall and winter hunting seasons and dress in highly visible attire. Call the Virginia Department of Game and Inland Fisheries (804-225-3867) for the opening and closing dates of hunting seasons for various game animals.

When everything starts to look the same, it's a good time to check your map.

Services: Water and camping are available at the primitive, 17-site Pines Campground. Many other services are available in the town of New Castle, and all others can be found a little farther away in Salem and Roanoke.

Hazards: Depending on your technical bike-handling skills, the single-track section of this ride across the northern edge of Barbours Creek Wilderness can be pretty challenging. The climb is not severe; it just seems like a long 3 miles coming right on the heels of the 5-mile ascent up FS 176. The 3-mile descent from Potts Mountain onto VA 617 is pretty steep and twisty. Riders should pay close attention.

Rescue index: Help can be found in the town of New Castle.

Land status: Jefferson National Forest—New Castle Ranger District.

Maps: Jefferson National Forest map of the New Castle Ranger District; USGS 7.5 minute quads: Jordan Mines, New Castle, and Potts Creek.

Finding the trail: From Interstate 81 take exit 41 heading north on US 311. Cross over North Mountain into Craig County and drive to the town of New

Castle approximately 25 miles west of I-81. Turn right at New Castle onto VA 615 and then left onto VA 609 until you reach VA 611. Turn left onto VA 611 and after 5 miles turn right onto VA 617. The Pines Campground is 5 miles ahead on the left.

Sources of additional information:

New Castle Ranger District of
the Jefferson National Forest
Box 246
New Castle, Virginia 24127
(540) 864-5195

East Coasters Cycling and Fitness
4341 Starkey Road
Roanoke, Virginia 24014
(540) 774-7933

Notes on the trail: This ride starts and ends at the Pines, a primitive campground with 17 sites scattered among the hardwoods, as well as running water and vaulted toilets. Leave the campground, turning right onto a slightly downhill stretch of VA 617. Enjoy this descent because you've got a healthy climb to look forward to after the first turn onto FS 176, Sweet Springs Turnpike. Although this wide dirt road over Potts Mountain probably doesn't resemble any turnpike you've seen before, many of the early roads were toll roads, and the word *turnpike* was used to describe the pole or pike that was turned to allow a wagon or other vehicle to pass after paying the toll.

The first mile of the climb is easy and will give you a chance to warm up your climbing muscles before the real huffing and puffing begins. Near the point where the climb gets steeper you'll also come to the intersection with FS 604-1. Turn right and continue to climb, passing gated Cove Branch Dead End Road on the left. A little more than a mile later, keep an eye out for an unmarked gravel road on the right, adjacent to Barbours Creek Wilderness.

You'll turn onto this double-track into the woods and continue to climb. The road becomes pretty rutted, and the fellow I met who was sporting clipless pedals fell several times while unable either to negotiate the technical sections or free his feet.

I enjoyed the 8-mile double-track/single-track section of this ride that runs southwest to northeast across the back of Barbours Creek Wilderness. The trail gets a good bit of mountain bike use and was easy to follow. A 1-mile section of downhill bisected a large clearing and then reentered the woods as a wonderful grassy double-track. The only slightly confusing section was a mile after this large "bald" where a section of the road has largely disappeared. It appears to cut left here, and you can follow this short detour or scramble across the gap in the road that's straight ahead.

As I approached what proved to be the crest of the last climb, another mountain biker appeared and told me that the best and hairiest downhill stretch was just ahead. And boy was he right! The last mile and a half of gravel double-track is steep and rocky with a large growth of verdant rhododendron for shade. After riding through Barbours Creek, you'll pass a gate and hit a short uphill that joins VA 617. Take a right here and continue heading downhill back to the Pines.

Any number of options can stretch this ride a little longer, including heading west on FS 177-1 to Potts Mountain Lookout or doing a second loop that will take you to Fenwick Mines and some real top-of-the-world views from Bald Mountain. Riders with surplus energy may opt to try out the area's newest racing trails to west of Barbours Creek.

RIDE 71 · Fenwick Mines

AT A GLANCE

Length/Configuration: 19-mile loop with other possibilities on hard-packed Forest Service roads

Aerobic difficulty: Includes a 4-mile climb

Technical difficulty: None

Scenery: Great views from the top of Bald Mountain and Fenwick Mines' unique biological habitat

Special comments: Families can select parts of the rail trail section for an easy outing

This 19-mile loop begins and ends at Fenwick Mines Recreation Area, site of a late-nineteenth-century iron-ore mining and manufacturing complex that covered 33,000 acres. You'll warm up with a four-mile climb before crossing the top of Bald Mountain, which offers limitless views that will take your breath away.

What goes up must come down, and you'll have a blast in the process. The initial stretch of this six-mile downhill appears as if the road simply drops off the end of the mountain. Then you'll discover the pleasures of riding a rail trail virtually unknown to the public. I guarantee you won't find it in any other guide. A picnic lunch or dinner at Fenwick Mines would be a perfect way to end the day. There are no technical challenges on this ride, so the only limiting factor for less-experienced riders is the distance. I guarantee you'll enjoy this ride.

General location: 30 miles north of Roanoke.

Elevation change: The ride starts at Fenwick Mines at an elevation of 1,422'. It begins climbing Bald Mountain, picking up the ridge line at 2,487'. It crosses the top, continuing to ascend to the site of the former lookout tower at 3,553'.

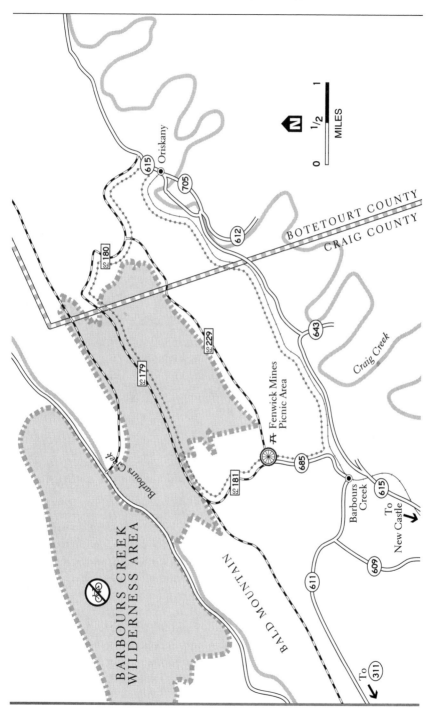

You'll drop to 1,128' after a 6-mile downhill. The next section stays pretty level on an abandoned rail bed, with a short climb back to Fenwick Mines.

Season: Year-round, although snow and ice at higher elevations in winter make this ride inadvisable. Riders should also use caution during fall and winter hunting seasons and dress in highly visible attire. Call the Virginia Department of Game and Inland Fisheries (540-782-9051) for the opening and closing dates of hunting seasons for various game animals.

Services: The Fenwick Mines Recreation Area offers hiking trails, picnic shelters, and interpretive information regarding the former Fenwick Mining complex and the reclamation efforts that resulted in a fertile wetlands habitat. Some services are available in the nearby town of New Castle, and all else is available in Salem and Roanoke.

Hazards: None.

Rescue index: Help can be summoned in the nearby town of New Castle.

Land status: Jefferson National Forest—New Castle Ranger District and Virginia Department of Transportation abandoned railroad right-of-way.

Maps: Jefferson National Forest map of the New Castle Ranger District; USGS 7.5 minute quads: Jordan Mines, New Castle, Oriskany, and Strom.

Finding the trail: From Interstate 81 take exit 41 and head north on US 311. Cross over North Mountain into Craig County and turn right at New Castle onto VA 615. Drive for 5 miles until you get to VA 611. Turn left onto VA 611 and, after one-half mile, turn right onto VA 685. Follow the signs for Fenwick Mines Recreation Area and begin this ride there.

Source of additional information:
New Castle Ranger District of the Jefferson National Forest
P.O. Box 246
New Castle, Virginia 24127
(540) 864-5195

Notes on the trail: Starting from the Fenwick Mines Recreation Area, head north on FS 181. After a short warm-up, the Bald Mountain climb starts in earnest. There are several breathtaking views as the road climbs higher. At the intersection with FS 179 from the left, continue straight and then bear right onto FS 179. After a short drop, the climb resumes and crests after 4 miles.

The first drop in the road is so sudden that this hard-packed surface seems to disappear in front of you. Mountains loom ahead and to the right as the descent continues through a series of switchbacks before you reach the intersection with FS 180 from the left. Continue straight ahead on FS 180 and descend past the gate. When you've reached a **T** intersection where the sign pointing left says Road Ends 0.1 Miles, turn right. After a hellacious downhill, turn right at the stop sign onto VA 615, and shortly afterward turn right onto

VA 774 and enter the old Chesapeake and Ohio rail line just behind the Oriskany Post Office.

The next stretch of the ride is on an abandoned railroad spur that the Chesapeake and Ohio freight trains used to carry iron ore out of the area while bringing supplies into the Oriskany community. The bed runs parallel to VA 615, but for my money there's simply no comparison between riding on one or the other. This spur runs through the Barbours Creek community and then on to New Castle. Although the Virginia Department of Transportation controls most of this right-of-way, a short section is posted against trespassing. Each of us has to use our best judgment in such matters, so my suggestion is to temporarily ride on VA 615 and then get back onto the rail bed after this section of private property. The rail trail at various places is accessible to VA 615 so it's not hard to go back and forth as necessary to avoid this one private section. Turn right onto VA 611 where the trail intersects and follow the signs back to Fenwick Mines. Be sure to spend some time exploring the Fenwick Recreation Area, with its swamp, waterfalls, and interesting collection of waterfowl. It's a unique environment for the mountains of western Virginia.

VIRGINIA'S BLUE RIDGE HIGHLANDS

By now you should realize that Virginia's uniqueness stems in part from its different regions. In terms of history, geography, and, of course, mountain biking, it is the sum of diverse parts. The Blue Ridge Highlands, Virginia's final frontier, is the exception to the other regions that make the rule. To many Virginians, this tucked-away corner of the Old Dominion is a hinterland that shares far less with its distant Virginia cousins than it does with its closer neighbors Kingsport, Tennessee; Whitesburg, Kentucky; and Bluefield, West Virginia.

On my first trip to these far reaches of the state during the homestretch of researching this book, I saw coal country up close. I was on my way to Breaks Interstate Park, which lies on the border adjoining Kentucky. This is an area where life is as hard as the anthracite "black gold" that has alternately given and taken the lives of highlanders for over a century.

While much of the mountain biking is as rugged and untouched as the local people and countryside, there are also converted railroad beds that make getting out on a bike a lot easier than you'd expect. Riding in the Blue Ridge Highlands ranges from 55 miles of smooth, easy sailing along New River State Park Trail to a variety of tough climbs and downhills along Iron Mountain in the Mount Rogers National Recreation Area. Other converted rail beds include the 33-mile Virginia Creeper Trail and the 5.8-mile Guest River Trail. In general, I found that Virginia's national forests have not embraced mountain biking the way its state parks have. But here in the Blue Ridge Highlands, the Mount Rogers National Recreation Area, under the administration of the Jefferson National Forest, touts itself thus: "Whoever invented mountain bicycles surely had the Mount Rogers National Recreation Area in mind!" So I guess there's another exception to the rule.

Geologically referred to as the Blue Ridge Province, this upland region is characterized by a steadily increasing mean elevation as you move in a southwestward direction from the Roanoke River. It is here in the Blue Ridge Highlands that you'll find the state's tallest peak, Mount Rogers (5,729 feet). However, given the relative elevation of the surrounding land, Mount Rogers doesn't really stand out from the neighboring peaks. In fact, Virginia's next four highest peaks are also in the Blue Ridge Highlands.

Thomas Jefferson omitted Mount Rogers in his *Notes on the State of Virginia* and said, "The mountains of the Blue ridge [sic], and of these the Peaks of Otter, are thought to be of greater height, measured from their base, than any others in our country, and perhaps in North America." Part of Jefferson's oversight may have stemmed from the fact that the Peaks of Otter are monadnocks that sit along the western edge of the Piedmont, standing out from the neighboring terrain in much sharper relief than Mount Rogers.

You can expect colder temperatures on any given day while mountain biking in and around the mountains of western Virginia, and the higher elevations of the Blue Ridge Highlands consistently register the state's lowest temperatures. A case in point is Virginia's lowest temperature of –30 degrees, recorded west of Blacksburg at Mountain Lake. This means that the mountain biker should pack and prepare for extremes of temperature when planning a ride in the mountains, but especially when riding at high elevations in the Blue Ridge Highlands. On the other hand, the summer humidity and heat are far less than you'll encounter along the coast.

Not only can the temperatures be extreme, they can also change rapidly. I got a firsthand look at this on an Easter weekend campout at 4,000 feet. I went to sleep with 70 degree temperatures and awoke before dawn under snow and blizzard conditions.

The Cumberland Gap in this corner of the Old Dominion was once the path to Kentucky and the country's true frontier, but you may find that much of Southwest Virginia has changed little since Daniel Boone and a few dozen other woodsmen contracted to build Wilderness Road. As you go farther and farther southwest, the high plateau will yield to a landscape whose rocky countryside is quite steep, as in the case of the Russell Fork River gorge, the "Grand Canyon of the East." The relentless power of moving water has cut a canyon through Breaks Interstate Park 1,660 feet deep and five miles long, the largest gorge east of the Mississippi River.

For most Virginians, a trip to the Blue Ridge Highlands is a considerable journey. However, I found that the more time I spent mountain biking in this part of the state, the more I came to realize that Mother Nature had saved some of her best work for this obscure corner where Kentucky, North Carolina, Tennessee, and West Virginia are closer neighbors than Virginia's capital city of Richmond. In some ways, the wide variety of mountain biking opportunities you'll find here typify the Virginia that is the sum of all her disparate parts.

RIDE 72 · Breeze across Brush Mountain

AT A GLANCE

Length/Configuration: 12.5-mile point-to-point
(or all-day 25-mile out-and-back)

Aerobic difficulty: Moderate ups and downs

Technical difficulty: None

Scenery: Great views from the top of Brush Mountain

Special comments: Visit the site of the plane crash that claimed the
life of war hero–movie star Audie Murphy, then enjoy a leisurely pedal

This 12.5-mile one-way ride (25-mile round trip) starts at the parking area
for the Audie Murphy Monument. This marks the site where Murphy,
World War II hero and subsequent star of more than 40 movies, died in an
airplane crash on May 28, 1971. Brush Mountain Road (Forest Service Road
188-1) follows the top of the mountain to US 460 where you can leave a second vehicle for shuttle purposes or turn around to create a good 25-mile
training ride.

Dave Shipp and I did this as a one-way ride with a shuttle vehicle after a
period of heavy rains, so there were quite a few mud holes along the hard-
packed forest road. Fortunately, there was also no shortage of outstanding
views from this 2,900-foot elevation.

Breezing across the top of Brush Mountain is something any rider with
basic bike handling skills and endurance can handle. It's important to remind
novice riders that mountain bike distance is considerably tougher than the
same distance on the road, especially in the mountains west of Blacksburg.
Wider tires and rougher terrain make a considerable difference when it comes
to doing an honest self-assessment of what you're capable of handling.

General location: 10 miles north of Blacksburg off US 460.

Elevation change: No killer hills but a steady array of ups and downs across
the top of Brush Mountain.

Season: Year-round, although snow and ice at higher elevations in winter
make this ride inadvisable. Riders should also use caution during fall and
winter hunting seasons and dress in highly visible attire. Call the Virginia
Department of Game and Inland Fisheries (540-782-9051) for the opening
and closing dates of hunting seasons for various game animals.

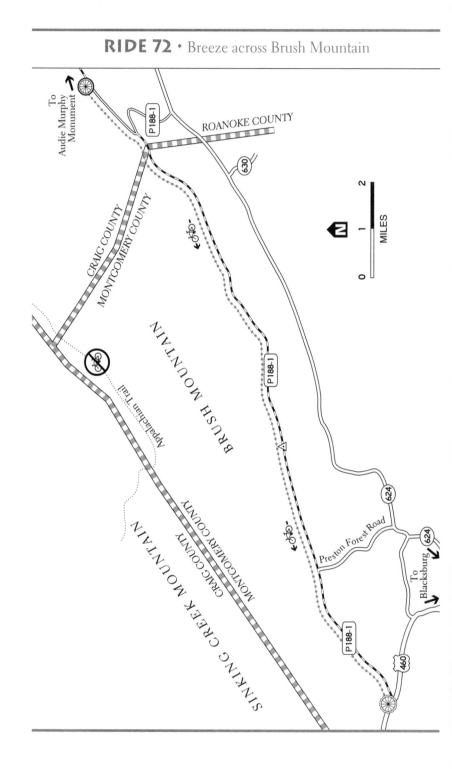

Services: All services are available in nearby Blacksburg.

Hazards: None.

Rescue index: Help can be found in nearby Blacksburg.

Land status: Jefferson National Forest—Blacksburg Ranger District.

Maps: Jefferson National Forest map for the Blacksburg Ranger District; USGS 7.5 minute quads: Glenvar, Looney, McDonalds Mill, and Newport.

Finding the trail: Take Main Street in Blacksburg to Mount Tabor Road/VA 624. Go 12 miles past VA 650 and turn left onto gravel FS P188-1. Start up the mountain and turn right at the top. Follow this road for 3 miles to the parking area for the Audie Murphy Monument.

Sources of additional information:

Blacksburg Ranger Station   East Coasters Cycling and Fitness
110 Southpark Drive   1001 North Main Street
Blacksburg, Virginia 24060   Blacksburg, Virginia 24060
(540) 552-4641   (540) 951-2369

Notes on the trail: Starting at the parking lot for the Audie Murphy Monument, you'll head away from the monument on FS 188-3. After a mile and a half you'll come to the intersection with well-defined gravel FS 188-1 on the left. Continue straight ahead on a dirt road into the woods just before some high-voltage lines and towers. There's also a sign at this intersection for the Audie Murphy Monument and Preston Forest.

The road you'll follow across the top of Brush Mountain is pretty obvious until you reach hard-surface Preston Forest Road on the left after about 9 miles. At this point turn right onto hard-surface Jefferson Forest Road and follow this to the intersection of VA 818 and VA 830. Continue straight on VA 818 past the sign that reads "Road Ends 0.7 mile." Shortly after this point, turn onto an unmarked dirt road that veers off into the woods on the right. You'll soon hear the drone of traffic on US 460. At this point you'll turn around and retrace your tracks or jump into the shuttle vehicle and head back into the college town of Blacksburg for some R & R.

RIDE 73 • Poverty Creek Trail

AT A GLANCE

Length/Configuration: 11- and 15.5-mile loops

Aerobic difficulty: Generally moderate with one difficult climb

Technical difficulty: Easy to moderate with a few tough spots

Scenery: Great views from the top of Brush Mountain

Special comments: Site of the autumn Rowdy Dog Race

Few places can boast of high-quality, diverse mountain biking *and* proximity to a major university town, but that's what you get at Poverty Creek. As you'd expect, it's a popular spot for Blacksburg's large contingent of mountain bikers. The effects of this popularity have been felt, and the adjoining Pandapas Pond is off-limits to bikes. Poverty Creek Trail itself saw recent changes at the hands of Forest Service personnel working to stem the stream's increasing channelization.

Novice bikers will enjoy the trail's relatively flat nature, but enough rises and falls are thrown in to make it interesting for more adventurous riders. Starting at the new parking area along US 460, you can ride an 11-mile loop that utilizes the Poverty Creek Trail and FS 708 to Boley Fields and back. It's not a true loop since it doubles back on itself in some places, but, given the area's assets, a little familiar terrain won't make much of a difference.

More advanced riders and those training for the annual Rowdy Dog Race will use the Poverty Creek Trail—the low-lying, flat section of Poverty Creek Trail running from the parking area to Boley Fields—as a warm-up to climb Brush Mountain via Jacob's Ladder and Horse Trails. Climbing from the Poverty Creek Trail to FS 188-2 at the top of Brush Mountain adds a 4.5-mile loop to the Poverty Creek/FS 708 loop to create a 15.5-mile loop.

General location: 3 miles northwest of Blacksburg off US 460.

Elevation change: The elevation along Poverty Creek stays fairly even at around 2,000'. The optional loop up Brush Mountain peaks along FS 188-2 at 2,800'.

Season: The best time to ride here is spring through fall when snow and ice no longer impede travel. It's also best to avoid Poverty Creek after periods of heavy rain, but areas of this trail stay muddy even during relatively dry periods. Riders should use caution during fall and winter hunting seasons and

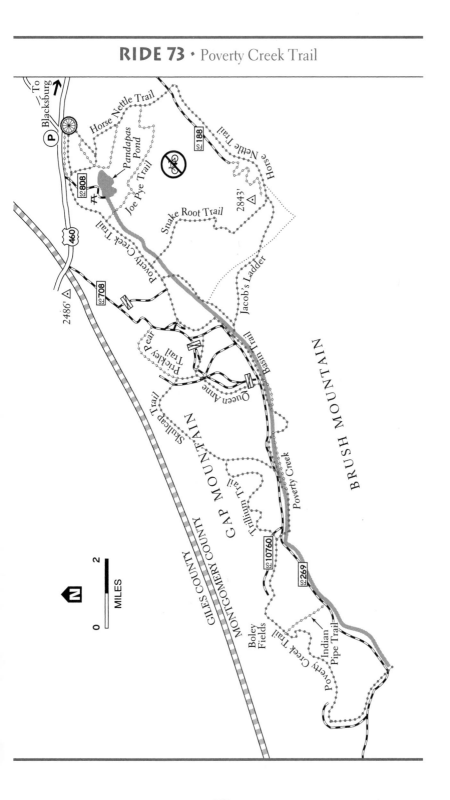

dress in highly visible attire. Call the Virginia Department of Game and Inland Fisheries (540-782-9051) for the exact opening and closing dates of hunting seasons for various game animals.

Services: All services are available in nearby Blacksburg.

Hazards: Two creek crossings near the trail's western end at Boley Fields can be hazardous depending on the depth and speed of the water as well as whether you walk or ride from bank to bank. The generally muddy nature of this trail can be difficult to maneuver. Be sure to yield the right-of-way to hikers and equestrians.

Rescue index: Although off limits to bicycles, Pandapas Pond is a popular spot, so you should be able to get help if necessary. Otherwise, assistance can be found in nearby Blacksburg.

Land status: Jefferson National Forest—Blacksburg Ranger District.

Maps: Jefferson National Forest map of the Blacksburg Ranger District; USGS 7.5 minute quad: Newport.

Finding the trail: Take US 460 west out of Blacksburg for 3 miles and turn left onto FS 708 at the sign for Pandapas Pond. The road splits very quickly; the parking area for horses and bikes is on the left. Turn here and park. The trailhead for Gap Mountain Trail is well marked and just across the main access road.

Sources of additional information:

Blacksburg Ranger District
110 Southpark Drive
Blacksburg, Virginia 24060
(540) 552-4641

East Coasters Cycling and Fitness
1001 North Main Street
Blacksburg, Virginia 24060
(540) 951-2369

Notes on the trail: Approximately 7 miles of trail along Poverty Creek were relocated away from from the increasingly abraded bottomland. Making a loop around Boley Fields now requires riding along FS 708, however this is an improvement for riders who can enjoy the sport without looking like the creature from *Swamp Thing*. Beginning the ride from the new parking lot along US 460, you'll cross FS 708 (which leads down to Pandapas Pond) to access the well-marked trail leading to Gap Mountain.

The Snake Root and Jacob's Ladder trails are the two most difficult in the network. A good rule of thumb to keep in mind: If you don't want to climb Brush Mountain, you should be wary of making any left turns toward the mountain. Prickly Pear, north of Poverty Creek is steep as well, but shorter. The Queen Anne, Joe Pye and Trillium trails also offer rider the opportunity to make several loops and figure-8's on that side of the main trail.

The Rowdy Dog Race generally ascends on the Horse Trail, crosses Brush Mountain heading west on FS 188-2 along the ridge, then descends on Jacob's

Ladder back to the Poverty Creek Trail. Blazes are presently used to designate the main trails, and a map is available from the Blacksburg Ranger District. Some older trails are still visible, though off limits. Riders should respect the work rangers recently put into revamping the Poverty Creek area trails.

The bottom line is this is a great place to ride if you don't mind getting wet. It's also pretty difficult to get lost given the well-used nature of this area. So go out to Poverty Creek, have a great time riding, and be sure to bring a large towel—you'll need it.

RIDE 74 · Mountain Lake Trail System

AT A GLANCE

Length/Configuration: 15 total miles, made up of trails 2.5 miles or less

Aerobic difficulty: Varies with trail; uphills are limited to short, steep inclines

Technical difficulty: Varies from well-maintained carriage roads to rocky, rooted single-track

Scenery: Mountain Lake is a grand resort overlooking one of Virginia's two natural lakes

Special comments: Pamper yourself with a stay at Mountain Lake; stop by the recreation office to purchase a bicycle trail pass

Enter Mountain Lake—the hotel that is, not the lake itself—and step into a bygone era of elegant resort hotels that served Virginia's upper crust. Arriving by a combination of train and carriage, families would spend their leisure time traveling to therapeutic springs and resorts such as Mountain Lake and along the nearby Salt Sulphur Turnpike, which took many vacationing travelers to the therapeutic waters at Salt Sulphur Springs, West Virginia. Most of these healing resorts have gone the way of the passenger pigeon, but here at one of Virginia's two natural lakes, you can still recreate the era when attention to the needs of the guest was a priority, before corporate bean-counters made customer service a secondary consideration. You owe it to yourself to stay here at least once to savor the complete Mountain Lake experience. Their brochure says it best: "We'll put you on top of the world." Don't shy away thinking that you can't afford such a treat. I spent about as much on a room in a fleabag motel in San Francisco several years ago.

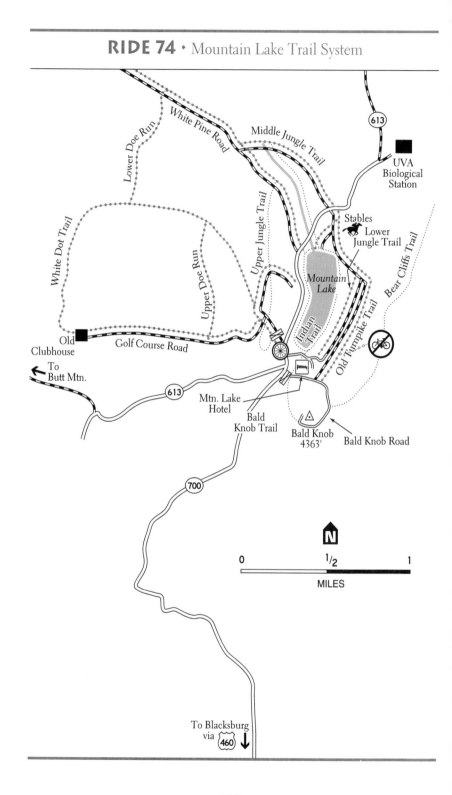

You can drive right to the door and go mountain biking on the resort's system of 1.5-to-2.5-mile trails on its own 2,600 wooded acres (or neighboring national forest). You can enjoy a soothing whirlpool in your lakeside cottage and a sumptuous gourmet feast in the hotel's dining room before finishing your day with a moonlit carriage ride along the lake. Sounds good to me!

While some of these trails have some short, steep sections, there's nothing here that even novices can't easily walk their bikes past if the ride becomes too steep. I haven't put together any specific rides, so the best thing is to go out with a map and explore the trails, many of which loop onto each other. Be sure to stick to those that are designated as bicycle trails. For a more adventurous outing, try the 22-mile Mountain Lake to Butt Mountain loop (Ride 76).

General location: 20 miles north of Blacksburg.

Elevation change: Rolling hills with no extreme changes.

Season: When the rest of the Old Dominion is sweltering hot, you can enjoy the lack of humidity and lake breezes at Mountain Lake's 4,000' perch. This is one of the few places in Virginia that stays cold enough during the winter to do a steady cross-country ski and ice skating business. In fact, Mountain Lake generally registers the coldest winter temperatures in the state, so plan on riding here from late spring through early fall.

Services: Food and lodging are available at the hotel. Bike rentals and minor repairs are available at the recreation office.

Hazards: Trails are multi-use, so yield right-of-way when necessary, especially to horse carriages on Lower Jungle Trail.

Rescue index: Help can readily be summoned at the hotel or rec. office.

Land status: Private resort.

Maps: A trail map and guide are available from the hotel.

Finding the trail: Take the Christiansburg exit from Interstate 81 and follow US 460 west past Blacksburg. Take the bypass around the home of Virginia Tech University to VA 700. Follow this road and the signs to Mountain Lake. The trail system is well marked and located primarily opposite the lake to the left of VA 700, although several are also on the other side of the lake.

Source of additional information:

Mountain Lake
Route 700
Mountain Lake, Virginia 24136
(800) 346-3334

East Coasters Cycling and Fitness
4341 Starkey Road
Roanoke, Virginia 24014
(540) 774-7933

Notes on the trail: A bicycle trail pass, which can be obtained from the recreation office, is required to use the hotel's trail system. A fee is charged for parking. Mountain Lake is situated on a high plateau at roughly 4,000', so you'll be surprised to find that your car did most of the climbing between here and Blacksburg. This is generally one of the cooler places in the state, a factor that more than likely resulted in the filming of the Patrick Swayze movie, *Dirty Dancing*, at this location. For this reason it is closed October through May, but makes an excellent summer destination, as it has for the last 100 years.

RIDE 75 · Mountain Lake to Butt Mountain

AT A GLANCE

Length/Configuration: 22-mile loop

Aerobic difficulty: No killer hills; climbs tend to be long inclines

Technical difficulty: None

Scenery: Splendid panoramic views, especially from the top of Butt Mountain

Special comments: Give this one a try if Mountain Lake's trails leave you wanting additional mileage

This 22-mile loop will take you across the tops of several mountains on terrain that is not flat by anybody's definition, but much flatter than you might expect. Riding on this elevated plateau across the top of Big Mountain, you'll understand Mountain Lake's claim, "We'll put you on top of the world." From Brushy Top to Butt Mountain (obviously named by some disgruntled mountain biker with a hard saddle), you'll think that you really are riding on the top of the world.

You'll cross Minie Ball Hill, where Union troops, with Johnny Reb hot on their trail, got stuck in the mud and had to jettison supplies to free their wagons. Rumor has it that lead bullets, known as Minie balls, can still be found if you look hard enough. Another point of interest is the Salt Sulphur Turnpike, which many vacationing travelers traversed to the therapeutic waters at Salt Sulphur Springs, West Virginia.

Mountain Lake is one of two natural lakes in Virginia; the other is Lake Drummond in the Great Dismal Swamp. However, some feel that Lake Drummond should relinquish any claim to being a natural lake since the system of drainage canals initiated by George Washington and continued by

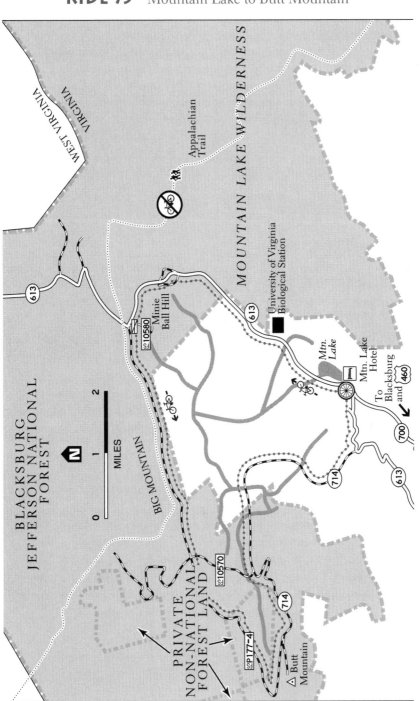

others has long since made it more dependent on people than on Mother Nature. Be that as it may, the jury continues to deliberate about the possible geologic causes for the formation of Mountain Lake. If that question seems too ponderous for a relatively easy ride such as this, see if you can recall the segments of the Patrick Swayze movie, *Dirty Dancing*, filmed here.

This loop offers little in the way of technical challenge and only moderate ups and downs on hard-packed and hard-surface roads, so the 22-mile distance is the only factor determining what level of rider could comfortably handle this ride.

General location: 20 miles north of Blacksburg.

Elevation change: This ride begins at Mountain Lake, elevation 3,875', and peaks near the top of Butt Mountain at around 4,000'. The overall change in elevation is relatively small, but quite indicative of the high plateau nature of the Blue Ridge Highlands.

Season: This is one of the few places in Virginia that stays cold enough during the winter to do a steady cross-country ski and ice skating business. In fact, Mountain Lake generally registers the coldest winter temperatures in the state, so plan on riding here from late spring through early fall.

Should you plan to extend the riding season, dress in highly visible attire during fall and winter hunting seasons. Call the Virginia Department of Game and Inland Fisheries (540-782-9051) for the opening and closing dates of hunting seasons for the various game animals.

Services: High-quality food and lodging are available at the Mountain Lake Hotel. Other levels of service are available in Blacksburg.

Hazards: None.

Rescue index: Help can be found at the Mountain Lake Hotel.

Land status: Jefferson National Forest—Blacksburg Ranger District and state-maintained roads.

Maps: Jefferson National Forest map of the Blacksburg Ranger District; USGS 7.5 minute quads: Eggleston, Interior, and Pearisburg.

Finding the trail: From Blacksburg follow US 460 west for 15 miles past the top of Brush Mountain. After several more miles turn right onto VA 700 and follow this road to Mountain Lake. If you can park along the ride, you will avoid a fee at Mountain Lake, and possibly an overcrowded lot.

Sources of additional information:

Blacksburg Ranger District of
    the Jefferson National Forest
110 Southpark Drive

Blacksburg, Virginia 24060
(540) 552-4641

Mountain Lake
Route 700
Mountain Lake, Virginia 24136
(800) 346-3334

East Coasters Cycling and Fitness
4341 Starkey Road
Roanoke, Virginia 24014
(540) 774-7933

Notes on the trail: Starting from the Mountain Lake resort complex, you'll head north on VA 613 and then follow this hard-surface road along the left side of the lake. The road shortly turns to gravel, and you'll bear left toward War Spur as you pass the entrance to the University of Virginia biological station. Make certain not to stray from the route into the nearby wilderness area, which is off-limits but not always marked.

You'll climb gradually to Minie Ball Hill on the left, where Confederate troops pursued a contingent of the Union army that got mired in the mud and had to hastily empty their wagons to escape capture. It's said that you can still find the Minie ball ammunition the soldiers discarded. At the crest of the climb to Minie Ball Hill, you'll pass a small parking area on the left and then turn left onto Forest Service Road P177-4. At this point, the Appalachian Trail joins this road at a rare spot where it's okay to ride on the trail.

From here on the road becomes rougher and possibly wet with large mud holes. It's easy to imagine Union wagons getting bogged down after heavy rains on this high plateau, where water runoff would be minimal. Much of the vegetation is small, scrubby second growth, but this adds to panoramic top-of-the-world views.

At an unmarked but very obvious intersection with FS 10570 in Bailey's Gap, continue straight toward the small Brushy Top peak as you climb your way toward the top of Butt Mountain. You'll begin to climb through a more mature hardwood section of forest as you approach the crest of Brushy Top. From here you can look ahead and see the Butt Mountain Fire Tower.

The panoramic views of neighboring and far-off peaks continue, and I was amazed at the relatively small climbs and downhills from this plateau. You'll reenter Jefferson National Forest and begin a gradual ascent toward the peak of Butt Mountain where the fire tower is located off to the right. The views from the edge just under the fire tower are pretty darn spectacular, so be sure to take a few minutes to savor them.

After the fire tower, VA 714 improves markedly over the mud hole–pocked Forest Service road. You'll descend to the intersection with FS 10570 and turn right to remain on VA 714. This is a nice 3-mile downhill that will carry you through a verdant section of mature hemlocks and mountain laurel and across the bridge over appropriately named Hemlock Branch. After several short ups and downs, turn left at the stop sign onto hard-surfaced VA 613. At the next stop sign you'll again turn left, remaining on VA 613 to finish the ride at Mountain Lake.

RIDE 76 • Flat Top Mountain

AT A GLANCE

Length/Configuration: 12-mile loop

Aerobic difficulty: Considerable; 2-mile killer climb

Technical difficulty: Minimal

Scenery: Endless groves of dense rhododendron

Special comments: The 5-mile downhill is a dream

Despite the name of this 12-mile loop and the mountain it traverses, there's nothing flat about it. After six miles of difficult climbing on hard-packed Forest Service road, you'll descend on some of the sweetest downhill I uncovered in all my riding through George Washington and Jefferson National Forests. This smooth section of horse trail weaves its way through endless groves of dense rhododendron towering over and shading the trail. It took me a while to get to this section of the Blacksburg Ranger District of the Jefferson National Forest lying in Giles County, not too far from the Virginia–West Virginia boundary, but wow—what a ride! Especially that downhill.

The climb is a killer because of its pitch as well as its length; it's the biggest determinant of what class of rider should tackle this ride. The downhill is relatively smooth, although there are some rocky areas adjacent to creek crossings toward the bottom. Overall, however, this descent is the stuff mountain bikers' dreams and memories are made of. In fact, some downhill fanatics may want to team up and leave cars at either end of this stretch of the ride and skip the climb altogether.

General location: 25 miles north of Wytheville.

Elevation change: The ride begins at 2,500' and climbs to 3,500' along Flat Top Mountain.

Season: This area in the far reaches of Virginia at 3,500' is one of the cooler places in the state. In that sense, it makes a great escape from summer's hottest days in mid-July. When the rest of the Old Dominion is roasting under temperatures in the 90s, it can be 10–15 degrees cooler here in God's country. However, the same is true for winter, so consider this as a good spring through fall ride. Should you decide to push your luck and extend the

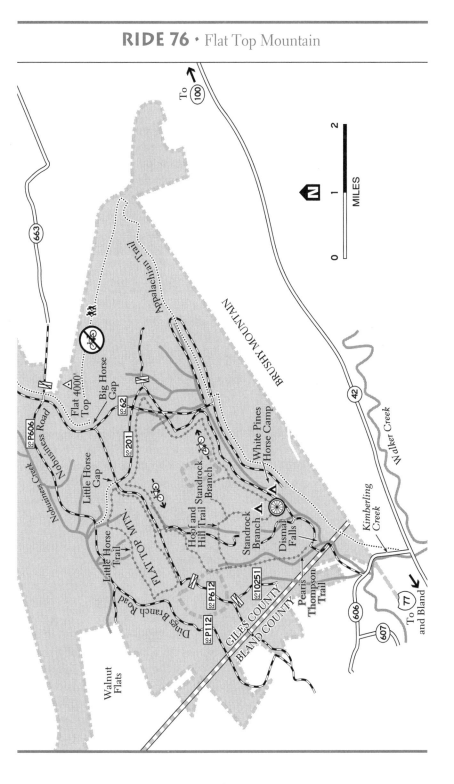

riding season into colder weather, be sure to dress in highly visible attire during fall and winter hunting seasons. Call the Virginia Department of Game and Inland Fisheries (540-782-9051) for the opening and closing dates of hunting seasons for various game animals.

Services: The ride starts from Walnut Flats Campground, which offers a toilet and little else except a quiet spot under the trees where you can pitch your tent. The nearby towns of Narrows and Pearisburg offer most basic services. A little farther away, Blacksburg offers a full range of food, lodging, and several bike shops.

Hazards: The downhill section is open to equestrians, so plan to share your space and yield to both horses and hikers. Toward the bottom of the downhill is a short, wooden bridge whose gaps could easily grab a wheel. For that matter, the wood itself is questionable.

Rescue index: This is fairly remote area, so if you aren't able to enlist the assistance of others around Dismal Falls and White Pines Horse Camp, drive back down VA 42 and request that personnel at the nearby Bland Correctional Center call for emergency help.

Land status: Jefferson National Forest—Blacksburg Ranger District.

Maps: Jefferson National Forest map of the Blacksburg Ranger District; USGS 7.5 minute quads: Rocky Gap and Mechanicsburg; online from www.dcr.state.va.us/parks.

Finding the trail: Follow Interstate 81 south past Radford and take exit 98 toward Dublin. Go north on VA 100 and turn left onto VA 42 at Poplar Hill. Continue on VA 42 for 10 miles and turn left onto VA 606 just before crossing Kimberling Creek. After a mile turn right onto FS 201/VA 671. Follow this road to Walnut Flats Campground (on the left), where you can park your car and start riding.

Source of additional information:
Blacksburg Ranger District—Jefferson National Forest
110 Southpark Drive
Blacksburg, Virginia 24060
(540) 552-4641

Notes on the trail: From Walnut Flats, go back down the short entrance road and turn left onto FS 201. This hard-packed Forest Service road has its ups and downs for the first 4 miles, but that will loosen you up before you take on the next 2 miles, which gain 1,000' in elevation. I don't know who named this Flat Top Mountain, but it definitely wasn't a mountain biker. As FS 201 bends sharply to the right at Little Horse Gap and continues climbing, you'll turn left into the woods at a small clearing. Take a left on the gated road that leaves FS 201. Heading to the right leads one towards Nobusiness

Creek—a name and location I took at face value. I was fortunate to meet several equestrians at this intersection who explained the various options.

This road begins a wonderful single-track descent. Lest you enjoy yourself too much, remember that this is an equestrian trail and mountain bikers should keep their mounts under control and be prepared to yield the right-of-way at any time to both hikers and horses. Otherwise, try to keep your grin to a controllable opening as you careen down Flat Top Mountain through profuse stands of wild rhododendron and crisscross Standrock Branch and the Pearis Thompson Horse Trail. When the gated road intersects the Hoof and Hill Trail, turn left. At the following intersection, turn left and finish the ride along Standrock Branch. After crossing a pair of dirt berms, you'll unceremoniously empty onto FS 201. Turn left and finish up with a short ride back to the start at Walnut Flats. By the time you've reached the end of this 5-mile descent, you'll probably be ready to head back up to the top.

RIDE 77 · Tract Fork and Polecat Trails

AT A GLANCE

Length/Configuration: 11.3-mile loop

Aerobic difficulty: Moderate

Technical difficulty: Rocky in places, especially along Tract Fork Trail

Scenery: Dense woods with creekside and mountain views

Special comments: Parts of Tract Fork Trail will be unridable after periods of heavy rain

After pushing my bike over innumerable blowdowns across miles of long-forgotten trails in Virginia's national forests for the last couple of years, I had little reason to believe that Tract Fork and Polecat Trails would be any different. However, I was pleasantly surprised to find these trails in good shape and among some of the best single-track riding I've uncovered in western Virginia. Of course, good single-track in the national forests doesn't occur by chance. The Adopt-a-Trail sign at the eastern end of Tract Fork Trail acknowledges members of the Southwest Virginia Packing and Pleasure Horse Association who have cleared and maintained this trail.

This 11.3-mile loop combines single-track with hard-packed Forest Service Road 707 to create a ride that offers advanced beginners and more experienced riders an opportunity to ride rocky single-track and forest roads along

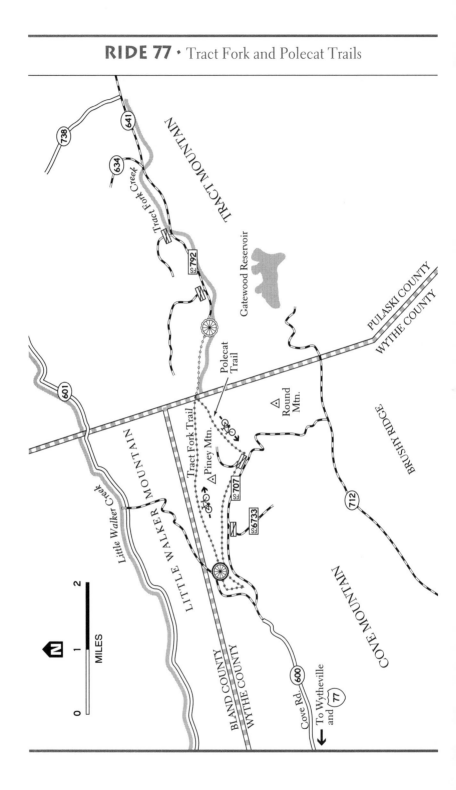

mountain streams. Although you may feel you're in the middle of nowhere, you're actually close enough to the towns of Wytheville and Pulaski that you can easily complete this ride and return to the comforts of civilization.

General location: 8 miles northwest of Pulaski.

Elevation change: Generally moderate climbs ranging from 2,400' to 3,000'.

Season: Year-round, although snow and ice in winter make this ride inadvisable. You should also avoid this ride after periods of heavy rain because of the dangers of flooding from low-lying streams. Riders should use caution during fall and winter hunting seasons and dress in highly visible attire. Call the Virginia Department of Game and Inland Fisheries (540-782-9051) for the opening and closing dates of hunting seasons for various game animals.

Services: All services are available in nearby Pulaski and Wytheville.

Hazards: Multi-use trail accessed by hunters and equestrians. The 2 crossings of Tract Fork Creek along VA 641 and multiple crossings by bike along the trail make riding inadvisable after periods of heavy rain.

Rescue index: Assistance can be found in nearby Pulaski or Wytheville; the choice will be dependent on your location on the ride.

Land status: Jefferson National Forest—Wythe Ranger District.

Maps: Jefferson National Forest map of the Wythe Ranger District; USGS 7.5 minute quad: Longspur; also available online at www.dcr.state.va.us/parks.

Finding the trail: To start from the eastern end of the trail, head out Pulaski's Randolph Avenue, which turns into VA 738 at the edge of the city. After it becomes Robinson Tract Road, turn left onto VA 641/Cox Hollow Road. This is an easy turn to miss. At the end of state maintenance, this road becomes FS 692. Tract Fork Trail begins where the forest road ends.

Sources of additional information:

Wythe and Blacksburg Ranger Districts
of the Jefferson National Forest
110 Southpark Drive
Blacksburg, Virginia 24060
(540) 552-4641

Kitty Grady
c/o Wytheville Visitors Bureau
P.O. Box 533
Wytheville, Virginia 24382
(540) 223-3355

Notes on the trail: This 11.3-mile loop starts as a gradual but steady uphill climb along the edge of Piney Mountain. You'll follow and alternately cross Tract Fork quite a few times before the trail empties onto FS 707. Turn left onto FS 707, which rises and falls over 5 miles of gravel Forest Service road with some wonderful views of Cove Mountain to the east. Watch for orange-blazed Polecat Trail and turn left onto it. Polecat Trail involves a great descent back to Tract Fork Trail. Turn right at the well-marked intersection with Tract Fork Trail and follow it back to the trailhead at the end of FS 692.

RIDE 78 · Grayson Highlands State Park

AT A GLANCE

Length/Configuration: 6 miles of double-track can be combined with park roads to form loops

Aerobic difficulty: Moderate

Technical difficulty: Moderate on rocky paths and double-track

Scenery: Incredible views from the top of the world

Special comments: A great place to camp, with access to Grayson Highlands trails as well as those in Mount Rogers National Recreation Area

Although Grayson Highlands State Park may be a bit out of the way for many Virginians, it's well worth the effort to get there. Lying on the southern edge of the Mount Rogers National Recreation Area, which proudly boasts its own mountain biking opportunities, Grayson Highlands is somewhat hidden from the public eye. However, like other state parks I've visited, its creature comforts mesh very well with a setting of incredible natural beauty.

Grayson Highlands should be commended for developing a mountain bike trail guide that specifically addresses where bikers can and cannot ride. I received this guide when I was having a hard time getting a consistent answer from other state parks to the question of mountain bike access on existing trails within their facilities. I didn't think these parks were being evasive; rather, it appeared to be an issue that was yet to be seriously considered.

Grayson Highlands comes by its name honestly, not just because of its location in Virginia's Grayson County, but because of its lofty position among the region's higher peaks. All trails open to mountain bikers are also open to hikers and equestrians, so sharing the trail is the order of business here. It's specifically recommended that you dismount at a healthy distance when horses are approaching so you don't spook them.

Utilizing the park's mountain bike trail guide, the hard-surface park roads, and the six miles of accessible gravel roads and trails, you can very easily put together several different loop and linear rides, so no specific route is given

RIDE 78 · Grayson Highlands State Park

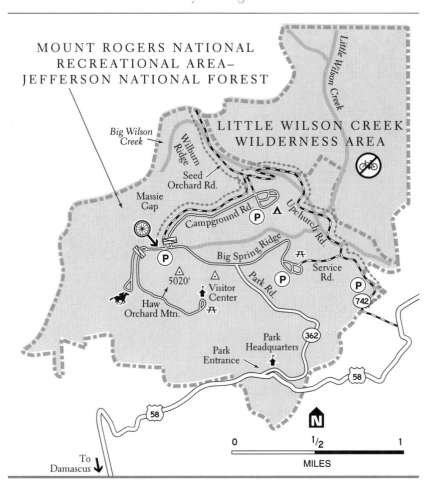

here. Just keep in mind that the Little Wilson Creek Wilderness Area across the northeast boundary from Grayson Highlands is off limits to bikes, as is the Appalachian Trail.

One definite stop on your itinerary should be a hike up to the 5,000-foot top of Haw Orchard Mountain. Bikes are not allowed in the meadow below where more than 150 wild ponies graze, but these critters seem oblivious to us two-legged animals walking among them to take in some panoramic views from this peak. Visitors are requested not to harass or feed the animals. The bloodline of some of these animals is thought to go back to animals kept by the area's earliest settlers, but this particular herd goes back to the time of the park's development 25 years ago.

Wild ponies graze at Grayson Highlands State Park.

General location: South of Marion and adjacent to the southern edge of Mount Rogers National Recreation Area.

Elevation change: Park elevations range from 3,000' to 5,000', although the bikeable trails exhibit considerably less up and down variation.

Season: Spring, summer, and fall, when snow and ice are not obstacles to safe riding. Winter at this elevation brings considerable snow and brutally cold temperatures.

Services: Camping and horse stables are available at Grayson Highlands State Park. All other services are available in nearby Marion.

Hazards: Rough, rocky sections of trail; roads could be tricky.

Rescue index: Park personnel at the entrance station, park office, and Visitor Center are readily available to respond to any need for help.

Land status: Grayson Highlands State Park.

Maps: The park's brochure shows trails and roads suitable for and open to mountain biking; USGS 7.5 minute quads: Park NC-VA and Grassy Creek NC-VA.

Finding the trail: Take exit 16 from Marion south on VA 16. Follow this for 30 twisty miles to VA 58 at Volney. Turn right onto VA 58, heading west toward Damascus, and after 5 miles turn right at the entrance for Grayson Highlands State Park.

Source of additional information:
Grayson Highlands State Park
829 Grayson Highland Lane
Mouth of Wilson, Virginia 24363
(540) 579-7092

Notes on the trail: There are 4 access points to the trails in the park's northeastern section, where mountain biking is permitted. These are shown on the map for this ride as possible starting points to form a loop of sorts with a mile-long spur going out Seed Orchard Road to the northernmost edge of Grayson Highlands State Park.

RIDE 79 · New River Trail State Park

AT A GLANCE

Length/Configuration: 55-mile point-to-point with shorter options

Aerobic difficulty: Slight uphill from milepost 9 to Galax at milepost 52; Steepest uphill from milepost 9 to milepost 5

Technical difficulty: None

Scenery: Bucolic farmland, dense woods, rocky cliffs, and 200-foot railroad trestles above the New River

Special comments: Good family ride in shorter bites

The New River Trail runs from milepost 2 at Pulaski to Galax, plus a five-mile spur going off to Fries (pronounced *freeze*). However, this 55-mile point-to-point converted railroad line runs *downhill* from Galax to Claytor Lake, some 43 miles. It's the kind of gentle incline you'd normally associate with rail-to-trail conversions, but any way you look at it, a 43-mile downhill is a 43-mile downhill. For this reason many riders will elect to start at Fries or Galax and, with the help of a shuttle from New River Bicycles, ride to the shop's location at Draper or continue all the way to Pulaski.

The ever-changing trail scenery includes waterfront views along the New River; secluded wooded settings on one side and sheer walls of granite on the other; and railroad trestle crossings hovering hundreds of feet above streams such as Cripple Creek, made famous by the popular bluegrass song of the same name.

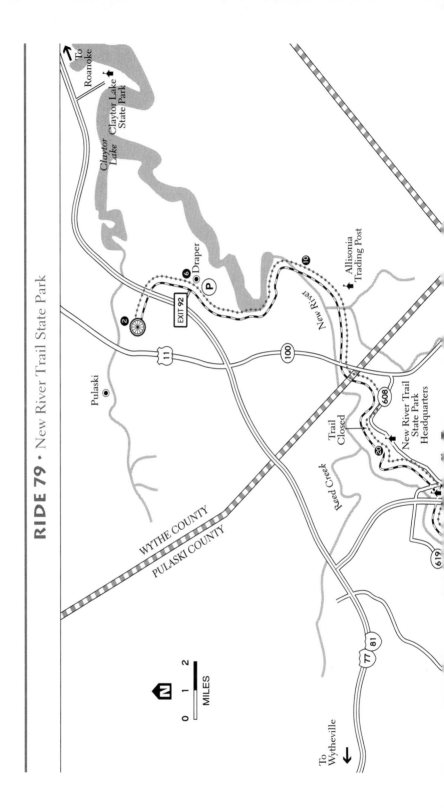

RIDE 79 · New River Trail State Park

To Roanoke

Claytor Lake Claytor Lake State Park

Claytor Lake

Draper

P

EXIT 92

Pulaski

New River

Allisonia Trading Post

11

100

608

Trail Closed

20

New River Trail State Park Headquarters

Reed Creek

WYTHE COUNTY
PULASKI COUNTY

619

77 81

To Wytheville

N
MILES
0 1 2

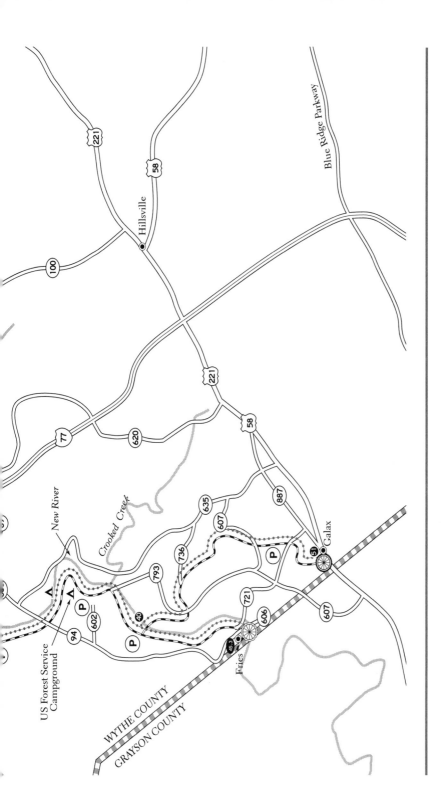

Take time to gaze at the oldest river in North America while riding along New River Trail.

General location: The trail runs from the town of Pulaski to Galax, with a 5-mile spur going to Fries.

Elevation change: The trail drops 500' between Galax and Claytor Lake (milepost 9). It gains 500' between there and milepost 5 and then drops another 300' before reaching the end of the line 2 miles from the Pulaski train station.

Season: Year-round.

Services: There is a state-operated campground and concessionaire at Foster Falls (milepost 24), complete with bike and tube rentals, food and drinks, and SSTs (sweet-smelling toilets). There is also a national forest campground at milepost 36 and the private Horseshoe Campground at milepost 9. Current plans call for State aquisition of these two campgrounds in the near future. All other services are available in the towns of Pulaski and Galax, located at opposite ends of the trail. In addition, New River Bicycles at milepost 6.5 makes it easy to arrange a shuttle, replace a tube, or purchase a new bike. This shop is just three-quarters of a mile from Interstate 81 at Draper exit 92.

Hazards: The trail closure between milepost 17 and milepost 19 has created a hazardous situation for novice cyclists attempting to ride the 8 miles of detour along state highways. Otherwise there is little of a hazardous nature on this smooth, well-graded former railroad bed.

Rescue index: The trail crosses state and county roads in numerous places so you're never too far from civilization and help when needed. There are generally state park personnel at the office next to historic Shot Tower at milepost 25.2.

Land status: New River State Park.

Maps: The *New River Trail State Park Map and User's Guide* is an excellent resource for learning the history and sights along the trail as well as for figuring out where you are at any given time; "Virginia State Parks' Trail Guide."

Finding the trail: The trail is accessible in any number of places between Pulaski at milepost 2 on the northern end, and Galax (milepost 51) and Fries (milepost 45) at the southern end. I've found it convenient to access the trail just one-half mile off the Draper exit from I-81. You can arrange a shuttle through New River Bicycles, located across the road from the trail, or just start pedaling in either direction from this spot at milepost 6.

Sources of additional information:

New River Trail State Park
176 Orphanage Drive
Foster Falls, Virginia 24360
(540) 699-6778

Allisonia Trading Post
HCO2, Box 15B
Allisonia, Virginia 24347
(540) 980-2051

New River Bicycles
Route 1, Box 175
Draper, Virginia 24324
(540) 980-1741

Tangent Outfitters
c/o Java River Company
1055 Norwood Street
Bradford, Virginia 24141
(540) 674-5202

For information about converting abandoned railroad beds into recreational trails:

Rails to Trails Conservancy
1400 Sixteenth Street, NW
Washington, DC 20036

Notes on the trail: Although some cyclists may hop onto New River Trail and pedal all the way to the other end with hardly a break, there's simply too much natural beauty and historic interest along the way to merely spin your cranks past them. Virginia's only linear park was created from the Cripple Creek branch of the Norfolk and Western's New River Division.

   This rail line was developed in an attempt to increase the production of pig iron from the natural iron ore mined in this part of the state, and in doing so, to attract more industry to the area. Numerous towns sprung up around railroad stops along the way. Shot Tower State Historic Park, headquarters for New River State Park, is definitely worth a stop; you'll learn how molten iron was dropped through air and then water to form ammunition. Pick up a $4 copy of the *New River State Park Map and User's Guide* from New River Bicycles to learn more about the rich history of this trail and its neighbors.

RIDE 80 · Mountain Bike Heaven

AT A GLANCE

Length/Configuration: 8-mile loop

Aerobic difficulty: Considerable on the 2.6-mile climb

Technical difficulty: Generally easy with some challenging parts along the single-track ascent

Scenery: Great views of neighboring peaks and ridges

Special comments: With an official name like Horse Heaven, expect some four-legged company

The Forest Service brochure calls this "Horse Heaven Loop," but the ride I took on a quiet weekday morning in the absence of horses, hikers, and bikers was mountain bike heaven for me. This 8-mile loop utilizes single-track, double-track, and Forest Service roads that are part of the Highlands Horse Trail. Except for rank novices, most mountain bikers can handle the mileage and terrain of this trail. For maximum enjoyment, I recommend riding this loop during the week when you can have the area to yourself. The 2.5-mile climb on double-track and single-track will be the most difficult part for most. When the going gets tough, don't be reluctant to stop and admire the outstanding views of neighboring peaks and ridges. The 3-mile double-track descent will leave you grinning for weeks.

Advanced cyclists will want to add the 1.5-mile (3 miles total) single-track out-and-back Henley Hollow Trail and then follow the Iron Mountain option, which will create a more challenging and somewhat longer 11-mile loop.

General location: 12 miles south of Wytheville.

Elevation change: The 8-mile loop starts at 2,680' and climbs gradually along FS 14 to 3,047'. The heartier climbing begins here and ascends to 3,873' before dropping back down to the start.

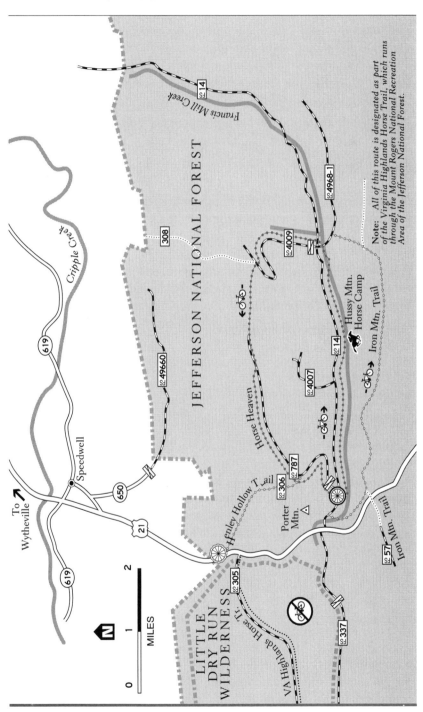

Note: All of this route is designated as part of the Virginia Highlands Horse Trail, which runs through the Mount Rogers National Recreation Area of the Jefferson National Forest.

Season: Spring through fall is the best time to ride in the Mount Rogers area, when snow and ice are no longer present at higher elevations. Be aware of the fall and winter hunting seasons and dress in highly visible attire. Call the Virginia Department of Game and Inland Fisheries (540-782-9051) for the opening and closing dates of hunting seasons for various game animals.

Services: All services are available in nearby Wytheville.

Hazards: Watch for and yield to horses along the way.

Rescue index: Help can be found in nearby Wytheville.

Land status: Jefferson National Forest—Mount Rogers National Recreation Area.

Maps: Jefferson National Forest map of the Mount Rogers National Recreation Area; USGS 7.5 minute quad: Speedwell.

Finding the trail: Go south from Wytheville for 10 miles on US 21. Those including the extra 3-mile (total) out-and-back on Henley Hollow Trail should park and start at the Henley Hollow parking area on US 21. All others will turn left onto FS 14 about .5 mile after Henley Hollow and start at the intersection of FS 14 and FS 787 on the left.

Sources of additional information:

Iron Mountain Trail Club
P.O. Box 1124
Damascus, Virginia 24236
www.naxs.com/people/thorsch

Virginia Highlander Bicycling
  and Flyfishing Association
347 Virginia Highlander Road

Sugar Grove, Virginia 24375
(540) 677-3600

Mount Rogers National Recreation
  Area of the Jefferson National Forest
3714 Highway 16
Marion, Virginia 24354-4097
(540) 783-5196

Notes on the trail: Start near the intersection of FS 14 and FS 787, heading away from VA 21. The gradual climb along this gravel road will limber you up. At the crest of a hill along this road, turn left onto FS 4009 and begin the real climb. This road ends after several miles and turns into single-track (follow the orange diamonds from this point), but you'll find it a ridable and manageable challenge. The final descent on wide Forest Service road is a blast, and it's easier to enjoy while maintaining safe control of your bike than if you had done this ride in the opposite direction.

For a greater challenge, head steeply up Henley Hollow before turning right at the intersection with the Highlands Horse Trail (FS 787) and heading downhill. Turn right onto FS 14 and then make a quick left onto Iron Mountain Trail. Follow the Iron Mountain Trail as it twists and turns among the pines and hemlocks until you turn left onto the Divide Trail, which will lead you across FS 14 and onto the same climb as the 8-mile loop. About two-thirds of the way along the descent, you'll turn right onto Henley Hollow Trail to return to Henley Hollow trailhead on VA 21. Whichever way you loop around this area, I think you'll agree that horse heaven and mountain bike heaven can be one and the same. Be sure to yield to horses and we'll all be angels in Mount Rogers' glimpse of eternity.

RIDE 81 • Skulls to Hurricane Gap

AT A GLANCE

Length/Configuration: 11-mile loop

Aerobic difficulty: Some good climbs

Technical difficulty: Overgrown crown vetch on old Forest Service Road 84 may hide obstacles; the rest of the trail covers rocky, sometimes rutted Forest Service road

Scenery: Dense woods with intermittent views of neighboring peaks

Special comments: A moderately challenging ride with no killer climbs and few technical obstacles

G aps were important to western Virginia's first pioneers and settlers. In an age that preceded earth-moving equipment and automobiles that would effectively lower the barriers mountains created for travelers, the first settlers found these naturally occurring low spots in a mountain range as the best— although by no means obstacle-free—places to cross the mountains that dominate the region.

Although Skulls Gap and Hurricane Gap can't rank up there in importance with the crucial Cumberland Gap in Southwest Virginia, through which our earliest pioneers passed on their way to the western frontier, these two minigaps did make it easier to cross the Iron Mountain range. This 11-mile loop circles Round Top and Double Top, two minor peaks along the top of Iron Mountain, on old FS 84 and returns on new FS 84. You can decide how progress has affected the replacement of the grassy double-track with a hard-packed wider forest road. This route has some pretty good climbs but otherwise should be suitable for a wide range of mountain bikers.

Timbering operations offered an economic boom to area residents, and the construction of railroads to move the lumber also gave local families the means to leave the hills and travel elsewhere. The sleepy community of Konnarock had greater prominence in the early 1900s, when its company store and electricity spelled real luxury in the hills and hollows of southwestern Virginia. The Lutheran Girls' School in Konnarock was built in the 1920s by the Hassinger Lumber Company, with wood siding from the all-but-extinct American chestnut.

General location: 15 miles east of Damascus.

Elevation change: This ride begins at an elevation of 3,300' at the Skulls Gap Picnic Area. It ascends and stays close to 3,800' along the old 84 double-track. The return from Hurricane Gap climbs to 4,320', going past Round Top (4,626') before dropping back to the start of the ride.

Season: The best time to ride this loop is spring through fall. Riders should also be aware of the fall and winter hunting seasons and dress in highly visible attire. Call the Virginia Department of Game and Inland Fisheries (540-782-9051) for the opening and closing dates of hunting seasons for various game animals.

Services: There is a small restaurant and convenience store in Konnarock, and all other services are available in Damascus.

Hazards: Obstacles such as rocks, limbs, and even the occasional hole may be hidden by the overgrown crown vetch on old FS 84.

Rescue index: You can get help from the store at Konnarock or in Damascus.

Land status: Jefferson National Forest—Mount Rogers National Recreation Area.

Maps: Jefferson National Forest map of the Mount Rogers National Recreation Area; USGS 7.5 minute quad: Whitetop Mountain.

Finding the trail: From the intersection of US 58 and VA 91 approximately 5 miles east of Damascus, go 9.5 miles to the intersection with VA 603. Continue through Konnarock on VA 603 for 4 miles and then go straight on VA 600. After driving 3 miles, turn left into the Skulls Gap Picnic Area, where you'll park and start the ride.

Sources of additional information:

Blue Blaze Bike and Shuttle Service
227 West Laurel Avenue
Damascus, Virginia 24236
(800) 475-5095 or (540) 475-5095

Iron Mountain Trail Club
P.O. Box 1124
Damascus, Virginia 24236
www.naxs.com/people/thorsch

Mount Rogers Outfitters
110 Laurel Avenue
Damascus, Virginia 24236
(540) 475-5416

Mount Rogers National Recreation
  Area of the Jefferson National Forest
3714 Highway 16
Marion, Virginia 24354-4097
(540) 783-5196

Notes on the trail: Start from the Skulls Gap Picnic Area and head east (away from VA 600) on FS 84. After an initial climb, this gravel hard-packed road levels off briefly before heading uphill and bending to the right. At this point, continue straight past a gate across unmarked old FS 84. After several miles of short ups and downs on this largely overgrown double-track you'll pass 2 or more tank traps before emptying into the parking area for Hurricane Gap.

RIDE 81 • Skulls to Hurricane Gap
RIDE 82 • Rowlands Creek Falls Circuit

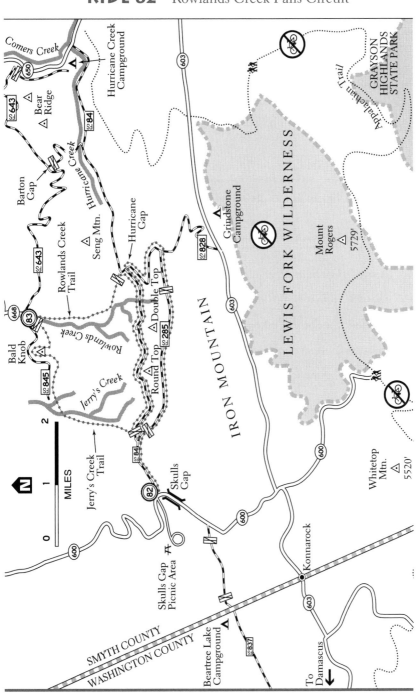

Turn right and head up to FS 285. As you climb higher you'll see some great views past Round Top and Double Top to the right. Iron Mountain Trail runs across the ridge just past a gate at the crest of one of several climbs along FS 285. This is a possible option for those who would rather ride a more demanding technical single-track. I had heard rumors about conflicts between mountain bikers and equestrians here, but the several I encountered along the way didn't pose any problems—although I'm careful to yield the right-of-way.

On one of the ride's better downhills—a 2-miler—you'll coast past old FS 84 on the right and finish up with a short climb back to the start.

RIDE 82 • Rowlands Creek Falls Circuit

AT A GLANCE

Length/Configuration: 11.7-mile loop

Aerobic difficulty: Some tough climbs

Technical difficulty: Moderate

Scenery: Several creeks and the falls

Special comments: A good challenge for intermediate and better bikers

This 11.7-mile loop is a combination of rocky single-track and wooded forest roads encircling Chestnut Ridge on the northern edge of Mount Rogers National Recreation Area. Its climbs and generally uneven riding surfaces make it a good challenge for intermediate and better bikers; however, less-experienced riders who are content to get off and walk when the going gets tough can enjoy much of the Rowlands Creek Falls Circuit.

The ride has two high points: One is the top of an infamous climb up Jerry's Creek Trail after gaining 900 feet in less than a mile. The second high point—one that more of us can appreciate—is the series of falls along Rowlands Creek that cascade through a dark, shaded area. This section of the Rowlands Creek Trail will tempt you to stop and admire the natural beauty of these environs. Don't be afraid to succumb; one of mountain biking's greatest joys for me is accessing areas such as this. This area stays cool and makes a great escape during the summer when the rest of Virginia is sweltering. Several creeks and branches make it especially nice to stop and dip your toes.

General location: 10 miles south of Marion.

Elevation change: Considerable ups and downs with an elevation range of 2,580–4,200'.

Season: Spring, summer, and fall, when snow and ice at higher elevations is no longer a viable threat. Riders should also be aware of fall and winter hunting seasons and dress in highly visible attire. Call the Virginia Department of Game and Inland Fisheries (540-782-9051) for the opening and closing dates of hunting seasons for various game animals.

Services: All services are available in nearby Marion.

Hazards: Creek crossings, especially when the water level is high.

Rescue index: Help can be found at Hurricane Creek Campground from Memorial Day to Labor Day. At other times, Forest Service personnel at the Mount Rogers Visitor Center on VA 16 can offer assistance.

Land status: Jefferson National Forest—Mount Rogers National Recreation Area.

Maps: Jefferson National Forest map of the Mount Rogers National Recreation Area; USGS 7.5 minute quads: Trout Dale and Whitetop Mountain.

Finding the trail: From the Mount Rogers Visitor Center, just south of Marion, follow VA 16 south for 3.5 miles to VA 601 at Sugar Grove. Turn right onto VA 601 and go another 3.5 miles until 601 becomes VA 670 at Teas. Continue on VA 670 for 4.5 miles and veer left onto VA 656. Go 1.7 miles and turn left onto VA 668. This road become FS 643 after .5 mile. Take the first right to reach the parking area and start riding from here.

Sources of additional information:

Mount Rogers National Recreation Area of the Jefferson National Forest
3714 Highway 16
Marion, Virginia 24354-4097
(540) 783-5196

Notes on the trail: Start riding just past the gate across FS 845. After several miles, this forest road ends just before crossing a branch of Jerry's Creek. Don't veer to the right; follow the orange blazes up a steep climb on Jerry's Creek Trail, which will lead to old FS 84 (now a gated gravel road that has been planted in crown vetch).

Follow old FS 84 as it winds around the northern flank of Round Top and Double Top. Pass the gate where old FS 84 empties onto Rowlands Creek Trail. Head downhill, crossing the creek several times before coming to the falls, which, depending on the amount of water, can be incredibly captivating. The trail gets somewhat rocky through here, but the sound of the creek cascading along will entertain you should you have to get off and walk through this verdant, heavily shaded area. Continue on Rowlands Creek Trail to FS 643, then turn left to return to the trailhead

---

RIDE 83 · Barton Gap

AT A GLANCE

Length/Configuration: 8.3-mile loop

Aerobic difficulty: Considerable with steady climbs

Technical difficulty: Easy

Scenery: Roadside streams lined with towering hemlocks and hardwoods

Special comments: Don't be too proud to use your granny gear

I hope you've learned not to assume short rides are easy ones. This 8.3-mile loop is relatively short but still quite challenging. Technical challenges are few, but you'll find yourself wishing you'd packed some oxygen while climbing steadily along a forest road and then a rough woods road. Fortunately, there are enough downhills in this densely wooded section of Mount Rogers National Recreation Area to make you forget the exertion by the time you finish at Hurricane Creek Campground.

Riders should have at least an average degree of fitness and not be too proud to use their lowest gears. Those looking for a longer ride in this area can combine Barton Gap and Rowlands Creek Falls Circuit to create an immense physical challenge.

General location: 15 miles south of Marion.

Elevation change: The ride begins at 2,700' at Hurricane Creek Campground. After a short drop to the creek, the trail climbs to 3,000' on Forest Service Road 643 at Barton Gap and continues to ascend to 3,500', before steadily descending to the start.

Season: Spring through fall, when snow and ice at higher elevations are no longer a viable threat. Riders should be aware of the fall and winter hunting seasons and dress in highly visible attire. Call the Virginia Department of Game and Inland Fisheries (540-782-9051) for the opening and closing dates of hunting seasons for various game animals.

Services: All services are available in nearby Marion.

Hazards: Crossing Hurricane Creek when the water is high.

Rescue index: Help can be found at Hurricane Creek Campground when this facility is open, from Memorial Day to Labor Day. At other times help can be found in Marion.

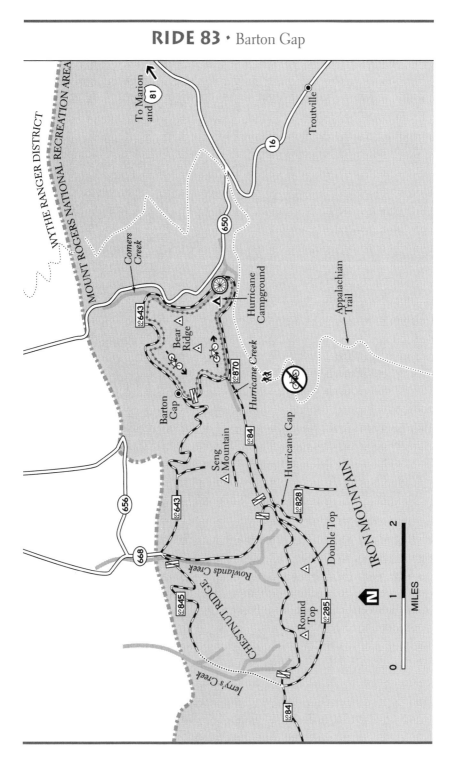

Land status: Jefferson National Forest—Mount Rogers National Recreation Area.

Maps: Jefferson National Forest map of the Mount Rogers National Recreation Area; USGS 7.5 minute quad: Whitetop Mountain.

Finding the trail: From the intersection of US 58 and VA 91 approximately 5 miles east of Damascus, go 9.5 miles to the intersection with VA 603. Continue on VA 603 for 10.5 miles to the intersection with VA 16 in the town of Troutville. Turn left onto VA 16 and go 2.5 miles to FS 650. Turn left onto FS 650 and follow the signs for 1.5 miles to Hurricane Creek Campground. Turn left onto FS 84 and start the ride from a parking pulloff on the left outside the campground.

Sources of additional information:

Blue Blaze Bike and Shuttle Service
227 West Laurel Avenue
Damascus, Virginia 24236
(800) 475-5095 or (540) 475-5095

Virginia Highlander Bicycling
  and Flyfishing Association
347 Virginia Highlander Road
Sugar Grove, Virginia 24375
(540) 677-3600

Iron Mountain Trail Club
P.O. Box 1124

Damascus, Virginia 24236
www.naxs.com/people/thorsch

Mount Rogers Outfitters
110 Laurel Avenue
Damascus, Virginia 24236
(540) 475-5416

Mount Rogers National Recreation
  Area of the Jefferson National Forest
3714 Hwy 16
Marion, Virginia 24354-4097
(540) 783-5196

Notes on the trail: Start by pedaling through Hurricane Creek Campground until you reach the trail at the end of the campground. This wonderful single-track follows Comers Creek and lies on a former rail bed. It may spoil you for the climbing that follows, so enjoy this bit of coasting while you can. The trail empties onto FS 643 (unmarked), where you'll turn left, heading away from and without crossing Comers Creek.

Slip your bike into low gear, sit back, and start cranking away. At one of the more pronounced flat spots along the way, you'll find yourself at Barton Gap between Plummer and Bear Ridge. Turn left past the gate onto unmarked FS 870 (also known as Barton Gap Trail) and continue to climb until an all-too-short descent through Hurricane Creek. After crossing the creek, turn left onto FS 84 and finish at Hurricane Creek Campground.

RIDE 84 · Whitetop Mountain

AT A GLANCE

Length/Configuration: 4.2-mile out-and-back (8.4 miles total)

Aerobic difficulty: Considerable 3-mile climb

Technical difficulty: Minimal, except where road gets rough near the top

Scenery: Great top-of-the-world views

Special comments: You will overlook the rest of Virginia from your perch at 5,500'

Whitetop's peak, or "bald," stands at over 5,500 feet. As such, it's the second- or third-highest peak in Virginia behind Mount Rogers at 5,729 feet. Pine Mountain tops Whitetop by six feet, although some consider Pine Mountain merely an extension of Mount Rogers and not a distinctly different peak. Be that as it may, Whitetop Mountain remains the highest point you can climb on a mountain bike since Mount Rogers lies in federally designated wilderness area. Those of you who are into bagging peaks or who merely want to look down on the rest of Virginia from this island in the sky, will want to make a run at this 8.4-mile out-and-back. You can also view mountain peaks in neighboring North Carolina and Tennessee from here.

Anyone who attempts (and expects to complete) this ride should be a strong climber, since you'll gain nearly 1,000 feet during the 4.2-mile "out" portion of this thigh-burner. As you might guess, the pitch of this ride makes it a tough one, so think about the vast panoramas from the top or the incredible descent on the second half of the ride to take your mind off your pain and suffering.

This altitude supports a biologically unique garden. In fact, a survey conducted by the Virginia Division of Natural Heritage found that Whitetop Mountain contains more threatened and endangered species than any other area in the state. The rock that underlies nature's carpeting in this vicinity is also quite unusual in that it is largely composed of rhyolites—the volcanic equivalent of granite—and the remnants of lava flows thought to have spewed forth from Mount Rogers about 720 million years ago.

This bald's name is more recent; references to it in 1747 use the name "Meadow Mountain." Many believe Native Americans in the area set fire to the mountainsides in late winter to clear areas for their spring gardens, so Whitetop's cleared meadow did not occur naturally.

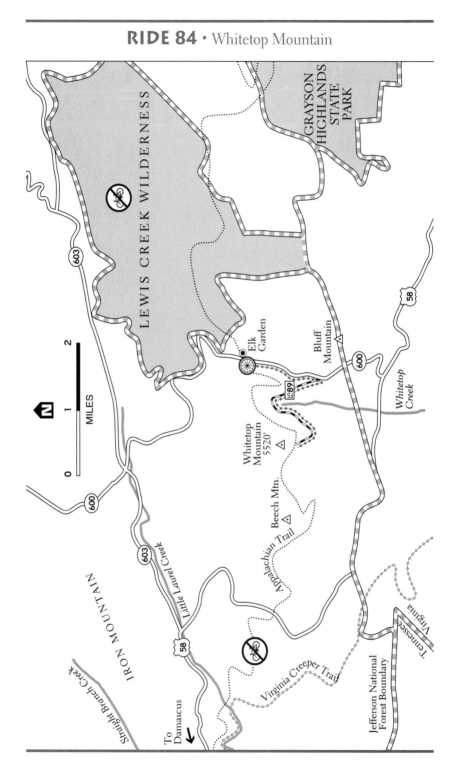

General location: 15 miles east of Damascus.

Elevation change: This ride begins at Elk Garden at 4,500'. You'll climb slightly along FS 600 before reaching 5,500' at the top of Whitetop Mountain.

Season: Spring through fall, when snow and ice at higher elevations are no longer a viable threat. However, given the 5,500-foot elevation at the top of Whitetop Mountain, you shouldn't be surprised to find cold white stuff at the top as late as May or as early as October. Riders should also be aware of fall and winter hunting seasons and dress in highly visible attire. Call the Virginia Department of Game and Inland Fisheries (540-782-9051) for the opening and closing dates of hunting seasons for various game animals.

Services: All services are available in nearby Damascus.

Hazards: Extreme and variable weather at high altitudes.

Rescue index: There is a pay telephone in the parking lot at Elk Garden. Should that be out of order, you can find help 15 miles away in Damascus.

Land status: Jefferson National Forest—Mount Rogers National Recreation Area.

Maps: Jefferson National Forest map of the Mount Rogers National Recreation Area; USGS 7.5 minute quad: Whitetop Mountain.

Finding the trail: From the intersection of US 58 and VA 91 approximately 5 miles east of Damascus, drive 9.5 miles east on US 58 to the intersection with VA 603. Turn right—staying on US 58—and continue for 8 miles to FS 600. Turn left onto this paved forest road and go almost 3 miles—past FS 89—and park in the large parking lot on the left at Elk Garden.

Source of additional information:
Mount Rogers National Recreation Area of the Jefferson National Forest
3714 Highway 16
Marion, Virginia 24354-4097
(540) 783-5196

Notes on the trail: From the parking lot at Elk Garden, head back down VA 600 before making a sharp right onto gravel FS 89. You'll have a chance to limber up those climbing muscles on a relatively straight section of road before reaching a series of switchbacks in the road. These occur just as the dense roadside woods of Fraser fir and other trees give way to the vast meadow at the top of the mountain. Keep pedaling until you reach the top. Even though the thought of the downhill to come is probably gnawing at you, spend adequate time at the top admiring this mountainous panorama.

RIDE 85 · Beartree Recreation Area

AT A GLANCE

Length/Configuration: 8-mile loop

Aerobic difficulty: Considerable climbing necessary

Technical difficulty: Lots of rock work

Scenery: Roadside streams and vistas from atop Iron Mountain

Special comments: You'll get a good technical workout along the top of Iron Mountain

This eight-mile loop starts and ends at the Beartree Recreation Area and includes enough riding on the Iron Mountain Trail to please anyone who likes rocky, technical single-track. Iron Mountain forms the backbone for the 115,000-acre Mount Rogers National Recreation Area, and the challenging Iron Mountain Trail is the magnet that attracts mountain bikers who insist that *hard* is the only way. There is also a short section of this ride on hard-surface road through the recreation area. Although not a long ride, this is a moderately challenging one and should be undertaken by those with moderate to advanced bike handling skills and physical abilities.

Beartree's 84 campsites, warm showers, location, and other amenities make this an excellent base from which to explore the array of trails and forest roads that the Mount Rogers National Recreation Area has to offer, including the 33-mile Virginia Creeper Trail. The 14-acre Beartree Lake offers fishing and the opportunity for a welcome dip after working up a good sweat on the trail.

General locatio East of Damascus.

Elevation change: The ride starts at 3,360' and climbs to Iron Mountain Trail at 3,840'. There are some ups and downs across Grosses Mountain, but the trail generally hovers around 3,800'. The descent from Shaw's Gap to Forest Service Road 837 running through the Beartree Recreation Area drops you down to 3,160', which will take you to the start.

Season: Spring through fall is the best time to ride in the Mount Rogers area. Riders should also be aware of the fall and winter hunting seasons and dress in highly visible attire. Call the Virginia Department of Game and Inland Fisheries (540-782-9051) for the opening and closing dates of hunting seasons for various game animals.

Services: Beartree Recreation Area is a fee area with facilities for camping, picnicking, fishing, and swimming. All other services are available in nearby Damascus.

Hazards: Technical parts of this ride may be hazardous to your health. Early spring and late fall weather can change quickly.

Rescue index: National forest personnel at Beartree Recreation Area can provide assistance when the campground is open. At other times help can be found in nearby Damascus.

Land status: Jefferson National Forest—Mount Rogers National Recreation Area.

Maps: Jefferson National Forest map of the Mount Rogers National Recreation Area; USGS 7.5 minute quads: Konnarock and Whitetop Mountain.

Finding the trail: Take VA 58 east from Damascus. Staying on VA 58, turn left at the intersection with VA 91. After 7.5 miles, turn left onto FS 837 into Beartree Recreation Area. If you plan to do this ride but don't wish to utilize the recreational facilities, park at the fishing parking area on the right before you enter the fee area.

Sources of additional information:

Iron Mountain Trail Club
P.O. Box 1124
Damascus, Virginia 24236
www.naxs.com/people/thorsch

Mount Rogers National Recreation
  Area of the Jefferson National Forest
3714 Highway 16
Marion, Virginia 24354-4097
(540) 783-5196

Notes on the trail: Start the ride on FS 837, heading slightly uphill on this hard-surface road. At the campground circle, continue past Straight Branch Trail and turn onto Lum Trail, partially hidden by the bathrooms at Beartree Campground. You'll notice a trailside shelter on the left before you come to the intersection with yellow-blazed Iron Mountain Trail. Turn left onto the trail and wend your way across the top of this range for several miles to the cloverleaf trail intersection at Shaw's Gap. According to local mountain bike enthusiast Tom Horsch, many of the trails east of FS 90 meet at this point, and it's a good spot to get oriented. Make 2 left turns to get onto the Shaw's Gap Trail, blazed with yellow squares. This will take you back to the Beartree Group Campground. From there turn left onto FS 837, or Beartree Gap Road, with Straight Branch accompanying you back to the start.

RIDE 86 • Feathercamp Ridge

AT A GLANCE

Length/Configuration: 2.75-mile out-and-back (5.5 miles total) with several longer loop options

Aerobic difficulty: Considerable for the 2.75-mile climb

Technical difficulty: Rocky, sometimes rutted Forest Service road

Scenery: A panorama of Virginia's highest peaks

Special comments: Pair this exhaustive climb and exhilarating down-hill with mileage on Iron Mountain Trail or intersect double-track to create longer, more challenging loops

This five-and-a-half-mile up-and-back (2.75 miles one-way) ride is pretty simple—you'll bust a gut getting to the top and have the ride of your life getting back down. All things in life should be that straightforward. Along the way you'll see views too heavenly for mere mortals, and you'll pass numerous access points for other rides fanning off in all directions from this peak, at 3,750 feet.

I believe the name for this ridge comes from the notion that only those mountain bikers who sprout wings ever make it to the top. Members of the Virginia Highlands Mountain Bike Club incorporated FS 90, Iron Mountain Trail, Beartree Gap Trail, and several other nearby trails in the route for their annual Virginia Mountain Bike Challenge in an attempt to disprove the need for feathers on this climb or anywhere else in the Mount Rogers area.

All kidding aside, this is a tough climb that only intermediate and stronger riders should attempt. However, you don't get to be an intermediate or stronger hill climber without taking a shot at ascents such as this. So if you're an experienced novice who's itching to ride with the big kids, switch into your lowest granny gear and get a running start.

General location: 6 miles east of Damascus.

Elevation change: The ride starts at an elevation of 2,800' and ascends to 3,400' in the first mile, and then levels briefly through Sandy Flats. From there it ascends once more to the former site of Feathercamp Lookout Tower at 3,750'.

Season: Spring through fall, when the presence of snow and ice at higher elevations is no longer a viable threat. However, having said that, it was here that I went to sleep in my tent on Easter Sunday after a balmy day with temperatures in the 80s and awoke before dawn under snow and blizzard conditions. So you never know.

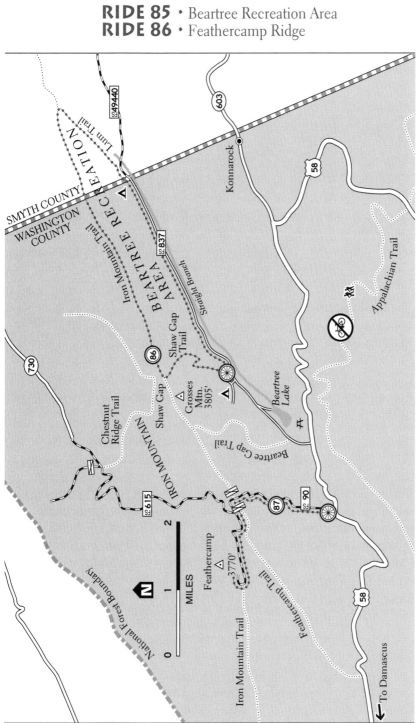

Riders should also use caution during fall and winter hunting seasons and dress in highly visible attire. Call the Virginia Department of Game and Inland Fisheries (540-782-9051) for the opening and closing dates of hunting seasons for various game animals.

Services: All services are available in nearby Abingdon and Damascus.

Hazards: Technical parts of this ride can be hazardous to your health, especially on the descent.

Rescue index: Help can be found in the nearby town of Damascus.

Land status: Jefferson National Forest—Mount Rogers National Recreation Area.

Maps: Jefferson National Forest map for Mount Rogers National Recreation Area; USGS 7.5 minute quad: Konnarock.

Finding the trail: Take VA 58 east from Damascus. Turn left at the intersection with VA 91, staying on VA 58. Turn left onto FS 90 a short distance ahead and park near the bottom as far off either road as possible.

Sources of additional information:

Blue Blaze Bike and
  Shuttle Service
227 West Laurel Avenue
Damascus, Virginia 24236
(800) 475-5095 or (540) 475-6262

Iron Mountain Trail Club
P.O. Box 1124
Damascus, Virginia 24236
www.naxs.com/people/thorsch

Mount Rogers Outfitters
110 Laurel Avenue
Damascus, Virginia 24236
(540) 475-5416

Mount Rogers National Recreation
  Area of the Jefferson National Forest
3714 Highway 16
Marion, Virginia 24354-4097
(540) 783-5196

Notes on the trail: There is no shortage of potential and well-trodden places to ride in this out-of-the-way section of the Blue Ridge Highlands. This ride offers some great views of Mount Rogers, Virginia's highest peak (5,729') whose location in a wilderness area is off limits to bikes. With the help of a national forest map, you can plot a course along Iron Mountain Trail west to Damascus or east to Shaw's Gap above Beartree Recreation Area, or head north to Chestnut Ridge. Look at this as a trial by fire and an introduction to what uphills and downhills can be like in the Mount Rogers National Recreation Area.

RIDE 87 · Virginia Creeper Trail

AT A GLANCE

Length/Configuration: 33.4-mile point-to-point with other mileages possible

Aerobic difficulty: 16.8-mile downhill grade from Whitetop Station to Damascus; slight uphill from Damascus to Abingdon

Technical difficulty: None

Scenery: Scenic Laurel Creek tumbles through a magnificent rocky gorge from Whitetop Station to Damascus; from there, the trail passes through open pasture to Abingdon

Special comments: Good family ride; shuttles allow you to create an easy 16.8-mile outing

The 33.4-mile Virginia Creeper Trail attracts countless cyclists, hikers, and equestrians to this corner of southwestern Virginia. The trail was once a Native American footpath and later was used by early white pioneers such as Daniel Boone. By 1905 Virginia-Carolina Railroad locomotives and their loads of lumber, iron ore, supplies, and passengers were creeping up the steep grades between Abingdon, Virginia, and Elkland, North Carolina.

The line's failure to earn its keep for several decades forced the Virginia Creeper to travel these tracks on its final run on March 31, 1977. However, the loss of this vestige of an American tradition has given us a recreational trail and access to a beautiful—often spectacular—section of Blue Ridge Highlands countryside.

There are a number of spots along this easy-to-pedal, point-to-point, converted railroad bed. You can park your car and easily get onto the trail, but you may want to take advantage of one of the local businesses that provide shuttles to Whitetop Station at the highest point of the trail. From there you can spread your wings and fly downhill to wherever you've decided to leave your vehicle. This trail is for everyone, particularly the 16.8-mile downhill stretch from Whitetop Station to the town of Damascus.

General location: This 33.4-mile linear trail runs from Green Cove near the farthest eastern point of Tennessee through the town of Damascus and on to the city of Abingdon.

Elevation change: The trail drops 1,576' between Whitetop Station and Damascus. It continues downhill past Damascus before climbing slightly to Abingdon for an overall gain of 65' between the 2 towns.

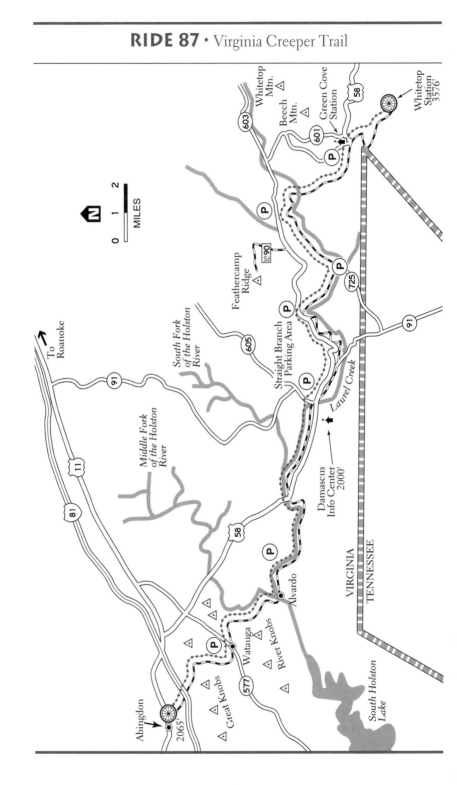

Whitetop Laurel Creek follows Virginia Creeper Trail into the town of Damascus.

Season: Late spring through early fall is the best time to ride.

Services: All services are available in Damascus and Abingdon, including shuttle service and bike rentals.

Hazards: Be careful of other riders on the trail since riders of all ages and ability levels bike here.

Rescue index: This is a very popular trail when the weather is nice, so it shouldn't be a problem to get help from other trail users.

Land status: Jefferson National Forest—Mount Rogers National Recreation Area and public right-of-way through private property.

Maps: Trail brochures from both the Abingdon and Damascus Chamber of Commerce contain maps; USGS 7.5 minute quads: Damascus, Konnarock, and Abingdon.

Finding the trail: To reach the end of the trail in Abingdon, take exit 19 off Interstate 81, heading toward Abingdon on US 11. Follow the numerous signs into Abingdon, where you'll find the end of the trail on Pecan Street S.E. If in doubt, look for the old Virginia Creeper locomotive in retirement at the Abingdon trailhead. To reach the trail in Damascus, take exit 19 off I-81, heading toward Damascus on US 58. Once you reach Damascus, approximately 11 miles from I-81, follow the numerous signs and US 58 to the very obvious red caboose information trailer, which the trail passes.

Sources of additional information:

Mount Rogers National Recreation
Area of the Jefferson National Forest
3717 Highway 16
Marion, Virginia 24354-4097
(540) 783-5196

Abingdon Convention and Visitors
Bureau
335 Cummings Street
Abingdon, Virginia 24210
(800) 435-3440

Damascus Town Hall
P.O. Box 56
Damascus, Virginia 24236
(540) 475-3831

Virginia Creeper Trail Club
P.O. Box 2382
Abingdon, Virginia 24212

Blue Blaze Bike and Shuttle Service
P.O. Box 982
Damascus, Virginia 24236
(800) 475-5095

Highlands Ski and Outdoor Center
P.O. Box 1944
Abingdon, Virginia 24210
(540) 628-1329

Mount Rogers Outfitters
110 Laurel Avenue
Damascus, Virginia 24236
(540) 475-5416

For information about converting abandoned railroad beds into recreational trails:

Rails to Trails Conservancy
1400 Sixteenth Street, NW
Washington, DC 20036

Notes on the trail: The section from Whitetop to the information caboose at Damascus has the greatest degree of incline, as well as—I think—the preferable scenery. This 16.8-mile section is part of Mount Rogers National Recreation Area, and the Damascus-to-Abingdon stretch is owned jointly by the 2 towns as a public right-of-way through private property.

The 15-mile Damascus-to-Abingdon section crosses pastureland along the banks of the South Fork of the Holston River. It works well as a 30-mile round-trip ride because of a minimal gain of 450 feet, as opposed to the 1,700-foot gain along the Damascus-to-Whitetop stretch. However, you'll have to open and close 10 cattle gates (20 for a round-trip) between Damascus and Abingdon. Take care not to stray from the trail, which is bordered by private land in some stretches. All in all, the Virginia Creeper Trail is a great ride that covers a beautiful cross-section of scenery in this corner of the state.

RIDE 88 · Guest River Trail

AT A GLANCE

Length/Configuration: 5.8-mile out-and-back (11.6 miles round-trip)

Aerobic difficulty: Steady downhill from trailhead to trail's end

Technical difficulty: None

Scenery: The scenic Guest River flows through a magnificent sandstone gorge

Special comments: Good family ride, but keep in mind the total distance and uphill return

The concept of taking an abandoned railroad bed and turning it into a recreational trail is so logical that it almost defies logic to do otherwise once the tracks are removed. Besides the obvious benefits of adding a smooth trail surface for nonmotorized users is the other, less obvious, perk such trails offer: access to otherwise inaccessible settings of incredible natural beauty.

This is certainly the case with the 5.8-mile (one-way) out-and-back Guest River Trail, which joined the better-known New River and Virginia Creeper Trails in the Blue Ridge Highlands in 1994 as one of Virginia's newer rail-trail conversions. The trail came about after its abandonment by the Norfolk and Southern Railroad, which in turn donated the land to the U.S. Forest Service. Students from the Flatwoods Job Corps Center improved the trestles that cross several mountain streams flowing into this stretch of the Guest River.

Along the way to the confluence of the Guest and Clinch Rivers are mileage markers and eight numbered points of interest. Families and beginning riders will enjoy this ride, especially the downhill on the way to the Clinch. Don't be ashamed to use the benches on your way out of the gorge on an uphill that may get you breathing hard.

The Forest Service's trail brochure speaks of Native Americans who lived in and around this gorge from 9,000 B.C. through the mid-1800s. I saw few other trail users on a clear, chilly, Sunday morning in late April. I felt a real sense of solitude, but it's probably only a matter of time before the word gets around.

General location: 10 miles southeast of Wise.

Elevation change: The trail descends steadily for 400' from beginning to end at the 5.8-mile point.

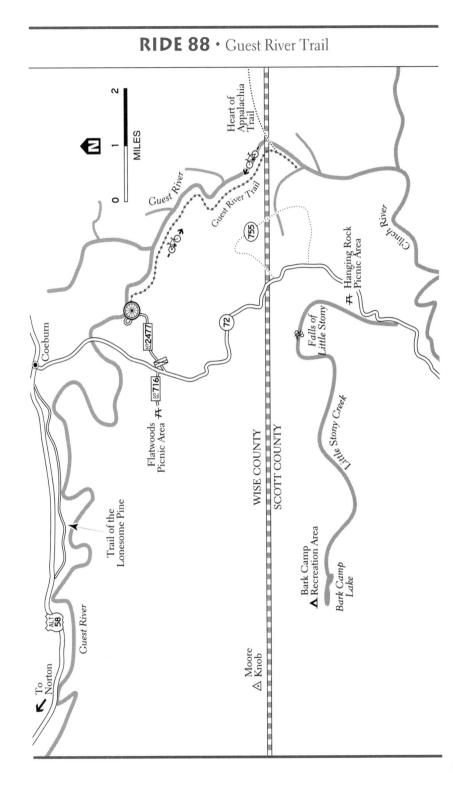

Season: Spring through fall is the best time to ride this trail. Winter weather is extremely cold. However, if you're willing to bundle up there's no reason not to ride here, as long as the trail is clear of ice and snow.

Services: There are toilet facilities at the trailhead and several restaurants and grocery stores in the nearby town of Coeburn.

Hazards: Although there are several safe access points to the Guest River along the trail, this scenic stretch of water generally lies at the bottom of a steep gorge. If you plan to go down to the river, do so at a level spot, and don't let the awesome natural beauty of this gorge allow you to forget the strength of the water current if you go wading.

Rescue index: Help can be found in the nearby town of Coeburn.

Land status: Jefferson National Forest—Clinch Ranger District.

Maps: Jefferson National Forest map of the Clinch Ranger District (The Guest River Trail is designated as Forest Service Trail 216 on the map of the Clinch District); USGS 7.5 minute quad: Coeburn.

Finding the trail: From the town of Coeburn drive out VA 58 Business Alternate. Turn onto Dungannon Road/VA 72 South. Continue for 2 miles and enter the Jefferson National Forest, and you'll see a sign for the Guest River Gorge on your left. Turn here onto FS 2477 and continue down the road to the parking loop at the end of the road. The entrance to the trail is clearly marked from the parking area.

Sources of additional information:

Clinch Ranger District of the Jefferson National Forest
9416 Darden Drive
Wise, Virginia 24293
(540) 328-2931

For information about converting abandoned railroad beds into recreational trails:

Rails to Trails Conservancy National Headquarters
1100 Seventeenth Street, NW
Tenth Floor
Washington, DC 20036
(202) 331-9696

Notes on the trail: Consider Mother Nature's force, which cut a 400-foot chasm through this 300-million year old Pennsylvania sandstone. This stretch of the Guest is so beautiful, it should be designated a State Scenic River. As I flew downhill toward the trail's end at the intersection with the Clinch River, I wondered who would stop to rest on the sturdy wooden benches erected along this fast 5.8-mile downhill. I discovered the answer as I panted my way uphill on the return trip.

You'll start your ride by entering Swede Tunnel, built in 1922 by local builders, some of whom— you guessed it—were Swedish. Chances are that once you begin pedaling downhill you probably won't want to stop at the

Mountain bikers will enjoy riding this former rail bed along scenic Guest River in Jefferson National Forest.

numbered points of interest or the innumerable points of natural beauty along the way. That's one advantage to this out-and-back configuration. On the return trip uphill, you can stop as often as you like—or need to—and enjoy the scenery as you catch your breath. According to Ed Grove in his *Classic Virginia Rivers*, "the Guest leaves the high country to plunge 550 feet at a rate of nearly 90 feet per mile to the Clinch River upstream of Dungannon. It is this rugged descent through all that sandstone that is responsible for one of the most challenging and intense whitewater runs in Virginia." If you find yourself doing a little huffing and puffing while pedaling back to the trailhead, just imagine what it would be like to try to paddle back upstream.

RIDE 89 · Breaks Interstate Park

AT A GLANCE

Length/Configuration: 2-mile loop

Aerobic difficulty: Mostly flat, with a few short ups and downs

Technical difficulty: Minimal

Scenery: Dense woods along the trail; be sure to check out the "Grand Canyon of the South"

Special comments: The park is a great family getaway

Breaks Interstate Park, often referred to as the "Grand Canyon of the South," joins a section of the Russell Fork River that has, over the last 250 million years, carved out a canyon five miles long with 1,600-foot, sheer rock walls. Nature's awesome persistence has created the largest canyon east of the Mississippi River.

The mountain bike trail itself is short but sweet. It's a fun single-track for those who like ups and downs to make it interesting, but not too many technical challenges. This is a very good beginners single-track because it addresses handling skills and not aerobic or physical endurance; it's suitable for older children ready for some fairly tame single-track. After driving eight miles up the mountain from Haysi, a relatively flat single-track is probably the last thing bikers expect to find.

It would have been easy to overlook this two-mile mountain bike trail at Breaks Interstate Park. But I'd never been to this part of the state in my two and a half decades of living in Virginia. And now I'm glad I took the time.

The park is pretty far from everything else in Virginia, lying as it does on the Kentucky border. The narrow, twisting access roads don't make it any easier. Even as the crow flies it's a long way to get here; but given the nature of the narrow, twisty roads that fought their way up and over some very serious mountains, I believe the crow probably beat me by a good two hours.

One excellent way to break up the long drive to the Virginia-Kentucky border is a stop at the Historic Crab Orchard Museum and Pioneer Park near Tazewell. Besides being southwestern Virginia's largest man-made tourist attraction, it's also Virginia's most comprehensive museum of Appalachian history. In addition to various special events held monthly, you'll see a gallery of artifacts dating back to early area Native American settlements, as well as 13 log and stone houses, crops in cultivation, and a replica of the first McCormick reaper.

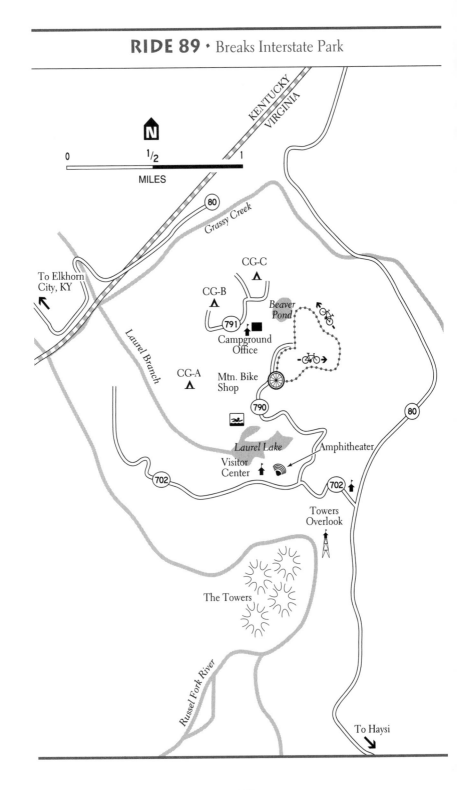

Early morning fog
coming off the "Grand
Canyon of the South" at
Breaks Interstate Park.

General location: On the Virginia-Kentucky border 67 miles northwest of Abingdon, Virginia.

Elevation change: Short, steep ups and downs with a minimal change in elevation overall. The highest point on the trail is around 1,740'.

Season: The most desirable time to ride is from the end of April through early October. Winters are pretty extreme out here in "coal country."

Services: The park itself offers camping, a 34-unit motor lodge (open April through December), cabins, an Olympic-sized swimming pool (open Memorial Day through Labor Day), bike rentals, fishing, a reasonably priced restaurant, and a schedule of monthly activities. A fee is charged to enter Breaks Interstate Park. The town of Grundy has several restaurants and grocery stores.

Hazards: The trail is narrow and twisty, which could be a problem depending on your bike handling skills.

Rescue index: Help can be found at the campground office or from 1 of the park employees patrolling the grounds.

Land status: State park administered jointly by Virginia and Kentucky.

Maps: Trail map available from the Visitor Center; USGS 7.5 minute quad: Elkhorn City, KY-VA.

Finding the trail: As I was told on several occasions when in Abingdon, there's really no good way to get to Breaks Interstate Park. However, you can get relatively close by following US 460 to Grundy, Virginia, and then completing the last 9 miles after a left turn onto VA 609. Once you enter the park, follow the signs for the mountain bike rental shack and trail. The trail starts across the road from the rental shack and is easy to find.

Sources of additional information:

Breaks Interstate Park
P.O. Box 100
Breaks, Virginia 24607-0100
(540) 865-4413

Campground Store
(bike rentals)
(540) 865-4413 extension 245

Crab Orchard Museum and Pioneer
  Park
Route 1, Box 194
Tazewell, Virginia 24651
(540) 988-6755

Notes on the trail: The trail starts across the road from the Mountain Bike Shed and there's only 1 way to go. After riding the loop, you'll empty out onto a service road that passes the stables and Beaver Pond before arriving back at the beginning. Plans call for a half-mile spur trail to open soon. While I wouldn't suggest making a special trip out to Breaks to ride 2 miles of single-track, the park would make an excellent destination for a longer vacation, especially for a family.

RIDE 90 · Sugar Hill Loop Trail

AT A GLANCE

Length/Configuration: 5-mile loop

Aerobic difficulty: Considerable on the 1.5-mile climb

Technical difficulty: None

Scenery: The beautiful Clinch River and views from atop Sugar Hill

Special comments: Good for beginner to intermediate riders; families can enjoy an easy 1-mile out-and-back (2 miles total) along Clinch River

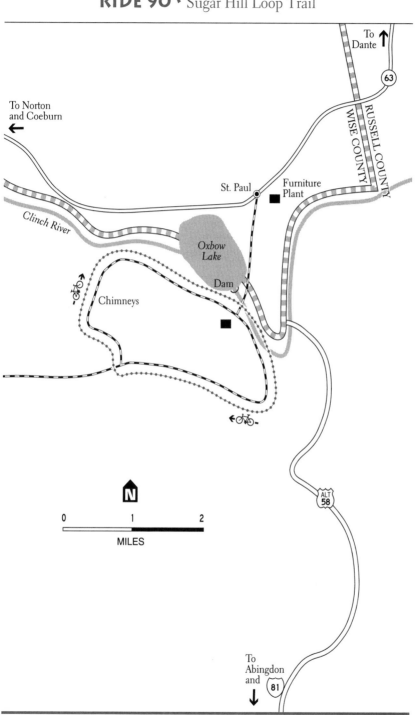

To Dante

63

To Norton and Coeburn

RUSSELL COUNTY
WISE COUNTY

St. Paul

Furniture Plant

Clinch River

Oxbow Lake

Dam

Chimneys

N

0   1   2

MILES

ALT 58

To Abingdon and 81

Many Virginians often overlook the state's far southwest largely because it is closer to capitals of neighboring states than to its own. However, there's an increased effort to let folks know that the terrain in this corner of the Old Dominion isn't strictly for coal miners and mountain goats; it contains the raw materials for a lifetime of memorable outdoor adventures including mountain biking.

The 5-mile Sugar Hill Loop Trail, in particular, offers beginning to intermediate bikers an opportunity to warm up along scenic Clinch River, said to be one of the cleanest rivers on the east coast. Even a family with young children can enjoy this first mile or so of flat biking before returning when the trail begins to climb at the first bend to the right. However, should you forgo the ascent to the top of Sugar Hill, you'll also miss out on an extremely hairy downhill back to the river. Along the way you'll encounter sharp hairpin turns—the stuff mountain biking memories are made of. It's such a sweet downhill you might guess the hill is named for it, instead of the maple syrup operations that occupied this knoll in the 1930s.

For those who wish to slow down and savor the experience, trees have been numbered and can be identified by using a trail brochure. History buffs will want to examine the site formerly occupied by François Pierre de Tuboeuf's hand-hewn cabin, circa 1791.

General location: 25 miles northwest of Abingdon.

Elevation change: Starting from 1,980' on the Clinch River, this trail rises to 2,380' at the top of Sugar Hill before dropping back to the trailhead.

Season: Year-round, although it's best to avoid this area after periods of heavy rain and when the frozen ground has recently thawed.

Services: Most services are available in the adjacent town of St. Paul; a wider array of food and lodging can be found 25 miles southeast in Abingdon.

Hazards: Hairpin turns along the downhill section.

Rescue index: You can readily summon help .5 mile away in downtown St. Paul.

Land status: Private land with public right-of-way on the trail.

Maps: USGS 7.5 minute quad: St. Paul.

Finding the trail: From Abingdon, follow VA 58-A west for 25 miles to St. Paul. The trail is just outside the commercial area and behind the Fournier Furniture Company at the intersection of VA 58-A and VA 63. The trail starts to the left of Oxbow Lake.

Source of additional information:

Heart of Appalachia Tourism Center   Big Stone Gap, VA 24219
Cloverleaf Square, Suite G3   (888) 798-2386

Notes on the trail: Although this 5-mile loop can be ridden in either direction, most of you will want to follow it clockwise. This direction allows you to warm up on the flat section bordering the Clinch River before you begin a relatively gentle but steady climb to the top of Sugar Hill. After climbing a short distance, you'll notice a trail running off to the left along the edge of a cultivated hillside. If you want to increase the length of this ride considerably, take a left here and the trail will lead to a portion of the 125-mile Heart of Appalachia Bike Route. Otherwise, continue to climb past the old cabin site marked only by its standing chimneys and a sign pointing toward St. Paul. Upon reaching the crest of this climb, take a deep breath, check your brakes, and then start descending. This one's short and sweet and may leave you with a real Sugar Hill craving. If that's the case, take another run. Great rides like this can be habit-forming, but definitely good for your health.

RIDE 91 · Heart of Appalachia Bike Route

AT A GLANCE

Length/Configuration: 125-mile scenic bike trail

Aerobic difficulty: Some hills, but the route strenuous by virtue of length rather than technical difficulty

Technical difficulty: None

Scenery: Rolling fields bordered by mountians complete with grazing livestock

Special comments: An excellent weekend getaway, with accomodations and side trips along the route

Virginia's far southwest has gotten a bad rap over the years. Although many outdoor lovers make the journey as far southwest as Mount Rogers National Recreation Area, the more western counties of Lee, Scott, Wise, Dickenson, Buchanan, Tazewell, and Russell see few sightseers. If it weren't for a local lawyer, I would count myself among those who still think the topography of this region is only suitable for coal mines and mountain goats.

Frank Kilgore, a lawyer and active mountain biker from St. Paul, Virginia, developed the five-mile Sugar Hill Loop Trail (Ride 91) along the scenic Clinch River on land that he owned and then turned it over to the town of St. Paul for use as a hiking and biking path. Most of us would give that act a "10" on the do-some-good-for-other-mountain-bikers scale. But that wasn't

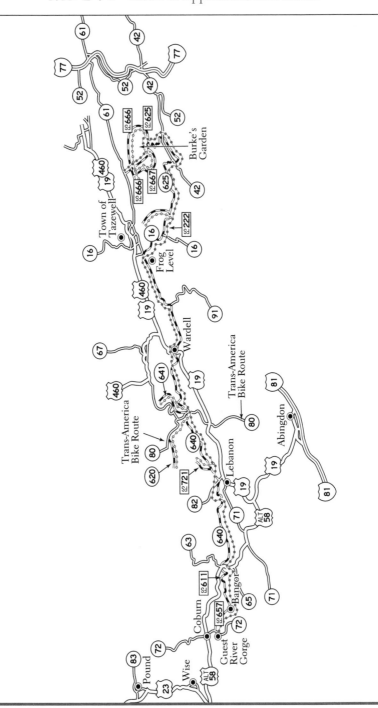

enough for Mr. Kilgore, who is a native of the region, a strong advocate to increase tourism, and an outspoken environmentalist.

In the course of a month, Frank mapped out the 125-mile Heart of Appalachia Bike route, which is roughly half paved/half gravel roads. That's pretty fast work, especially when you consider that he was even able to get the necessary rights-of-way across privately owned land.

This 125-mile point-to-point route starts at Burke's Garden and runs in a southwesterly direction before ending at the parking lot for Guest River Trail (Ride 89). Burke's Garden is unique in many ways. This circular valley lies at an elevation of 3,100 feet and is completely surrounded by a sandstone ridge, giving it the aerial appearance of the Garden of Eden in a lunar crater. This area is Virginia's largest rural historical district and national landmark, as well as the state's "premier biological hotspot" according to the Virginia Museum of Natural History.

General location: Wise, Russell, and Tazewell counties

Elevation change: Plenty of rolling hills

Season: The most desirable time to ride is from the end of April through early October. Winters are pretty extreme out here in "coal country."

Services: Available in towns along the route, including St. Paul, Lebanon, Wardell, Tazewell, and Frog Level.

Hazards: Watch out for cars and other vehicles along the ride, which is also billed as a scenic drive.

Rescue index: tSome stretches seem desolate, but the route is regularly traveled by tourists and locals.

Land status: A combinbation of federal, state, local and private land.

Maps: Trail map available from the Virginia Coalfield Regional Tourism Developement Authority, and specifically its Heart of Appalachia Tourism Center.

Finding the trail: The recommended trailhead is at Burke's Garden, east of VA 623, which runs between Route 61 to the north and Route 42 to the south.

Source of additional information:
Heart of Appalachia Tourism Center
Cloverleaf Square, Suite G3
Big Stone Gap, VA 24219
(888) 798-2386

Notes on the trail: From Burke's garden, follow the Heart of Appalachia Bike Route through beautiful rolling hills on VA 623, Highway 42 (not for long), and VA 625. You will ride up and over a mountain or two and through

Tazewell's verdant pastures (the setting for the movie *Lassie*). Continue through lesser-traveled sections of Jefferson National Forest on FR 222, and past some of Virginia's most spectacular real estate. State Routes 16, 91 and 609 will wind you past Frog Level and Wardell. Once you reach VA 640 you can relax and forget about navigation for a while. The road comprises approximately one-third of the trip. It also bisects the Trans America Bike Route. Eventually, you will head north on Route 657 to reach the Guest River Trail.

There are also 50 miles of out-and back side trips linked to the Heart of Appalachia Bike Route. These detours allow riders to view such awesome sights as the Pinnacle at Big Cedar Falls and Russell Creek Falls before ending on the 5.8-mile Guest River Trail along a scenic section of the Guest River.

Although the intent of the route is a trail the average rider can handle, with lodgings spaced intermittently, many of you may want to park and ride a section of this route as an out-and-back or a point-to-point with shuttle vehicles at each end. Fairly regular intersections with state roads make this an easy undertaking, and the future placement of signs marking the trail will also help. Others may want to explore specific areas such as Burke's Garden, gravel roads that pass reclaimed coal mines, and backcountry roads through a beautiful and often overlooked part of the Old Dominion. Whatever you do, don't wait too long to explore this area of Virginia's southwest.

GLOSSARY

This short list of terms does not contain all the words used by mountain bike enthusiasts when discussing their sport. But it should serve as an introduction to the lingo you'll hear on the trails.

ATB   all-terrain bike; this, like "fat-tire bike," is another name for a mountain bike

ATV   all-terrain vehicle; this usually refers to the loud, fume-spewing three- or four-wheeled motorized vehicles you will not enjoy meeting on the trail—except, of course, if you crash and have to hitch a ride out on one

bladed   refers to a dirt road which has been smoothed out by the use of a wide blade on earth-moving equipment; "blading" gets rid of the teeth-chattering, much-cursed washboards found on so many dirt roads after heavy vehicle use

blaze   a mark on a tree made by chipping away a piece of the bark, usually done to designate a trail; such trails are sometimes described as "blazed"

blind corner a curve in the road or trail that conceals bikers, hikers, equestrians, and other traffic

BLM   Bureau of Land Management, an agency of the federal government

buffed   used to describe a very smooth trail

catching air taking a jump in such a way that both wheels of the bike are off the ground at the same time

clean while this may describe what you and your bike *won't* be after following many trails, the term is most often used as a verb to denote the action of pedaling a tough section of trail successfully

combination this type of route may combine two or more configurations; for example, a point-to-point route may integrate a scenic loop or an out-and-back spur midway through the ride; likewise, an out-and-back may have a loop at its farthest point (this configuration looks like a cherry with a stem attached; the stem is the out-and-back, the fruit is the terminus loop); or a loop route may have multiple out-and-back spurs and/or loops to the side; mileage for a combination route is for the total distance to complete the ride

dab touching the ground with a foot or hand

deadfall a tangled mass of fallen trees or branches

diversion ditch a usually narrow, shallow ditch dug across or around a trail; funneling the water in this manner keeps it from destroying the trail

double-track the dual tracks made by a jeep or other vehicle, with grass or weeds or rocks between; mountain bikers can ride in either of the tracks, but you will of course find that whichever one you choose, and no matter how many times you change back and forth, the other track will appear to offer smoother travel

dugway a steep, unpaved, switchbacked descent

endo flipping end over end

feathering using a light touch on the brake lever, hitting it lightly many times rather than very hard or locking the brake

four-wheel-drive this refers to any vehicle with drive-wheel capability on all four wheels (a jeep, for instance, has four-wheel drive as compared with a two-wheel-drive passenger car), or to a rough road or trail that requires four-wheel-drive capability (or a one-wheel-drive mountain bike!) to negotiate it

game trail	the usually narrow trail made by deer, elk, or other game
gated	everyone knows what a gate is, and how many variations exist upon this theme; well, if a trail is described as "gated" it simply has a gate across it; don't forget that the rule is if you find a gate closed, close it behind you; if you find one open, leave it that way
Giardia	shorthand for *Giardia lamblia*, and known as the "backpacker's bane" until we mountain bikers expropriated it; this is a waterborne parasite that begins its life cycle when swallowed, and one to four weeks later has its host (you) bloated, vomiting, shivering with chills and living in the bathroom; the disease can be avoided by "treating" (purifying) the water you acquire along the trail (see "Hitting the Trail" in the Introduction)
gnarly	a term thankfully used less and less these days, it refers to tough trails
hammer	to ride very hard
hardpack	a trail in which the dirt surface is packed down hard; such trails make for good and fast riding, and very painful landings; bikers most often use "hardpack" as both a noun and adjective, and "hard-packed" as an adjective only (the grammar lesson will help you when diagramming sentences in camp)
hike-a-bike	what you do when the road or trail becomes too steep or rough to remain in the saddle
jeep road, jeep trail	a rough road or trail passable only with four-wheel-drive capability (or a horse or mountain bike)
kamikaze	while this once referred primarily to those Japanese fliers who quaffed a glass of sake, then flew off as human bombs in suicide missions against U.S. naval vessels, it has more recently been applied to the idiot mountain bikers who, far less honorably, scream down hiking trails, endangering the physical and mental safety of the walking, biking, and equestrian traffic they meet; deck guns were necessary to stop the Japanese kamikaze pilots, but a bike pump or walking staff in the spokes is sufficient for the current-day kamikazes who threaten to get us all kicked off the trails

loop	this route configuration is characterized by riding from the designated trailhead to a distant point, then returning to the trailhead via a different route (or simply continuing on the same in a circle route) without doubling back; you always move forward across new terrain, but return to the starting point when finished; mileage is for the entire loop from the trailhead back to trailhead
multi-purpose	a BLM designation of land which is open to many uses; mountain biking is allowed
ORV	a motorized off-road vehicle
out-and-back	a ride where you will return on the same trail you pedaled out; while this might sound far more boring than a loop route, many trails look very different when pedaled in the opposite direction
pack stock	horses, mules, llamas, et cetera, carrying provisions along the trails . . . and unfortunately leaving a trail of their own behind
point-to-point	a vehicle shuttle (or similar assistance) is required for this type of route, which is ridden from the designated trailhead to a distant location, or end point, where the route ends; total mileage is for the one-way trip from the trailhead to end point
portage	to carry your bike on your person
pummy	volcanic activity in the Pacific Northwest and elsewhere produces soil with a high content of pumice; trails through such soil often become thick with dust, but this is light in consistency and can usually be pedaled; remember, however, to pedal carefully, for this dust obscures whatever might lurk below
quads	bikers use this term to refer both to the extensor muscle in the front of the thigh (which is separated into four parts) and to USGS maps; the expression "Nice quads!" refers always to the former, however, except in those instances when the speaker is an engineer
runoff	rainwater or snowmelt
scree	an accumulation of loose stones or rocky debris lying on a slope or at the base of a hill or cliff

signed	a "signed" trail has signs in place of blazes
single-track	a single, narrow path through grass or brush or over rocky terrain, often created by deer, elk, or backpackers; single-track riding is some of the best fun around
slickrock	the rock-hard, compacted sandstone that is *great* to ride and even prettier to look at; you'll appreciate it even more if you think of it as a petrified sand dune or seabed (which it is), and if the rider before you hasn't left tire marks (from unnecessary skidding) or granola bar wrappers behind
snowmelt	runoff produced by the melting of snow
snowpack	unmelted snow accumulated over weeks or months of winter—or over years in high-mountain terrain
spur	a road or trail that intersects the main trail you're following
switchback	a zigzagging road or trail designed to assist in traversing steep terrain: mountain bikers should *not* skid through switchbacks
technical	terrain that is difficult to ride due not to its grade (steepness) but to its obstacles—rocks, roots, logs, ledges, loose soil . . .
topo	short for topographical map, the kind that shows both linear distance *and* elevation gain and loss; "topo" is pronounced with both vowels long
trashed	a trail that has been destroyed (same term used no matter what has destroyed it . . . cattle, horses, or even mountain bikers riding when the ground was too wet)
two-wheel-drive	this refers to any vehicle with drive-wheel capability on only two wheels (a passenger car, for instance, has two-wheel-drive); a two-wheel-drive road is a road or trail easily traveled by an ordinary car
waterbar	An earth, rock, or wooden structure that funnels water off trails to reduce erosion
washboarded	a road that is surfaced with many ridges spaced closely together, like the ripples on a washboard; these make for very rough riding, and even worse driving in a car or jeep

whoop-de-doo	closely spaced dips or undulations in a trail; these are often encountered in areas traveled heavily by ORVs
wilderness area	land that is officially set aside by the federal government to remain *natural* —pure, pristine, and untrammeled by any vehicle, including mountain bikes; though mountain bikes had not been born in 1964 (when the United States Congress passed the Wilderness Act, establishing the National Wilderness Preservation system), they are considered a "form of mechanical transport" and are thereby excluded; in short, stay out
windchill	a reference to the wind's cooling effect upon exposed flesh; for example, if the temperature is 10 degrees Fahrenheit and the wind is blowing at 20 miles per hour, the windchill (that is, the actual temperature to which your skin reacts) is *minus* 32 degrees; if you are riding in wet conditions things are even worse, for the windchill would then be *minus 74 degrees!*
windfall	anything (trees, limbs, brush, fellow bikers . . .) blown down by the wind

INDEX

Abingdon, Virginia Creeper Trail, 347–51
Alexandria, 102
Appomattox-Buckingham State Forest, 83
Ashland, Poor Farm Park, 74–76
ATV trail, 141, 143–44

Back Bay National Wildlife Refuge, 13–19
Back Creek Mountain, 219
Back Creek Trail, 205–6
Backbone Trail, 42–44
Bail-Out Trail, 45–47
Bald Knob, 237
Bald Mountain, 292, 294–95
Bald Mountain Road, 254, 256
Barbours Creek Wilderness, 287–92
Barger Wildlife Pond, 191
Barton Gap, 336–38
Basin Trail, 302–5
Bath County, Hidden Valley, 215–19
Beach trails, False Cape State Park, 13–19
Bear(s), in Great Dismal Swamp, 25, 27
Bear Creek Lake State Park, 88–90
Bear Wallow Trail (Elizabeth Furnace), 136

Beartree Recreation Area, 342–44
Bearwallow Trail (Laurel Fork), 221, 224
Beast Trail, 302–5
Beaver Lake, 66–70
Beaver Pond, 42–44
Beaverdam Reservoir park, 37–41
Behavior code, 6–7, 368–69
Belle Isle, 53–55
Benson Run, 197
Big Hollow Trail, 160
Big Levels Reservoir Loop, 247–52
Big Levels to Blue Ridge, 252–56
Big Mountain, 308
Black Horse Gap, 277, 279, 280
Blacksburg Ranger District.
   See Jefferson National Forest, Blacksburg Ranger District
Blue Ridge Highlands, 297–363
   Barton Gap, 336–38
   Beartree Recreation Area, 342–44
   Big Levels to Blue Ridge, 252–56
   Breaks Interstate Park, 355–59
   Brush Mountain, 299–301
   Butt Mountain, 308–12
   Feathercamp Ridge, 345–46
   Flat Top Mountain, 312–15
   Grayson Highlands State Park, 318–21

Blue Ridge Highlands (continued)
Guest River Trail, 351–55
Heart of Appalachia Route, 362–63
Horse Heaven Loop, 327–30
Hurricane Gap, 330–33
Mountain Bike Heaven, 327–30
Mountain Lake to Butt Mountain, 308–12
Mountain Lake Trail System, 305–8
New River Trail State Park, 322–27
Polecat Trail, 315–18
Poverty Creek Trail, 302–5
Rowlands Creek Falls Circuit, 334–35
Skulls Gap to Hurricane Gap, 330–33
Sugar Hill Loop Trail, 359–61
Tract Fork Trail, 315–18
Virginia Creeper Trail, 347–51
Whitetop Mountain, 339–41
Blue Ridge Parkway
Otter Creek Outing, 272–76
Spec Mines, 277–80
Blue Suck Falls, 242–45
Blueberry Trail, 168–71
Bogan Run Trail, 219
Braley Pond, 192, 195
Brandywine Lake Overnighter, 151–55
Breaks Interstate Park, 355–59
Bridge Hollow Trail, 192
Bridgewater.
See George Washington National Forest, Dry River Ranger District
Browns Creek, 274, 276
Brush Mountain, 299–301
Brushy Top peak, 311
Buchanan
Pine Mountain Trail, 270–72
Thomas Mountain, 268–70
Buck Lick Run, 162, 164
Buena Vista
Pedlar River Loop, 257–61
Shady Mountain Trail, 261–63
Buggs Island Lake, 80–82
Bullpasture Mountain/Gorge/River, 206, 208–12, 214

Burd, Colonel William, II, 25
Burke's Garden, 362
Butt Mountain, 308–12

Cabell Trail, 91–94
Camp May Flather, 185
Camp Roosevelt, 138, 140–41
Camp Run, 154
Camp Todd, 176, 186–87
Camping
Brandywine Lake Overnighter, 151–55
Massanutten Campout, 137–47
Cape Henry Trail, 19–22
Carillon, Dogwood Dell, 59
Carrollton Nike Park, 27–31
Carter Taylor Trail, 83–87
Carvins Cove Reservoir, 281–83
Cave Mountain Lake, 264–68
Cave Mountain Lake Recreation Area, 264
Chair Rock Road, 280
Charcoal Trail, 131
Charlottesville
Observatory Hill, 98–100
Walnut Creek Park, 94–97
Chesapeake & Ohio Canal National Historic Park, 112–17
Chesapeake & Ohio Railroad bed, 295
Chesterfield County, Iron Bridge Park, 70–73
Chestnut Ridge, 334
Chimbarazo Park, 56–58
Civil War sites
Carter Taylor Trail, 83, 85
Chimbarazo Park, 56
Confederate Breastworks, 197
Elizabeth Furnace, 131, 144–47
McDowell, 208
Massanutten Mountain, 129–30
Minie Ball Hill, 310, 311
northern Virginia, 102
Petersburg National Battlefield, 77–79
Piedmont, 52

Clarksville, Occoneechee State Park,
    80–82
Clayton Mill Creek, 204
Claytor Lake, 322
Clinch Ranger District, Guest River
    Trail, 351–55
Clinch River, Sugar Hill Loop Trail,
    359–61
C&O Canal National Historic Park,
    112–17
Coastal Virginia, 11–49
    Beaverdam Reservoir park, 37–41
    Cape Henry Trail, 19–22
    Carrollton Nike Park, 27–31
    False Cape State Park, 13–19
    First Landing State Park, 19–22
    Great Dismal Swamp, 23–27
    Harwoods Mill Trail, 34–37
    Marl Ravine Trail, 45–47
    Newport News Park, 31–33
    Waller Mill Park, 47–49
    York River State Park, 42–47
Colon Hollow, 269, 270
Colonial Historic Park, 33
Comers Creek, 338
Confederate Breastworks, 197
Coursey Spring Fish Hatchery, 213
Cove Branch Dead End Road, 291
Covington, West Virginia
    Dry Run, 237–40
    Fore Mountain Trail, 240–42
    Longdale Recreation Area, 229–33
    North Mountain Ridge, 233–36
Cowpasture River, 206, 208, 212, 214
Cryptosporidiosis, prevention of, 8
Cumberland Gap, 298
Cumberland State Forest, 88–90

Damascus
    Beartree Recreation Area, 342–44
    Feathercamp Ridge, 345–46
    Hurricane Gap, 330–33
    Virginia Creeper Trail, 347–51
    Whitetop Mountain, 339–41
Day Creek Horse Trail, 280
Deer Trail, 284, 286–87

Deerfield Horse Trail, 195–98
Deerfield Ranger District.
    See George Washington National
    Forest, Deerfield Ranger District
Deerfield Valley, 201
Dice Run, 155
Dillwyn, Cumberland State Forest,
    88–90
Dogwood Dell, 59–61
Dogwood Half Hundred Race/Hike,
    135
Dogwood Trail, 47–49
Dolly Ann CCC Camp, 232
Dolly Ann Work Center, 242
Double Top, 332, 335
Douthat State Park
    Blue Suck Falls, 242–45
    Middle Mountain Ridge, 245–47
Dragon's Back, 284–87
Drinking water, 7–8
Drummond, William, 25
Dry Branch Gap, 200
Dry River Ranger District.
    See George Washington National
    Forest, Dry River Ranger District
Dry Run, 237–40
Duncan Hollow, 147–51
Dyke Marsh, Mount Vernon Trail,
    119

Eastern Virginia Mountain Bike
    Association, 11–12
Edinburg, Elizabeth Furnace,
    131–36, 144–47
Edinburg Gap, 141–44
Edinburg Reservoir, 136
Elevation changes. *See specific trails*
Elizabeth Furnace, 131–36, 144–47
Elkhorn Lake, 189–91
Elliott Knob, 198–202
Etiquette, trail, 6–7, 368–69

Fairfax Station, Fountainhead
    Regional Park, 106–9
Fall Line, geography of, 11
False Cape State Park, 13–19

Feathercamp Ridge, 345–46
Fenwick Mines, 292–95
First Landing State Park, 19–22
First-aid kit, 9
Flagpole Knob, 158, 159
Flat Top Mountain, 312–15
Fluid requirements, 7–8
Fore Mountain Trail, 240–42
Fort Seybert, 155
Fort Valley, 131, 134
Fountainhead Regional Park, 106–9
Fries, New River Trail State Park,
    322–27
Front Royal, Elizabeth Furnace,
    131–36, 144–47
Furnaces
    Elizabeth, 131–36, 144–47
    Longdale, 229–33

Gap Trail, 151
Gauley Ridge, 160
Gauley Ridge Road, 164, 167
George Washington National Forest
    biking guidelines for, 130
    Deerfield Ranger District
        Deerfield Horse Trail, 195–98
        Elliott Knob, 198–202
        Walker Mountain, 202–6
        Wallace Tract, 210–14
        West Augusta Trail, 192–95
    Dry River Ranger District
        Blueberry Trail, 168–71
        Brandywine Lake Overnighter,
            151–55
        Great Lakes Loop, 188–91
        Lake to Lake, 156–60
        Little Bald Knob Climb, 186–88
        Long Run, 164–67
        North River Gorge Trail, 180–85
        Reddish Knob, 156, 176–80
        Sandspring Mountain Trail,
            172–75
        Slate Lick Lake, 160–64
    James River Ranger District
        Dry Run, 237–40
        Fore Mountain Trail, 240–42

Longdale Recreation Area,
    229–33
    North Mountain Ridge,
        233–36
Lee Ranger District
    Duncan Hollow, 147–51
    Elizabeth Furnace, 131–36,
        144–47
    Massanutten Campout, 137–47
Pedlar Ranger District
    Big Levels, 252–56
    Big Levels Reservoir Loop,
        247–52
    Otter Creek Outing, 272–76
    Pedlar River Loop, 257–61
    Shady Mountain Trail, 261–63
Warm Springs Ranger District
    Hidden Valley, 215–19
    Laurel Fork, 219–25
Giardiasis, prevention of, 7–8
Gladstone, James River State Park,
    91–94
Glasgow, Otter Creek Outing, 272–76
Glenwood Horse Trail, 277
Glenwood Ranger District.
    See Jefferson National Forest,
    Glenwood Ranger District
Glossary, 368–73
Gloucester, Beaverdam Reservoir
    park, 37–41
Gorge Road, 218
Grand Canyon of the South
    (Breaks Interstate Park), 355–59
Grayson Highlands State Park,
    318–21
Great Dismal Swamp, 23–27
Great Falls Park, 120–22
Great Lakes Loop, 188–91
Green Hill Pond, 93
Green Mountain, 134–36
Green Pastures Forest Camp, 232
Green Ridge Trail, 281
Guest River Trail, 351–55

Hanover County, Poor Farm Park,
    74–76

Harrisonburg
  Blueberry Trail, 168–71
  Brandywine Lake Overnighter,
    151–55
  Lake to Lake, 156–60
  Long Run, 164–67
  North River Gorge Trail, 180–85
  Sandspring Mountain Trail,
    172–75
  Slate Lick Lake, 160–64
Harwoods Mill Trail, 34–37
Haw Orchard Mountains,
  320–21
Hazards. *See specific trails*
Heart of Appalachia Bike Route,
  362–63
Henly Hollow, 330
Hidden Valley, 215–19
High Knob, 156–57, 159
Highland Country, Williamsville
  Loop, 206–10
Historic Crab Orchard Museum
  and Pioneer Park, 357
Hite Hollow Road, 200, 202
Hogback, 202
Hogpen Mountain, 167
Holliday Lake State Park,
  Carter Taylor Trail, 83–87
Hollywood Rapids, 53
Hone Quarry, 156, 158
Hoop Pole Gap, 268
Horse Heaven Loop, 327–30
Horse Trail, 302–5
Horse Trough Hollow, 186, 187
Horsehair Trail, 302–5
Hot Springs, Hidden Valley, 215–19
Hunting season precautions.
  See specific trails
Hupman Valley Trail, 210
Hurricane Creek, 336–38
Hurricane Gap, 330–33

International Mountain Bicycling
  Association Rules of the Trail, 6–7
Iron Bridge Park, 70–73
Iron Mountain, 332

Iron Mountain Trail, 342–44
Isle of Wight County, Carrollton Nike
  Park, 27–31

Jackson River, 216–18
James River, Belle Isle, 53–55
James River Ranger District.
  See George Washington National
  Forest, James River Ranger District
James River State Park, 91–94
Jamestown historic site, 12
Jefferson National Forest
  biking guidelines for, 130
  Blacksburg Ranger District
    Brush Mountain, 299–301
    Flat Top Mountain, 312–15
    Mountain Lake, 308–12
    Polecat Trail, 315–18
    Poverty Creek Trail, 302–5
    Tract Fork Trail, 315–18
  Clinch Ranger District, Guest
    River Trail, 351–55
  Glenwood Ranger District
    Cave Mountain Lake, 264–68
    Pine Mountain Trail, 270–72
    Spec Mines, 277–80
    Thomas Mountain, 268–70
  Mount Rogers National Recreation
    Area, 298
    Barton Gap, 336–38
    Beartree Recreation Area,
      342–44
    Feathercamp Ridge, 345–46
    Hurricane Gap, 330–33
    Mountain Bike Heaven,
      327–30
    Rowlands Creek Falls Circuit,
      334–35
    Skulls Gap, 330–33
    Virginia Creeper Trail, 347–51
    Whitetop Mountain, 339–41
  New Castle Ranger District
    Barbours Creek Wilderness,
      287–92
    Dragon's Back, 284–87
    Fenwick Mines, 292–95

Jefferson National Forest (continued)
Wythe Ranger District
Polecat Trail, 315–18
Tract Fork Trail, 315–18
Jerry's Creek Trail, 334

Lake Accotink Park, 103–6
Lake Drummond, 23–27
Lake Gaston, 80–82
Lake Occoquan, 106–9
Lake Robertson, 225–28
Lake Sherando, 250–51, 256
Lake to Lake, 156–60
Lakeshore Trail, 83–87
Land-use controversy, 365–67
Laurel Fork, 219–25
Lee Ranger District.
See George Washington National
Forest, Lee Ranger District
Lexington
Blue Suck Falls, 242–45
Lake Robertson, 225–28
Longdale Recreation Area, 229–33
Middle Mountain Ridge, 245–47
North Mountain Ridge, 233–36
Little Bald Knob Climb, 186–88
Little Fort Recreation Area, 141–44
Little Irish Creek, 257, 263
Little Passage Creek, 134, 135, 147
Little Switzerland, Williamsville
Loop, 206–10
Locust Spring Run Trail, 223
Locust Springs Campground, 221
Long Run, 164–67
Longdale Recreation Area, 229–33
Lum Trail, 344
Lynchburg Reservoir, 164

McCormick Observatory, 98–100
McDowell, 208
McLean
Great Falls Park, 120–22
Mount Vernon Trail, 117–19
Maple Festival, Highland County, 208
Maps. See also specific trails
chronologic list of, xii–xiv

index map, x–xi
legends, ix
topographic, 4–5
Marion. See Jefferson National Forest,
Mount Rogers National Recreation
Area
Marl Ravine Trail, 45–47
Massanutten Campout, 137–47
Massanutten Mountain, 129–30
Duncan Hollow, 147–51
Massanutten Mountain Trail West,
136
Massanutten Story Trail, 149
Meadow Mountain (Bald Mountain),
339–41
Meneka Trail, 136
Mid-Atlantic Off-Road Enthusiasts,
101–2, 106
Middle Mountain, 149, 151
Middle Mountain Ridge, 245–47
Millboro, Middle Mountain Ridge,
245–47
Mills Creek Trail, 251, 256
Mine(s)
Fenwick, 292–95
Spec, 277–80
Mine Gap, 146
Minie Ball Hill, 310, 311
Mitchell Knob Hunter Access Road,
155
Mole Hill, 174, 175
Monterey
Laurel Fork, 219–25
Wallace Tract, 210–14
Williamsville Loop, 206–10
Moreland Gap, 143
Mount Jefferson, Observatory Hill,
98–100
Mount Rogers National Recreation
Area. See under Jefferson National
Forest
Mount Vernon Trail, 117–19
Mountain(s)
Blue Ridge.
See Blue Ridge Highlands
western. See Western mountains

Mountain Bike Heaven, 327–30
Mountain Lake to Butt Mountain, 308–12
Mountain Lake Trail System, 305–8
Mouth of Wilson, Grayson Highlands State Park, 318–21
Mud Pond, 168
Mud Pond Gap Trail, 171
Muddy Run Trail, 218
Mudhole Gap, 134, 135, 146, 147
Murphy, Audie, 299–301

Narrow Back Mountain, 168
National Battlefield Park, in Chimbarazo Park, 56–58
National Off-Road Bicycle Association, code of behavior, 366
Natural Bridge Station
    Cave Mountain Lake, 264–68
    Pine Mountain Trail, 270–72
    Spec Mines, 277–80
    Thomas Mountain, 268–70
Natural Chimneys, 184
New Castle
    Barbours Creek Wilderness, 287–92
    Fenwick Mines, 292–95
New Castle Ranger District.
    See Jefferson National Forest, New Castle Ranger District
New Market, Duncan Hollow, 147–51
New Market Gap, 149
    Massanutten Mountain campout, 138, 140–41
New River Trail State Park, 322–27
New Year's Ride, 281
Newport News, Harwoods Mill Trail, 34–37
Newport News Park, 31–33
Nickel Bridge, 59–61
Nobusiness Creek, 315
Norfolk and Southern Railroad bed, Guest River Trail, 351–55
North Creek Campground, 269–71

North Mountain, 129
    Dragon's Back, 284–87
    Lake Robertson, 225–28
North Mountain Ridge, 233–36
North Mountain Trail, 201, 202, 231
North River Dam, 191
North River Gorge Trail, 180–85
Northern Virginia, 101–26
    C&O Canal National Historic Park, 112–17
    Fountainhead Regional Park, 106–9
    Great Falls Park, 120–22
    Lake Accotink Park, 103–6
    Mount Vernon Trail, 117–19
    Prince William Forest Park, 123–26
    Wakefield Park, 103–6
    W&OD Railroad Regional Park, 109–12

Oak Recreational Trail, 187
Observatory Hill, 98–100
Occoneechee State Park and Wildlife Management Area, 80–82
O-Hill (Observatory Hill), 98–100
Old Mill Trail, 66–70
185 Miles of Adventure: Hiker's Guide to the C&O Canal, 116
Opossum Pass Trail, 228
Orebank Creek Road, 251–52, 255–56
Otter Creek Outing, 272–76

Page Valley, 149
Pandapas Pond, 304
Panther Falls, 261
Passage Creek, 140
Paw Paw Tunnel, 114
Pedlar Ranger District.
    See George Washington National Forest, Pedlar Ranger District
Pedlar River Loop, 257–61
Peters Mill ATV Trail, 141, 143–44
Peter's Ridge, 237
Petersburg National Battlefield, 77–79

Piedmont, 51–100
  Belle Isle, 53–55
  Carter Taylor Trail, 83–87
  Chimbarazo Park, 56–58
  Cumberland State Forest, 88–90
  Dogwood Dell, 59–61
  Iron Bridge Park, 70–73
  James River State Park, 91–94
  Observatory Hill, 98–100
  Occoneechee State Park and Wildlife
    Management Area, 80–82
  Petersburg National Battlefield,
    77–79
  Pocahontas State Park, 66–70
  Poor Farm Park, 74–76
  Powhite Park, 62–66
  Walnut Creek Park, 94–97
Pig Iron Trail, 131
Pine Mountain, 339
Pine Mountain Trail, 270–72
Pines Campground, 290–91
Pocahontas State Park, 66–70
Polecat Trail, 315–18
Poor Farm Park, 74–76
Potomac River
  Chesapeake & Ohio Canal
    National Historic Park, 112–17
  C&O Canal National Historic
    Park, 112–17
  Great Falls Park, 120–22
  Mount Vernon Trail, 117–19
Potts Mountain, 291
Potts Mountain Trek Escape, 289
Pounding Mill Run/Creek, 241–42
Poverty Creek Trail, 302–5
Powell's Fort Valley, 131, 134
Powhite Park, 62–66
Prince William Forest Park, 123–26
Pulaski, Tract Fork Trail, 315–18

Railroad beds
  Chesapeake & Ohio, 295
  Guest River Trail, 351–55
  New River Trail State Park, 322–27
  Slate Lick Lake, 160–64
  Virginia Creeper Trail, 347–51

Ramseys Draft Wilderness, 192
Reddish Knob, 156, 176–80
Rescue index. *See specific trails*
Reservoirs
  Beaverdam, 37–41
  Big Levels, 247–52
  Carvins Cove, 281–83
  Edinburg, 136
  Lynchburg, 164
Richmond
  Belle Isle, 53–55
  Chimbarazo Park, 56–58
  Dogwood Dell, 59–61
  Pocahontas State Park, 66–70
  Powhite Park, 62–65
Ridge Trail, 122
Riverview Trail, 42–44
Roanoke
  Barbours Creek Wilderness,
    287–92
  Carvins Cove Reservoir, 281–83
  Fenwick Mines, 292–95
Rock Shelter Trail, 218
Rockbridge County, Lake Robertson,
  225–28
Rough Run, 155
Round Top, 332, 335
Rowdy Dog mountain bike race, 305
Rowlands Creek Falls Circuit, 334–35
Russell Fork River
  Breaks Interstate Park, 355–59
  gorge, 298

Sailor's Creek Historic State Park, 83,
  85
St. Paul
  Heart of Appalachia Bike Route,
    362–63
  Sugar Hill Loop Trail, 359–61
Salem, Dragon's Back, 284–87
Salt Sulphur Turnpike, 310
Sandspring Mountain Trail, 172–75
Scenic Drive, Prince William Forest
  Park, 123
Scothorn Gap, 149
Services. *See specific trails*

Shady Mountain Trail, 261–63
Sharpsburg, Maryland, Chesapeake &
  Ohio Canal National Historic Park,
  112–17
Shaw's Gap Trail, 344
Shenandoah Mountain,
  154, 155, 156, 159
  Deerfield Horse Trail, 195–98
  Wallace Tract, 210–14
Shenandoah Mountain Trail, 197
Shenandoah River, 144
Shock-a-Billy Trail, 108
Shot Tower State Historic Park, 327
Siege Road, 77
Signal Knob, 131, 136, 145–46
Sinking Creek, 229–33
Skulls Gap to Hurricane Gap,
  330–33
Slabcamp Run Trail, 221, 224
Slacks Overlook and Trail, 256
Slate Lick Lake, 160–64
Slate Springs Mountain, 159
Snakes, in Great Dismal Swamp, 27
Spec Mines, 277–80
Springfield, Lake Accotink Park,
  103–6
Spur Trail, 136
Squirrel Run Trail, 228
Stagg Creek, 74–76
Staunton
  Deerfield Horse Trail, 195–98
  Elliott Knob, 198–202
  Great Lakes Loop, 188–91
  Little Bald Knob Climb, 186–88
  North River Gorge Trail, 180–85
  Reddish Knob, 156, 176–80
  Walker Mountain, 202–6
  West Augusta Trail, 192–95
  Williamsville Loop, 206–10
Staunton Dam, 191
Stony Run Trail, 246–47
Straight Branch Trail
  (Beartree Recreation Area), 344
Strasburg, Elizabeth Furnace,
  131–36
Suffolk, Great Dismal Swamp, 23–27

Sugar Grove, West Virginia, 178, 179
Sugar Hill Loop Trail, 359–61
Super Bowl Sunday ride, George
  Washington National Forest, 156
Swede Tunnel, 355
Swift Creek Lake, 69
Switchbacks
  Big Levels, 254–56
  protection of, 367
Switzer Lake, 156, 158, 159

Taskinas Creek, 42–44
Taylor Mountain Trail, 257, 259
Tazewell, Breaks Interstate Park,
  355–59
Thomas Mountain, 268–70
Tidal rivers, 11
Timber Ridge Peak, 172
Timber Ridge Trail, 174–75
Todd Lake, 189, 191
Tools, for bike repair and mainte-
  nance, 8
Topographic maps, 4–5
Towpath, C&O Canal National
  Historic Park, 112–17
Tract Fork Trail, 315–18
Trail etiquette, 6–7, 368–69
Trek Escape, 289
Triangle, Prince William Forest Park,
  123–26
Turkey Pen Ridge, 251
Turkey Roost Trail, 228
Turkey Trail, 284
Tye River Overlook Trail, 93

Union Springs Run, 171
United States Geological Survey,
  topographic maps, 4–5
University of Virginia, Observatory
  Hill, 98–100
Utah Wasatch-Cache National Forest
  Office, code of ethics, 366–67

Virginia Beach
  False Cape State Park, 13–19
  First Landing Park, 19–22

Virginia Championship Mountain
Bike races, 284
Virginia Creeper Trail
(Jefferson Forest), 347–51
Virginia Creeper Trail
(W&OD Railroad Regional Park),
109–12
Virginia Mountain Bike Challenge,
345
Virginia-Carolina Railroad, Virginia
Creeper Trail, 347–51

Wakefield Park, 103–6
Walker Mountain, 202–6
Wallace Tract, 210–14
Waller Mill Park, 47–49
Walnut Creek Park, 94–97
Walnut Flats, 314, 315
Warm Springs
Hidden Valley, 215–19
Laurel Fork, 219–25
Warm Springs Ranger District, Laurel
Fork, 219–25
Wash Woods community, 16, 18–19
Washington Ditch Road, 23–27
Water supplies, 7–8
Waterbars, protection of, 367
Wateredge Trail, 281
Waterfall Mountain, 151
Waynesboro, Big Levels Reservoir
Loop, 247–52
West Augusta Trail, 192–95
Western mountains, 127–297
Barbours Creek Wilderness,
287–92
Big Levels Reservoir Loop, 247–52
Big Levels to Blue Ridge, 252–56
Blue Suck Falls, 242–45
Blueberry Trail, 168–71
Brandywine Lake Overnighter,
151–55
Carvins Cove Reservoir, 281–83
Cave Mountain Lake, 264–68
Deerfield Horse Trail, 195–98
Dragon's Back, 284–87
Dry Run, 237–40

Duncan Hollow, 147–51
Elizabeth Furnace, 131–36
Elliott Knob, 198–202
Fenwick Mines, 292–95
Fore Mountain Trail, 240–42
Great Lakes Loop, 188–91
Hidden Valley, 215–19
Lake Robertson, 225–28
Lake to Lake, 156–60
Laurel Fork, 219–25
Little Bald Knob Climb, 186–88
Long Run, 164–67
Longdale Recreation Area, 229–33
Massanutten Campout, 137–47
Middle Mountain Ridge, 245–47
North Mountain Ridge, 233–36
North River Gorge Trail, 180–85
Otter Creek Outing, 272–76
Pedlar River Loop, 257–61
Pine Mountain Trail, 270–72
Reddish Knob, 156, 176–80
Sandspring Mountain Trail,
172–75
Shady Mountain Trail, 261–63
Slate Lick Lake, 160–64
Spec Mines, 277–80
Thomas Mountain, 268–70
Walker Mountain, 202–6
Wallace Tract, 210–14
West Augusta Trail, 192–95
Williamsville Loop, 206–10
Westvaco Corp., 240–42
White Oak Flat, 166, 167
White Rocks Trail, 256
White-Tail Trail, 42–44
Whitetop Mountain, 339–41
Whitetop Station, 347–51
Wildcat Mountain Trail, 264–65, 268
Wildlife Road, 286
Williamsburg
Waller Mill Park, 47–49
York River State Park, 42–44
Williamsville, Wallace Tract, 210–14
Williamsville Loop, 206–10
Willis River Trail, 88–90
Winston Lake, 88

Wise, Guest River Trail, 351–55
W&OD Railroad Regional Park,
  109–12
Wolf Ridge, 174
Woodstock Gap, 143–44
World Cup Downhill Championship,
  130
Wytheville
  Mountain Bike Heaven, 327–30

Polecat Trail, 315–18
  Tract Fork Trail, 315–18
Wythe Ranger District, Jefferson
  National Forest
  Polecat Trail, 315–18
  Tract Fork Trail, 315–18

York River State Park, 42–44
Yorktown, 33

RANDY PORTER calls himself a born-again Virginian. He has lived in the Old Dominion since 1968, when he moved to Williamsburg to attend the College of William and Mary. After earning a B.S. in Psychology, he returned to school at Virginia Commonwealth University in Richmond for a

M.Ed. in Special Education and since 1979 has lived in the Shenandoah Valley and taught students with disabilities.

His bicycle ventures have included partial ownership of a bicycle shop in Williamsburg in the early 1970s, cofounding Virginia's first commercial bicycle touring company in the early 1980s, and coauthoring his first guidebook, A *Cyclist's Guide to the Shenandoah Valley*, in the early 1990s. Only time will tell what the early part of the new century will bring.

Besides his love for his ten-year-old son, Chris, and mountain biking, Randy is fixated on his next book, which will be a psychological crime novel set in Richmond, Virginia. Traveling all over Virginia to uncover the Commonwealth's best mountain biking destinations convinced him that there is no finer place to live and bike.